THE LAST
GOOD
SEASON

Brooklyn,

the Dodgers, and

Their Final

Pennant Race

Together

Doubleday

New York   London   Toronto
Sydney   Auckland

THE LAST
GOOD
SEASON

Michael Shapiro

PUBLISHED BY DOUBLEDAY
a division of Random House, Inc.

DOUBLEDAY and the portrayal of an anchor with a dolphin are
registered trademarks of Random House, Inc.

Book design by Donna Sinisgalli.

Library of Congress Cataloging-in-Publication Data
Shapiro, Michael.
The last good season: Brooklyn, the Dodgers, and their final pennant
race together /
Michael Shapiro.—1st ed.
p.   cm.
Includes bibliographical references (p. 333) and index.
1. Brooklyn Dodgers (Baseball team)—History. 2. Baseball—New York
(State)—New York—History—20th century. 3. Brooklyn
(New York, N.Y.)—History—20th century. I. Title.

GV875.B7 S43 2003
796.357'64'0974723—dc21   2002071410

ISBN 0-385-50152-8

April 2003

First Edition

1   3   5   7   9   10   8   6   4   2

For

BARNEY KARPFINGER

And For

LENNY WEXLER

CONTENTS

The last parade for the Brooklyn Dodgers began just after noon on the third Monday of April, 1956. It was a cool day. The sky was cloudy and the sun never quite came out.

Two thousand marchers gathered near Albermarle Road, converged on Flatbush Avenue, and headed north to the Dodgers' ballpark, Ebbets Field. A squad of mounted police led what felt like a small town's parade. The ROTC marching band from the Pratt Institute, downtown Brooklyn's college of art and design, was joined by the young men and women of the Pershing Rifles drill team. Miss Flatbush, a local beauty queen, rode in an open car. The Navy Yard Boys Club marched behind, along with the orphans from the St. Vincent's Home for Boys. There were drum majorettes in short skirts and white leather boots. There were marching Boy Scouts, Little Leaguers, and, in white uniforms and toques, five bakers from Ebingers, which made Brooklyn's finest chocolate blackout cake. There was a navy band and an army band and marching units from Long Island, too, from Lake Ronkonkoma, Babylon, Baldwin, and Bay Shore. Thousands lined the two-mile route to watch.

The floats and cars stopped at the stadium gate while those on foot marched inside. Women were warned not to wear high heels, so that they would not churn up divots in the new outfield grass. They marched around the field, and at 1:42 precisely, the team's manager, Walter Alston, and the captain, Pee Wee Reese, joined two chosen fans, Barbara Billinks of New Jersey and Anthony Micari of Brooklyn, in centerfield at the scoreboard flagpole, for the high point of the day: the raising of the 1955 World Championship banner over Ebbets Field.

The Dodgers had never before been champions. But in October they had at last defeated the New York Yankees, who had beaten them in the

World Series five times before. Brooklyn never had a more glorious night. Downtown, near the Borough Hall, the streets were covered with torn telephone books and ankle-deep confetti. People lit firecrackers and carried paper banners that read, as only a Brooklyn victory slogan could, "I told you so." Nearby, police barricaded the street in front of the Dodger offices, but a great crowd surged down Montague Street to the Hotel Bossert, where the players were arriving for their victory party. People called for the Dodgers, and when they stepped from their cars the crowd surrounded them for autographs as the bellhops tried to get them inside. Those lucky enough to squeeze inside the marble and gilded lobby serenaded Walter Alston with "For He's a Jolly Good Fellow" with such unfettered joy that for a moment it appeared that the taciturn manager fought back tears. He tipped his hat and headed inside the ballroom with his players, their wives, and anyone, it seemed, who could scam an invitation for a party that lasted until dawn and ended so happily and drunkenly that Johnny Podres, who'd pitched the clinching game, tried in his stupor to pass his room key to the daughter of one of the team's vice presidents.

Now, seven months later, the moment had come to raise the flag that in Brooklyn had felt as elusive as the Holy Grail. The flag was enormous. It was twenty feet wide, all blue with white lettering that read: World Champions 1955 Dodgers. Barbara Billinks, chosen by chance as she walked through the stadium turnstiles, stood with Alston, Reese, and Anthony Micari, who was fourteen years old and had been picked for the job by lottery from among the members of the Dodger Knot-Hole Gang fan club who were invited to attend the team's annual "welcome home" dinner the night before at the Hotel St. George in Brooklyn Heights. He was perfect for the part. He played shortstop on his neighborhood team, the Pythons. When someone asked him how the Dodgers would do on Opening Day, he answered, "With me there, they gotta win. Today and every day."

The Dodger players received their champion's rings. Roy Campanella, the catcher, accepted the plaque for the league's most valuable player, and Johnny Podres, newly drafted and dressed in his navy uniform, accepted his for being chosen the star of the World Series. The Dodgers and the day's opponents, the Philadelphia Phillies, stood along the first and third base lines. The baritone Everett McCooey, a familiar Opening Day performer, stepped to the microphone to sing the national anthem. People rose. The band began to play. Then they stopped. A brief and awkward silence followed.

Finally, Everett McCooey leaned into the microphone and asked for all to hear, "Who's going to raise the flag?"

It had all gone so well. But then this was Brooklyn, for years the home of baseball's also-rans and so a place filled with people who understood what it meant to see even the best moments deflated. Men and women now looked at each other and wondered what might happen next. Finally, the members of the Marine Color Guard volunteered to raise the flag. Everett McCooey sang. And those old enough to remember joked that this was nothing: on Opening Day 1913, the first at Ebbets Field, they forgot the flag altogether.

The Dodgers took the field. It was, with two exceptions—Jim Gilliam in left field, Charley Neal at second—the same team they'd been fielding for almost ten years: Reese, their leader, at shortstop; the home run champion Duke Snider in center; Carl Furillo, master of the carom, in right; Gil Hodges, tall and elegant, at first; Campanella, three times the league's Most Valuable Player Award, catching; and, at third, graying and thickening around the middle, Jackie Robinson. On the mound stood Don Newcombe, towering and, from a hitter's perspective, menacing.

Things began well. Reese led off by doubling against Robin Roberts, the Phillies' ace. Snider walked. But Campanella grounded into a double play. They did score in the second, but in the third Newcombe, who could not find the plate, gave up five runs. And though Campanella and Jim Gilliam did homer, the champions fell, 8 to 6.

In his box overlooking his stadium, the team's owner, Walter O'Malley, saw a sight far more disturbing, but hardly surprising: eight thousand empty seats. All through the winter and on into the spring, the team had been pushing tickets for Opening Day. The ticket people worked the phones, calling likely buyers. But only twenty-four thousand people had come to Ebbets Field to see the championship banner raised. And while losing to the Phillies was the stuff of sighs and rolled eyes—Philadelphia had finished fourth in 1955, 21½ games out—the empty seats were, for O'Malley, further evidence that he had not been hasty when he had announced nine months earlier, in August of 1955, that the team would play only two more seasons at Ebbets Field.

Walter O'Malley was a man with a problem he was not disposed to ignore. He was president of a championship baseball team that played in a ballpark he had years before deemed obsolete, a ballpark situated in a neighborhood in which he no longer wished to remain. He recognized that in the euphemistic parlance of the business schools he had a "maturing product." His players were aging and his ballpark was impossibly cramped, and though he still owned the most profitable team in baseball—yes, more profitable even than the Yankees, with their bloated front office and vast cathedral of a ballpark in the Bronx—he sensed that he was not going to be making money on his corner of Bedford Avenue much longer.

But Walter O'Malley still believed that he could make money, very good money, owning a baseball team in Brooklyn, but only if he could move the Dodgers to a new stadium in the borough. For four years he had been using every skill and ploy he could muster to acquire the land where he might build a new ballpark. But the Dodgers were still in Ebbets Field. Walter O'Malley had no wish to leave Brooklyn. He was, in fact, desperate to stay.

THE BROOKLYN DODGERS were the most local team in baseball. They did not represent a city, as did each of the other fifteen major league teams. They represented a *part* of a city. Brooklyn had once been a city, a very large and booming city. But in 1898, caught in growth so rapid that it could no longer afford to build the roads, schools, and sewers it needed, Brooklyn reluctantly voted to consolidate with Manhattan and thereby became a part of New York City. Brooklyn was downgraded statutorily and emotionally to the status of "borough." Centuries earlier a borough would have been a place that stood within thick, protective walls. But by the twentieth century being a borough meant little more than being an administrative entity that fell under the sway of a greater city of which, presumably, it was fortunate to be a part.

Just over a million people then lived in Brooklyn, four times as many as thirty years before. By the mid-1950s its population would top two million, eclipsing that of every other big-league town but for Chicago, Philadelphia, and all of New York itself. For years Brooklyn would welcome visitors with signs boasting of its self-proclaimed ranking as the nation's "fourth largest city." But this only underscored the feeling that Brooklyn had once been something more than it now was—that it had been an important city, a rival to Manhattan, that skinny island on the far side of the Brooklyn Bridge. But it was Manhattan, the smallest of New York's five boroughs—the others were the Bronx, Queens, and Staten Island—that had become the *New York* of grandeur and power, so much so that when Brooklyn people crossed the East River they spoke of going to "the city." Dreamers came to Manhattan to see what they might make of their lives. And while some of those lofty dreamers gravitated to Brooklyn, many more people came there bearing less fanciful dreams: a good job, a pleasant home where a family might live.

Manhattan was an island, but it was Brooklyn that sat apart. It was a vast tract of land—eighty-one square miles—shaped liked a fist and surrounded on three sides by water. Manhattan lay to the west. To the east, sharing a border, was Queens. The geography provided a metaphor of sorts: water separated Brooklyn from Manhattan; but nothing separated Brooklyn from Queens, and beyond Queens, Long Island. Brooklyn was wedged between a reminder of what it no longer was—a great city—and what it seemed destined to become—a symbol not of the future, but of the past.

In the many years when Brooklyn had good reason to think of itself as an important place—from the late nineteenth century when it was home to fifty oil refineries, to the 1930s when its waterfront boasted the largest docking and terminal station in the world, through the war years when seventy thousand people worked at its navy yard—Long Island was a little more than an interminable stretch of potato farms broken by the occasional estate, park, and fishing village. But with the end of the war and the coming of new homes to new towns, it was Long Island that came to represent the shape and face of the Good Life. For generations Brooklyn had been a patchwork of neighborhoods where people of varying ethnicities but of similar classes lived close by one another. But beginning in the late 1940s, many people who could not otherwise find or afford a place to live—New York had been housing returning veterans in Quonset huts—had headed east, through Queens and out to Long Island. The island's population was growing so quickly that in the town of Plainedge, whose student enrollment had mushroomed from 76 in 1945 to 4,800 in 1956, the local schools put out an urgent plea to college-educated mothers to fill in as substitute teachers because there simply weren't enough professionals to go around.

Long Island beckoned, especially for people living in, say, a rented two-bedroom apartment over a Brooklyn candy store who, for a thousand dollars down, could buy a little house with a yard in front and back. They followed the moving vans to towns like Oceanside and Merrick, where even the roads had alluring names like the Sunrise Highway. In their place, to Brooklyn, came people from elsewhere, from the South, from the Caribbean, from Puerto Rico. There had been black people in Brooklyn since the 1600s, and Puerto Ricans since the turn of the century. But the numbers in which they now came proved disconcerting to many white people who may have not minded the occasional black or Latino family in the neighborhood but who now found themselves fretting about being the last white people on the block.

In 1956, Brooklyn no longer had its own newspaper: the *Brooklyn Eagle* had folded the year before. But it still had the navy yard, which was now pressing to compete with distant shipyards like Newport News for the big and profitable jobs. It had an art museum, a rustic park, a botanical garden, a zoo. It had neighborhoods that had changed little over the past generation, and other neighborhoods that bore less and less resemblance to what had existed even ten years before. It had a music academy, a waterfront promenade, an amusement park. And it still had a major league baseball team.

MEN HAD BEEN playing baseball in Brooklyn for a hundred years. They had played for such long-forgotten teams as the Mutuals, Excelsiors, Superbas, Robins, and Eckfords—the first team ever to pay a player's salary. Men became stars in Brooklyn, like Candy Cummings, who in the late nineteenth century threw what was believed to be history's first curveball. Other, less skilled men watched with such dedication that it was in Brooklyn, too, that the profession of baseball writer was born in the person of Henry Chadwick, an Englishman who covered games for the *Eagle* with an occasional sidekick, his colleague Walt Whitman. Baseball's infancy was a chaotic time, beset by competing leagues and teams. The major league game assumed a recognizable form in the early twentieth century, and in 1905 the often-renamed Brooklyn franchise found a name that stuck: the Trolley Dodgers. The name derived from a Manhattanites' taunt—Brooklyn people, they said derisively, were forever forced to "dodge" cars rumbling over the borough's web of trolley tracks.

This was a nickname meant to last—an outlander's barb that would become a point of cockeyed pride, a name that fairly screamed *"Oh yeah . . ."*

No Muse could have chosen a finer or more fitting name for Brooklyn's team. And no alignment of the stars, nor acts of the Fates, nor divine intervention could have so artfully conspired to bless that team with a destiny better suited for the place, and the people for whom it played.

Had the Dodgers always been a good team—not necessarily a championship team, but a team that won more often than it lost—its relationship with Brooklyn would have lacked a certain intimacy. The Dodgers would have been admired; but they would not have been loved. Great teams are like beautiful people—the focus of the imagination, though not necessarily the heart. Great teams have a wide following, but the devotion hinges on performance: the fans stay as long as the team is winning; and when it stops winning there is nothing much left.

A losing team has fewer admirers, but their allegiance endures, year after year. It is a relationship built upon hope and disappointment. And then, in the spring, that most romantic season, longing again. Losing teams are like potboiler novels, predictable but addictive in their capacity to sustain the dream that one day the clouds will part. The relationship between a losing team and its admirers is more complex and compelling than the simple delight in conquest enjoyed by the winners' fans. Winning teams are grand and heroic, qualities that lack a human dimension. But losing teams are all too human. They are cursed by chance, by their own limitations, by failures of will and desire. But when they win, their victories speak to fans who, having witnessed so much misery, can draw lessons from those triumphs.

The Brooklyn Dodgers spent most of their history being a bad team. They played in two early World Series, in 1916 and 1920, losing both. They did not win another National League Championship until 1941. The Dodgers fielded such players as Snooks Dowd, whose career lasted all but two days, and Moose Clabaugh, who enjoyed only one brief appearance on the field for Brooklyn. And though some of the Dodgers were very good— Jake Daubert, who led the league twice in hitting, Babe Herman who once hit .393, and Hall of Famers outfielder Zack Wheat and pitcher Dazzy Vance—the team was so hapless that the dyspeptic columnist Westbrook Pegler dubbed them "the Daffiness Boys."

But the decades of awful play were crucial in the relationship between the Dodgers and Brooklyn: they rendered the team an object of perverse but genuine affection. Rooting for the Dodgers was a painful business. But they were Brooklyn's team, the losing team in the only big-league town that didn't have its own city hall. They were *"da bums,"* a nickname bestowed by Sid Mercer, a sports columnist who heard the words "Ya bums, ya," screamed endlessly by one particularly angry fan at Ebbets Field. Mercer dubbed the fellow "The Spirit of Brooklyn." A winning team can do many things, but it cannot be the agent of its followers' redemption. Only losing teams can do that.

The Dodgers started to be a good team in 1941. The war stalled, but did not halt, their progress. They won a pennant in 1947, and another in 1949. They might have won again in 1951, *should have won,* had they not squandered a 13½-game lead in August to the rival Giants, ended the season tied for first place, split the first two games of a three-game playoff, and carried a 4-to-1 lead into the top of the ninth inning at the Polo Grounds only to see their championship vanish when Bobby Thomson homered against Ralph Branca—the accursed and immortalized *"shot heard 'round the world"*—giving New York the pennant and inflicting upon Brooklyn a cruel lesson on what fate has in store for those who believe themselves destined for second place: Brooklyn and its Dodgers were doomed by the curse of the self-fulfilling prophecy.

The Dodgers did win again in 1952 and 1953. Both times they faced the Yankees in the World Series. And both times they lost. Then came 1955, and the world championship made infinitely sweeter by all the pain that came before.

It is safe to say that between 1947 and 1955 the Dodgers were the best team in the National League, and the second-best team in baseball. That they were perennial runners-up to a *New York* team only strengthened the bond with their fans, who needed only to look across to the glittering world on the far side of the Brooklyn Bridge to feel like runners-up, too.

Still, Walt Whitman was drawn to write about Brooklyn. So too were Thomas Wolfe, Carson McCullers, Henry Miller, Betty Smith, Marianne Moore, Irwin Shaw, Isaac Bashevis Singer, Truman Capote, Hart Crane, and Bernard Malamud. More than a hundred movies and documentaries have been made about or in Brooklyn. Brooklyn and the Dodgers were William Bendix's dying thoughts in the movie *Lifeboat.* Brooklyn was the Bridge, the parachute jump at Coney Island, the brownstone stoop. The name, and legend, traveled. Brooklyn was the name an Italian candy company gave its chewing gum. It was the accent that people who had never been there still attempted—*"toidy-toid and toid"* (read: Thirty-third and Third). A quarter of all Americans, wrote historian Kenneth Jackson, can trace their lineage to someone who once lived in Brooklyn.

But to come from Brooklyn was to be part of a culture riddled with contradictions. Brooklyn was at once vast but small-town: not for Brooklyn the glitter of Manhattan's skyline. Brooklyn's landscape was flat, an urban prairie where the buildings, homes mostly, seldom rose higher than six stories, and where street upon street, in neighborhood upon neighborhood, gave the impression of endless rows of gray and brownstone houses, shoved together with no light in between. Brooklyn was a place where parents came to live but where their children so often left. For a place that prided itself on stability it was nonetheless a transient's town, a one-generation stopover on the path to someplace else. Brooklyn was a place that had a common mythology but where unanimity came only in a sense of inferiority to Manhattan, and in rooting for the Dodgers. Otherwise Brooklyn was so defined by its neighborhoods, and by neighborhoods within neighborhoods, that the most common way that Brooklyn people drew distinctions between one another was to ask people where they went to high school. Middle-class Jews went to Midwood, poor blacks to Jefferson, working-class Italians to Lafayette: the instant, if woefully oversimplified, sizing-up of race, faith, and class.

If there was a single metaphor that captured both Brooklyn's sense of pride and occasional shame, it was the accent. Only the most romantic urbanist could think it charming. The Brooklyn accent was hard and coarse and could diminish the words of even the wisest speaker. A Brooklyn accent was, at turns, either a mark of distinction to be accepted and flaunted or a handicap to be battled and conquered. Fighting it meant remembering to use the letter R and resisting the habit of running many words together—*"Waddaya tawkin' about?"* But then, inevitably, in a moment of anger or delight, the facade slipped, revealing the speaker for who he was: *"You from Brooklyn?" "Yeah, what of it . . . ?"*

In 1956, Brooklyn's ballpark, Ebbets Field, was only forty-four years old, hardly a relic. It was older than Yankee Stadium, which opened in 1923, and younger than Philadelphia's Shibe Park, built in 1909. But

Ebbets Field had aged poorly. By the 1940s the plumbing was so bad that the walkways sometimes stank of urine, a state of disrepair made sadder still by the fact that when it had opened in 1913, Ebbets Field was the model of the modern ballpark. Unlike the stadium it replaced—Washington Park, which sat near the stench and industry of the Gowanus Canal—and unlike so many other ballparks of the day, it was fireproof. It was made not of wood, but from steel. The floors were reinforced concrete. The walls were brick and terracotta. The architect, Charles Van Buskirk, added touches of grandeur never before seen at a ballpark: the main entrance was a rotunda made from Italian marble. The domed ceiling was 27 feet high, and in the center of the 80-foot rotunda floor was a tile relief of a baseball surrounded by the words, Ebbets Field. The stadium cost the Dodgers' owner, Charles Ebbets, $750,000. It seated twenty-five thousand patrons. More seats were added over the years so that by 1946, Van Buskirk's once open ballpark felt like a box, enclosed and tight.

There was no room to stretch at Ebbets Field. The shape and size of the place directed every eye toward the field. There was no escaping the person in the next seat, or the drunk a few rows down. The fans' close proximity to the field, which made it possible to talk with outfielders during a pitching change and to hear voices from everywhere in the park, felt as confining as life in a brownstone with neighbors who asked too many questions. Ebbets Field was a row house street, a railroad flat, a kitchen window looking out onto a red brick wall. It was not the way people wanted to live anymore.

THE TEAM, TOO, was aging, but with infinitely more grace. Reese, the captain, was thirty-seven. So too was Jackie Robinson, who had played in only 105 games in 1955 and batted a meager .256, the first time in his career he had fallen below .300. Even the younger men had aches that would not go away. Carl Erskine was twenty-nine, but his pitching arm had been hurting since 1952 and he slumped badly in the second half of 1955, pitching only once, and poorly, in the World Series. His best friend, Duke Snider, had had a marvelous championship season. But at twenty-nine his right knee hurt badly. New faces appeared, among them the pitchers Don Drysdale, who was just nineteen, and Sandy Koufax, twenty years old, impossibly wild and only two years out of Lafayette High School near Coney Island. There was

Don Zimmer, a twenty-five-year-old infielder who had a penchant for getting hurt but whom people thought might yet replace Reese at shortstop. Roger Craig, who was twenty-six, pitched well in 1955, as did twenty-four-year-old Ed Roebuck, who had a wonderful arm, even if he lacked the confidence to believe in it. Carl Furillo was thirty-three but played right field as well as any man in the game. Gil Hodges was thirty-two and could still hit for power. Roy Campanella, the ebullient catcher, was thirty-four but beset by questions about the condition of his worn and surgically mended hands.

The core—Campanella, Reese, Robinson, Hodges, Furillo, Snider, Erskine, Newcombe, and relief pitcher Clem Labine—had, in a baseball sense, grown old together. Reese had arrived in 1940 and was joined by Furillo in 1946. Robinson became the first black man to play in the major leagues in 1947, the same year that Snider and Hodges arrived. Campanella and Erskine came in 1948, Newcombe in 1949, and Labine in 1950. Now, six years later, having at last won the world championship that had so long eluded them, the people who followed them in the press box, in the stands, and, more and more, on television were left to wonder whether they had another championship run left in them. The Dodgers had won the 1955 National League pennant in a walk, winning 21 of their first 23 games. But things would not be so easy in 1956.

The Milwaukee Braves were younger and possessed both the pitching of Warren Spahn and Lew Burdette, and the hitting of Henry Aaron, Eddie Mathews, and burly Joe Adcock. The Cincinnati Reds were weaker on the mound but had a lineup that threatened pitchers with Frank Robinson, Gus Bell, and the biggest of baseball's big men, Ted Kluszewski.

THE GAME ON the field was not, strictly speaking, Walter O'Malley's problem: he left the running of the team to baseball people, his vice presidents, Fresco Thompson and Buzzie Bavasi. His worries were on a grander scale: the world in which he operated and profited was changing and, in his view, for the worse. Yet all around him were people who thought and behaved as if all were as it had always been, and always would be. The Brooklyn politicians he courted were narrow men whose interests seldom extended beyond deciding who would run for, say, the vacant seat on the Surrogate's Court. His players marked time in the most relentlessly incremental way— by pitching and batting, by inning and game, one at a time, with thoughts of the future regarded as a risky proposition that only made for worry and doubt. His baseball people thought in terms of tired arms and prospects, of raises and pay cuts measured in the thousands of dollars, not, as he thought, in the millions. His patrons had new diversions. They had television, and not just in the taverns where so many had started watching their first shows just ten years before. Now there were millions of televisions in living rooms, and with two competing teams, the Giants and Yankees in his own market, O'Malley had no choice but to broadcast Dodger games for people who might have once paid to see the team at Ebbets Field but who could now watch them at home, for free. Those eager to get out could go to Roosevelt Raceway, where the trotters ran eight times every night out on Long Island in Westbury. Roosevelt was a novelty. O'Malley's Dodgers, and Ebbets Field, were not.

When his front office began hunting for marchers for the Opening Day parade, they fanned out across Brooklyn and then to the Island where so many who'd once come to Ebbets Field now lived. The faithful among them still sent their sons to the Dodgers summer camp at Vero Beach. It was filled with Jewish kids from the Island. The team even hired a Jewish coach, Stanley Seidman, who always suspected he got the job by virtue of his being a teacher, his ball playing skills, and his last name. The now-distant fans still performed such acts of loyalty as naming a child for their heroes—Walter Alston Ketchum was baptized on Opening Day at Rugby Congregational Church in Brooklyn. But then his parents drove him back home to the Long Island town of West Islip.

O'Malley was in a muddle; the numbers did not look promising. Even in the championship season of 1955, the Dodgers had averaged just 13,400 spectators a game, their lowest number since 1945. Attendance at Ebbets Field had been slipping since 1947, when in Jackie Robinson's first year in Brooklyn, the Dodgers' home attendance averaged 23,300. The team never had a better year. But then this was a franchise that drew 5,000 or 6,000 spectators a game during the 1920s and '30s; the team had hit bottom in 1918, when, in wartime, they averaged 1,331 patrons a game. Since Walter O'Malley became the team's president in 1950, the Dodger home attendance ebbed and swelled between 13,000 and 16,000 patrons a game, with no evident sign of recovery.

The 1955 Dodgers bettered the National League average of 12,500, just as they had every year since 1937. But this brought little comfort to O'Malley, who had only to look no further west than Wisconsin to see riches the game could bring to even the most humble ball clubs. In 1953, Lou Perini, who owned the Boston Braves, secured the permission of his fellow National League owners to do what no team had done since 1903: move his franchise. Perini wanted to relocate to Milwaukee. O'Malley had objected. But not for long.

In 1952 the Boston Braves drew so few patrons that their average crowd of 3,677 made Braves Field feel like a bus station at midnight. The next year, at brand-new County Stadium, they averaged 23,700. The numbers only got higher in Milwaukee—26,000 in 1955—as they slid in Brooklyn. Lou Perini's Braves were now Brooklyn's competition, both on the field, and at the gate. Like his players, who'd grown used to their World Series checks, Walter O'Malley was not a man who cared for losing. And now the losing was only getting worse.

O'MALLEY WAS NOT the sort to wait for events to unfold around him. He was not at all like his rival Horace Stoncham, who owned the New York Giants. Stoneham was an owner by way of inheritance, a rich boy with too great a fondness for Dewar's White Label scotch. Horace Stoneham's Giants drew half the fans the Dodgers did, and their sorry attendance was bolstered only by those eleven games when the Dodgers traveled to northern Manhattan, to the Polo Grounds. Stoneham talked about moving his team out of New York altogether, maybe even to Minneapolis. But he was a man whose talk did not merit serious attention. He was not a mover. He was not Walter O'Malley.

In truth, among his baseball-owner colleagues, no one was. The men who owned the other major league teams were, like Horace Stoneham, wealthy sons who had taken over their fathers' teams, or scions of families that had made their money elsewhere—like Phil Wrigley, who owned the Cubs and whose family made chewing gum—or self-made men like Perini, who had made his money in construction, or John Galbreath, who used his real estate fortune to buy the Pittsburgh Pirates. Walter O'Malley made his money in baseball. Or more specifically, he was a businessman whose primary holding was the baseball team he owned. Bill Veeck, who had owned the St. Louis Browns and the Cleveland Indians, was a baseball man, a ballpark lifer and hustler whose pleasure, and profits, came from a delight in the game. O'Malley had other financial interests. But he spent his days running the Dodgers, which meant he could not afford to sit and risk having the Dodgers wilt into Horace Stoneham's Giants.

Nine months before, in August 1955, O'Malley decided that he had to act. The Dodgers, he announced, would play seven "home games" not at Ebbets Field, but at Roosevelt Stadium, across the Hudson River, in Jersey City. Not that he had any intention at the moment of *necessarily* making the move permanent.

His intent, he insisted, was quite the opposite: "Our present arrangements with Jersey City can be viewed as guaranteeing the continuance of the franchise at the nearest possible point to Brooklyn during the period when the new stadium might be under construction."

The *new* stadium. That was Walter O'Malley's answer. He had a site. He had a plan to get it built. He even had a model. It would be unlike any stadium ever seen. He had money in the bank. He had everything he needed, except what he needed most, and that was the man who had spent a generation building and shaping New York: Robert Moses. Moses, like Walter O'Malley, also looked to the future. Their views, however, were not the same.

TWO CONTESTS WERE unfolding on Opening Day in Brooklyn, 1956. One, of course, was the pennant race. Less visible was the battle Walter O'Malley was fighting against Robert Moses for a new ballpark in Brooklyn. Both contests were taking place against the backdrop of great upheaval across the borough, a transformation being witnessed by a Greek chorus of Brooklynites: the pastor of a black church, a couple leaving for Long Island, two teenage boys coming of age in two very different neighborhoods, a seminarian working among Brooklyn's poorest newcomers, a member of the borough's gentry, a veteran with three drug-addicted brothers. Each saw the change, and what it would mean to their lives, differently. Some ran from it; others embraced it. And still others insisted that nothing was really changing in Brooklyn, and never would.

A baseball season's Opening Day is a moment filled with possibility. A long season stretches out ahead, and even an Opening Day loss is hardly reason for concern. There are still so many games to play.

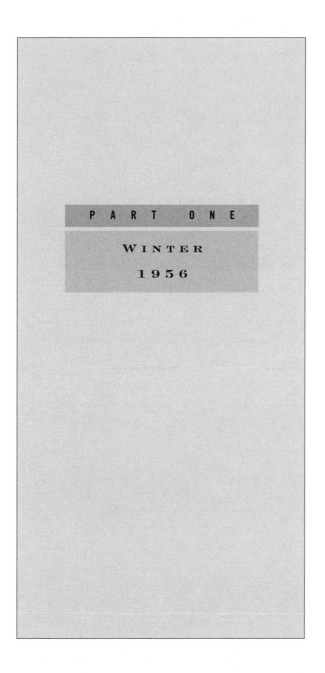

PART ONE

WINTER

1956

The first time Billy Kleinsasser saw Walter O'Malley was in November of 1955, at Princeton, when O'Malley had come looking for a new ballpark. Billy Kleinsasser was twenty-six years old, a graduate student in architecture, and that fall he enrolled in a graduate seminar taught by the great architect, R. Buckminster Fuller. Fuller had devised the geodesic dome, the great igloo that arched across the sky without benefit of intrusive struts and beams. Domes were the subject of the semester, specifically, the feasibility of creating a dome of the grandest scale, one that would, if done correctly, fit over a baseball stadium. This dome, however, was not Buckminster Fuller's idea. It was Walter O'Malley who had suggested to him just this sort of stadium for his Dodgers, in Brooklyn. Fuller, intrigued, enlisted his students who set about building a model for O'Malley. They worked through the fall and by Thanksgiving it was ready.

O'Malley came to Princeton with an entourage, which was to be expected; he was not a man who traveled alone. He brought an engineering friend, Emil Praeger, with whom he had been talking about a new stadium for years, and his public relations man, Red Patterson. And because O'Malley had been speaking of this stadium as a matter of great importance not only to the Dodgers and to Brooklyn but to the entire city of New York, he invited the press, who followed knowing that Walter O'Malley had a keen understanding of the nature of a good story.

It was snowing in Princeton, an early storm that O'Malley commented upon as he walked into the architecture school's laboratory. The storm, he said, was further evidence of the wisdom of the plan: bad weather would never again wash out a Dodger game, which was good for the fans and for him, too. He had calculated that he lost $200,000 for every rained out game. The savings from the dome, however, did not stop there. He explained to Fuller and his students that he stood to save an additional $21,000 for a tarpaulin large enough to cover an infield, the pro-rated salaries of twenty-one groundskeepers who pulled the tarp out and then, when the skies cleared, rolled it back up, and fifty cents to repaint every weatherworn seat in his ballpark each spring. This final savings represented one of the incidentals that especially pleased him: he told admirers of his spring training stadium at Vero Beach, Florida, that he had purposely sunk the park into the ground and surrounded it with a berm to eliminate the need for an annual paint job.

Billy Kleinsasser had never before helped design a project for a real client and was excited to be moving from the theoretical stage of his budding career to the practical. Now he watched as O'Malley approached the model stadium. It was round, and as wide as a loveseat. Fuller explained the design of the dome. The top came off and the two men peered inside. There was no grandstand; there were no seats at all, only a ball field with pegs to show where the players would stand.

"This is great. I'm just thrilled with it," O'Malley said. "I'm absolutely delighted. Let's slip off our coats."

Fuller told him that there would be no shadows, that the sun would shine through the translucent roof but would not burn the patrons. "The grass would grow greener, too," he said. "That has been proved."

"That's an important point, Bucky," O'Malley replied. "That's extremely important psychologically because baseball is traditionally an outdoor game. Bucky, what seating capacity does your model suggest?"

"Walter, we thought 100,000."

"I think 52,000 would be more practical, Bucky."

"It could be 52,000 just as easily," said Fuller.

O'Malley looked at his cigar, a prop he was never without. He smoked big Antonio y Cleopatras. He lit each fresh one from the smoldering butt of its predecessor. Wherever he went ash and smoke trailed behind him.

"Oh," he said, "the advantages are endless." He noted the absence of posts and pillars, and the unobstructed view from every seat. He proceeded with a recitation delivered at length and with such grammatical and syntactical precision that it not only strained the note-taking skills of the assembled hacks, but sounded, in print at least, as if he knew precisely what he was going to say before he ever started talking. He did this effortlessly, without benefit of notes. He was a marvelous talker.

"Well, where do we go from here?" he asked, rhetorically. The moment had come for his pitch. He had his audience, pens at the ready. "Can we purchase the land we need for a stadium? Well, the City of New York has appropriated $100,000 for the study of the Flatbush and Atlantic Avenue area in Brooklyn. Perhaps, in the solving of many problems that must be solved in that area, perhaps as an incident in the rehabilitation of that area, some land will be made available for purchase by the Brooklyn Dodgers."

But that was getting ahead of things. In the meantime, he said, he was very pleased by the work, so much so that perhaps if he were ever allowed to buy the land where he might build his stadium, it would indeed be a domed stadium, which, he added, was both "practical and economical."

As if on cue, the publicist Red Patterson returned to the morning's refrain. "This stadium would be tremendous from the air," he said. "It would be a landmark of New York."

O'Malley tossed away his cigar. "It would be big enough to enclose St. Peter's in Rome," he said, his deep baritone rising for emphasis. "It would be one of the wonders of the world."

HE RETURNED IN January of 1956 to see the finished model, not R. Buckminster Fuller's, but the work of Billy Kleinsasser. While his classmates moved on to other assignments, Kleinsasser decided to make the domed stadium the final project for his degree. He took Fuller's model and added 55,000 seats, 2,000 of them in hanging boxes. He shrunk the dome: Fuller wanted it 300 feet high and 750 feet in diameter. Kleinsasser made his 550 feet in diameter and 250 feet high, which, he reasoned, was still too tall for any fly ball to reach. He added a parking garage large enough for 5,000 cars. And, as a lark, he added a tramway that would run across the top of the dome. He thought it might be fun for children.

O'Malley was pleased, so pleased that he wanted to put Billy Kleinsasser's model on display. He took it back to Brooklyn, and soon had it placed in the lobbies of banks so people could pause and see what he had in mind for the Dodgers and for Brooklyn. He did not bother asking Billy Kleinsasser's permission to do this. Kleinsasser objected. O'Malley wrote to advise him that things might be made difficult for him if he made a fuss. Kleinsasser relented and was rewarded with an invitation to a dinner at which he was seated next to Sandy Koufax, a pitcher of vast but thus far unfulfilled potential.

Billy Kleinsasser, of course, was happy that Walter O'Malley liked his stadium. Yet there was something about O'Malley and the way he talked about the ballpark that perplexed him. "He seemed a little too nice, a little too enthusiastic," Kleinsasser recalled many years later. "He didn't ask the right kinds of questions. He talked about the idea. But he didn't push." In time, Billy Kleinsasser would learn a good deal about clients, about the way they asked questions and the sorts of questions they asked. The interested ones probed.

But that day in Princeton, Walter O'Malley did not probe. And this left Kleinsasser to wonder whether the whole exercise with Fuller and the class project and his own refinements of the dome had less to do with building a stadium than with building a model that Walter O'Malley could show as evidence of his *desire* to build a stadium. Billy Kleinsasser recognized, however, that he was only guessing. But then Walter O'Malley, a gregarious man, a talker, an infinitely accessible sort, nonetheless often left people who believed they knew him well wondering what, precisely, he was thinking.

2 | HIMSELF

Walter Francis O'Malley was then fifty-two years old and in his manner and bearing cultivated the air of prosperity. He was thick in the middle and in the face; his jowls were so heavy they swallowed his chin. His onetime manager, the vulgar and trenchant Leo Durocher, called him "whale belly." His appearance had changed little over the years, other than in the thickening. His hair was dark and oiled, parted in the middle and combed straight back. He wore frameless glasses and double-breasted suits, the better to conceal his gut. He smoked too much and exercised too little; he golfed occasionally at Vero Beach, but mostly he gardened.

He and his wife, Kay, were approaching their twenty-fifth wedding anniversary. They had two children, a twenty-one-year-old daughter, Terry, and Peter, an eighteen-year-old son. They lived in the Long Island town of Amityville. The house had been his parents' summer home. O'Malley had remodeled it and relocated his family there from Brooklyn in 1944. The house stood next door to the house where Kay O'Malley had grown up and where her parents still lived. There was no fence between their yards, and the O'Malley children had had a wide field in which to run. He commuted to his office on Montague Street in Brooklyn in a big black Buick chauffeured by his driver, Tony DeMeo. Like so many of the people who used to come to his ballpark, he had moved his family from Brooklyn to the Island and went to work in a car.

He always tried to be home for dinner. The family gathered at one end of the long dining room table built from a thick, varnished piece of wood that sat on two tree stumps. Papers were piled on the other end, and that is where he worked after dinner. In the longer evenings of spring and summer, he retired with his wife to the small greenhouse on the side of the house and tended the orchids they kept.

His first act upon rising was to light a cigarette. Then, a devout Catholic, he dropped to his knees and said his morning prayers. He made breakfast for his wife and children before leaving for work. He attended Mass every Sunday with his family. Sometimes, after Mass, they went to eat at a diner in Massapequa. He liked to cook and he liked to eat and he swore to his family that even though he could not abide the taste of fish he would one day come up with a recipe that would satisfy both him and the church's prohibition against eating meat on Fridays. He tended toward lecturing when disciplining his children, especially when they fought—an only child, he did not understand how siblings could fight—and he launched into a refrain about how children fighting led to neighbors fighting, led to cities fighting, led to nations fighting which, during the war years, left his children thinking, guiltily, that they were somehow to blame for the battles in Europe and the Pacific. He made a practice of attending his son Peter's football games at LaSalle Academy. He and his wife chaperoned their daughter's dances, once prevailing upon one of his pitchers, Rex Barney, to join them at a high school party. His daughter was thrilled, but not nearly as much as she was when she was sixteen and received her driver's license. That day her father told her to pack her pajamas, her toothbrush, and a hairbrush because now that she had a license it was time for her to drive. He gave her the wheel and that day they drove for hours. They stopped at his uncle's farm and the next day they drove to Cooperstown, to see the Baseball Hall of Fame. On summer weekends he took his children sailing on his boat, *Dodger*.

If there was trouble at work he might talk about it at the dinner table but did not display rage or frustration. Sometimes he told stories that his storytelling catcher, Roy Campanella, had told him. When his wife, Kay, spoke, he and the children turned to face her so that they could read her lips. She spoke only in a whisper. Shortly before they were to be married, Kay O'Malley was diagnosed with cancer of the larynx. To save her life, doctors advised the new technique of removing her voice box and then treating her with x-rays. She would be rendered mute, and her doctors warned her that the x-rays could make her infertile. Walter O'Malley's father advised him to break off the engagement. He refused. She would be, he told his father, the same girl he loved, whether or not she could speak. When Kay told him that she might never be able to have children, he replied that if God intended them to have children they would have children and if he did not he would be married to her just the same. His parents did not attend the wedding.

He looked just like his father, Edwin, who had been a middle-level functionary in the New York City Democratic Party—commissioner of markets, a ward heeler's plum—and who made his money in the dry goods business. His father was the son of Irish immigrants; his mother's parents were German. Walter O'Malley let the world think of him as Irish.

He grew up in the Bronx. He rooted for the Giants as a boy, or so he said years later, establishing his bona fides as a baseball fan. He would talk of his devotion to the game as "a virus"—"It's in my Irish bloodstream, and I revel in it"—and of how his uncle Clarence would take him to the Polo Grounds. He would tell, impishly, of sneaking into the Polo Grounds— "There were ways, ho, ho, there were ways." He insisted that he once traded ten Dodger pictures that came with packs of Sweet Caporal cigarettes for a single picture of the great Giant pitcher, Christy Mathewson.

He also liked to hint at a rough-and-tumble childhood, growing up "with the rock-throwing gangs of Crotona Park." Still, he did become a Boy Scout, rising to the rank of Star, two grades below Eagle. He also organized a unit of scouts, the Pine Tree Patrol, an early foray into politics—his father's world—that foreshadowed the sort of life he would fashion for himself. His father sent him to the Culver Military Academy in Culver, Indiana. He did not want to go; "my parents," he later said, "made me." He arrived at Culver a husky boy with a penchant for joining and organizing: corporal of "the Battery," his military unit; manager of the company baseball and tennis teams; member of the executive staff of the *Vedette*, the student newspaper; member of the Hospital Visitation Committee, the Debating Team, the Bible Discipline Committee, and the YMCA. The comment about him in the 1922 *Roll Call* student yearbook read: "A pleasing personality is perhaps his greatest asset, and with it he has won himself many friends." His teachers regarded him as "a very promising student" with "an excellent attitude." Friends thought he might one day become a newspaperman. He played baseball but stopped when a ground ball bounced badly, struck him in the face, and broke his nose. He graduated in 1922 and enrolled at the University of Pennsylvania.

At Penn he was a decent student and a legendary politician. He did not dance, friends said years later; he ran the dances and made money doing it. He built his own political machine—"O'Malley's Tammany"—by organizing the students who did not join the fraternities. He also prudently joined the ROTC and the Cardinal Newman Club; he chaired the junior class committee. And with those votes he became the only student ever to be elected president of his junior *and* senior classes. When he graduated, the yearbook prediction for him for 1946 read: "Now District Attorney in New York City and leader of Tammany Hall, a feat hitherto never performed. Walt certainly has a knack for breaking traditions." He took a double major in psychology and engineering, and for a graduation present his parents gave him forty-two-foot yacht. In the fall of 1926 he entered Columbia Law School.

But he could not stay. His father's dry goods business was failing and Walter O'Malley was forced to leave school and go to work. Years later he would talk of the good things that came with hard times: "It was," he said, "the best thing that ever happened to me because it made me buckle down and be serious." He continued studying law at night, at Fordham. By day he hustled work as a fledgling engineer. He was in his early twenties, and as he had done when his father sent him off, gloomily, to Culver Military Academy, O'Malley displayed a capacity to adapt rather than wallow.

He was also adept at using his father's political connections. The city's Board of Transportation hired him to conduct surveys for the Independent Subway lines. When he went into business—first with a partner and then on his own—he found work making engineering reports for several public schools, borings for the West Side Highway, geological surveys for the Queens Midtown Tunnel, and engineering reports for the Triborough

Bridge Authority. He earned his law degree but needed to spend a year clerking for a lawyer. When he could not find a lawyer who could afford to hire him, he gave a struggling lawyer space in his offices and paid for his own Depression-era clerkship.

He dreamed big. He came up with a plan to publish a legal manual for builders; they sold for five dollars a copy but did not make him much money. Then he won a bid to build the American embassy in Lima, but lost the job when the government canceled the contract. He tried winning contracts to drill freshwater wells in Bermuda, and to set up portable rigs to comb Alaskan waterways for gold. "Youth," he later said, "is a wonderful thing."

But there was no money to be made in engineering. So he turned to law. Long after he became a wealthy man, he liked to tell the story of his start in the law. It was a wonderful and useful yarn, folksy and impossible to confirm: one day, just after he opened his practice, he took a call from a man with a thick Irish brogue. "D'you do wills?" the man asked. O'Malley could not tell if the man said "wills" or "wells." Still, he took the man's address and arrived on East Fourteenth Street in Manhattan at the door of a Catholic church. It was the priest who had called; a wealthy parishioner was dying. The fellow had land in Ireland and needed to settle his estate. "Tell me, Father," O'Malley asked, "how did you come to pick me? I only opened my law practice yesterday."

"I just looked in the lawyer's directory till I found a name that looked like it came from County Mayo," replied the priest.

Around him were many people in difficult straits. And having attended to one dying man's affairs, Walter O'Malley sensed that there was money to be made assisting others in desperate circumstances. Apocryphal or not, the story of the priest and the dying man served a larger purpose: it gave an impish veneer to the work that launched O'Malley's career—Depression-era bankruptcy lawyer. He became, in the parlance of the times, "a grave dancer."

BY 1933 HE and his partner had offices in midtown Manhattan and twenty lawyers working for them. O'Malley was now thirty years old and cultivating wealthy clients, calling on old friends who might be useful. One was George V. McLaughlin, who had been New York's police commissioner in

1926 and who knew his father. Walter O'Malley had met him when he was still at Penn; they went to Athletics games together when McLaughlin visited Philadelphia. McLaughlin had since become a man with many powerful friends and connections, especially in banking and politics. He was president of the Brooklyn Trust Company and also a member of Robert Moses' Triborough Bridge (and later Tunnel) Authority. Tall and blustery, his intimidated subordinates secretly called him "George the Fifth." He was Walter O'Malley's kind of man.

Brooklyn Trust, like so many banks, was then awash in mortgages on properties whose value had all but evaporated. So it was that O'Malley stopped by McLaughlin's office and offered his firm's legal assistance in finding ways to extract money from those seemingly worthless mortgage properties, either by rewriting the payment terms, by foreclosure, or by selling off the collateral on the promise of future profits. McLaughlin declined. O'Malley suggested that his plan might make Brooklyn Trust $50 million. McLaughlin offered him a cigar and invited him to stay for a while. As it happened, tucked away among Brooklyn Trust's holdings was the estate of Charles Ebbets, which included half of the stock his family owned in the Brooklyn Dodgers.

IT WAS NOT an attractive property. The team was a million dollars in debt and on the verge of bankruptcy; the phone company once shut off their service when the Dodgers stopped paying the bills. Ebbets, who had built the team and its once-modern ballpark, had died in 1925. He had been a humorless, taciturn man who began his career with the Dodgers as a twenty-four-year-old scorecard and peanut vendor. The team promoted him to ticket seller, and, in time, to assistant to Joseph Boyle, an owner who made his money running gambling casinos. Ebbets bought shares of the team and though he only owned 10 percent of the club when Boyle died, he managed to get himself elected president. Ebbets' Dodgers played in an old wooden stadium, Washington Park, where business was never better than when the New York Giants came to play. Ebbets, however, wanted to get out of Washington Park. The place was crumbling. It was thick with mosquitoes and rusting so badly that foul balls tore through the chicken wire fence in the press box. The beat fellows each offered Ebbets a dollar for repairs. Ebbets quietly went looking for a site, finally settling on a tract of shanties surrounding a garbage dump. It was called "Pigtown." Ebbets spent four years buying the forty parcels of land he needed.

But to finance his new stadium, Ebbets needed partners. He found them in the McKeever brothers, Edward and Stephen, Irish immigrants who had begun making their money by carting dead horses from Brooklyn's streets. Their fortune came later in construction. In 1912, Ebbets had sold half his stock to the McKeevers. Suffice to say that from the beginning the arrangement was destined for complications. Ebbets and the McKeevers had set up two corporations, one for the team, one for the ballpark. Ebbets presided over the Dodgers; Edward McKeever was president of the ballpark corporation.

Thirteen years later Ebbets died. At his funeral Edward McKeever caught a cold. The cold turned into pneumonia. Within a week he, too, was dead. His brother Stephen wanted badly to be team president. Stephen McKeever was an ebullient man who called everyone "judge" and asked that the courtesy be returned. He was also a fan, taking in Dodger games from an elevated bench in the grandstand. But because ownership of the team was split evenly between McKeever people and Ebbets' heirs, the directors were compelled to turn to a compromise president, Wilbert Robinson, the corpulent manager whom people called "Uncle Robbie."

This proved unwise. Robinson was a middle-aged baseball man who had played the game in the late nineteenth century. Though well liked in the manner of a mascot, he was less than dynamic. Nor was he one for juggling responsibilities. While he had twice managed the Dodgers to the World Series under Ebbets' stewardship, he could do no better than fourth place on his own. In each of the first six years of his presidency the Dodgers finished in sixth place. When the directors forced him out in 1931, they once again broke Stephen McKeever's heart and chose another man, Frank York, as president. York lasted two years. Finally, in 1933 the directors turned to the aging McKeever. The title pleased the old man, even if the team's play and finances could not. The Dodgers finished no better than fifth place, in 1935, under manager Casey Stengel.

The team's debt, meanwhile, was growing and the directors were forced, time and again, to seek loans from George V. McLaughlin's Brooklyn Trust Company. Stephen McKeever died in 1938 at the age of eighty-six. By 1939, with the heirs squabbling and with the team coming off a seventh-place finish, McLaughlin had had enough. So too had Ford Frick, president of the National League. Frick advised the team's directors that they needed new management. He recommended Larry MacPhail.

MacPhail was a maddening and angry drunk who nonetheless knew how to fashion a winner and turn a profit. He had done wonders in Cincinnati with the Reds, having introduced in 1934 the revolutionary idea of playing baseball at night under lights. In four years under MacPhail the Dodgers paid off their debts and won the 1941 National League pennant. When he left to join the army in 1942 there was $250,000 in the bank. When the McKeever heirs decided to sell their quarter of the team in 1944, McLaughlin helped put together a consortium of buyers: John Smith, president of Pfizer pharmaceutical company; the baseball impresario Branch Rickey, who after making champions of the St. Louis Cardinals had succeeded MacPhail in running the Dodgers; and a little-known lawyer, in baseball circles at least, named Walter O'Malley.

He was by now a wealthy man, having parlayed his increasingly lofty legal fees—he claimed to have earned as much as $100,000 on a single case—into wise and profitable investments. In time his holdings would include full ownership of the New York Subway Advertising Company, 6 percent of the stock of the Long Island Railroad, one of seven ownership stakes in the Brooklyn Union Gas Company, and holdings in the J. P. Duffy building materials company.

His patron, McLaughlin, had helped make him the team's lawyer in 1942. By 1944, McLaughlin had midwifed the sale that made O'Malley a part owner, as well as team secretary and vice president. A year later, again with McLaughlin's assistance, O'Malley, Smith, and Rickey bought another 50 percent of the team—the shares from the Ebbets estate held by Brooklyn Trust. The three men agreed that no partner could sell his shares to an outsider without first offering them to the others. This would pose a problem, because Walter O'Malley did not like Branch Rickey and Rickey did not like him.

O'MALLEY THOUGHT RICKEY a sanctimonious prig; Rickey, who did not swear or drink, disapproved of men who drank scotch in the company of other men drinking scotch—he advised guests at his daughter's wedding that if they wanted a drink there was a bar nearby. O'Malley believed that the way he cultivated people and did his business was no concern of Rickey's. Besides, O'Malley was offended by Rickey's appearance: he dressed badly and his clothes were flecked with ash and food. All of this, however, seemed a pretext for a deeper rift.

Rickey was a baseball man; he'd been a catcher in the days of paper-thin mitts. He had built the first great farm systems, first in St. Louis and later in Brooklyn, networks of minor league teams that provided a vast pool of talent. He was an early proponent of management by "creative tension": a young player who arrived at the Dodger spring training camp in Vero Beach could well find himself with that rarest of baseball uniforms: one with a triple-digit number on the back. The Dodgers had as many as eight hundred players under contract, and the sight of so many of them at Vero Beach was sufficient evidence for any prospect that a bad day could well mean that someone else would take his place tomorrow.

Rickey had been especially prescient in harvesting talent after the war. And by the late 1940s, the Dodgers were heavily stocked with good players, all of whom came to Vero Beach and learned the "Dodger way"—the proper way to slide and catch and play the field. Every minor league in Rickey's constellation played the game just like the big team did.

This was, in a baseball sense, Rickey's triumph. The awful Dodger teams of the twenties and thirties were mythologized because the team that Rickey later built was so good. But creating the champion Dodgers paled before Rickey's great and enduring accomplishment: the transcendent act of hiring a black man to play in the major leagues when he signed Jackie Robinson in 1946. Rickey was a principled man and did this at great risk to his team, to Robinson, and to his own considerable reputation. His partner, O'Malley, did not attempt to block the signing. That is noteworthy, but up to a point. O'Malley did not sign Jackie Robinson. And no one has ever suggested that the idea would have occurred to him.

Breaching baseball's "color line" required vision beyond the game, and beyond the profits it might generate. Rickey was such a visionary. Walter O'Malley was not. He was, above all, a practical man, expedient and clever. He was also a political man, and political people adjust, making up the script as they go along. And because they see the world so differently, they often distrust visionaries, who are most interested in charting a path to the future.

Walter O'Malley was in the business of making money, and to do this in baseball he needed a good team and an inviting place for people to come to see it play. "Money," he once said, "are the only chips we have." He was speaking of his game, which was business. Branch Rickey's business was baseball. He liked making money just as much as Walter O'Malley did, so much so that he was reluctant to spend it on paying his players.

O'Malley had been keenly interested in different ways of striking it rich before he ever thought of trying to make his fortune in baseball. He was not of the school of "always leave the other fellow with something." He was not much interested in leaving the other fellow with anything. He spent his days thinking and plotting ways to do this, in ways that people close to him admired—he was a master at his game—but which years later they conceded diminished him. "Walter," his vice president Buzzie Bavasi once said, "would have been a wonderful guy except he loved money too goddamn much."

THE PARTNERSHIP ENDURED for six years. Rickey ran the club; the Dodgers won pennants in 1947 and 1949. O'Malley, so adept at cultivating men of means and influence, created an ally in the third partner, John Smith: when the teetotaling Rickey tried to block the sponsorship of Schaefer Beer, O'Malley and Smith outvoted him. And when Smith died in 1950, O'Malley extended his solicitude to his widow, May. By 1950, O'Malley was poised to push Rickey out.

Rickey, then sixty-nine years old, was not going to step away without exacting a price from Walter O'Malley. He offered his share of the team to William Zeckendorf, a real estate developer, for $1 million. Zeckendorf, an old friend of Rickey's, agreed. But Rickey had to let his partners match any offer for his shares. O'Malley and May Smith wanted his shares. Rickey explained that he had a problem: Zeckendorf had already put money down; he would need to be compensated by O'Malley and Smith. This "reimbursement fee" would together cost them $50,000. O'Malley paid; but he would not forgive Rickey, and one way or another he was going to get his money back.

Still, in the fall of 1950, Walter O'Malley had what he wanted, which was control of the team. He would run it in a way altogether different than Rickey had. He did not concern himself with players or their salaries.

Fresco Thompson ran the farm system. Buzzie Bavasi hired, fired, haggled with, and signed the players. Bavasi and Thompson were rarities in O'Malley's universe: holdovers from the Rickey days. O'Malley so detested even the absent Rickey that anyone in the office who mentioned his name was fined a quarter. Luckily for Bavasi and Thompson, they had first worked for Larry MacPhail, which granted them dispensation from the sin of association with Branch Rickey.

While Rickey had traveled widely, scouting players and watching his minor leaguers play, O'Malley remained in Brooklyn and turned his attention to such matters as attendance, his ballpark, and the revenue potential from television. O'Malley had taken over Branch Rickey's corner office in downtown Brooklyn at 215 Montague Street. It was a dark office with a heavy desk next to which was a trash can whose contents often burst into flames; O'Malley would drop a smoldering cigar butt into the can, set the paper on fire, and then, barely missing a beat, reach into his desk for a small fire extinguisher.

As he had done since his father sent him out into the world, he set about identifying and seducing people who could be of use. He started with the press. A month after taking over the club, he invited Jimmy Powers, sports editor and columnist of the *New York Daily News*—his column "The Powerhouse" had well over a million readers—to the house in Amityville. It was a clever choice: Powers had hated Rickey, dubbing him "el cheapo" for the miserly salaries he paid his players. O'Malley offered him something new, not the sermonizing wise man whom the beat writers called "the Mahatma." Instead, he assumed the role of Friend of the Little Man.

He invited him to dinner, and made sure that Powers knew that he did the cooking. He drew Powers in—suggesting the manly task of getting the fire going while Kay O'Malley made the salad. No chef, Powers noted. No help. Walter O'Malley himself would carve the turkey.

They chatted while he worked. Oh yes, O'Malley explained, he had the other businesses. But really, he was not so much different from the men who came to see his team. "My big wish, Jimmy, is to get the ball club back close to the fans. This Dodger team, you know, used to be the darling of the whole country. Now, for one reason or another, we've drifted apart from the Little People." (Powers, eating this up, felt compelled to capitalize.)

O'Malley went on. "How do we make the cab driver and the milkman feel that they are part of this club—that's what worries me."

But Powers was not worried. For here was an owner unlike any other; yes, he was a wealthy man, but he was not remote. He "does not consort only with big brass." He wrote nice notes to his manager. He had gone to games before he ever owned a piece of the team. He cheered up his players when they lost. He was "no stuffed shirt." He lived in a "modest" home with a "lovely" wife and two "fine youngsters." And when O'Malley told Powers that he had learned what the Little People wanted by "sitting in with the fan and suffering as he suffers" Powers noted this, like Boswell recounting yet another gem of Dr. Johnson's.

Jimmy Powers left Amityville well-fed and seduced. The column recounting his visit was all that Walter O'Malley could have wanted. "It looks like a brighter day in Brooklyn," Powers wrote, "and, we sincerely hope, better things ahead at Ebbets Field."

3 | THE ICE STORM

In early January 1956 a rare and nasty ice storm struck New York. Ice started falling after dinnertime and by late that night the streets were so slick that in Brooklyn the buses stopped running. The borough felt paralyzed. People tried to walk but slipped and fell. It was not safe to drive. Telephone lines at the police precinct houses were jammed with calls from all the people who had hurt themselves and needed help. Hospital emergency rooms were crowded with still more people waiting hours to see a doctor. Ambulances were so busy that the police started ferrying injured people to hospitals in patrol cars. One police officer broke his back when he slipped and fell helping a man who had suffered a heart attack. Another broke his hip leaving his station house. Two officers delivered a child whose parents could not get an ambulance to take them to the hospital. People waited in long lines for buses that did not come. Only the two remaining trolley car lines ran on time.

By midmorning, however, the temperature rose and the falling ice turned to rain. The sidewalks thawed, the streets began to flood, and by the end of the day attention had shifted back to the concerns of the moment, both great and small. Troubles abounded, or so it felt. The Transit Authority announced that its ridership had dropped for the seventh year in a row. A third fewer passengers were now riding the subways and buses, and for this the authority blamed all the new cars, and all the many people who had moved to the suburbs.

The boxing promoter Max Joss died, and his death was yet another reminder of the passing of a time when men and influence and reputation in Brooklyn flocked to the ringside seats at the Broadway Arena on Halsey Street for the Tuesday night fights. Joss's shows, which featured the likes of Solly Kreiger, Bernie Friedkin, and Morris Reif, were long gone, and by the time he died the Broadway had become a factory and Joss was left to peddle storm windows. "Milton Berle," he said of the king of television, "finished us."

And now, on top of it all, Robert Moses wanted to build a highway through the heart of Brooklyn.

The mere *suggestion* that Robert Moses wanted to build a highway propelled people to worry and perhaps to act—as much good it might do them. The highway would connect the Brooklyn-Queens Expressway with the Belt Parkway, cutting through such neighborhoods as Midwood, Canarsie, Flatlands, and East New York. Citizens living in the highway's proposed path formed the Save Brooklyn Committee. The committee joined with the Save Bay Ridge Committee, which had already formed to try to block yet another of Moses' plans: connecting Staten Island to Brooklyn with a great bridge that would, inevitably, mean destroying homes in Bay Ridge to make way for access roads. These people had good reason to fret, because if Robert Moses wanted to build a highway, or a bridge, if he wanted to tear down homes or condemn entire blocks, if he wanted to empty a neighborhood to make way for something new and grand, he did it. No one stopped him. No one, not presidents, governors, or mayors stopped him. Nor did the voters, because Robert Moses held no elective office. He had run for governor of New York State in 1934. He was trounced. But he soon found a route to power far greater than any governor ever enjoyed.

Moses was, in the narrowest definition, an appointed official—narrow, because once he was appointed to a position that post became *his*. The men who appointed him did not ask for Moses' resignation if he somehow displeased them; it was Robert Moses who periodically threatened to resign if the men with the loftier titles displeased *him*. Moses headed the Triborough Bridge and Tunnel Authority, as well as the New York Parks Commission, Construction Commission, and Slum Clearance Committee. He had held appointed positions since 1924. In those positions he built seven great bridges, sixteen expressways and highways, over a thousand housing project buildings, over six hundred playgrounds. He built parks and dams. He built the United Nations. He built the roadways that made it possible for New Yorkers to be able to drive around and out of the city—north to the suburbs of Westchester County, and east, to Long Island. Billions of dollars flowed through his offices, and it was with that money along with the perception that he was a man who *got things done* that he was able to do as he pleased, without oversight, without dissent, without question. He was sixty-seven years old, tall, powerfully built; he swam every day. He was smarter than almost everyone around him, and he knew this, and if people did not know it he was quick to remind them. He was charming with the people he needed. He was an overbearing brute, a bully when it came to dispensing with people who had the temerity to disagree with him.

Like Branch Rickey he was also a visionary. Educated at Yale and Oxford, he had come to government an idealistic reformer, a Good Government crusader intent on rooting out corruption, and on making better the lives of the less fortunate. He was a protégé of Al Smith, the populist New York governor of the 1920s who had revolutionized government's relationship with the poor and powerless. Before Franklin Roosevelt's New Deal, there was Al Smith, the waif from the Lower East Side, who had championed the idea of government's *responsibility* to the dispossessed. Moses came to work for Smith as a young man of privilege, a Jew who grew up with an elitist sense of noblesse oblige. Though Moses would cite Smith often in his letters and writings, the essential lesson of Smith's doctrine of social responsibility became ever more lost to him. Unlike Smith, Moses was above all a builder, and people tended to get in his way. People needed to be moved, and if the least fortunate among them somehow disappeared from view, if they ended up not in the housing projects he was building to replace their tenement homes but instead in the ramshackle bungalows in the distant reaches of New York, this did not appear to sadden him. Moses was building a great city and in this pursuit he was tireless. In his head he possessed a map of what this new New York would—not might, but *would*—look like. He was not about to stop or slow down until it was all filled in.

In 1956, Robert Moses was at the height of his powers. In addition to the "Cross-Brooklyn Expressway" he had plans for yet another multimillion-dollar "slum clearance," which would mean three more housing projects for Brooklyn alone. Moses and his public works were everywhere in the borough: the new Coney Island Hospital was all but complete; there were new libraries in Coney Island and New Lots, and health centers in Crown Heights and Sunset Park. Moses had razed "slum" neighborhoods across the city, cleared out the rubble and the poor people who lived there, and built in Brooklyn nineteen housing projects—high-rises with elevators and modern conveniences, and 26,500 apartments. He was far from done. He was building another seven projects—another 7,800 apartments—and had plans for another five, which meant another 5,300 apartments, which like all public housing was intended not for poor people but for the working and middle-class people who could afford the rents. He needed them if the city were to compete for those desirable renters with their lifestyle that he had, in good measure, helped create: the suburban-home-of-one's-own, especially on Long Island, which he made accessible for commuters with the highways he had built twenty years before. In Brooklyn and across the city, Moses built and built quickly, and in the second week of January 1956 he announced plans to clear a wide swath behind the Long Island Railroad Station in downtown Brooklyn and build housing for another 1,800 families. Clearing the land was not difficult. The federal government gave him the power and the money to do it. In fact, Moses had the power to clear the land and do with it what he wanted, so long as the purpose served the public good. Suffice it to say that Robert Moses was a lone and powerful voice in defining the public good.

He had begun his career in a New York that was, literally in some spots, a sinkhole—a city awash in corruption, a crowded and often fetid town where it was impossible to drive from one end to the other without having to stop at endless red lights. His intent was to change that, and he did. But he did more than condemn, flatten, and build. He changed the character of the city, of its neighborhoods, of its delicate ethnic and racial mix. This did not trouble him. Robert Moses was, for all his considerable flaws, a bold man capable of envisioning and creating a grand New York, a New York of tall buildings, vast parks, great cultural centers, and highways over which people could come and go. Walter O'Malley wanted to be a part of Robert Moses' New York.

O'MALLEY HAD STARTED talking about a new stadium for the Dodgers well before he ever became the team's president. He had first broached the idea in 1946 to John Cashmore, the Brooklyn borough president. In 1952, his second year as Dodger president, O'Malley began a public campaign for a new ballpark. That spring he invited the industrial designer, Norman Bel Geddes, to Vero Beach. Bel Geddes came to help design a new spring training stadium, and to talk, too, about a replacement for Ebbets Field. Bel Geddes, a big thinker, had an idea for a stadium with a retractable roof, foam rubber seating, automatic hot dog vending machines, artificial turf that could be painted any color, and a 7,000-space parking garage. Parking was essential. More and more of O'Malley's patrons were driving to the park, especially those Dodger loyalists who had moved to Long Island. But Ebbets Field had only 700 spots, scattered in service stations and small parking lots around the stadium. Those who got to the game late were left to search for parking on the street.

In 1953, O'Malley announced that the Dodgers were planning a new ballpark, a 52,000-seat stadium. He was looking at several unnamed sites and insisted that they were all in Brooklyn. He hoped to get started on construction in six months. "In any event," he said, "I am certain that we will have a new stadium within the next five years. The Dodgers will own it but it will also be constructed to accommodate other enterprises."

He was, of course, free to buy land and build on it, so long as those plans conformed to zoning requirements. But land in Brooklyn was not nearly as cheap as it had been forty years earlier when Charles Ebbets was bargaining with the squatters and shanty-dwellers of "Pigtown" who were thrilled to take his five hundred dollars for their seemingly worthless plots. To afford land that was centrally located and near the major roadways and subway stops, O'Malley needed Robert Moses. Specifically, he needed the condemnation power Washington had granted Moses as the city's Slum Clearance Commissioner under Title I of the Federal Housing Act. It was up to Moses to determine where new housing would replace tenement housing, and where other amenities of urban life—parks, hospitals, schools, libraries—might go. A ballpark, O'Malley reasoned, *could* serve a public purpose, so long as it included an amenity that both he and Moses needed: a parking garage. He was not asking Moses to build him a stadium. In fact, a publicly-owned stadium was the last thing O'Malley wanted. He did not want to be a renter. In order to profit, he reasoned, he needed to own. Despite the wealth he had accumulated, O'Malley could not afford both to buy land at a good location and then build a ballpark and garage. But if Moses condemned the land, thereby reducing its cost drastically, O'Malley could afford it. Perhaps, O'Malley calculated, Moses might see the public good in his plan.

On September 8, 1953, O'Malley invited Moses to Brooklyn, to a gathering at the Brooklyn Club, an exclusive club housed in a brownstone around the corner from the Dodger offices on Montague Street in Brooklyn Heights. They met with a host of Brooklyn's political and civic leaders in a room called the Coal Hole. Moses hated the room. But he was prepared to listen.

Walter O'Malley talked about the needs of the little fellow. He talked of Brooklyn's love affair with its Dodgers. He talked of the orphans who came to Ebbets Field as the team's guests. Robert Moses was amused. "That was a wonderful spiel Walter O'Malley gave us," he wrote the next day to his chief lieutenant at the city construction commission, George Spargo. "I had heard a considerable part of it before and he has perfected it with some lovely embroidery. George McLaughlin tells me that the poor little orphans, etc. are allowed in free now and then, spend 60 ¢ apiece for popcorn, coca-cola, etc [sic]."

Transparent as the pitch was, it had nonetheless worked. "On the other hand," Moses went on, "I am ready to concede that Brooklyn is crazy about the Dodgers. Whether it is crazy enough to support a $6,000,000 stadium is another matter."

If this were so, Moses was willing to be accommodating. He even had a site in mind, and as it happened a very attractive one. Chief among his Brooklyn projects was the creation of a civic center in the borough's downtown. The civic center was Moses at his most vainglorious. Here he saw not only the seat of Brooklyn's government, but a new courthouse, a new home for Long Island University, the Brooklyn Polytechnic Institute, an expanded Brooklyn Hospital, new and wide boulevards leading to the Brooklyn and

Manhattan bridges, and a larger campus for Pratt Institute, the design school. The neighborhood was filled with factories and tenement homes. These would be relocated or demolished, making room for housing projects. The housing, of course, would be for those who could afford it. These new tenants would then be within walking distance of the downtown Brooklyn department stores, like Martin's and Abraham & Straus, whose vice president, Robert Blum was, not surprisingly, a booster of Moses' plan. This support was essential. Robert Moses could plan, condemn, and bring millions of federal dollars to his projects. But he could not simply order buildings to rise. He needed bankers and builders to invest in his projects. He needed politicians to back his plans. He needed the newspapers to write glowingly of his vision, to remind the hesitant politicians and reluctant bankers of the wisdom in aligning themselves with him. The very people Walter O'Malley had been soliciting to help him with his new ballpark were many of the same people Robert Moses had also felt compelled to court: among them John Cashmore; Robert Blum; Frank Schroth, Sr., publisher of the *Brooklyn Eagle*; and Jack Flynn, publisher of the *New York Daily News*. Moses wrote them letters and attended their parties and sent them congratulatory notes. The more prominent the person, the more fulsome the letter—his notes, for instance, to Arthur Sulzberger, publisher of the *New York Times*, were almost as fawning as those Moses wrote to Sulzberger's wife, Iphigene.

The Brooklyn Civic Center would need the support of all these people. It would need parking, a lot of parking. This was where Walter O'Malley might be useful. O'Malley needed fifteen acres to build a ballpark and the requisite parking garage. "We might expand the Pratt Institute project and let the Dodgers have part of it, or let them bid against a residential sponsor," Moses wrote in a memo to Spargo. The Dodgers, he suggested, might include Ebbets Field in the deal, so that Moses could tear it down and build yet another housing project. He and Spargo would go to downtown Brooklyn to see whether the plan might work.

He sent word of the idea to O'Malley, who had every reason to feel confident that his plan might work: Moses was not only considering a choice location but, just as important, was willing to include the park and the garage as part of a slum clearance project.

Yet, whatever dreams O'Malley enjoyed of a new and affordable stadium rising in the heart of the Brooklyn Civic Center lasted only a few days. A week after their meeting at the Brooklyn Club, Moses had inspected the site and written to William Lebwohl, his counsel at Triborough, that it was "wholly impractical." Adding the stadium, he had concluded, would "jeopardize" the entire Pratt Institute project. Still, he was not ruling out a new Dodger stadium in Brooklyn: "We shall have to look at some other neighborhood."

ON THE EDGE of Bedford-Stuyvesant, on the border of Brownsville, in the very place where Brooklyn was undergoing its most dramatic and widespread transformation from racially and economically mixed to increasingly black and poor, sat the House of the Good Shepherd, a home for teenage girls who'd run afoul of the law. The shelter was a complex of buildings that dated to the late 1800s, and which were in poor repair. The same day that he rejected granting O'Malley leave to build in downtown Brooklyn, Moses sent a memo to Spargo asking that someone look into the site as a possible home for the Dodgers.

This was not, however, the kind of location that O'Malley had in mind. Although it abutted a major thoroughfare, Atlantic Avenue, it was, Moses wrote, "a bad rundown neighborhood" filled with "lousy negro [sic] tenements." But Moses saw possibilities in the site: because the property was so unattractive, the land would be cheap—cheap enough for O'Malley to buy it. Moses could condemn the surrounding slums, build new housing and perhaps a playground and school, and, in so doing, add a valuable and lucrative property to the city's tax rolls. He would also get another parking garage. And, if O'Malley sold and abandoned Ebbets Field, he could use that site for housing. "The stadium people, of course, would get less revenue from parking than if they were in some other neighborhood," he wrote in a memo to Spargo. But that was not his problem. Walter O'Malley was becoming a problem, and now Moses believed he had found a way to make him go away.

Whatever charm or amusement Moses found in O'Malley that day at the Brooklyn Club was quickly vanishing. On September 24, just three weeks after the gathering, Moses wrote to borough president Cashmore, apprising him of his plans. He characterized the work as "the chore assigned to me." He could not have sounded less pleased. But worse still for

O'Malley, Moses was having second thoughts about whether the stadium could, in fact, be part of a slum clearance project. The sticking point was the "public purpose" proviso; a privately owned stadium did not, in Moses' new thinking, fulfill such a purpose. He offered no written explanation for changing his mind. It was one thing for O'Malley to buy some cheap land and, with the stadium and parking garage as an anchor, for Moses to redevelop the rest of a poor neighborhood with the federal government's assistance. Washington paid two-thirds of the cost of demolishing slums and clearing the land, so long as half of that land was set aside for housing. But this gave Moses ample room to do as he pleased. It was therefore appropriate, in his view, to condemn land on Manhattan's Upper West Side for the New York Coliseum because even though the Coliseum would host such events as the trade and boat shows, it would still be owned and operated by a public agency, a Moses agency, and therefore serve a public purpose. And it was also in the public's interest for Moses to condemn land further north in Manhattan for the "Manhattanville" housing project and then allow the buildings to sit untouched while the politically connected developers to whom he had awarded the project squeezed the remaining tenement dwellers for two more years of rent. The federal government would, from time to time, ask Robert Moses to explain how he was using its Title I money, but generally it allowed him to proceed as he wished. The newspapers, for their part, were foursquare behind Moses, quick and generous to praise his efforts on the city's behalf.

O'Malley's stadium plan did not fit Moses' vision. Whether this reflected a genuinely held belief on the misuse of Title I money or whether he simply did not like O'Malley, Moses did not say. "We obviously cannot select areas to be cleared for the primary purpose of providing a fifteen acre location for a new privately owned stadium," he wrote to Frank Schroth of the *Eagle*. He sent a copy of this letter when he wrote to Walter O'Malley on October 20.

"It is obviously your thought that we can some how [*sic*] go out and condemn property for a new Dodger field just where you want it. . . . This is absolutely out of the question." The Bedford-Stuyvesant site, he added, "is your best bet."

Moses had made his offer. Now he waited to see if O'Malley would take it. "Let's see if O is serious," he wrote to Spargo on October 26. "Pin it down to the purchase by him of the old institution on Atlantic Avenue. If he won't do this, he's kidding us." But if by "kidding us" Moses meant that O'Malley was not serious about wanting to move the Dodgers to a new location in Brooklyn, the reply he got a week later made it clear that he was very much mistaken.

O'Malley possessed the soul of a salesman: just because Moses had made him a take-it-or-leave-it offer did not mean he was disposed either to take it or to leave. His response sounded like that of a man who, having heard bad news, simply changes the subject.

"My dear Bob," he wrote on October 28. "Your letter . . . leaves me with some hope that when we get together after the election a way will be found for a new Dodger stadium."

Moses, he was now suggesting, had misunderstood him. Forget the stadium for the moment. They were talking about a parking garage. The stadium was simply part of the package. "Let us suppose it costs $3,000 a car to build a parking garage," O'Malley wrote, offering an unnecessary lesson on the economics of parking facilities: a 2,000-car garage would cost $6 million. Adding a stadium, he calculated, would cost another $2.5 million. Fees from the parking garage would make it possible for him to afford to build both the garage and the stadium. There was, however, a catch: "It is obvious that location becomes a matter of great importance when planning for the parking garage feature." He did not mention that the use of a parking garage on nongame days would be far greater in downtown Brooklyn than it would in Bedford-Stuyvesant.

O'Malley may not have minded opening with an obsequious tone, if only because it masked his steelier side until he was ready to display it. Now that moment had come: "I am aware of your encouragement to industry to finance, build and operate public parking garages and I was hoping my plans were in that direction.

"I want a new baseball stadium. You want a parking garage to ease a public problem. It is my hope we can combine the two needs, using public authority to assemble the plot and private money to finance it."

Moses' reply came five days later. He sounded like a man trying hard to control his temper. "Dear Walter," he began. "Let me see if I can simplify this matter." He ticked off O'Malley's arguments on the mutual benefits of his plan. He chose his words carefully, the better to leave O'Malley no room to wiggle.

"First, neither the City nor any existing public authority has any power or right to acquire by eminent domain property for the purposes you outline . . . it is obvious that the garage is financially incidental to the stadium and that the real purpose is to build a new Dodger Stadium."

As to combining the stadium with the garage, "I would personally have the gravest doubts about the practicality of this plan." Impractical, he explained, because building a garage on land that is either vacant or "relatively inexpensive" (read: Bedford-Stuyvesant) would not cover the cost because no one would park there except on game days. In other words, I have no quarrel with a garage except one that is well-located and next to a ballpark, and which sits on land that I have condemned (read: downtown). "There is an indication in your letter that you still have in mind the possibility of locating a stadium and garage within a Title I Slum Clearance Project at a central location where the garage would carry the stadium. As previously indicated to you, I can see no way in which this can be done."

He did give O'Malley his blessing to buy land in Brooklyn, if that was what he wanted. And if he did choose to buy some affordable land, Moses was confident that officeholders "from the Borough President on down" would be happy to help with widening roads and building schools and parks as part of a "general neighborhood improvement."

He closed icily: "I would earnestly suggest that you and the others interested proceed along these lines which seem to offer the best prospect for success."

Not that Moses necessarily thought he would. Nor, it appeared, did Moses much care. "I don't believe Walter O'Malley has the slightest interest in buying the old institution on Atlantic Avenue for a new Dodger Stadium," he wrote on November 16 to Philip Cruise, chairman of the city's housing authority. Perhaps, he added, a housing project might go there after all.

But if Moses thought he could make O'Malley go away he was wrong, more wrong than he could imagine. People listened when Moses spoke. O'Malley heard him. But it was as if he paid him no mind.

Spurning the Bedford-Stuyvesant site was, from a financial point of view, the prudent move, even if it seemed harsh in what it said about the prospects for turning a profit in what was a largely black neighborhood. Even setting aside the neighborhood's economic erosion, the site was not attractive. It sat in a hard-to-reach corner of Brooklyn, far from any highway and with only one subway line running close by.

With the civic center dream doomed from the start, and with Bedford-Stuyvesant offering a location even worse than the one where he still found himself, Walter O'Malley needed help. He had positioned himself well to get it. Less than six months after his chilly letter from Robert Moses, O'Malley was rewarded for all the flattery he had bestowed upon important people with a cheery note from John Cashmore. The letter reached him in Vero Beach, where the Dodgers were preparing for the 1954 season.

"Dear Walter," wrote the borough president. "This is the letter which I promised to send to you."

The letter had come to Cashmore in January from a man named Joseph Kaufman. Kaufman was president of the New York Council of Wholesale Meat Dealers. He had a problem, "a serious situation which exists in the heart of the borough of Brooklyn, which I am sure you can correct." On the corner of Flatbush and Atlantic Avenues, across from the Brooklyn terminal of the Long Island Railroad, on the edge of the Brooklyn Civic Center, sat the vast and fetid Fort Greene meat market. The market, wrote Kaufman, was "deteriorating very rapidly." The equipment and buildings were old. Traffic jams were common. The owners were small merchants who could not afford to relocate. The market was filled with "health hazards." Kaufman was pleading for help so that "in the greatest borough" the market could be moved, en masse, to a new location.

Walter O'Malley did not need John Cashmore to spell out the possibilities. Joseph Kaufman was offering a jewel: a large, wonderfully located eyesore. It sat on the confluence of two major roadways, both of which connected with the highways that ringed the borough. Better still, it sat above the Brooklyn terminus of the Long Island Railroad, which meant that Dodger fans who'd relocated to the Island would not even need to drive to a game; the train would deposit them at the front gate. If Brooklyn were Manhattan, then this location would have been Times Square—smack in the middle of everything. It was impossible to envision a better site for a new Brooklyn ballpark, because no better site existed. Surely, Robert Moses could see the public purpose in helping him make a ballpark—and a parking garage—rise on this woebegone corner of Brooklyn.

4 | LUXURY ROW

In late February 1956, the Brooklyn Dodgers boarded the DC-3 that Walter O'Malley had bought for the team and flew south, to Vero Beach, Florida, to begin spring training.

Duke Snider agreed to a $40,000 salary, a $7,000 raise that made him the team's second highest paid player; Roy Campanella made $42,000. Clem Labine signed for $18,000 and instead of bragging about his terrific pitching joked about the three home runs he had somehow hit in 1955. Jackie Robinson walked out when Buzzie Bavasi, who handled all contracts, told him his salary was being cut by $4,500—a common practice after a poor season. Bavasi waited. Robinson relented, called, and signed for $33,000. The cut itself, he said, was no more than a "hill of beans"; but his pride had been hurt. The hurt worsened when the team signed Randy Jackson, a third baseman picked up in a trade with the Chicago Cubs. Jackson was thirty, six years younger than Robinson. He hit for power, fielded his position deftly, and was expected to challenge Robinson, now too slow to play second base, for the starting job at third.

The Dodger front office dispatched representatives across the borough, and out to Queens and Long Island, searching for fans who had proven their loyalty and who would be invited to step onto the field on Opening Day. Ticket sales for the opener were slow. Jersey City, however, was another story. The Jersey City Dodgers Boosters managed to pack the local armory with ten thousand people for a rally. Walter Alston spoke, as did the mayor, the governor, and Walter O'Malley, who said he was "optimistic" about how well the team would draw in Jersey City.

Meanwhile, the Save Brooklyn Committee met at the grand Hotel St. George in Brooklyn Heights to begin planning its campaign to block the Cross-Brooklyn Expressway. Even though Robert Moses' Triborough Bridge and Tunnel Authority insisted that the highway was far down on its list of priorities, the committee's chairman, Vincent Kassenbrook of Bay Ridge, was suspicious: that, he replied, was the same thing they said about the bridge from Bay Ridge to Staten Island, and now planning for the bridge was racing along. Kassenbrook painted a picture of a Brooklyn split and devastated by the highway: 60 blocks razed in Flatbush, another 100 in Flatlands, 2,000 homes flattened in Bay Ridge. The committee dispatched its members across the borough for "educational meetings" so that people might know what Moses had in mind.

The Brooklyn they were trying to save was the quiet Brooklyn that a generation earlier was the sort of enclave that Long Island had now become. Midwood, which sat in the highway's proposed path, was a neighborhood of tree-lined streets and brick-and-stucco houses filled with middle-aged people who thirty years earlier had had the money to escape the row houses of Williamsburg, Brownsville, and South Brooklyn, or the apartment houses on Ocean Parkway. Midwood was not the Brooklyn of two-room-plus-kitchenette apartments for $77 a month, or a basement room with a private bath on Ocean Avenue for $12 a week.

Midwood was roomy. Streets were wide and the closest apartment buildings were blocks away. It was so quiet that in the summer it was possible to hear the sound of sprinklers watering the small front lawns, a steady patter seldom interrupted by the sound of children running through the spray. There were blocks with only a scattering of children; their parents, who themselves might have grown up in places like Midwood, could not afford to buy there; a semidetached, one-family in Flatbush for $12,500 was more within reach, but then not as roomy and affordable—or as attractive to the banks and mortgage companies—as a $10,000 house with a yard out on the Island in Syosset. If they stayed in Midwood they might have no choice but to live in the remodeled second-floor apartments in their parents' homes. Midwood was by no means the wealthiest district in Brooklyn. It was not the Heights, which the rest of Brooklyn did not regard as Brooklyn at all, with all the Wall Street people who lived there (only a subway stop away on Clark Street), the handsomely preserved brownstones and the High Wasp toniness. It was not Manhattan Beach, a neighborhood of grand houses out near the bay, nor elegant Maple Street in Crown Heights, perhaps the most beautiful stretch of old homes in the borough. Midwood was the burghers' Brooklyn, prosperous, sedate, and, for young parents, dull. It was the Brooklyn of shopping streets like Avenue J, where the prices at women's clothing stores like Rosalie's were just as high as they were on

Madison Avenue; of Catholic blocks and Jewish blocks—Christmas was the giveaway; either lots of houses with holiday lights, or with no lights at all; of Friday night dinners at Junior's and Sunday dinners at Lundy's great barn of a seafood restaurant in Sheepshead Bay, and birthday parties at Jahn's Ice Cream Parlor on Nostrand Avenue where the all-you-could-eat was called "the kitchen sink." In Midwood the only black faces were those of the cleaning women, "the girls," who came by subway from Bedford-Stuyvesant and Bushwick. The used-clothing man still walked down the middle of the street calling out, "I cash clothes." Children who attended the local parochial schools rode to places like the Yeshiva of Flatbush in the wide backseats of black limousines driven, it was said, by low-level functionaries of the Brooklyn crime families.

There were other neighborhoods, too, where little if anything had changed: a few miles from Midwood stood a shantytown known ironically on the city survey maps as Luxury Row. Luxury Row was a reminder of the crumbling New York to which the young idealist Robert Moses had come in the early 1920s. What was remarkable was that in Brooklyn such a place still existed at all. The streets of Luxury Row were mud and at night were filled with rats and dogs and chickens. The twenty homes were wooden shacks that rented for eight dollars a month and seemed a carelessly thrown matchstick away from bursting into flames. This could have been Steinbeck's Brooklyn, homes without running water, where people shared an outdoor privy that sat near the well they pumped by hand for their water, and who believed it best not to rile the landlord, Joseph De Maria, who lived over on Coney Island Avenue. He'd once warned a reporter to stay away from Luxury Row if he wanted to remain "in one piece." The city, eager to level Luxury Row, was powerless to do anything about it. Even with Robert Moses' seemingly limitless condemnation powers, the law made it clear that just because houses were old did not necessarily mean that together they constituted a "slum." A slum had to be judged unsafe. But when building inspectors came out to Luxury Row, they could not get inside the houses: people never appeared to be home, or at least were reluctant to open their doors. "I don't know anything," one old woman told a reporter who knocked on her door. "I just mind the children. Go away."

The Save Brooklyn Committee did not concern itself with Luxury Row. Its troubles felt greater and deeper. The coming of the highway, like the now-inevitable coming of the bridge from Bay Ridge to Staten Island, were harbingers that to people like Vincent Kassenbrook, who headed the Save Brooklyn Committee, only a fool could ignore. Kassenbrook did not believe Robert Moses when he said the highway was not high on his list of things to do. But if Kassenbrook was Brooklyn's Jeremiah, his talk of the dire things to come did not resonate. Signs of change were easy to dismiss: for every bit of discouraging news, there still came word that Brooklyn was not really changing after all.

The navy announced that it was laying off 600 workers at the Brooklyn Navy Yard. But then 16,300 civilians still worked at the navy yard. While there was talk of more layoffs in March, and the requisite protests by the local congressmen, the navy yard was having a busy year. Meanwhile, the Board of Education was planning twelve new schools for Brooklyn alone, and modernizing another five. The cost, $40 million, was more than the board was spending on any other borough. Burlesque, once dead, was being resurrected in Brooklyn: the city was ordered to issue the license that Thomas Phillips had applied for in 1954 to bring burlesque to the old Orpheum Theater on Fulton Street.

And at spring training in Vero Beach, Roy Campanella dismissed any concerns about the state of his scarred and battered hands, insisting that the Dodgers did not have to think about replacing him. "They ain't gonna need no catcher," he said. "I'm raring to go."

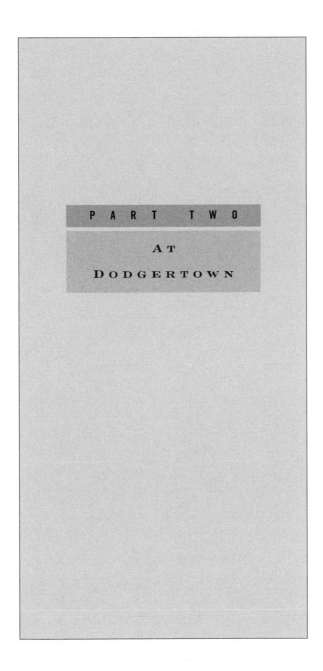

PART TWO

AT

DODGERTOWN

Clem Labine did not mind the company of hitters, but he liked pitchers better. He could talk to pitchers. He could say the things that pitchers said to each other like "bow your neck," an elliptical expression a hitter would not understand, meaning "get your body into the pitch." On the road he roomed with pitchers. In fact, on the Dodgers, pitchers often roomed with other pitchers, except for Carl Erskine, who roomed with Duke Snider. But then Erskine was so polite and agreeable that he could get along with anyone, even Snider, who tended to sulk when he was not hitting well. Erskine and Snider were best friends, a pitcher and a hitter, an unlikely pair.

Labine was different. He was a reader, and this alone set him apart. His teammate and fellow pitcher Ed Roebuck thought Labine took his reading, and himself as a reader, too seriously. He decided that Labine carried books because he wanted everyone to know how smart he was. Labine was a college man—he had attended the University of Rhode Island—and this made him even more of a rarity in the big leagues. He read on trains when everyone else was playing cards or talking or heading to the bar car. Sometimes, when Labine was not looking, Roebuck snatched his book and cut out the last few pages. This way, he figured, Labine would never know what happened.

Roebuck would ask, "How did it turn out?"

"Wonderfully," Labine would reply.

"How do you know?" Roebuck would ask. "There are pages missing."

Labine would say, "Did you know you can go to the library and get the very same book. You can go to a book store and read the last five pages."

He especially liked the poems of Robert Service, poetic yarns like "The Shooting of Dan McGrew" that pitted a lone and rugged man against the Yukon's perils. The heroic imagery—"were you ever out in the Great Alone when the moon was awful clear . . ."—appealed to Labine, who was the best relief pitcher in the game. Once a starter, he now liked coming into games when his team was in trouble. He threw two pitches for strikes, a slider and a sinker. But more than the nasty break on his slider—a sharp spin exaggerated by the crooked way a broken finger on his pitching hand had healed—Labine welcomed the pressure of cleaning up a starter's mess. Summoned in the late innings, he tucked his mitt into his back pocket, threw back his shoulders, and slowly walked through the dugout. His fellow pitchers, Roebuck and Roger Craig, would watch him and shake their heads in admiration and amusement at the man's cockiness.

He was twenty-nine years old, six feet tall, wore his hair in a crew cut, and was broad across the chest and shoulders. He had grown up poor near Providence, Rhode Island, during the Great Depression. He played hockey, basketball, and football, but mostly baseball, and, in the thin years of World War II, when scouts were looking for anyone who could play, he began getting noticed, especially after striking out nineteen batters in a high school game. The Cardinals gave him a tryout while he was still in college, but never called back. The Dodgers, too, had a look—his high school coach knew a friend of Leo Durocher, who then managed in Brooklyn. Durocher was interested but Labine hesitated, wondering whether he might be drafted into the military, or whether he should finish school. He was eighteen years old and, again, as had so many of his teammates, he had married his high school sweetheart. He took the money, signed, left school, and reported to Newport News in the Piedmont League. Graduation would come later. He pitched until his draft notice came. He spent two years with the 82nd Airborne Division. When the war ended he resumed his career, pitched well as a starter—good enough to make the big club, but never as the ace of the staff.

Relief pitching then was not, strictly speaking, new: pitchers were always getting knocked out and new men had to come in to save them. But the idea of a specialist, a man who appeared day after day, for a few innings at a time, was still novel. More and more the Dodgers used Labine this way, and soon he found his place. Besides, he liked to say, the Dodgers paid him well to do this; by 1956 he was the team's highest paid pitcher. He was well suited for the work, especially to the theater in relief pitching. He could play with a batter, varying the tempo of his pitching, keeping his opponent off stride. He could play with the crowd, too, especially on the road, when the fans booed like mad when he threw to first base, again and again, to keep a runner close. By the 1955 championship season he was appearing in sixty games a year and the Dodgers, it was generally acknowledged, could not have won without him.

For all the reading and the college courses and the extension-school art classes, Labine still considered himself a "red ass": he liked to fight and he liked to talk about his good fights. But then he also liked arty movies like *Moulin Rouge*. On the road he often visited men's clothing stores to study the season's line. The son of a weaver, he spent his winters designing men's clothing for Julius Finkelstein & Son of Woonsocket, Rhode Island. Which was why, just before pitchers and catchers were scheduled to report for spring training at Dodgertown in Vero Beach, he was the featured speaker at a luncheon hosted by his winter employer at Toots Shor's saloon in Manhattan, and why he came to Shor's not to drink—a violation of custom and of Shor's own credo—but to talk about the look for spring. The local wags, never ones to turn down a lunchtime invitation to the third-floor dining room at Toots Shor's, a room called the Bucket of Blood for all the red meat served, came to eat and drink and maybe spin a quick and easy piece. Labine was always a good one for copy—smart, polysyllabic, and with terrific control of his grammar.

"We agree," he began, "with those abroad who say day dresses will again be simple, that coats will favor open-side seams with criss-cross lacing of small fabric and with small knife pleats in afternoon skirts."

"Hey," someone called out. "How's your arm?"

"Good," replied Clem Labine. "Very good, thank you." With that he turned to the matter of ladies' sport coats and butterfly-winged skirts.

"When do you plan to leave for spring training?" someone called out.

"Spring," he replied. "That reminds me of beach wear."

"You better start thinking specially about gettin' your legs in shape," called out another.

The loud and fleshy Toots Shor entered the room. He listened and asked, "Hey, has this guy been drinking?"

Hearing all he needed to hear about the nature of the event and of Labine's part in it, he said, "A Dodger designin' clothes. It don't seem human."

———

IT HAD BEEN that sort of winter for the Brooklyn Dodgers—speeches and testimonial dinners, keys to their hometowns, and attention in the papers that befit their newfound status as world champions. They had scattered after the victory party at the Bossert—Pee Wee home to Louisville, Duke to Southern California, Newcombe to Newark, Furillo to Reading, Pennsylvania, Erskine to Anderson, Indiana. Only Hodges stayed in Brooklyn. But then his wife, Joan, was from Crown Heights, and they had a brick house on Bedford Avenue in Midwood. The Dodgers did not see each other for five months, which was just as well because they would soon begin spending every day together until October.

His appearance at Toots Shor's over, Labine returned to Rhode Island, said good-bye to his wife Barbara and his three children, and headed to Vero Beach, wondering what sort of team he would find. He was used to beginning spring training as an also-ran, and had come to believe that losing gave the beginning of the season a useful edge: "What made you lose?" Losing gave a team something to think about, together—was it attitude or ability? But now the Dodgers were winners and he wondered whether this might make his teammates lazy and content.

But he detected no complacency at Dodgertown. Instead, what he saw was a group of men who, having won once, badly wanted to win again, if only to prove that 1955 was not a fluke and that they were every bit as good as they believed they were. They had believed they were great in 1951, but collapsed at the end of the season and lost the playoff to the Giants on the terrible day when Bobby Thomson hit his home run against Ralph Branca. They had believed that they were never better than they were in 1953, when the Yankees beat them in the Series in six. Now, Labine sensed that his teammates had come to camp thinking, "We can't just make it a one-time thing."

That was good, but it did not hide the fact that all around him the men he knew were wearing down. That was the early talk of camp. Was someone going to push Pee Wee out at short? Could Campy repeat his marvelous 1955? Was Jackie going to be a part-time player? All this added to the larger and more elusive question that came with the players' arrival at Vero Beach: "the blending" as Labine called it. How would this version of the Brooklyn Dodgers come together as twenty-five individuals and manage to get along for the next eight months? This was not just a matter of people all liking each other; that, he believed, was impossible. Besides, harmony was not always a good thing: a little tension, a little edge was useful, if only to show that things mattered. Labine liked the idea of a team that sustained a manageable degree of anger—"It shows you're not lethargic about what you're doing"—so long as it did not flare. This meant that while it was fine for Ed Roebuck to cut out the last pages of his books, it was a bad idea, a very bad idea, to stuff chewing tobacco into Carl Furillo's shoes. Furillo, quiet and dark, was not, under any circumstances, ever to be teased. He was to be left alone and never bothered, and if someone were foolish enough to take a bite of his sandwich when he wasn't looking—and yes, some fool would always try—everyone else waited while Furillo looked down at his food and then looked around the clubhouse and asked, "Whose foolin' around here?" Best not to raise a hand.

Labine had the measure of his teammates. He knew that Don Newcombe's temper was "anger personified," that his rages were not purposeful and directed as Jackie Robinson's were. Snider moped and, in Labine's view, acted childishly, which was unfortunate because he had never seen a more talented player. Campanella was a joy to be around, funny and easy and never one to let things linger. Erskine was so congenial and pleasant that people wondered whether he was too nice to be a baseball player. Hodges was quiet and strong yet capable, when sitting in the backseat of a car, of putting his big hands over the driver's eyes. Furillo, a poorly educated man, believed that his teammates thought him a fool and did not want to be his friend because they thought he was dumb. He did not come to their parties and barbecues because he did not think they wanted him around. Robinson thought about ideas and about the world beyond baseball and that alone set him apart and, for Labine, made him a good man to spend an evening with, just talking. That is if Jackie was not in his hotel room, in the middle of a putting contest, playing, always, for money. Because then Jackie did not want to talk about being a black man, or about things he read. If Jackie was playing a game, any game, he *had* to win. And then there was Pee Wee, the captain, whom Labine and all the others looked up to and admired, and whom they saw at the center, as the nucleus of their small and potentially fractious universe.

2 | PEE WEE'S TEAM

The spring began, as had so many springs before, with talk of the team finding someone new to play shortstop. Pee Wee Reese, it was said, once again, was slowing down, and, at thirty-seven, could not range as far as he once had. The succession story had become a spring training chestnut, a reliable and predictable piece that, for a day or two at least, satisfied the relentless need for copy from Vero Beach—to say nothing of the break from a predictable snore like "Alston Likes Brooks' Chances." Each spring there was a new candidate prepared to bounce Reese to second base or third—Chico Carrasquel, Billy Hunter, Bobby Morgan, Rocky Bridges, Stan Rojek, and now Don Zimmer and Chico Fernandez. And each camp broke with Reese at short, where he had been starting for the Dodgers since 1940, when Leo Durocher, who'd been playing short and searching for a successor, quit the field to manage the team from the bench. Reese had arrived in Brooklyn just as the team, so awful for so long, was beginning to jell. His tenure—sixteen seasons, broken only by three years in the navy during the war—was not only longer than anyone else's but connected the team to its past, to the Dodgers of Whitlow Wyatt, Hugh Casey, Billy Herman, Mickey Owen, and Dixie Walker. And while some of those men had still been around in the late 1940s, now only Reese remained.

His teammates thought of the team as *his* team, even though Walter Alston was their manager. Even with all the strong and forceful personalities among them, there was no question that Reese was the leader. He accomplished this with few words, a fitting approach in baseball, where extended and serious talk is regarded with suspicion. His teammates could recall no particular moments that cemented his position among them, no defining words or acts or encounters after which they all accepted his role. Branch Rickey himself had appointed him captain in 1949—and gave him a meager five-hundred-dollar raise—but the title went only so far in explaining the way they saw him. Reese was not loud or forceful; he was not, in the parlance of the trade, a "holler guy." He was not the best player on the team: he was a splendid fielder and reliable hitter who performed well in the clutch, but he possessed neither Snider's skills nor Robinson's fire. He never sat a teammate down for a heart-to-heart or took a new man aside and explained the Dodger way. He *was* a stickler for players not hurrying out of the clubhouse after a game, believing that *baseball* talk was important—*you missed the cutoff man*—especially in reviewing what went wrong. He drank and smoked, but in moderation; he was no longer the young man who, on the train ride back to Brooklyn after the 1941 pennant clincher in Boston, ran through the cars with a jackknife, merrily cutting off any necktie he could find.

He was an adult and many of them were not—the nature of the game and the gilded ascent of great athletes worked against this. He seemed to know just what they were feeling or thinking, and with an economy of words knew precisely what each of them, at a given moment, needed to hear. He possessed a rare and remarkable capacity for empathy, although to have suggested it at the time and in that setting would have been dismissed as effete and alien. Better to leave it at, Pee Wee always knew what to say.

Like the time Preacher Roe was having a hard time getting Yankee batters out in the 1949 World Series and Reese called time, walked over to the mound, and said, "Preacher, why don't we have a little talk." What about, Roe asked as Tommy Henrich waited to bat. "Anything," Reese said, "fishing or hunting." Just to get his mind off things, but also making sure to glance at the dugout and let his manager, Burt Shotton, know that Roe would be fine. Or the time Carl Furillo came to him, weary and fearful that he was about to spiral into a batting slump but afraid to ask Shotton for a day off. The next day Reese told Shotton to scratch Furillo's name from the lineup. Which Shotton did, on Reese's word alone. Or the way he would scold Snider for yet another foolish comment in the papers, like the time in 1955 when the Duke whined that the Brooklyn fans are the worst in the league. Reese first chastised him—"your mother wouldn't like that. . . ." Then he walked Snider out to the field to offer his protection against the bottle throwers.

Of course, the moment the writers returned to, time and again, was in Cincinnati in 1947, Jackie Robinson's first year as the first black man in the major leagues, when the fans were taunting Robinson mercilessly and Reese walked over, and in full view of the jeering masses, draped an arm over Robinson's shoulder. (Carl Erskine, who was close to Reese, was convinced that as the two men stood together on the field, Reese said, "If you think this is bad, wait 'til we get to New York," because that was just the sort of thing he would say. Whatever Reese did say remained a mystery.) No one had better press than Reese; the man never had a harsh word written about him, other than about lapses on the field. The sportswriters wrote glowingly of that moment in Cincinnati, of how remarkable a gesture this was: a white man from Louisville displaying great courage by extending himself to a black man in such dire and public need. Reese would have none of this, none of the praise and celebration of his embrace of Robinson: he is my teammate and he can play and that, he said, was the end of it. His teammates, appreciating his refusal to grandstand, admired him all the more. They knew, too, that despite Robinson's praise and Roy Campanella's, too, that Reese said precisely what he meant: that Robinson was a teammate and a good one; and even though Reese was from Kentucky and risked the enmity of some of the other southerners on his team—good, popular, and bigoted players like Dixie Walker and Bobby Bragan among them—he was not going to sign a petition, as some wanted, insisting that no black man play with them. But Reese also made clear to his teammates and to Robinson that he had not turned on his past and the people he saw back home every winter—"you *shower* with that guy; you *eat* with him?"—and embraced a new and enlightened view on race. "I'm not going to be your great white father," Carl Erskine recalled his telling Robinson. No marches. No rallies. Just the game, as teammates. On the team for which he was responsible, as the captain.

HE HAD COME to the Dodgers as an innocent, frightened and nervous, with none of the arrogance, hidden or displayed, of a young man who had grown up a better ballplayer than anyone else. Reese was a late bloomer, small and, by his own assessment, forgettable.

He grew up in Louisville in a family that did not have much money. His father, Carl, had moved them from their farm near the village of Ekron to Louisville when he took a job as a rail yard detective for the Louisville and Nashville Railroad. Pee Wee sold newspapers and box lunches at the yard. He played all the sports; he did not like sitting still and though he did not go out for his high school baseball team until his senior year, he played baseball, football, and basketball—his favorite sport—in the Louisville park leagues. His nickname, while fitting at the time, had nothing to do with being slight: he earned it after finishing second in the Kentucky state marble shooting championships using his favorite, a pee wee. His given name was Harold.

When he graduated from DuPont Manual High School in 1936 he weighed only 115 pounds. He took a job as a line splicer for the Louisville phone company and over the next year grew, finally; he added three inches and thirty pounds, most of it muscle. By now he was playing shortstop for the New Covenant Presbyterian Church team in the Louisville church league and was beginning to gain a reputation and the confidence that went with it. He approached the manager of the minor league Louisville Colonels about a job. He wanted $200 a month, a hefty raise for an $18-a-week phone line splicer. The manager told him he'd have to start on the Colonels' second team. Reese asked whether the Colonels were still fielding the same players they had the year before. The manager told him he was. "Well, I can play as well as they can," Reese replied. The Colonels signed him to play short. His foreman at the phone company warned him that he was giving up a good job, with a pension and benefits. Reese, with his parents' backing, decided to try playing baseball for a living.

He was very good, very quickly—he fielded wonderfully and also led the American Association in stolen bases and in triples, a combination that suggested not only speed but daring. Word of his spirited play spread and in 1938, two years after he'd graduated high school as a skinny boy with modest prospects, the Boston Red Sox offered $195,000 to buy the Louisville franchise, primarily for its star shortstop. He might have joined the Red Sox had the team's manager, Joe Cronin, not insisted that he still had a few good years left playing short. Cronin did not want Reese pushing him out, not just yet, and so the Red Sox, famous for jettisoning men like Babe Ruth who became stars someplace else, sold him to Brooklyn.

It was not the place Reese wanted to be: the Dodgers had been losers for years. But these were the Dodgers of Larry MacPhail and Leo Durocher; they were not only respectable, they were getting better. Durocher, like Cronin, also was a shortstop who managed from the field; in his time Durocher was considered among the best fielders in the game. But unlike Cronin, Durocher was ready to groom a successor. In spring training he watched Reese field just two ground balls and announced that he had seen all he needed to see: Reese would be taking his place.

They formed a curious bond. Durocher was spectacularly crude; he credited his great success with women (his wives included the actress Laraine Day) with a willingness to ask, in simple terms both verbal and not, whether the woman who'd caught his eye was in the mood. He swore and drank and cared about little but winning and himself. But he loved Reese. He and his wife of the moment, Grace Dozier, took him into their home and treated him like an adopted son, which was a good thing for Reese, whose own father had died, at fifty-three, without ever seeing him play in the big leagues. He called the manager Mr. Durocher.

REESE WAS TWENTY years old and babyfaced when he arrived at the Dodger training camp at Clearwater, Florida; years later he told Frank Graham of the *Sun* that he wished he could have had a few more years in the minor leagues, just to get ready for the majors. Instead, he was thrust into the starting job at shortstop and Durocher, who in any sporting contest was incapable of a gentle word, screamed at him, believing that this was the best way to mold his protégé. Mercifully, Reese's older teammates, out of kindness or pity, watched out for him; when they played golf or went to the movies they invited him along. The team stayed at the Hotel Bel Air, and Reese had never before been in a place where men wore evening clothes to dinner and women wore gowns. He owned two suits. Although he was not inclined to ask many questions, he did approach Durocher one day to ask for advice. Durocher, a man always eager to share his wisdom, asked what was on his mind. Reese asked, "Where do you get your clothes?"

Reese could field beautifully. He was quick to the ball and, in the ultimate test for a shortstop, could go deep into the hole between second base and third and make a play. His throwing, however, was erratic, a result of trying to throw the way Durocher threw—"People said I imitated him," he told Jimmy Cannon of the *New York Post*. "Maybe I did." No one was faster than Durocher at getting the ball out of his mitt, into his throwing hand, and on to first base. But he was thirty-five years old and needed more and more to rely on tricks and guile. Reese's arm was young and powerful; finally a friend pointed out that he did not need to rush his throws—that he had slipped into the habit of imitating an old man who was compensating for vanished years. His throwing improved.

Durocher started the 1940 season on the bench, with Reese at short.

And when the younger man stumbled, when he committed errors, Durocher stayed with him, resisting MacPhail's ranting to bench him. Reese's mother came to see him play when the team visited Cincinnati and, because it was that kind of season, he made an error in the ninth inning and cost the Dodgers the game. After the game his coach, Red Corriden, saw him lingering in the shower and asked whether his mother had been in the stands. Reese mournfully replied that she was, and that she had seen his error. "I know how to make her feel better," Corriden told him, seizing the moment to pass along the timeless baseball lesson of stoicism in the face of adversity. "When you go out to meet her give her the biggest smile you've got." Reese greeted his mother as Corriden had advised, and in a season of so many lessons on how to play and look and behave like a big leaguer, he absorbed this one, too: handle your troubles with grace and silence.

All was going well enough until June, in Chicago, when Jake Mooty of the Cubs hit Reese in the head with a pitch. The blow was so severe that the club called Reese's mother to the hospital. Though he suffered only a concussion, his teammates waited to see if the beaning would make him tentative at the plate, fearful of being hit again. It did not, and he returned to the lineup, until August, when he broke his heel and missed the rest of the season.

Still, he was the team's future, a pair with his teammate Pete Reiser. He and Reiser were the anointed ones, joined at the hip, a generation of baseball ahead of them. They were everywhere together—*Life* magazine staged a shot of the two of them impishly sneaking down the hallway of the Hotel Nacional in Havana after curfew, shushing each other; in another they are sipping papaya juice through long straws in the company of two young women who, the caption noted "taught Pee Wee and his reluctant teammate Reiser how to rumba." They even got married on the same day: Reese and his fiancée Dorothy Wilson, who lived a few houses down from his aunt in Louisville, were witnesses at Reiser's wedding at city hall. Later that day, they decided to get married, too. Reiser was proclaimed the reincarnation of Ty Cobb: he could hit and field and played with abandon, perhaps too much. In 1942 he ran into a concrete wall making a catch and was never again the same player. Reese played on.

The following year, 1941, was harder still. Now there was no question of Reese starting, only of his ability. He was beset by doubt and worry, a view of his play he was sure his teammates shared. "I knew the only one the players weren't sure of was me," he told Frank Graham. "They were afraid that I might blow the pennant. If they had been able to conceal their feelings it would have been easier for me but they couldn't. I know they never intended to hurt me but I could tell, just the way they looked at me, how they felt."

Every error seemed pivotal; if it did not cost the team a game, it made winning that much harder. The team had not won a pennant in twenty-one years and when they returned to Brooklyn from a road trip the fans were waiting for them, which made Reese worry more that "if I failed I would be throwing all these people down. There were days when I dreaded to go to the ballpark."

Durocher stayed with him, once telling him after a particularly disastrous game that he did not care if he committed a dozen errors in a game; he was staying at short, which is just what he did through that championship season—it ended with the Dodgers winning the National League pennant and the first of five World Series losses to the Yankees. The loss was made memorable and emblematic when catcher Mickey Owen dropped a third strike that would have ended a game that the Yankees went on to win. In 1943, Reese enlisted in the navy. He had an easy war, playing baseball on the service teams in Guam and Hawaii. But the two years overseas were years well spent: Reese gained another twenty pounds. In the spring of 1946 he returned to spring training with all the other veterans who'd been in the service. Durocher, an astute judge of character, if only to assess another man's weaknesses, saw a change: Reese was no longer the stripling of 1940. He had, at last, grown up.

He was at ease with himself—the worries about failing his teammates having abated—and wise about himself, too. More than anything else, he understood his place. As it happened he left the navy with the rank of chief petty officer, the highest rank for a noncommissioned officer; in the context of the navy he was a top sergeant. And that is precisely what he became on his team. The men with whom he had played before the war were gone, and by the early 1950s he was surrounded by talented but nervous young men who looked to him as the veteran—his was a name they had read in the papers when they were still in high school. In 1953 the Dodgers' manager Charlie Dressen quit after Walter O'Malley refused his demand for a three-year contract. (O'Malley believed only in annual renewals.) There was serious talk of Reese succeeding Dressen; no one was better liked among the Dodgers, or more respected. The team *seemed* interested, as did Reese. And while O'Malley did not extend a formal offer, Reese began confiding in the beat writers; he was, at best, ambivalent about being in charge. On the one hand, he told Michael Gaven of the *New York Journal-American*, he didn't want to get a reputation as a man who played hard to get—who'd want him then? And what about fights? He could avoid fights as a player, but could he do that as a manager? And what about the burdens of the game; "What if I start bringing the game home with me as a manager? If I did, and I thought it was disrupting my family life or injuring my health?" And he'd surely need the help of good coaches because for the life of him he couldn't tell a good pitch from a bad pitch and he'd need help with the pitching staff. And what about the writers, who'd been so kind, and who would have to be critical if he were manager—"I think I could take it." And then there were his teammates, which was the greatest problem of all. He'd have to yell at them, and bench them, and when they were slumping send them down to the minors—"They tell me I would get over that." But would he? These were the men he played golf with, and whose wives were friends with his wife. "Drawing the line might be difficult."

Reese's candor was remarkable: he was admitting doubt, which might be construed as *weakness*. But Gaven took his doubts seriously; he did not so much as hint at a failure of character, or lapse in manhood. Of course, while Reese's questions were all reasonable, taken together they sounded like the ruminations of a man trying to talk himself out of being in love. In the end, all the prudent arguments dissolve in the face of the argument that goes: I want it. His teammates, too, sensed his uncertainty. They knew that while he was comfortable with leading them, he preferred doing so as a baseball equivalent of a noncommissioned officer. Let someone else decide who plays and who sits. Let someone else make the pitching changes and cut men in spring training. The feeling among his teammates, Duke Snider said years later, was that when faced with what being their manager meant, Reese thought, "I don't want you guys to hate me."

O'Malley hired Walter Alston, a bland and taciturn minor league manager—a sportswriter could die waiting for a decent quote from the man. But Alston was nonetheless capable of taking over a pennant-winning team (the 1953 Dodgers had again lost a World Series to the Yankees) and, even having barely played in the majors could still tell his proud and talented men as they slumped early in 1954, "You guys are pros and you know what to do to win. If you don't do the job we'll get someone else."

Pee Wee Reese returned to the rocking chair that sat in front of his locker in the clubhouse at Ebbets Field. He golfed with his teammates and drank with them on the road. His wife played bridge with the other Dodger wives. He returned to the role of go-between for players and management, and kept order and harmony in Walter Alston's clubhouse. In time the players, who had been suspicious of Alston, came to respect him. But unlike their regard for the captain, they did not love him.

3 | THE BASEBALL FACTORY

There was no happier man at Vero Beach that spring than Randy Jackson. Jackson had been playing third base for the Chicago Cubs since 1951 and had twice made the National League All-Star team. He hit for power, if not always for average, and fielded his position well. Jackson had decided to keep his family in Chicago for the winter. This proved a disaster; he was born in Little Rock and went to college in Texas and had never experienced anything like the cold of a Chicago winter. But in December he took a call from a sportswriter who had news to report.

"You've been traded," said the writer.

"To who?" Jackson asked.

"Guess," said the writer.

"Pittsburgh?" replied Jackson, not wanting to get his hopes too high.

"No," said the writer. "The Dodgers."

Jackson told the writer he had to be teasing because this news was too good. The next day he read in the paper that the Cubs, who never bothered to call, had traded him for Don Hoak and Walter Moryn, young men who appeared to have promise. Chicago, it seemed, had wearied of Jackson, their only all-star, because he did not like to yell. The Cubs' front office liked its players to be "holler guys," men of passion and gusto who compensated for their modest play with the sort of grunts and threats that showed that, at the very least, they cared. Randy Jackson was a phlegmatic man, a college graduate—his father had played ball at Princeton—with an easy manner that the Cubs interpreted as a lack of spirit. His pedigree suggested otherwise: having never played football before going to college, he went on to star as halfback as the University of Texas.

No matter: the Cubs, legendary for trading players who would become stars elsewhere—the boneheaded dispatching of the great Lou Brock to St. Louis would haunt Wrigley Field for years—had mercifully sent him to the best team in the league. Brooklyn mailed him a contract matching his 1955 salary. Jackson sent it back, reminding Buzzie Bavasi that he had made the All-Star Team. Bavasi told him he had thus far accomplished nothing in Brooklyn, but because he, Jackson, was such a nice fellow he'd throw in another thousand dollars.

Randy Jackson had never seen anything like Dodgertown. There were four diamonds. There were mechanical pitching machines: Branch Rickey had even tinkered with one that threw curves, but the machine was wild and hit too many batters. There was a "sliding dolly" that fairly spilled runners into second base. There were hanging-string strike zones and pitching targets. The Cubs trained in Arizona, where they had a single field, and on Catalina Island—a property of the Wrigley family, who made chewing gum and owned the team. The Cubs had curious ideas about physical conditioning. One year the team ordered its players to come to Catalina a week early. The island is a rugged place, a terrain best suited for the goats whose tracks covered the mountains. All players were told to climb the goat paths, which the team believed might get everyone's legs in shape. Instead, everyone got shin splints and could not practice for a week. That was life with the Cubs, a team that, in Jackson's view, opened each game already two runs down to the Dodgers through intimidation alone. It was not that his teammates were afraid of the Dodgers or in awe of the other men; rather, it was a realistic understanding that Brooklyn was superior, that they pitched better and hit better, and while the Cubs might win a game here and there, Brooklyn had the better team and better teams generally won.

The Dodgers assigned Jackson to room with Donald Drysdale, a nineteen-year-old pitching prospect from California's San Fernando Valley who was so awed of the presence of major leaguers that he called him "Mr. Jackson." Jackson's new teammates were friendly and accessible—he'd known them a little over the years from occasional game-time chats between pitches when he got on base. The Dodger clubhouse was an altogether different place than the one he'd known in Chicago, where Phil Cavarretta, a fine hitter, had emerged as the leader because he'd been around forever. Cavarretta's clubhouse was not Pee Wee Reese's, where Jackson quickly detected a professionalism he had never felt in Chicago. The Dodgers talked baseball; and that alone was a departure, so much so that men who left the Dodgers would tell, many years later, of how much they missed the lingering, and the conversation. Ben Wade, who pitched for the Dodgers and later returned as chief scout, was traded to St. Louis, where Stan Musial, the team's best player, would be content after games to play his harmonica while his teammates showered, dressed, and went their separate ways. "Once you're on the club," Wade said of Brooklyn, "you don't want to leave."

But coming to the Dodgers was not without its perils for Randy Jackson. The Dodgers had traded for a third baseman, even though they already had one: Jackie Robinson. And on Jackson's first day in camp the writers descended on him, poking a bit, looking for a little blood in the water.

Robinson, they told him, was talking of fighting for the job. He had arrived in camp—after playing, the writers noted, in a "Negro" golf tournament—at 218 pounds, lighter than he'd been in years; he'd finished the 1955 season at 230. And while Robinson insisted that he had never said "Randy Jackson will play third base over my dead body," he made it clear that he intended to start, somewhere on the team. The writers picked away; Jackson, a wise man, was cautious and complimentary—"Robinson has been a great player through the years, I'll say that"—and offered so little that Roscoe McGowan of the *New York Times,* the éminence grise of the beat fellows, was sure he detected a hint of edge in Jackson's use of the past tense in the kind words about Robinson. No, he'd never been a "fire and vinegar" guy, Jackson said, and yes, he'd always hit well at Ebbets Field. With that the talk turned to his weight and some bland jokes about how few bases he'd stolen, which was fine with Jackson, who was just happy to be no longer climbing goat paths on Catalina Island.

DAYS AT DODGERTOWN began at six in the morning when Charles DiGiovanna, "The Mighty Brow" himself, went to work. First he hung three hundred uniforms and pieces of equipment, doing so in precisely the same order as he had done the day before. Then he fetched lunches, which he placed in each locker. Next he shined the shoes. The players had called him "The Brow" because his eyebrows were bushy (they added "Mighty" after they won the World Series).

The Brow was twenty-five years old, the oldest batboy in the game. Married and the father of three, he lived in the Long Island town of Malverne. He had been the Dodger batboy for six years and took his responsibilities seriously, including the artful forgery of many of the Dodgers' autographs. Players were forever being presented with boxes of balls to sign; they passed them along to the batboys for forgeries. The Brow, like the batboy he succeeded, Stan Strull, was gifted at imitating many of the scrawls, in particular that of Pee Wee Reese, whose autograph was always in demand.

The Brow, like Strull, reported to John Griffin, the clubhouse manager, a doughy buffoon of a man who was always putting on silly hats and making a spectacle of himself in front of the players, to whom he was deferential to the point of being obsequious. The batboys loathed him. Griffin left them to do the heavy lifting while he stood guard over the cooler where the team stocked soda and beer, none of which was on the house. Griffin kept a running tab on who took what from the cooler. The batboys, meanwhile, cursed him and packed the players' trunks.

Still, The Brow had worked himself up to an enviable position, having graduated from turnstile boy—a job he landed after hanging around outside Ebbets Field long enough to get the players to know and like him—to visiting team batboy to batboy for the Dodgers. He wanted to stay with the team forever, even though the days at Dodgertown started so early and he had so many uniforms to clean and hang with all the minor leaguers in camp. The minor leaguers, the hopefuls, lived in the Dodgertown barracks, where the walls were thin and where it was so cold at night that the clever ones grabbed the rubber shower mats and pulled them on top of their meager blankets. The new men woke at eight in the morning, hounded out of bed by Herman Levy, an Ebbets Field usher whom the team brought to Florida to serve as night watchman.

Veteran players did not live in the barracks. The Reeses rented a cottage by the ocean, as did the Sniders and Erskines, who had started sharing a place when their children were still too young for school. They began trickling down in mid-February; Gil Hodges and Carl Furillo came early for the fishing. Don Newcombe arrived by train from Newark, a fifteen-hour trip that he spent in his berth, fighting a virus. Newcombe, prone to testiness even on good days, got a shot of penicillin from Harold Wendler, the team doctor, and told a writer who'd asked when he'd start working out, "I didn't come down here to go to bed. I came here to work. If I wanted to stay in bed, I would have stayed at home."

But Newcombe seemed otherwise happy. In fact, most everyone did, which made this camp so different from the year before. The spring of 1955 had not been a good time: Jackie Robinson was angry at Walter Alston for holding him out of games and Alston, in return, was angry at Robinson. Roy Campanella was angry because Alston dropped him to eighth in the batting order, and there was little that even Pee Wee Reese could do to lessen the tension between the players and the new manager. They tested Alston that spring and finally, in May, Newcombe, who could be so unpredictable, a hard case one moment, a gentleman the next, committed a mutinous act when he refused to pitch batting practice. Every pitcher threw batting practice on off-days, but Newcombe refused, for no apparent reason other than pique. Alston, faced with open insurrection, ordered him off the field in full view of his teammates. Newcombe walked into the clubhouse and began stripping off his uniform. Roy Campanella ran after him. Campanella was his roommate and the one person on the team to whom Newcombe would listen.

"Don't you take that uniform off!" bellowed Campanella, who after so many years of triple-headers in the Negro Leagues waiting for a chance to play in the majors, knew, just as well as Newcombe did, how long the uniform was in coming. "You never take that uniform off. You make them tear it off you." Newcombe relented; the rebellion ended. Alston managed the team to its first World Championship. And now, in Dodgertown, he went about assembling a team, his worries confined largely to the question of pitching.

Dodgertown was a Branch Rickey invention, and reflected his approach to life and the game: it was a baseball ascetic's paradise. There was little to do but play ball. Rickey got the place for a song and quickly converted the open fields of what had been a naval air station into a factory for the production of baseball teams. In addition to the fields and machines and extra pitching mounds, there were a swimming pool, basketball and tennis courts, and later, a golf course. The Dodgers, and those who hoped to make the team, played baseball all morning and had their afternoons and evenings free, which was not the gift it seemed: Rickey had built his factory in a place where there was little to do but play ball. His players could play basketball or read their mail or shoot pool, although it was not wise to play Newcombe, a shark. They could try to chat up one of the very few women around, like the young woman who worked in the press office and who, at any given time, might be dating six different players, including three from the Norfolk minor league club.

There was a Ping-Pong table at Dodgertown and a jukebox, too. And when the players got tired of hearing that spring's hits like "Tutti Frutti" and "Rock and Roll Waltz," they went looking for Ralph Muriello, a pitching prospect who owned a car. They drove to town, which was small and often dead, or fifteen miles away to Fort Pierce to go to the movies. Sometimes they just talked, mostly about what they read in the papers about other men they'd met along the minor league trail and who now stood a decent chance, even if they did not, of making a big league club—*Him? He can't hit a lick. . . .*

The best chance of sticking with the Dodgers—a slim chance at best—belonged to young pitchers of promise. After the morning's practice, Alston and his coaches retired to his office, a spartan room with a wooden desk and folding chairs, a navy leftover. They stripped down to their underwear and tried to decide what, if anything, Billy Loes had left, and whether Karl Spooner's arm was ever going to stop hurting and what to do about the big void left by Johnny Podres' draft notice. Loes vexed them. On his good days he looked like the best pitcher in the game, terrific speed and control and an assortment of curves. But his prospects were undercut by a chronically sore arm and a disposition that, to be charitable, was curious. Loes was a man of limited intellect who nonetheless spoke his mind. He won fourteen games in 1952, and when Buzzie Bavasi offered him a bonus contingent on winning twenty, he replied that he did not want to win twenty because then the team would expect him to do it all the time. Loes was sad-eyed and put-upon, a decent fellow who believed himself cursed by fate; how else to explain losing a *ground ball* in the sun—"I seen the first bounce but then I jerked up my head and the sun hit me right in the eyes. . . ." Loes' arm hurt so badly in 1955 that he could barely pitch at the end of the season, and he appeared only once in the World Series. Now, he told the writers that he just wanted to go home because he couldn't pitch anymore. Spooner would have to remain in Florida to nurse his sore arm. Erskine would always pitch, even in pain. Podres was ordered to report to Bainbridge Naval Air Station, which meant that Alston and his coaches were compelled to look hard at the younger men.

Ken Lehman was the ace for the Montreal affiliate. Donald Drysdale and Chuck Templeton seemed capable, as did Roger Craig, who had come up in 1955 and pitched well. So too did Ed Roebuck. But Roebuck had developed an ulcer playing winter ball in Puerto Rico and was ordered to rest and eat a modified diet. There was also Sandy Koufax, whom no one could seem to figure out. Koufax threw very hard, but the ball tended to arrive at unpredictable destinations—twenty feet in front of home plate; high over the catcher's glove and into the backstop. When he pitched batting practice, the veterans passed on their turns in the cage, insisting they needed work fielding grounders.

Koufax was a Jimmy Murphy discovery, which meant that he had joined the anointed ones, The Worthy Young Men of Brooklyn. Murphy had been the sports editor and columnist of the *Brooklyn Eagle* for thirty years, and when the *Eagle* folded he moved with many of his colleagues to the *New York World-Telegram*'s Brooklyn edition. Murphy was a creator of heroes, and his prose, in the spirit of Grantland Rice, veered toward hagiography; to be selected for one of Murphy's "All-Scholastic" teams could well mean a football scholarship at, say, Notre Dame or Columbia. Murphy's audience extended beyond parents and school principals and included college coaches, too. He favored young men of character; his columns celebrated athletic accomplishment, decent grades, solid attendance, and extracurricular activities—"Donnelley, a brilliant end on the varsity football team, was recently awarded a gold medal for his portrayal of Brutus in 'Julius Caesar'. . . ." Koufax had been something of a fluke. He played basketball at Lafayette High School and third base, too. He pitched a little, very little in fact, in the Coney Island League, just nine games. Yet Murphy, having seen him play at the Parade Grounds on Ocean Avenue, alerted Alex Campanis, a Dodger scout. Koufax had accepted a basketball scholarship at the University of Cincinnati. Campanis watched him throw at Ebbets Field, and later said that the sight and sound of Koufax's fastball made the hairs on the back of his neck stand up. The Dodgers signed him for a twenty-thousand-dollar bonus and Koufax enrolled at Columbia. He never pitched a day in the minors and, in fact, had pitched well late in 1955, his rookie season—two shutouts among his twelve appearances. But at Vero Beach his control was miserable and he looked so out of sorts that people told him he "threw like a girl." Koufax, a shy fellow—Tommy Holmes of the *Herald-Tribune* noted that "it was easy to forget he was around"—sought the solitude for which he would one day become famous, and did his throwing behind the barracks where no one could see.

The hitting was of little concern to Walter Alston. Gil Hodges tinkered with his swing—where to plant his feet in the batter's box to raise his home run total from a seven-year low of twenty-seven in 1955. Don Zimmer, so enthusiastic at the plate, tried choking up on the bat to cut down on his ferocious swing. Roy Campanella hit a few home runs and pronounced his mangled hands so healthy he planned to play for another ten years. Duke Snider carped about the extended exhibition season, playing in thirty games that "did not count"; maybe, he suggested, the owners should give a thousand dollars to every man on the team that finished the spring season with the best season record. Asked if he might press his case, Snider, prone to moping, sighed, "What good would it do?" He parked himself in the back of the batter's box at Dodgertown's Holman Stadium, taking pitch after pitch because he did not like the park's hitting backdrop. The fans booed him.

The Snider story was good for a day. Meanwhile, Dodgertown that spring was a sportswriter's nightmare: the Podres draft story made for a few days of copy, especially when Boston's Ted Williams, who'd seen combat in Korea and was never one to leaven an opinion, called Podres's draft board "gutless"; he was convinced they'd called him up because he was a World Series hero. A physiologist came to camp with a carload of timing devices and concluded that Snider had the "fastest brain" on the team—okay, the writers conceded, fastest in reacting to a pitched ball—and that Jackie Robinson still possessed the quickest start to second base.

Pee Wee Reese told the writers that his legs were feeling better than they had in 1955—he admitted that the year before his legs hurt so badly that he told his wife that perhaps the end of his career was finally at hand. But now, after a running coach told him to stop jogging on hard indoor running tracks, his legs felt fine. With that he went about the rituals of his captaincy, among them trimming his teammates' winter moustaches. Two weeks into camp Reese was chasing a ground ball when his foot slipped. He straightened up and felt a sharp pull in his back. He did not play golf that afternoon, or the next. The injury was diagnosed as nothing more severe than a pulled muscle. Still, it seemed to take forever to heal.

4 | "HURRICANE DODGER"

Walter O'Malley, who avoided excess in exercise, liked to play cards with the beat writers at Dodgertown, and liked to let them win. He played golf, too. But he found his greater pleasure in his garden, an elaborate seedbed where he tended his orchids and cultivated rare and primordial metasequoia tree cuttings; a delicate business, this required dipping the cuttings in a special hormone and transplanting them in peat moss and vermiculite. He had little to say about his players; Snider's grousing about exhibition games did not concern him. He preferred to boast to anyone who'd listen about the ancient history of his cutting—"These trees were around millions of years ago. . . ."

He spent a week with his cuttings in Vero Beach. Then he returned to Brooklyn to resume his campaign for a new ballpark. The battle was entering its fourth year.

The quick demise of the plan to make the stadium part of the Brooklyn Civic Center project, and O'Malley's unwillingness to relocate to Bedford-Stuyvesant had, temporarily at least, left him without options. But then, in March 1953, John Cashmore, the borough president, had sent him a copy of the letter from the president of the wholesale meat sellers association, pleading for Cashmore's help in moving his members out of the antiquated Fort Greene market on the corner of Flatbush and Atlantic Avenues, near the Long Island Railroad station. It had taken O'Malley several months to put together a proposal for Robert Moses. Once again he asked Moses to condemn the land so that O'Malley could afford to buy it, and build a stadium on it and, of course, a parking garage. And once again Moses would have none of it. A stadium, even one with a large parking facility, was not "public purpose" and therefore not eligible for federal Title I money and condemnation. The area may have been a slum; but a ballpark was not, Moses decreed, a suitable replacement.

That should have been the end of it. It was not. Because once again Walter O'Malley turned to friends who might have leverage with Robert Moses. They wrote letters on his behalf. And because they were prominent men, men who Moses needed, too, he felt compelled to reply, testily. "This is positively my last Dodger spasm," an exasperated Moses wrote to Frank Schroth, publisher of the *Brooklyn Eagle* in June 1954. "If Walter O'Malley would stop beefing, threatening, foxing and conniving . . ." Maybe, he suggested, O'Malley would accept improvements at Ebbets Field, like street widening and more parking. But O'Malley wanted out of Ebbets Field. Moses knew it and tried to persuade O'Malley's allies both of the wisdom of this strategy, or in taking his Bedford-Stuyvesant offer. It was futile, he wrote, to ask for his assistance in condemning such well-situated land as the Fort Greene market. "We have been over and over this ground," he wrote in May 1955, wearily, to Walter Rothschild, chairman of Abraham & Straus department store. "A new stadium . . . couldn't possibly be an incident at this location." But still the letters came, from O'Malley's friends, and from the man himself.

"Dear Bob," he wrote on August 10, 1955. "We may not be in agreement on some points but we, at least, get a kick out of fighting." He asked that Moses take another look at his plans for the market, for relocating the butchers and easing the chronic traffic bottleneck at the intersection. The stadium could be round, or pear-shaped, depending on how much land Moses gave him. "If you get any further ideas," he closed, "I know you will let me have them. . . ."

Moses did, five days later. He did not even feign civility: "I can only repeat what I have told you verbally and in writing, namely, a new ball field for the Dodgers cannot be dressed up as a Title I project." He went on to remind O'Malley that he was free to use his money to buy land where he could afford it. He was also free to walk away: Moses suggested that he could also sell the Dodgers "and make a substantial profit." And if he sold to someone who did not wish to remain in Brooklyn, "then, in spite of any feeling I might have of the need for keeping as many attractions in Brooklyn as possible, I would have to agree that you would certainly be within your rights."

His contempt now turned to anger. "On the other hand, I don't see how you can have the nerve to indicate that you have not received proper support from public officials involved." If O'Malley had done this it had not come in his letter, whose tone was characteristically fawning. "Every reasonable, practical and legal alternative we have suggested has been unsatisfactory to you. The record shows we have made many suggestions, even though it is not part of our official duties." The record showed that he had made two: renovations at Ebbets Field, and buying in Bedford-Stuyvesant.

O'Malley had heard enough. The following day, August 16, he announced that the Dodgers would play seven games in Jersey City. The team would play two more seasons at Ebbets Field. In 1958, he added, the Dodgers would be in a new stadium, hopefully in Brooklyn. If O'Malley had failed to get Robert Moses to take him seriously, he had quickly succeeded in getting the attention of most everyone else. His announcement was front-page news. The *Times* added its considerable weight to the story with the carefully worded proviso that the announcement did "not necessarily foreshadow a shift of the Dodger franchise to another city, although such a change is not impossible at some future date."

That was, of course, precisely what O'Malley meant, even if he had not said it. He was down to only one chip, but the chip was his team, which he believed no city official wanted to lose on his watch. As if on cue, Mayor Robert Wagner announced that he was "very anxious to keep the Brooklyn Dodgers in New York City." In fact, Wagner, a bland and cautious man, was so eager to show his concern that he hastily invited O'Malley to a meeting at Gracie Mansion, his official residence. He also invited John Cashmore, who helped things along with his own statement championing O'Malley's idea of a new park on the corner of Atlantic and Flatbush Avenues. Cashmore's office released a map of the site. O'Malley made himself available for questions about the cost, the site, and what the stadium might look like. "I would like to make it plain that we are not going into this thing hat in hand," he said. Other cities—Milwaukee, Cleveland, Baltimore, Kansas City—had built stadiums with public money. He had sold his shares in the Long Island Railroad and in the Subway Advertising Company. He had $6 million in the bank, $1.5 million of which he had set aside to buy the land. The rest would go toward the stadium and the parking garage that, O'Malley explained, would be essential if the team were to continue drawing its many fans who had moved to the suburbs. The park itself would have no pillars to obstruct his patrons' views. The seats would resemble theater seats and be arranged so fans would not have to crane their necks. There would be plenty of bathrooms, and refreshment stands, too.

O'Malley was so pleased with the way things had gone that when Arthur Daley, the *Times* sports columnist, stopped by his office on Montague Street, O'Malley allowed himself a moment of delight. "If you wish," O'Malley told him, "you may call it Hurricane Dodger. And the core of the hurricane is now passing over Brooklyn."

WALTER O'MALLEY CAME to Gracie Mansion on Friday morning, August 20, to find the assembled press and Robert Moses, too. This was to be a public chat, which meant that O'Malley and Moses had come to perform: O'Malley would play the worried owner of the beloved ballclub to Moses' dedicated if irritable public servant. Wagner played the concerned host. Cashmore was there to hold O'Malley's coat.

They met outside on the terrace, where the late summer wind was whipping the awnings and making it hard to hear. Wagner attempted a joke at the expense of Horace Stoneham. Stoneham had not been invited, even though he'd sent Wagner a telegram the day before asking to come; the Giants, he wrote, had problems, too.

"That must be Horace Stoneham," Wagner quipped, when the wind drowned out O'Malley's voice.

"Oh, no," said O'Malley, laughing, "there's not that much wind."

Still, he tried using the absent Stoneham to his advantage in raising the stakes still further: the city, he said, was not just facing the loss of one of its National League clubs. It risked losing both. He offered attendance figures to show just how much the Giants needed the Dodger rivalry to stay afloat—half the team's paltry attendance came from the mere eleven home games against Brooklyn; they played another sixty-six games at the Polo Grounds.

"If one goes, the other will go," O'Malley said. "It is serious, Mr. Mayor, very serious."

O'Malley had one certain ally, and that was John Cashmore, who performed well when his turn came to speak. He asked Wagner to spend fifty thousand dollars to pay for an engineering study of the meat market site.

Wagner replied that he would raise the idea at the next meeting of the city's fiscal governing body, the Board of Estimate, but warned of legal and financial problems in getting the land cleared and the park built.

Wagner then asked O'Malley whether he might consider building on another site.

"We would be willing to build there with Dodger money because of its accessibility," O'Malley replied. "But we wouldn't want to invest our money if a site is proposed at another, less favorable location." So much for Bedford-Stuyvesant.

With that Wagner asked Moses to explain why condemning the land might prove difficult. Moses spoke of the legal complexities of land condemnation. And then, keeping in character, he turned on O'Malley. "What you're saying is that unless a way is found to make a home for the Dodgers in this location, you'll pick up your marbles and take them away."

It was not phrased as a question. If Moses meant it as a dare, which he was certainly capable of doing, O'Malley was not inclined to double it.

"Oh, no," he said. "I don't even want to consider ever having the Dodgers leave New York." But then, as if to assure Moses that he was no pushover, he added, "You, Mr. Moses, never got anything without fighting for it. Well, I'm fighting for this. If I go down I want the record to show I went down swinging."

O'Malley told him of the $6 million in the bank and the $1.5 million set aside for land.

Not enough to buy on Flatbush Avenue, Moses said.

Rebuked, O'Malley fought back. "Other cities have gone further," he said. "They've built the ballparks and rented them to clubs. Other cities can't understand why we can't do it when they can. We have to start trying to find out how it can be done, not why it can't be done."

So, Moses asked, was it Flatbush Avenue or nothing?

"I don't know," O'Malley replied. "This is not a threat. But we're down to what we believe is our last chance."

It was a threat, and it had worked. O'Malley had made it possible to consider the possibility of the Dodgers abandoning Brooklyn. Two days later, on a visit to Jersey City, he squeezed the pressure a notch higher. The Dodgers were willing to invest, he said, "provided we can get the only practical site in Brooklyn. If that isn't possible we have to look elsewhere." Perhaps in New Jersey, or Queens, or Long Island.

Suitors appeared instantly. The Long Island town of Patchogue offered thirty acres in what the local Chamber of Commerce described as the Island's "densest Dodger fan concentration." Staten Island, the most remote of the city's boroughs, also offered a home. "Come to Staten Island," Louis Russo, a state assemblyman wrote to O'Malley, "where you will find all the land you need for baseball and parking."

Those were to be expected; they were local bidders. Far more surprising was the overture that came to O'Malley from, of all places, Los Angeles. The city council was dispatching two of its members, Rosalind Wyman and Edward Roybal, to travel east and see if either O'Malley or Stoneham might be enticed to move their teams to California.

Wyman heard back quickly from Walter O'Malley. "I doubt very much I can see you in this period," O'Malley wrote, although perhaps they could meet at a "later date." But then, to cool whatever enthusiasm Wyman may have been harboring about a Dodger move to Los Angeles, he added, "Los Angeles has two teams in organized baseball [by this he meant the city's minor league teams] and we would not want to be party to any publicity that might be construed as detrimental to their franchise." Wyman, knowing a brush-off when she heard one, let the matter drop.

O'Malley was similarly dismissive of the offers from Patchogue and Staten Island. He had made his play for Brooklyn, and things were unfolding nicely. Within days of his encounter with Moses at Gracie Mansion, the city's Board of Estimate voted to spend one hundred thousand dollars to study the feasibility of building a stadium on the corner of Flatbush and Atlantic Avenues. O'Malley, however, knew enough of the city's political workings to recognize the vote for what it was: not necessarily an endorsement of his plan, but rather a courtesy to John Cashmore.

THE FIVE BOROUGH presidents sat on the Board of Estimate, along with the mayor, the city council president, and the controller, who was the city's chief financial officer. The board controlled the city's money. The problem was, the city did not have nearly as much money as Robert Moses. Moses' money came in large denominations from Washington, and in a veritable flood of nickels and dimes from all the tolls collected, without pause, at the bridges and tunnels controlled by his Triborough Bridge and Tunnel Authority. This meant that the city, and its respective boroughs, desperately needed Moses to get things built with public money. Still, the members of the board were men with some pride. The borough presidents may have been hacks, men selected to run as shoo-ins by the powerful borough political bosses. But they were still officeholders, men who were invited to give speeches and whose comments were noted in the newspapers and who, as in the case of John Cashmore, were credited with such accomplishments as having the forsythia designated as Brooklyn's official flower. Cashmore was the front man, the smiling face and ribbon cutter for such men as Irwin Steingut and Joseph Sharkey, who ran the Brooklyn Democratic machine. Like the other borough presidents, Cashmore did as he was told. He had been a city council member and later a state assemblyman, and when a borough president named Raymond Ingersoll died in office, the political men chose Cashmore to succeed him. That was in 1940 and he had been borough president ever since.

It was the wise borough president who understood the limits of his power, if only so that he could enjoy the perquisites that came with the office, such as the kindnesses his fellow borough presidents extended to one another. Among these was the understanding that if a borough president wanted a project in his borough, the others would not stand in his way. So it was that while the city could not afford to assist with the cost of buying land for a new Dodger stadium, it could afford the hundred thousand dollars that Cashmore wanted for a study. Never mind that Robert Moses had now made it clear that the only way O'Malley was going to buy that land was if he somehow found the money in his own pockets. Cashmore's fellow borough presidents knew what it meant to be humiliated by Moses. The least they could do was grant Cashmore the hundred thousand, and with it the illusion of the power that resided in the borough presidency.

Like Steingut and Sharkey, O'Malley needed a front man, too. And like the bosses, he had one in John Cashmore. But Cashmore served a larger purpose. O'Malley needed to sustain the momentum of his campaign, and to do that he needed to keep his plan before the press and the public. He needed to make the stadium plan sound real, and look real if it was, in fact, ever to become a reality. He needed announcements and schematic drawings in the newspapers. He needed the columnists to ask about the latest on the stadium project, and for the bankers and businessmen he'd befriended to mention it in their letters to Robert Moses. He had heard enough from Robert Moses, both privately and now publicly, to know that the only way he could fight him was by threat, and by acting as if Moses' rejection of his plan was simply the opinion of one unelected official who now could only look on in frustration and dismay as a team of city-appointed engineers descended on the Fort Greene meat market and began surveying the land for the ballpark that Moses insisted was never going to go there.

BUT MOSES WAS not above using for his own purposes the same letter writers whom O'Malley had been inflicting upon him for four years. The day after O'Malley's announcement about the Jersey City games, Jack Flynn, publisher of the *Daily News*, had written on O'Malley's behalf, noting that "the risk of losing the Dodgers provides a spark which may bring together all interests. . . ." Flynn ran the biggest newspaper in the country, which meant that Moses was compelled to answer and explain himself. This time, however, he wrote that O'Malley's plan was "a dead issue." Nor, he added, was there another place in Brooklyn "at which the Dodgers are willing to spend real money." Then, because he was eager to show that he was not spurning the Dodgers, he suggested an alternative: "a field in Queens." The site was in Jamaica. It was close to the geographical center of the city. Perhaps, and this he acknowledged would not be easy, the land might be used for housing, and a ballpark, too. In closing, he wrote, "We see nothing else in the picture."

He may not have. But all through the fall and into the winter the letters kept coming, from bankers and from John Cashmore. Walter O'Malley continued to play the press, inviting reporters on his trip to Princeton to see, of all things, a model for a domed stadium designed by Buckminster Fuller and later, one of his architecture students, Billy Kleinsasser. Now Moses was finding himself forced to answer questions about a dome, a gimmick he later dismissed as a work of an "ambitious graduate student reporting to a rather wild professor of architecture." The story was not dying down. In January 1956, when Duke Snider arrived at the annual sportswriters' dinner to be honored as player of the year, he came wearing a double-sided baseball cap: the familiar Dodger "B" on one side; but on the other an interlocking

"JC"—Jersey City. The Duke was not one for joking, but the writers had to laugh. It was that kind of night: the entertainment included a song a group of the wags sang to the Dodgers to the tune of "Home on the Range": "Oh, give me a home, with a translucent dome . . ." Then, with a bow to *Guys and Dolls*, they saluted the Dodgers as the "oldest established permanent floating franchise in New York." Not that anyone thought that Walter O'Malley was *really* thinking of permanently relocating. "The last thing The O'Malley wants to do is have the Dodgers leave Brooklyn," Arthur Daley wrote in the *Times*. Likewise, wrote Red Smith in the *Herald-Tribune*, "It is difficult to believe that he could seriously entertain the idea of leaving. . . ."

5 | "A NEW DAY"

In the late winter of 1956 it was reasonable to believe that there were no greater powers in Brooklyn than the will and whims of Robert Moses. This was not true. Moses may have been the object of fear and envy. But he was merely a facilitator of an epochal change that was easy to spot but difficult to explain: many people were leaving Brooklyn and many others were moving in. They were being propelled by forces greater than any single man's vision: jobs, sanctuary, dreams. In comparison to these forces, Robert Moses merely built the roads leading out of Brooklyn and the homes where the newly arrived might, if they were fortunate, live.

The change, of course, was happening everywhere: since the end of the war the nation felt like a place on the move, with great shifts in people from country to city and from city to suburb, from east to west, from south to north. The change was especially dramatic in Brooklyn, at least in spots. While neighborhoods like Midwood and Marine Park felt untouched, others, like Brownsville, East New York, and Bedford-Stuyvesant were seeing a steady departure of white residents and the arrival of many new black people. Some of the white people moved to other Brooklyn neighborhoods, like Crown Heights, to the new high-rise housing projects that Robert Moses was building. Others were leaving altogether, for Long Island, for New Jersey. This movement in, through, and out of Brooklyn was nothing new. It was only the larger scale and greater speed that made it different and so important.

Long before 1947, when William Levitt built his eponymous town of mass-produced houses on what were once Long Island potato fields, *Brooklyn* was the destination for people escaping the crush, terrors, and sin of urban life. Brooklyn, of course, was the city. From the early nineteenth century on it had been a riverbank town bordered by a series of distant farm villages—Midwood, Flatlands, New Lots, Flatbush. By the turn of the twentieth century, however, Brooklyn had become the prototype of the American city: busy, dirty, and crowded at its core, bucolic on the fringes. It was to the fringes, to the open spaces, that people escaped.

America has never had much use for its cities. The decent life had long been defined by what was left behind by all the young men and women who flocked from the countryside to the cities in the early nineteenth century. Many came for the simplest of reasons: to make money, because there was too little money and opportunity on the farm. Immigrants came to the cities, too, first German, then Irish, then Italians and Jews. So did criminals and people of questionable ideologies and opinions. And although the murder rates in the romanticized rural South were higher than in the urban North—which was not afflicted by such traditions as revenge killings—the cities were still regarded as dangerous places, dangerous to the body and to the soul, too. The countryside offered salvation which was why, for instance, Charles Loring Brace, founder of the Children's Aid Society, thought that the best thing he could do for tens of thousands of abandoned or merely poor children was to place them on what became known as the "orphan trains" and ship them to farm towns, to be taken in by decent Christian people.

It is no small irony that beginning in the late nineteenth century, urban Americans embraced as their new diversion a country game, baseball, which was played on large and open expanses of grass; these fields, of course, were by the early twentieth century surrounded by concrete-and-steel walls, and by thousands of wooden seats to accommodate all the city people who came to see the country boys play.

As a city and later a borough, Brooklyn had its burghers, but it was primarily a working-class town—a dockside-factory-warehouse-construction site place. This, in turn, went a long way toward molding the borough's character, a character that Brooklynites self-consciously mythologized: pugnacious, a bit rough in manner, and more than a little defensive about

the swells who lived in the tall buildings on the other side of the East
River.

This is not to suggest that Brooklyn people shared some sort of communal harmony, an us-against-them unanimity. The people with money did not
want to live where they worked, and most certainly not near the people
without money, the laboring classes. So they moved out, in the late nineteenth century, to East New York and Bedford and Bushwick. They commuted by trolley and later by train. Working people followed them, moving
along with the new trolley lines, so that by the 1920s developers were building the first rows of mass-produced, cookie-cutter homes in places like
Canarsie, which, in turn, became suburban redoubts. The lines of demar-
cation were not always neat and clean—this despite the often successful efforts by realtors to make sure that white people lived on one side of the
divide and black people on the other. Neighborhoods often evolved along
class lines, and in this way Brooklyn people came to embrace another view
of themselves, and their world: that in Brooklyn's neighborhoods everyone
got along—Italians, Jews, Irish, Scandinavians, and the sprinkling of blacks
and Puerto Ricans. And often this was true, at least temporarily.

But Brooklyn was a transitory place, for those who stayed there and for
those who wanted out. People rented in Brooklyn more than they owned,
and this meant that as circumstances improved it was time to move, from a
nineteenth-century hovel with no indoor plumbing in Williamsburg to a
coldwater flat in Borough Park to, at last, a home with amenities in Windsor
Terrace. The lucky ones moved south, following the arterial roads like Flatbush and Coney Island Avenues and Ocean Parkway to brick houses by the
water. Others headed east, to Queens. In Brooklyn the moving had a pattern, and generally it was about moving on, and eventually out. In the winter of 1956 it was Abe and Ruth Steinberg's time to leave.

They were then living in an apartment in Bensonhurst, a neighborhood
that was mostly Italian but with a scattering of "ethnic whites," the euphe-
mism for immigrants and immigrants' children. They had two rooms and a
kitchenette. They had been married for three years and their first child,
Linda, was a year old. Their neighbors were pleasant but were for the most
part older; the women came to visit Ruth in their housedresses. There was
nothing wrong with the building, or with their neighbors or with Brooklyn.
Ruth, who was twenty-eight, had grown up in Brooklyn and had committed

the petty heresy of marrying not only a man from the Bronx, but a Yankee fan. On their honeymoon in October 1953, Abe sent a telegram from Bermuda to Ruth's brother in Brooklyn after the Yankees had defeated the Dodgers in yet another World Series: it read, simply and gleefully, "Ho hum." Ruth could not have been pleased: her first crush was on Pete Reiser, who had captured her heart in the 1940s.

The Steinbergs needed space and not once did the thought occur to them to look for it in Brooklyn. They wanted a house, and the houses they could afford on Abe's salary as an accountant and with the mortgage benefits he enjoyed as a veteran were on Long Island. Besides, the houses in Brooklyn were attached. They were smaller and had only modest patches of grass growing in the front and back. But beyond these practical considerations was the desire to live among people their own age. Young people in Brooklyn moved to Long Island. Those from the Bronx looked for homes in Westchester because it was closer and that was where the Bronx highways led. Brooklyn was Ruth's parents' world. Brooklyn was old. "The image of the island," she would later say, "was very appealing." The Island also held a certain romantic appeal for Ruth. One night, when she was a child, she went with her parents and three brothers to a roadside restaurant in the town of Oceanside. There was no highway then and the drive seemed to go on forever. The sky was black and Ruth felt as if they were heading to "the end of the earth." But when they got there Ruth saw that her parents had taken them to a popular destination, to a fancy place where men wore white dinner jackets.

Now her brother Jack lived in Oceanside and Ruth and Abe began visiting on Sundays. The town was a place of empty lots where builders were planning developments. One Sunday, Abe, who was thirty-one, took a walk in the neighborhood with his niece and nephew and happened upon a builder who had opened a model home. The home was a "front to back split"—the front door opened onto a playroom and up a short flight of stairs to the kitchen and den; the bedrooms were on the second floor. Abe liked the house and was especially taken with all the trees that surrounded the property, including a big oak in the back. The builder told him he was planning eight more houses on that same block, which was otherwise vacant. Abe went to fetch Ruth, who liked the house just as much as he did. He asked the builder if the model was for sale. When the builder told him it was, Abe gave him a $10 bill and told him he'd meet him the following day to draw up a contract. "You'll give me credit for this $10," he said. Just like that, Abe and Ruth Steinberg began their exodus from Brooklyn. The house cost $19,500. The down payment was $3,500, and with a $16,000, thirty-year mortgage at 4 percent interest, the monthly cost would be $125.

The decision to leave came for Ruth without sadness or nostalgia. She had gone to Midwood High School in Brooklyn, and then on to Brooklyn College. She had been married in the Avenue R Temple in Brooklyn and until Linda was born had worked as a legal assistant in a downtown Brooklyn law firm. Yet when the time came to move, she did not for a moment feel any sense of loss. If she wanted to find people like Abe and her, a young couple with a baby who were capable of being so quickly smitten by the prospect of a "front to back split" with an oak tree in the back, she would have to go to Long Island to find them. Her new neighbors, it turned out, were Brooklyn people, too, young and a little restless. The Island, she would later say, "was an extension of Brooklyn." This was true but, as Walter O'Malley had calculated, only up to a point.

When he spurned Patchogue's offer of thirty acres of land surrounded by a legion of Dodger fans, O'Malley did so knowing that while people liked to live on Long Island, they still came back into Brooklyn to work and sometimes play: that is just what he had been doing since moving his family from Brooklyn to Amityville in 1944. The congestion of downtown may have been unappealing for those who wanted space and green. But it was still the district of jobs and restaurants, of movie houses, theaters, and, O'Malley hoped, a ballpark. Robert Moses thought this way, too, with the exception of the ballpark.

But Moses was working two tracks at once: making downtown Brooklyn's Civic Center grand, vital, and attractive to those who wanted to live in his new housing projects; at the same time making it easier for those who wanted out of Brooklyn to make the commute back for work. In March the *World-Telegram* broke the story that construction on the great bridge across the Verrazano Narrows from Brooklyn to Staten Island would begin not sometime in the distant future, but in a mere eighteen months. No longer would it be necessary to commute from Staten Island by ferry. For Moses had looked across the Narrows and envisioned the longest suspension bridge in the world.

While Bay Ridge fretted, and worked futilely to prevent the demolition of the hundreds of homes that stood in the path of the bridge's access roads, the people of Midwood experienced that rare pleasure of learning that a Moses highway was not going to run through their neighborhood after all. It was Moses himself who announced that the Cross-Brooklyn Expressway was not even a line on an official map. If it was to be built, no date, timetable, or precise path existed.

If the shape of the future was becoming painfully clear in Bay Ridge, then in Midwood it was possible to slip back into the comforting belief that things could remain as they were. Yet even in Midwood fissures were developing, even if they were barely noticeable. At Midwood High School the principal, Jacob Bernstein, sent a letter home to parents warning them that their children risked an unpleasant visit to his office if they came to school wearing that unfortunate emblem of youthful rebellion, dungarees. The student body was split. The student council, a conservative body, had already voted to ban jeans. But some students insisted they would wear what they wanted. Bernstein, a taciturn man whom the students nicknamed "Jake the Flake," warned that while dungarees themselves were not a problem they were still the uniform of "youngsters showing an indifference to convention."

Elsewhere in Brooklyn the reports were even more disquieting. John Cashmore was trying to block folksinger Pete Seeger's concert at the Brooklyn Academy of Music, the borough's premier concert hall. Veterans' groups were protesting the show, which was being sponsored by a Brooklyn private school. "There is no room—on stage or even in the wings—for left wingers. . . ." Cashmore fulminated. He went to court, seeking an injunction to halt the use of a city-owned concert hall by "left-wing termites." Meanwhile, in Brooklyn Heights, the Protestant Episcopal Church of the Holy Trinity had been fighting for months to rid itself of its pastor, the Reverend Howard Melish, a man of questionably liberal thinking. Yet despite court challenges and canonical rulings, he was still at the pulpit.

But in other sections of Brooklyn, change was not so much acceptable as it was eagerly anticipated. On March 29, a week after his conviction for leading the four-month boycott of the Montgomery, Alabama, bus system, the twenty-seven-year-old Reverend Martin Luther King, Jr., came to speak in Bedford-Stuyvesant. Ten thousand people tried to squeeze into the Concord Baptist Church to hear him.

Concord Baptist's pastor, the Reverend Gardner C. Taylor, was an old friend of the King family: his father had been a friend of Martin Luther King, Jr.'s grandfather. Taylor was thirty-eight and emerging as a prominent voice in the civil rights movement. He presided over one of the most prestigious pulpits of any black church in America, and competed with Adam Clayton Powell, Jr.'s Abyssinian Baptist Church in Harlem as the largest Protestant congregration in the nation. Powell, a member of Congress and a powerful man in his own right, was not a booster of King. So it was that when King headed north, the most welcoming and important podium awaited him at Gardner C. Taylor's church.

The church itself had replaced a sanctuary destroyed by fire in 1952. The new building had just been completed. It was a vast room, a seemingly endless row of dark wooden pews, arrayed beneath a beamed, vaulted ceiling. A balcony surrounded the room on three sides and, in the front, on a wide, low riser, sat an immensely pleased Gardner C. Taylor.

He had come to Concord Baptist in 1948 from Baton Rouge, Louisiana, where he had been pastor of the Mount Zion Baptist Church. Mount Zion had been his father's pulpit and was the largest congregation in Baton Rouge. Baton Rouge was a city of thirty-five thousand, which meant that even at a well-attended church like Mount Zion, the Sunday congregation was perhaps three hundred. He had arrived in Brooklyn thirty years old and restless. After his father's death, his mother had supported the family by teaching. Her salary of fifty-two dollars a week was half that of white teachers. It was yet another humiliation among so many. "I was always angry in the South," he would later say. The civil rights movement "was right up my alley."

He knew little of Brooklyn when he arrived to inherit a congregation being transformed by all the many new people arriving in Bedford-Stuyvesant—fifteen or twenty were coming to Concord Baptist each week. They were not, strictly speaking, his people. Migrants from Louisiana had followed the Illinois Central line to Chicago. Bedford-Stuyvesant was filling up with black people from the coastal states: Virginia, Georgia, the Carolinas. The newcomers were not always popular. They were for the most part country people, and those who had come a generation before them were quick with such denigrating labels as "Geegees"—bumpkins from Georgia.

The older congregants, Taylor learned quickly, were a conservative lot,

Republicans who insisted upon a certain sense of propriety. They were postal workers, Pullman porters, bus drivers. The women who worked did so as domestics. There was a small coterie of professionals. But it was understood that one did not ask what someone else did for a living.

The newcomers found work at the navy yard, but not the well-paying union jobs. They were the janitors and porters, the members of his congregation most intent on forcing changes in the way big employers did their hiring. The Concord pulpit was a position of considerable political influence, if only because of the congregation's great and swelling numbers: Taylor now preached to audiences as large as two thousand. He had been quickly approached by the congregation's activists, most of whom were women.

Taylor also saw how well-placed men like John Cashmore felt compelled to be solicitous, if only because he spoke to and for so many voters. He met famous people, too, among them Jackie Robinson. Things, however, had not gone well with Robinson. Taylor had asked him the pastor's standard question—when was he going to see him in church? But Robinson recoiled and grew defensive. Taylor let the matter drop.

By 1956, Taylor had emerged in his role as leader of a vast and growing flock. The church's fire had, ironically, been his test: without a sanctuary the congregation had turned to its pastor to hold it together. That he did. And now, in his newly opened building, Taylor took his seat at the front of the church and saw a sight unlike any he had ever witnessed. In a sanctuary built to hold as many as twenty-two hundred people on Easter morning, three thousand managed to find room inside to hear Martin Luther King.

They cheered and wept as he spoke. He told them that he was prepared to take to the United States Supreme Court the battle that had begun with the arrest of Rosa Parks for refusing a driver's order that she move to the back of his bus. "We will not degrade ourselves with hatred," King said, and with that pans, cardboard boxes, and wastepaper baskets were passed through the aisles; four thousand dollars was collected that night to aid the boycott. It was for Gardner C. Taylor a glorious night. He sensed that his congregation was, as he later put it, "on the edge of something new and hopeful." Bedford-Stuyvesant may have been becoming a largely black neighborhood. But this did not mean it was sinking. Quite the opposite. "There was bright promise and great hope," Taylor later said. "A new day had come. We were on our way."

———

THE EVENTS IN Montgomery may have felt remote to many in Brooklyn, but not for the Dodgers, who found themselves, for a few days at least, in the thick of it. In February, Buzzie Bavasi announced that the team would not play an exhibition game against the Milwaukee Braves in Birmingham, which prohibited blacks and whites from participating together on the same field of play. "If they don't want all of us, the hell with them," Bavasi said. There were five black men on the team's twenty-five-man roster. And while four were not overtly political men, one, Jackie Robinson, most certainly was. The "gag" that Branch Rickey had imposed on him early in his career had ended years before, and now Robinson, a man of passionate and bluntly expressed opinions, said what he pleased and thought. Robinson had cultivated important and well-connected friends: Richard Simon, a founder of Simon and Schuster, had been instrumental in smoothing the way for Robinson to buy a home in Stamford, Connecticut, a leafy and white suburb. He gave speeches and testified before congressional commit-tees and wrote guest newspaper columns about his experiences as a *black man* in the major leagues.

His politics placed him further at a remove from his teammates, whose visions of the future often extended no further than the next at-bat. As it happened, Robinson had brought a group of barnstorming all-stars—including some Dodgers—to segregated Birmingham in 1953. But faced with the ban in mixed-race playing, he kept the white men, Gil Hodges, Ralph Branca, and Bobby Young, out of the lineup. Bavasi told Robinson, and the papers, that he was wrong, that prejudice cut two ways. Robinson, however, replied that had he forced the issue, Birmingham's police chief, Bull Connor, a racist of the most virulent sort, would have used the game to advance his political career (he was running for sheriff) by arresting every-one on the field. Robinson refused to give him the satisfaction, or what he sensed would be the boost.

The Dodgers broke camp and began working their way through the South, bypassing Birmingham but playing the Braves in a series of exhibi-tions in several other southern cities, among them New Orleans, Nashville, Jacksonville, and Mobile. The team hired a couple of Pullman cars and a dining car and along the way rented a few hotel rooms where the players could shower. It had been a desultory spring; the team won as often as it lost. Pitching still remained a worry—the sore-armed Karl Spooner would stay in Florida, Billy Loes could not yet pitch, Erskine would soldier on, and Don Drysdale would make the club. But the Dodgers felt solid, even if they had not always played like champions. Their route took them into the Jim Crow South, where the papers were filled with news of trouble with, and over, black people.

In New Orleans an investigator with the Senate Internal Security Subcommittee announced that he had uncovered documentary evidence of a Communist-led plan to foment a "civil war in the South" that would topple the existing order and replace it with a "Southern Negro empire." The committee chairman, Senator James Eastland of Mississippi, called the findings "informative" and evidence "of conspiracy of the Soviet Union in the United States." In Birmingham, six white men rushed onstage and attacked singer Nat King Cole as he performed for a white audience. The men, who had hatched their plan to disrupt the concert several days before at a filling station, had hoped to lure a mob of 150 men into the Municipal Auditorium to stop the show. But the other men did not show up. The attack came a few days after the White Citizens Council began a campaign against "Negro music" in Alabama. Cole returned to the stage, where he was greeted with a five-minute ovation. In Montgomery the bus boycott continued as protestors renewed their call for open seating, polite service, and jobs for black drivers.

In city after city the Dodgers and Braves attracted few white fans, even with the promise that these were the two teams that would battle each other for the National League pennant. But black people came in such numbers that the whites-only seating sections in the bleachers and in the grandstands were opened to accommodate them.

The sight was a familiar one for Clem Labine; year after year the team had followed the same route, playing in many of the same minor league parks. And always it was black people who came to see them—to see Jackie, of course, and Campy and Newk. Labine would stand in the infield and look out at the stands, scanning the bleachers from end to end, and all he could see were black faces. There sat a vast, untapped audience that major league baseball would neglect and ignore, and whose attendance it would never actively solicit once the real games began.

PART THREE

APRIL

Buzzie Bavasi thought playing seven games in Jersey City was a bad idea. He believed the ploy was a foolish one, not worthy of O'Malley's talents as a manipulator of events: it could too easily backfire, alienating not only people in Brooklyn but Robert Moses, too.

Bavasi was forty-one years old, tall, and blunt. He had been with the team since 1939, which meant that while he had worked for Branch Rickey he was not, strictly speaking, a Rickey man. This was fortunate because Walter O'Malley had so detested Rickey that too close an association was potentially damning. Bavasi, however, was Larry MacPhail's hire.

His given name was Emil. He picked up the nickname as a child, from his younger sister who could not pronounce the word "brother." He grew up in Queens and later went off to college at DePauw, in Greencastle, Indiana. There he became good friends with the son of Ford Frick, who later became the commissioner of baseball. Frick was well connected in the game, and when he learned that Bavasi was spending his year after college driving around the country in the new car his mother had given him as a graduation present, Frick offered to introduce Bavasi to MacPhail, who might have something for him.

He went to work for the Dodgers for ninety-five dollars a month and, except for the war years, which he spent on the front lines in Italy, that was where he stayed. He stayed through MacPhail and through Rickey, too. Still, O'Malley liked him. Bavasi suspected this had a good deal to do with his handling of the peanut sales for the Montreal franchise. Bavasi had worked for and later run the Dodger franchises in Valdosta, Georgia; Durham, North Carolina; and Nashua, New Hampshire, before being promoted to oversee the Dodgers' top minor league team. O'Malley came up for a visit, and in the course of their talk Bavasi mentioned that he had increased the team's take on peanut sales by cutting the number of peanuts in a bag from 35 to 34, thereby saving the team the cost of 4,000 peanuts a night.

O'Malley saw promise in Bavasi. He had Bavasi and his wife, Evit, to the house in Amityville and to his son Peter's football games. He had entrusted to Bavasi the signings, trades, and sales of his players—the latter of which was an important skill on a team that had little room for flab in the budget. Bavasi had had to sell players just to meet the team's payroll. He'd sold Benny Taylor, Billy Cox, Preacher Roe, Bobby Morgan, and even twice sold a less-than-stellar pitching prospect, Tom Lasorda.

O'Malley had given Bavasi a great responsibility: spending his money. Bavasi handled all trades and contracts. He worked closely with O'Malley, close enough to offer a dissenting opinion, and close enough, too, to have taken the measure of his boss. Bavasi saw Jersey City as a loser on all fronts, except for one and that was the gate. He knew Walter O'Malley well enough to recognize his attraction to the promise of a quick and considerable buck. Jersey City was a legendary baseball town—less so for the quality of play (it was strictly a minor league city) than for ticket sale revenue. The Giants' top farm club had played in Roosevelt Stadium there, and on their Opening Days, the local lore had it, drew 63,000 patrons. This feat was made all the more remarkable by the fact that Roosevelt Stadium had only 30,000 seats. This miracle of attendance was accomplished by Frank "I Am the Law" Hague, longtime mayor of Jersey City. It was Boss Hague himself who convinced President Franklin Roosevelt to have the WPA build him a stadium, which Hague prudently named for the president. Hague's power in Jersey City was such that all city employees felt compelled to buy *two* tickets for the Jersey Giants' Opening Day games. And though Hague was gone, Bavasi sensed that O'Malley looked at those bloated attendance figures and did not need an adding machine to convince himself that he might score nicely there, too.

So O'Malley announced his plan for the seven games and shook hands with the current mayor, Bernard Berry. When Bavasi tried to talk him out of going, O'Malley replied that it was now too late: he'd committed himself. With that O'Malley dispatched Irving Rudd to Jersey City to see what sort of business he could drum up.

IF IRVING RUDD had not existed, Central Casting could have sent a replica over to Montague Street to play the part of the Brooklyn-guy-whose-dream-comes-true-when-he-goes-to-work-for-*Da-Bums*. Rudd was the Dodgers' front man, their publicist, their director of promotions. The work made him exceptionally happy. He was a small man with grand ideas, a Brownsville guy who resisted the pretense of insisting, as others there did, that he was from the more respectable sounding East New York. Brownsville was a Jewish neighborhood, but of a sort considered déclassé in such tonier places as Midwood and Flatbush. The Jewish gangsters of Murder, Incorporated came from Brownsville, and though the most vicious among them, Abe Relis, was defenestrated elsewhere—at the Half Moon Hotel in Coney Island—he was, to the end, a Brownsville guy, as was the eager and endlessly inventive Irving Rudd.

Rudd came to work for the Dodgers in 1951 because Walter O'Malley thought he was Protestant. O'Malley was concerned that the Dodgers front office might appear to be too Catholic. Ethnicities, however, challenged him. He hired Lee Scott, the traveling secretary, in the belief that Scott was a Jew. Only afterward did he learn that Scott was an Italian with an abbreviated surname. Rudd was hired for five thousand dollars a year to get people into the stadium seats. He endeared himself to O'Malley when, by dint of such events as meet-the-players cabana parties, he accomplished the heretofore impossible task of filling the seats of Miami Stadium when the Dodgers came to visit during the exhibition season. It was he who worked to make sure that Ebbets Field was packed to capacity for "Pee Wee Reese Night" in 1955—the only regular season sellout that year. So in December 1955, O'Malley dispatched him to the Hotel Plaza on Journal Square in Jersey City, where he hung up the team's shingle and set about selling the idea of the Jersey/Brooklyn Dodgers. Irving Rudd, who was now making fifty-eight hundred dollars a year, did not want to disappoint, especially after having asked O'Malley for a thousand-dollar raise.

O'Malley promised him no money, but did have him featured prominently in the team's newsletter, *Dodgers Line Drives*; Rudd, the team's "irrepressible promotion man" was the "guiding genius" behind Pee Wee's night, a man known "from Coney Island to Miami Beach." The words, Rudd later admitted in his memoir, *The Sporting Life*, emboldened him. He planted some lovely items in the papers—Could you believe it, the first two kids who lined up to buy tickets for the Jersey City games were named, and this he swore "just happened," Willie Mays and Bill Rigney, the *very same names* as the Giants center fielder and manager. Really and truly, he later wrote. He couldn't make this up.

Rudd was a clever man and not without an ego. But he was not a powerful man, nor, he recognized, an important one in Walter O'Malley's ordering of his universe. Like the other lesser men who worked for the Dodgers, Rudd loathed the man he called "The Dragon." All the whiskey-soaked and hail-fellow-well-met charm that O'Malley heaped on the men he cultivated had just the opposite effect on the men who worked for him, in good measure because he used it so liberally against them when they asked for a raise. One of the standing parlor games played behind O'Malley's back was trying to decide, once and for all, who was the greater miser: "The Oom" or Branch Rickey. The differences were so slight they could be measured in nickels and dimes; neither man spent more than necessary on an employee. For a party, yes. But not on a salary. O'Malley had fired Charlie Dressen, a good if self-important manager ("Just stay close to 'em, I'll think of something. . . ."), when Dressen, on the advice of his wife, asked for a three-year contract and an expense account. Dressen's successor, Walter Alston, worked on a one-year contract, which the Dodgers would renew nineteen times.

O'Malley would feign the common touch with his employees—"Call me Walter"—then head out for lunch with his moneyed friends at his clubhouse just down Montague Street, Room 40 of the Hotel Bossert. Downtown Brooklyn had a limited selection of dark-wood-and-leather-chair places where prominent men could find each other at lunch and for a scotch-and-water at the end of the day. So O'Malley made Room 40 his own. At Room 40 he could have lunch with George V. McLaughlin, still president of the Brooklyn Trust Company, and with the assortment of appellate court judges and businesspeople who, along with O'Malley, embodied a certain Brooklyn provincialism: they were wealthy, to be sure, but not quite as numerous or as powerful as the men who met for lunch in midtown Manhattan.

O'Malley never publicly berated an employee, never raised his voice or belittled a man. Still, Irving Rudd, Harold Parrott, the ticket manager, and Frank Graham, Jr., who also handled the press, could not abide him. Graham, a Columbia graduate who went on to a career as an author first on sports and later on the environment, found what he called the "Irish pol manqué" just too transparent. Graham was luckier than the others; O'Malley invited him to lunch from time to time. Graham was not flattered; he understood that he was being asked out only because his father was one of the best-known sports columnists in New York, for decades a fixture at the *Sun*. Graham watched as O'Malley effected a bond with the common man, yet he was never seen at Ebbets Field anyplace but in his private box. He tried to be charming with women, but this, too, felt false; Graham's wife told him that O'Malley's presence made her "shiver." O'Malley's people talked about him and groused about him and in all the time he spent working for the Dodgers, Graham never heard any of them express affection for him. His only redeeming quality was his devotion to his wife; and that affection they did not doubt.

Irving Rudd did send O'Malley a note reminding him about the raise, and when he heard nothing he called. O'Malley made it clear that the question was not appreciated. "I don't like being pushed, boy," he said. Later he told Rudd that perhaps he might find better pay elsewhere; there was no money to be made in baseball. He said this in an attempt at commiseration. Irving Rudd, who did not leave Brownsville a fool, knew when he was being conned.

ALL THROUGH THE winter and on into the spring Irving Rudd worked like a dervish and by the second week of April he was looking at a disaster. Roosevelt Stadium was a mud pit; an April snowstorm had turned the field to ankle-deep muck. Ice-skating and car racing had long since replaced baseball at the park; workmen had torn out the rink and sodded over the cinder-and-shale racetrack. But worse still were the ticket sales: without the strong arm of the departed Mayor Hague, the locals no longer felt compelled to buy two tickets, let alone one.

Still, the field was ready the day before the opener and the Dodgers came out to practice. Rudd opened the workout to the public, free of charge, and ten thousand people, children mostly who'd been dismissed early from school (the local pols were eager to help) came to watch. The players looked at the distant fences—330 feet down the right field line, 33 feet longer than at Ebbets Field—and took note of the wind that blew *in* from Newark Bay, a veritable gale that, it was said, had kept any fly ball from ever clearing the fence in center field, an otherwise manageable 411 feet away. The workout and inspection complete, the children ran onto the field and the Dodgers retreated to the clubhouse. Irving Rudd announced that there were still 8,000 seats available each for $1.25 in the "open pavilion"—the bleachers, really, but grander sounding—and another 1,600 in the reserved section for $2 and $3 a throw. And plenty of parking, too, 10,000 spots in the sandlots by the bay, a buck a car.

April 19, "Opening Day" in Jersey City, dawned cloudy, windy, and cold, a curse of nature that dominated the conversation during batting practice.

"It's gonna be cold on the fans," said Rube Walker, the backup catcher. "They'll have to sit in the stands without moving."

"It's gonna be cold on me, too," replied Don Zimmer, another reserve. "I'll be sitting on the bench without moving."

"I don't know what you fellows are complaining about," said Gil Hodges. "It's not cold. It's all in your head."

Hodges was a quiet man, but he was a kidder, too. He had to be kidding. Roy Campanella blew on his hands and said, "It's in my hands."

Twelve thousand people came to see them play, which left half the seats vacant—in plain view of Walter O'Malley who shared a box with Mayor Berry. The mayor was supposed to throw out the first ball, but when the moment arrived none was at hand. Lee Scott raced into the clubhouse, returned with a ball, which the mayor, prudently wearing a topcoat, tossed to Campanella. The Dodgers and Phillies took their positions along the base paths. The fans booed them both.

CARL ERSKINE STARTED, pitched well, and might have won had the Dodgers not committed a week's worth of errors—five—including two *on the same play* by Reese. Balls flew unpredictably. Fly balls that would have been home runs in Ebbets Field fell yards short in Roosevelt. A Reese pop fly, which appeared to go foul, instead lurched fair in the wind, its flight so perplexing to the Philadelphia third baseman that he fell down and Reese had himself a single. Balls that appeared catchable off the bat suddenly gained loft just as outfielders thought they'd drawn a bead.

Still, the Dodgers managed to squeeze out a win on Walker's pinch-hit double in the tenth, which came after a lovely piece of run construction: a single by Snider, a run-scoring double by Campanella, an intentional walk to Hodges, a sacrifice by Robinson (yes Robinson, whom Alston had elected to start at third, without protest from Randy Jackson), an intentional walk to Furillo that filled the bases. Zimmer, who with Walker assumed he'd spend the day sitting and shivering, ran for Campy and scored on Walker's first-pitch double, which evened the team's record at a win and a loss. In the clubhouse, however, Jackie Robinson got into an argument with a Jersey sportswriter who wanted to talk about the way the fans booed him; they were on him from the fourth inning, when he committed an error and got so angry that he threw his cap on the ground and kicked it. The reception of Robinson was tinged with historical irony: in was in 1946, at Roosevelt Stadium, that he became the first black man to play in a minor league game.

But now he fumed. "The way they acted," he said of his error, "you'd think I did it on purpose." And with that he ranted for a while about the town and the people. The writers asked him to repeat some of the juicier lines for the record. Robinson declined; the man from the *Jersey Journal* pressed. Robinson grew testy. The writer snapped, "Why don't you act like a gentleman?"

Robinson erupted and Red Patterson, the team's press handler, stepped between them. At this moment Irving Rudd, who'd worked long and hard in the hope of his thousand-dollar raise, tried, one last time, to squeeze something good out of the misery of this second Opening Day.

"Jackie didn't say they could give Jersey City back to the Indians," he explained. He said the Jersey Dodgers will be back here to play an exhibition with the Cleveland Indians April 30. "Isn't that right, Jack?"

"I don't think I mentioned the date, Irv," Robinson replied.

2 | A BRIEF, FALSE SUMMER

On the last Saturday of April the Brooklyn Dodgers won their fifth straight game. Their record stood at 8 and 2, good enough for first place, if only by a slender game and a half over the Milwaukee Braves. They'd beaten the weaker teams—the Phillies, Giants, and Pirates—winning on the road, and at home, where evening temperatures hovered in the mid-forties, keeping attendance low. But just before the month's final weekend, the days of rain stopped. The sun burnt off early morning fog, sending temperatures soaring by almost forty degrees. It was 81 degrees on Friday afternoon, and on Saturday, with temperatures still in the mid-seventies, one hundred thousand people flocked to Coney Island. Many came in bathing suits, and though the Atlantic was still too cold for swimming, people gathered across the wide beach, approximating the experience of summer. At Ebbets Field, Don Newcombe pitched the team's fifth consecutive complete game victory. Only Jim Gilliam was hitting well, but the pitching worries that had dogged the Dodgers at Vero Beach appeared to have vanished. Saturday was Ladies' Day, a baseball tradition in which women fans were admitted for free. Seventeen thousand people came to Ebbets Field that afternoon, and the park, deserted on the chilly nights for a week, now felt again like a place where people wanted to come.

For all of Walter O'Malley's grousing about his ballpark's poor location, Charles Ebbets had chosen the site for his stadium wisely: the land was cheap, and, though it would one day want for parking, was nonetheless well-situated. Ebbets Field rose up if not precisely in the geographic center of Brooklyn, then certainly in the middle of its cultural heart.

Two blocks from home plate stood the Brooklyn Botanical Garden, fifty idyllic acres that had opened in 1910. The Garden featured rows of exotic trees and plants, and a Japanese garden so serene that it could easily be mistaken for one in Kyoto. Adjoining the Garden was Prospect Park, a vast expanse of bluffs and meadows designed by Frederick Law Olmsted and Calvert Vaux, who drew upon their success with Manhattan's Central Park to create in Brooklyn a place where people might go to feel as if they were in the country. The park, which opened in 1873, had a carousel, a miniature boathouse, and a zoo. The park stretched over five hundred acres, and when it at last gave way to streets it opened onto Brooklyn's great thoroughfare, Eastern Parkway. The Parkway, too, was an Olmsted and Vaux creation. When it opened in 1868 it was the first six-lane highway in the world. Along its borders ran leafy promenades, where people could walk and sit and, in the years to come, stop at the Brooklyn Museum, which featured one of the world's great collections of ancient Asian, African, Egyptian, and American art. The museum was the creation of architect Stanford White, whose original but unrealized plan was for a museum even larger than the Louvre. Just up the boulevard was the Brooklyn Public Library and when

Eastern Parkway finally ended, it did so gloriously, at the great Soldiers' and Sailors' Memorial Arch at Grand Army Plaza. The arch, like the Parkway and the parks, was the creation of James S. T. Stranahan who, decades before Robert Moses was even aware of Brooklyn, headed what was then that city's park and boulevard system. So grand was Stranahan's vision that he was called "the Baron Haussmann of Brooklyn" after the man who had rebuilt Paris. But Stranahan, like Moses, also saw Brooklyn's limitations: he was a backer of the bridge connecting Brooklyn to Manhattan, and then of its consolidation into New York.

Ebbets Field sat on the edge of a neighborhood called Crown Heights. It had once been called Crow Hill, disparagingly dubbed after all the many freed slaves who'd come to live there in the early nineteenth century. Realtors, sensing that association with black people would keep white buyers away, succeeded in having the name changed to Crown Heights. Black people continued to live in Crown Heights and always would. But the realtors did lure white people, in such numbers, in fact, that a century later Crown Heights would rank among the most highly populated districts in Brooklyn. By the mid-1930s some 150,000 people were living in Crown Heights, a number that would remain steady through the mid-1950s. People came to Crown Heights from Russia (or more precisely, the Pale of Settlement, where the Jews were compelled to live), Poland, Austria, Germany, Romania, Hungary, Italy, Ireland, Greece, Lithuania, and Czechoslovakia. These were the white immigrants, who with their American-born children comprised roughly three-quarters of Crown Heights' population. The rest, most of them blacks with a scattering of Puerto Ricans, came from the rural South and the West Indies. Crown Heights was, by and large, a place where people came to live, though not necessarily to work—there was some light industry and commerce on the main shopping streets. It was a neighborhood of apartment buildings with Tudor facades on Eastern Parkway, of brownstone row houses around the corner on Lincoln Place, and of more modest three-story homes mostly filled with renters, not owners. Crown Heights was, for the most part, a neighborhood where working and middle-class people lived, among them Sam Qualiarini, who in the spring of 1956 was sixteen years old and confident in the belief that life in Crown Heights would proceed only in the way he had known it.

Sam lived on Lincoln Place between Troy and Schenectady Avenues and his world was limited to ten city blocks. He did not know anybody who lived anyplace else. He had seldom *been* anyplace else, except for the times when he and his friends traveled thirty blocks away to Betsy Head Park in Brownsville to play hardball against the black kids.

Lincoln Place was a one-way street of private homes and small apartment buildings and maybe two-dozen kids roughly Sam's age. Everyone's parents, it seemed to Sam, had arrived in Crown Heights at just about the same time while about the same age and at the same station in life. Sam's father and grandfather owned a bar on Park Place and Troy Avenue. It was called Sargeant's Bar, after the rank Sam's grandfather had achieved in the Italian army or the Italian police—Sam was never sure which. There was a jukebox in the bar as well as a miniature shuffleboard game and a television. Sometimes the Dodger game was on the television but it did not occupy everyone's attention. On the bar itself, in the back by the liquor bottles, was a cardboard 3-D cutout of the 1955 Dodgers. Sargeant's Bar also attracted the neighborhood bookmakers and loan sharks.

Sargeant's Bar was originally on Bergen Street, near the St. John's home, an orphanage. But in 1950 the city condemned the land and leveled the bar and St. John's home, too, and in their place built St. John's Park and the Albany Houses. Albany Houses was a project built on what architects called the "star" model—a high-rise core surrounded by spokes stacked with apartments. In the core was an elevator, which was a first: everyone Sam knew lived in a building that had stairs. Albany Houses, like the other projects the city was building, was designed to give the working people who lived there amenities denied them in the tenements they'd left: light, space, and, in the eternal American quest to return to the good and bucolic life, greenery. There was "open space" between the buildings, and in that space went trees, grass, and shrubbery. Albany House was an urban oasis with modern kitchens and working toilets.

Some of the people who lived there had lived in the demolished neighborhood houses. Others came from East New York and Brownsville, where the city was tearing down other houses, too. The migrants from East New York were like the people in Crown Heights: Italian, Irish, and a few Jews. They had a lot of kids, too. Sam knew parents whose older kids were twenty and whose youngest were babies. The older ones sometimes left to go into the service and when they came out they got married. Sometimes they had to move in with their parents and sometimes they moved away, to a Brook-lyn neighborhood like Bay Ridge or to Bensonhurst, where they could find a one-bedroom apartment for $60 a month. They were not moving to Long Island, not yet. They didn't have the money for the down payment. This was not 1947, when a veteran could put $50 down for a house in Levittown. If you wanted to buy a house in Syosset it would cost you $10,000 with $1,000 down, which meant you had to go to your parents for the money and maybe they were not ready to see you move to the "country," so far away.

In the world as Sam had come to know it, grandparents lived with their children (his did) and relatives lived nearby (his Aunt Sadie was three blocks away) and only the Jews seemed to be moving away. Black people lived on Sam's block, but not many of them, so their presence felt manage-able and tolerable to the white neighbors. Black people also lived on East-ern Parkway, but this was a different social class: lawyers and doctors and judges.

Ebbets Field was on the border of Sam Qualiarini's ten-block corner of the world, but Sam did not go there so much anymore, for no reason other than his friends did not go to Ebbets Field, and joy was to be found in the company of his friends. He was friendly with kids from school but they were not his true friends. The kids with whom he went to Brooklyn Techni-cal High School came from far away, from Canarsie and Flatbush and other points around Brooklyn, and while he might go out for a Coke with them after school and talk in class, that was the extent of their association. His friends were Anthony Emanuel, John Greshick, and Frank Boccavella. They had been friends since they were ten years old, the age when they were first allowed to cross an avenue, with two-way traffic, by themselves. This was a liberating event: it meant they could go anywhere. They went to Patty's Pool Room, where they did not go to shoot pool but to stand outside, or to St. John's Park.

There were girls at St. John's Park, too. They sat on the stone tables by the fence and listened to their radios. Sam and his friends went to confra-ternity gatherings in the gymnasium of St. Matthew's Church on Eastern Parkway and Utica Avenue, and girls were there, too. Sometimes they danced with the girls, but not often.

Sam's life proceeded with little to no planning. He knew where his friends would be and what they would do and knew, too, the options they had for diversion. Sometimes their plans were firm, like when they had an American Legion baseball game at the Parade Grounds across from Prospect Park on Ocean Avenue. The year before he had even played in Ebbets Field. Actually, he sat on the bench, a third-string infielder, when Brooklyn Tech lost to Boys High in the public school championships. That was the extent of his formal team-sport associations. If it was a Saturday and there were a lot of other kids at St. John's Park they played softball and if no one was around they played stickball, for which all you needed was two kids, a broomstick, a wall, and rubber ball, a Spalding (pronounced Spaldeen) or a Pensy Pinky, which possessed the superior bounce.

Sam still talked about the Dodgers and cared about the Dodgers but they no longer occupied their once elevated position in his hierarchy of concerns. They were someplace ahead of school, which wasn't saying much, and someplace behind girls, a matter of great interest that was still a bit fuzzy. The Dodgers had mattered a lot to Sam when he was, say, twelve and thirteen, and together with his friends, or by himself, he would stand outside the rotunda at Ebbets Field at the end of day games and wait for the players to come out so that he could run after them, asking for autographs. When class let out, Sam pursued autographs with the sort of precision and dedication that would have made his teachers sigh, as if to say, If only he would apply himself the same way to algebra. They chased anyone. Sometimes they waited outside the right field gate and, like a safecracker listening for the tumblers to slip into place, waited for the telltale sign of the chains to rattle, which meant that someone inside was raising the gate so that a player could emerge. The boys were on him like locusts and the good autographers learned to sign as they walked. And if they were rushing or did not feel like signing—*wasn't that kid here yesterday?*—they took and did not too obviously discard the stamped, self-addressed one-cent postcards. Sam loved many things about the Dodgers, not the least of which was that none of them was ever rude or nasty to a boy who wanted an autograph, even if some of the boys, upset that the signing had stopped before their turn had come, would squirt ink on a player's shirt.

Sam's Italian friends did not collect autographs. His Jewish friends did. In Sam's view of his universe, Italian kids thought that autograph hunting and collecting were unmanly and Jewish kids were not the ballplayers the Italians were. He regarded his Jewish friends as more bookish, and so it was with the Jewish kids that he shared in the passion for autographs. Sam ordered his world into clear and immutable lines. And because there were so many kids around, he could move between groups and never feel alone.

Going to Ebbets Field was a crossover event; everyone went. Sam and his friends waited until the second inning, when the ticket takers might let them slip under the turnstiles. Sometimes they just sneaked in; no grown-up was going to chase a group of kids. He had started going to Ebbets Field when he was seven, when his Uncle Pete took him. Sam's father did not have time to go to the ballpark. In fact, Sam's father, trapped by a saloon-keeper's hours, had little time for anything but work; he never did come to see Sam play ball.

It is hard to be aware of everything when you are sixteen. This meant that for Sam it was easy to pay little heed to the moving vans that came from time to time to transport families away from Lincoln Place. It was impossible to see that Albany Houses would become a way station on the journey from Brownsville to Bensonhurst and out to the Island or New Jersey. And even if the older children were leaving and not coming back, there were still so many kids in St. John's Park, and so many ballgames. For Sam Qualiarini the future looked very much like the past and the present, except with the added dimension of all the girls who suddenly started appearing at the park, as if they'd emerged from the fog.

ON THE LAST Sunday of April, twenty-two thousand came to Ebbets Field to watch the surging Dodgers play two against the Pirates. Sore-armed Billy Loes started the opener and lasted all of an inning and a third, giving up five runs, and headed to the showers under a cascade of boos. The troubles did not stop there: Robinson hurt his thumb and was taken for x-rays. Snider, who was hitting an embarrassing .162, sprained his wrist. The Pirates scored early and often, taking the first game 10 to 1 and the second 11 to 3, thereby erasing any thoughts of a repeat of the 22 and 2 sprint that had opened the 1955 season.

They left that night for Cincinnati, but first made a detour in Jersey City for an exhibition game against the Cleveland Indians, an American League team, a meaningless contest that would stretch the train trip to Ohio to eighteen hours and necessitate their having to face their old nemesis, Sal Maglie. Maglie had tormented them when he was with the Giants, and the Dodgers detested "The Barber," the master of the brushback pitch. But Maglie was now thirty-nine, a down-on-his-luck castoff trying to stick in Cleveland. Still an evening dodging Maglie's curveball was the last thing they needed before an overnight trip to Cincinnati with nothing to think about but the recent thrashing by the Pirates, who never seemed to beat anyone else.

3 | CASSANDRA

Jane Jacobs had lived in Brooklyn in the 1930s and from time to time returned there from Manhattan to bicycle. But by the spring of 1956 she was maintaining her connection to the borough mostly through the newspapers. What she read troubled her. Tucked between items about the marriages of Grace Kelly and Margaret Truman, and news from the campaigns of Adlai Stevenson and Estes Kefauver for the Democratic presidential nomination, were the local stories of slum demolitions, housing project construction, and plans for new and wider highways. Jacobs saw these not as isolated events—as, she believed, so many did—but as a vast plan to transform New York into the sort of city she could not abide: a place of concrete and highrises and endless schemes aimed at creating the sorts of lives that people *ought* to lead, rather than the lives they cared to.

Not that her voice drew much attention—that would come several years later with the publication of her seminal book, *The Death and Life of Great American Cities.* That spring Jacobs was a writer at *Architectural Forum* magazine, writing pieces on the designs of hospitals and schools but finding little interest among her editors for what she had to say about the way cities should look. Because her writing was punchy and stylish they tended to be kind in their criticism. Her view of cities, they told her, was "nostalgic."

To them it lacked grandeur, and grandeur was the watchword of the moment. The famous men who wrote about cities, who taught architecture and who planned those cities, thought about cities in Olympian terms. Robert Moses, who was building *his* vision of a city, could not stand academics, whom he dismissed as woolly-headed theorists, and academics did not much like Moses. But they did share a view of cities: that they were supposed to be *big*. That was how the famous celebrants of cities then thought about them—men like Lewis Mumford, who wrote at length and at times impenetrably about cities as utopian clusters, as the place where a great civilization reached its zenith. Of course there were still others who thought that cities were terrible places and that the best thing a government could do was to find ways to get people—actually, people of similar incomes and class—out of cities, to small and carefully planned villages where they might come together around the green and breathe the good air.

Jane Jacobs thought all of this was nuts. Jacobs was a heretic: she liked neighborhoods. She was neither an academic nor a planner. She was a writer and a walker. She did her walking in city neighborhoods, in places like South Boston, Greenwich Village, and in Brooklyn's Red Hook. She walked and watched and began noticing remarkable things in neighborhoods that the planners and academics and politicians had dismissed as poor and shabby and in need of quick and radical replacement. She noticed that people in neighborhoods got along, that they had established not Mumford's idealized Athens-Upon-the-East-River, but a civilization of a very different sort. City people had devised ways to get along with each other without the assistance of the great thinkers. Because there were so many people and because their homes forced them to look out, at the street and at each other—as opposed to a suburban street that accomplished just the opposite; people could sit in the back and look at the grass—they had to find ways to avoid driving each other crazy. Jacobs noticed that people in the places she lived and visited were friendly with each other *without* being friends. They said hello in the butcher shop and nodded good morning on the street and engaged in meaningless chatter while waiting for the bus. But they did not step over the line and assume that because they had been friendly it stood to reason that they should start inviting one another over for coffee. Those invitations were for friends. Not neighbors. The neighbor who made that mistake, who asked a question too many—*So, where are you off to today?*—was the neighbor to be avoided as too nosy.

City people maintained this equilibrium because they had no choice: they had all somehow come to live in close proximity to one another, in a collection of homes that were not built for them—as was the case in the planned communities in the suburbs—but which had existed before they arrived, and where other people had lived in much the same way. They were a mix, ethnically and socially. They were not all any one thing—not all rich, nor all poor, nor all Italian or Irish. They shared little but the same block and maybe children who happened to be roughly the same age. Jacobs noted all this and noted, too, on her bicycle trips to Brooklyn with her sister, the coming of the housing projects to places like Red Hook. New and tall buildings now stood in the place of older buildings. And while the buildings were sturdier and more attractive, the scale and what it did to neighborhood life was all wrong. "I thought it was very sterile," she said years later. "I wondered how people could be happy there." True neighborhoods evolved, as did the relationships among the people who lived there. They were messy places, and Jacobs believed that such messiness was an accurate reflection of life. Not so the planners, who saw only clutter and dreamed of a new order they could impose.

She came to believe that in each story she read about opposition to a highway there was a neighborhood about to vanish. She recognized, too, that while people could protest and sometimes prevail, there were too many powerful forces arrayed against them, not the least of which was the federal government itself. In the 1930s the Home Owner Loan Corporation gave realtors the guidelines and pretext they needed for blockbusting and redlining when they devised the criteria for assigning value for every block in a city. These guidelines determined where the government would be willing to assist with mortgages. But its impact was devastating to the very places Jacobs liked best. The most attractive neighborhoods in the eyes of the government's evaluators were new, homogeneous, and always in demand. They were populated with the families of "American business and professional men." Jews did not fit this category—not sufficiently American. A good block had space and greenery—and a complete absence of black people.

The value of a block dropped as the homes got smaller, older, and closer together, as the green spaces shrank, and as the population grew more varied and the proportion of black people grew. The values were color-coded: green for the best; a red line outlined the blocks to be avoided. The evaluators then went a step forward, looked toward the future, and, assuming that city neighborhoods always got worse, never better, started judging blocks on their *anticipated* declines. Self-fulfilling prophecies followed. Neighborhoods got worse because the very stability they needed to prevent their decline—home ownership and all it engendered in a neighborhood—

was prevented by government evaluators who did their work in the belief that the people living in, say, Crown Heights and Brownsville would not want to keep living there anyway. Why would they when the government was offering to help them buy a new house on Long Island whose models had grand names like The Kent or The Mayfair?

And so it went, block after block, city after city, where, in Jacobs' view, people had created a life and a world that the planners and thinkers could neither appreciate nor understand. As it happened, Jacobs and her husband had bought their home in Greenwich Village in 1948. They could not get a loan, so they used family money. Had they wanted to move to the Island, money would not have been a problem: "They would have pushed it down our throats."

Jacobs hated when planners talked about "people." She did not believe the planners actually saw people, but rather "interchangeable cogs" who could be shifted from one place to another and who would perform well in that new setting. She also hated the idea of "togetherness," the idea that people could be brought together in a planned community and would, because the planners had only their best interests at heart, would come to like being with each other. But that is not what happened. Instead, those planned communities did not so much bring people together as put them in the awkward position of having to choose whether to be very close, or not close at all. It is hard to be a little friendly with someone whose circumstances are so similar to your own that you assume you *have* to be friends. Those "created neighborhoods" did not allow the luxury of being physically close to other people, and enjoying the feeling (if you wanted it) of being part of a place, while at the same time being free to shut your door, opening it only for intimates. But then how could a planner understand this if he saw people as the little pegs he moved around on a scale model of a cluster of tall buildings, with little trees and bushes dotted between them? Planners did not intend to do harm. Robert Moses, she said, "always thought he was doing good."

Planners could no more see the impact of their ideas than Walter O'Malley could see what was happening among the spectators at his small and dingy ballpark. Because O'Malley sat in his box he could not see that the very same dynamic of the neighborhood was taking place in the stands, where people sat close together, and close by the players, too. It had always been a part of the game; and it always would be. People come to the ball-park to be entertained. But they also come to sit next to strangers with whom they know they are free to talk. They talk about the score, or the pitching or the lousy at-bat they all had to watch. They offer to buy each other beers and watch the kids when they run to the john and offer to get the next round. And in this way they pass the nine innings together. And when the game is done, they turn away from each other and head home, knowing but not necessarily thinking about the fact that they will never talk to each other again. But that's fine. That's the understanding. No one offers a ride home or an invitation out. It was just about being together at the game, and having company for the afternoon or the evening. It is easy to forget that of the many reasons people come to the ballpark, one of them is for the conversation.

Jane Jacobs would always be a romantic about cities and their neigh-borhoods. But she was not naïve. She also saw how people did *not* get along, how the balance of interests was a tricky thing to maintain. For years, however, she bristled when she heard, once again, the received wisdom of what was happening to places like Brooklyn in 1956: that *everyone* (read: white people) wanted out; that black people were pouring in. Because that view suggests that by 1956 civilization as it had come to be mythologized in places like Brooklyn was gone—and that in its place stood a vast tract of empty homes and city streets, waiting only for the poor to take them over. But that was not the case at all. The transformation of Brooklyn from a place of well-functioning neighborhoods, she would always insist, was not inevitable. It reflected the mood of the time, dictated from above—by the planners, the monied and political interests—and from below, too. Every week the newspaper real estate sections ran pictures of the new ranch and detached houses being built on the city's edge—the good life, right there on the page. Meanwhile, realtors were quick to remind prospective buyers that black people were coming, lots of them. Just ask anyone from Brownsville. And when the buyers looked again, their block did not seem the same any-more. They had no reason to think it would ever be as it once was. And no one wanted to be the last one left.

It would take a generation before the children of the people who left the neighborhoods that had so captivated Jane Jacobs began to feel that a desirable but elusive quality had been left behind in their parents' rush to get out: the company of so many familiar and friendly strangers.

4 | A KISS GOODBYE

Even cynical readers could have picked up the Brooklyn edition of the *World-Telegram and Sun* on April 19 and allowed themselves a moment or so to contemplate the possibility that the Brooklyn Dodgers might be opening the 1958 baseball season on the corner of Flatbush and Atlantic Avenues, in a new stadium crowned by a translucent roof.

Granted, no one was actually saying that the ballpark would be ready in two years, when the Dodgers would vacate Ebbets Field. But it did not seem naïve to dream. Because on Saturday, two days hence, Governor Averill Harriman would descend from Albany and come to Brooklyn Borough Hall and, in the presence of the borough president and his boss, Joseph Sharkey, and representatives of the Long Island Railroad and, of course, Walter O'Malley, sign the bill creating the Brooklyn Sports Center Authority.

The title itself sounded almost too grand. And better still, once Harriman signed the bill, the "authority" would have the power to issue $30 million in bonds to pay for land and a stadium. The bill had survived a bit of rough going in the state assembly. Upstate Republicans complained that the deal was a giveaway for Walter O'Malley. But the opposition wilted and the bill had sailed through the assembly, 114 to 32, and now awaited only the governor's signature. And Harriman swore he was a Dodger fan.

The sports authority bill had been Mayor Robert Wagner's idea. He had proposed it in early February when together with John Cashmore he had announced plans to create a "sports center" on the site of the old Fort Greene meat market. The precise location, dimensions, seating capacity, placement, and financing of the stadium still needed to be studied. But the engineering and architectural firm that the city's Board of Estimate had dispatched in the fall of 1955 to study the site had reported that the plan could, in fact, work. "An appropriate and suitable location could be found within this area for a stadium to accommodate 50,000 persons," Gilmore Clarke, one of the city's most prominent landscape architects, wrote to

John Cashmore. Clarke's was the voice of authority; his firm had worked on many of Robert Moses' projects. Three days after Cashmore received Clarke's report, he and Wagner made their announcement, boosting O'Malley's plan as an enterprise worthy of consideration, and of supporting legislation, too. Wagner called upon the city's representatives in Albany to carry his plan to the legislature, where they might get the approval necessary for creating a three-member authority to oversee the project.

O'Malley was "elated." He also presented himself as the spirit of civic cooperation. He announced that he was prepared to buy land, or bonds, to build and operate the stadium, or even serve as its tenant, which was something he had long insisted he did not want to do. Then he paused, briefly, to salute what was for all appearances a soon-to-vanish past: "It's sad to kiss Ebbets Field good-bye."

But now there was much to be done—relocating the Long Island Railroad tracks that ran under the site, moving the meat market to Canarsie, rerouting traffic, surveying the land, assessing costs. Clarke's encouraging report was only a first step. The mayor would still have to find three men to serve as the authority's members. Robert Moses would insist upon being consulted on the choices, and on their agenda and on the progress of engineering and financial studies. But on the morning of April 19, Moses' involvement appeared almost peripheral. His name, in fact, hardly came up at all. It was as if the governor, legislature, the mayor, the borough president, and Walter O'Malley had somehow found a way to proceed without him.

IN JANUARY 1956, Jack Flynn, publisher of the *Daily News*, invited Moses to join him, Cashmore, and O'Malley for lunch at his offices to talk about the progress of the stadium project. The invitation did not please Moses, for now he had other plans for the meat market site, and a ballpark was not one of them.

Flynn's invitation coincided with yet another dutifully recorded announcement by Moses of yet more mammoth housing projects, five in all, spread around the city. But one stood out, a middle-income cooperative that he envisioned rising on the corner of Flatbush and Atlantic Avenues—the same place Walter O'Malley had in mind for his ballpark. This was a fact not easily ignored: just the day before, John Cashmore had announced that Gilmore Clarke's firm had completed its work and that he was going to the Board of Estimate to ask for another $80,000 to pay for the firm's report.

It was virtually impossible to imagine a functionary like John Cashmore performing an end-run around Robert Moses. But that is how things appeared in Moses' office on the morning of January 12. For there, in the *Times*, was a prominent story giving credence to Cashmore's support for the ballpark, and to an engineering study about which Moses had somehow been kept in the dark. Now Jack Flynn wanted him to come to a lunch where he'd be forced to answer questions for which he did not necessarily have the answers. He dispatched his aides to learn what they could of the progress of Clarke's study, and sent a note to Cashmore, asking for an update. There was, however, a bigger problem.

On the front page of the same paper was a story whose implications, if sorted out, could be even more troubling: Moses' plan for the Upper West Side of Manhattan, a great arts center and housing development to be called Lincoln Square, was ballooning in size and in cost. What he had presented initially nine months before as a thirty-two-acre, $75 million project had somehow grown to include fifty acres at a projected cost of $160 million. Not that anyone was suggesting this was a bad idea: the center's plan called for leveling the tenements in the area, and in their place building apartment buildings, a new campus for Fordham University, a hotel, a shopping mall, and, most gloriously and conspicuously, new homes for the Metropolitan Opera Company and the New York Philharmonic Orchestra. These were nonprofit organizations, not organizations whose primary purpose was to enrich Walter O'Malley.

Moses had insisted that he could not use the power and money that the federal government gave him to acquire land for a private purpose. But he knew this was not true. He knew it because he had initially considered allowing O'Malley to build his stadium on the site of his Pratt Institute project in downtown Brooklyn. He knew it because he had offered to condemn land in Bedford-Stuyvesant for a ballpark. His rejection of O'Malley's plan then was not based on principle. And even if the condemned land in Lincoln Square was designated for nonprofit organizations, the distinction was a legal one, and legal distinctions generally matter only to lawyers. Moses recognized that he had to find a way to make it appear as if his rejection of O'Malley's stadium was something other than personal.

So on the morning of January 12, he sent a note to his deputy, George Spargo, detailing what information he would need to avoid being embarrassed, or exposed, at the *Daily News* luncheon. "I don't propose to be put in a position by the Daily News or John Cashmore of refusing to discuss a matter of this kind," he wrote. Then, he went on, "I think we can agree in advance on what the outcome will be so far as the Dodgers are concerned, but it is necessary to show that our opposition is based on something other than prejudice. This is particularly true in view of the larger neighborhood improvements proposed in other boroughs, such as the Lincoln Square."

He concluded, "I am not going to be labeled as an obstructionist without evidence to support conclusions."

He need not have worried. No one was going to label Robert Moses an obstructionist, because no one knew, or had bothered to learn, or had begun to see that that was just what he was.

WALTER O'MALLEY'S cultivation of the press, inviting Jimmy Powers out to the house in Amityville, letting the beat fellows believe they were beating him at poker, was like puppy love courting compared to Robert Moses' seduction of almost every important editor and publisher in town.

O'Malley might have been the object of amusement and admiration; it was generally conceded that he was a clever man. But Moses' standing in print bordered on hagiography. He was not only the man who "got things done." He was the selfless public servant, the visionary shaping New York, a man to be admired, feared, and, most of all, held in awe. He was not a politician, after all. He was something more, and presumably better: all around him was evidence of his good and munificent deeds—the highways, the housing, the bridges, the hospitals and libraries, all of it. And if Moses was at times a bit rough around the edges, that was okay: it showed just how real so Olympian a figure could be. The adulation spanned the political and intellectual spectrum.

"That obstinate, truculent, and . . . engaging man was at the undisputed top of his form and as well worth taking the measure of as any great force of nature we know," gushed *The New Yorker* in 1956.

Or, "At 67 he is too busy, too dedicated, and too actively engaged in looking boldly into the future to think of quitting," echoed the *World-Telegram and Sun* in April of that year. The hosannas from the *Telegram* were particularly striking because this had been the only daily paper in New York ever to go after Moses, raising serious questions about the way he had gone about condemning and selling the Manhattanville Title I project in 1954. The reports, however, had never touched Moses directly, only those to whom he had sold the land. He remained, in the most profound way, above it all.

No paper was more solicitous than the august *Times*, which twice a year turned over pages of its Sunday Magazine so that Moses could weigh in on the future of the city. These great heaves were solicited by the *Times'* Sunday editor, Lester Markel, whose letters dripped with praise and gratitude for such Moses tomes as "New Highways for a Better New York." Moses' submissions came with notes asking that the pieces run without cuts, an impossible request to honor considering that Moses wrote like a man who believed that there was no better way for readers to spend their Sunday mornings than to curl up with yet another missive on grade crossing elimination on the Cross Bronx Expressway: "The cartoonist's idea of a complicated modern traffic interchange is, of course, caricature, but caricature has its serious lessons for those who realize how much common sense lurks in the exaggerations of slapstick American fun."

Those who crossed or angered Moses in print felt his wrath, quickly. So it was that on the morning of January 13, as stories were breaking all around him about Lincoln Square and Flatbush Avenue and the Dodgers, he hurried to halt the spread of news not to his liking. He turned on the city editor of the *Herald-Tribune,* another friendly paper. He excoriated him for having the temerity to run a piece that pointed out that the site he envisioned for a new housing project in Brooklyn was in the middle of the same tract that city engineers were studying as the site of a new home for the Dodgers. "Your story . . . seems to be one of those seemingly irresistible impulses of the press to stir up official dissension," he began. Never mind that—in principle at least, that is what newspapers are supposed to do. Moses went on to rehash his now-familiar objections to using the land for a ballpark, and closed with a sharp slap to the wrist: "Why stir up the animals? Something constructive will no doubt be worked out with or without the Dodgers."

He had shown a draft of the letter to George Spargo, who replied that it seemed just fine if the intent was "to soften the controversy." But even Spargo, the loyal deputy, felt compelled to point out that the boss's

argument that the land could not be used for any purpose other than housing was flawed. "As you know, part of the area could be used for other than
residential purposes," Spargo wrote. Moses ignored him. The letter served
its purpose. The story died.

But Moses was not done using the press to finish his business with
Walter O'Malley. He did this work methodically, so that he could maintain
the illusion that, civil servant that he was, he would carry out the wishes of
the city and state and assist in guiding the stadium project along. Having
quickly gathered the intelligence he needed on the status of Clarke's report,
he went to meetings to talk about the stadium project. He offered to be of
help. He wrote to Frank Schroth, former publisher of the *Eagle* who now
ran the Brooklyn edition of the *Daily News*, offering names of potential
members for the sports authority board as well as agenda items for its first
meeting. When a group of Brooklyn business leaders formed the Committee for a Sports Stadium, he accepted their invitation to attend a luncheon
to find ways to keep pressure on reluctant state legislators weighing the
sports authority bill. He even called Frank Schroth and suggested that the
proceedings be recorded and broadcast by the city's radio station, WNYC,
that the *News* publicize the broadcast, and that the tape be played on an Albany radio station, too. And while he was at it, Moses suggested, it might be
a good idea to "play down Walter." He suggested that the station "omit the
big O'Malley build up and the embroidery of wolfhounds, shamrocks and
harps when he speaks." Schroth replied that he had arranged to have the
broadcast aired in New York and in Albany, and offered no defense of Walter O'Malley.

5 | AN EVENING WITH THE BARBER

Life seemed to be getting only worse for Irving Rudd. The Dodgers' return
to Jersey City was, if possible, even worse than their first visit. The night
was cold. Only ten thousand people showed up. They came to boo the
Dodgers, or so it seemed. No one was sure why the fans had turned on the
Dodgers, but there was no question that after a mere two games they had.
They cheered for the Indians. So relentless was the jeering that the fans

even turned on men who were not in the field. They were especially hard on Jackie Robinson, who had been so caustic about their town. Alston had decided to rest him, but the Jersey City fans still heckled him when he came out of the dugout to warm up a pitcher. Robinson doffed his cap and smiled.

Alston sat Snider and Reese, too, and saved his better pitchers for games that counted. He started the little-used Chuck Templeton, who pitched well enough to win—had the Dodgers managed more than two hits. Bob Feller started for Cleveland. Feller had once been a legend in Cleveland, the farm boy with the unhittable fastball. But he was aging, and other pitchers had moved ahead of him in the Indian rotation. Now he and Sal Maglie were competing to be the fifth and final starter. Maglie, who had made his name in the National League, recognized the perils of competing with a local legend. He did not stand a chance.

The Giants, for whom he had starred for years, had waived him in 1955, a move calculated to unload his thirty-three-thousand-dollar annual salary and give the younger men a chance. The Dodgers were delighted when they heard he had switched leagues: no pitcher gave them more trouble, beat them more consistently, and so often left them dusting off the seats of their pants after yet another pitch too close to the face. Sal Maglie looked like a mortician. He was tall, gaunt, and always in need of a shave. His eyes were dark and mournful. But he possessed an assortment of curves that kept batters forever off-stride. Robinson hated him, as did Furillo, for his penchant for claiming the inside part of their plate at their expense. The others merely feared him.

But now Sal Maglie was a castoff whom Cleveland had signed only as a way to keep the rival Yankees from grabbing him. The Indians had little use for him, not with their strong pitching staff. So Maglie pitched intermittently and waited to see if he might catch a break.

That night in Jersey City he entered the game in the seventh. Feller had been perfect for three innings and the Dodgers had managed only two hits off his replacement, Buddy Daley. Maglie first struck out Gino Cimoli and then got Charley Neal to bounce out weakly. He pitched through the eighth and ninth, and, in the tenth, with the Indians up by a run, he set down the Dodgers in order. Later in the clubhouse, Roy Campanella wondered aloud why anyone thought The Barber was finished. The curve was the same, just as sharp, just as elusive. His teammates agreed: Maglie was as he'd always been, a master of gamesmanship, a hitter's nightmare.

Maglie's performance and the impression he made was not lost on Buzzie Bavasi, who always thought that playing in Jersey City was a bad idea, but with one bright spot: Sal Maglie might still have something left. And he would come cheap.

PART FOUR

MAY

The West, as the National League defined it, began in Cincinnati, extended to Chicago and Milwaukee, and ended at St. Louis, gateway to Kansas City, an American League town. From there it was nothing but bush leagues all the way to the Pacific. On the first of May the Brooklyn Dodgers arrived in Cincinnati, checking into the Netherland Plaza. After an eighteen-hour train trip, a cold night in Jersey City, and with the memory of last week's five-game winning streak a fading memory, they had little to be thankful for other than the fact that it was a Tuesday and not a Sunday. Cincinnati was a dry town on Sundays and if you wanted a drink after the game you had to start calling everyone's hotel room to see who'd been smart enough to bring a bottle.

The Cincinnati Reds were far better than the Pirates, and the Pirates had just shellacked the Dodgers. The Reds had a brawny lineup: Gus Bell, an outfielder who hit for power and average; the young left fielder Frank Robinson; and brawny Ted Kluszewski. Their pitching was suspect, but they could hit and they were winning—four in a row when the Dodgers arrived at Crosley Field. Carl Erskine started and by the end of the first inning was down by one, on a home run over the center field wall by Frank Robinson. The Reds scored twice more and the Dodgers could barely touch Johnny Klippstein, a pitcher of modest talent who seemed always to be at his best against them; he'd beaten them four times out of five in 1955. The losing streak now stood at three.

They returned the next night and this time brought their bats, scoring six times. This did them little good. Cincinnati scored ten runs, feasting on Roger Craig and a succession of relievers. They were back on the train that night, heading to St. Louis, their losing streak at four.

The Cardinals were somehow in first place, although no one believed this would last: Stan Musial was a marvelous hitter, Ken Boyer was among the league's best third basemen, and Red Schoendienst was a star at second. But the quality of the team dipped sharply after them. It was a warm night, and when Pee Wee Reese came to bat in the top of the first he looked out to the mound and saw the antidote to all that ailed his teammates: Ben Flowers. It was not to be Flowers' night; this was apparent immediately. Reese doubled. Snider walked. Campanella singled and after Hodges flied out, Robinson tripled everyone home. Flowers took an early and barely necessary shower. Furillo doubled Robinson home and the Dodgers had all they would need. Don Newcombe, who had won twice since his Opening Day loss to Robin Roberts, was solid through eight and when he faded, Clem Labine came on to finish.

But the rebound lasted only a day. Chuck Templeton, who had looked so sharp against the Indians in Jersey City, might have escaped the sixth down only by a run against the Cardinals had Reese himself not botched a double play by throwing wide to Charley Neal at second. The Cardinals went on to score seven runs and took the game 10 to 3. It got no better the next night: Ken Boyer hit a grand slam homer off Roger Craig in the first inning and that was all the Cardinals needed. The losing had taken on a disturbing pattern in that there was no consistency at all: a well-pitched game with no hitting followed by a poorly pitched game with terrific hitting followed by a close game with sloppy fielding and ending with a poorly pitched game with barely any hitting. Their record stood at 8 and 8, dropping them to fifth place. Luckily, no team had caught fire the way the Dodgers had in 1955. Now they were on to Milwaukee, where the first-place Braves and their noisy fans waited.

MILWAUKEE WAS WALTER O'Malley's kind of baseball town. The Braves, who'd played and lost games, fans, and money in Boston, had found salvation in Milwaukee: a stadium built "on a come"—as in, let's build it and see if we can get someone to play in it; fans so dedicated to the game that for years they had filled old Borchert Field to see the minor league Milwaukee Brewers. Milwaukee had been O'Malley's inspiration: if Lou Perini, the Braves' owner, could squeeze two million fans into Milwaukee's new County Stadium, imagine what he could do with a new park in Brooklyn. The Braves also had a very good team. Their lineup was a powerful one—Henry Aaron, Eddie Mathews, Joe Adcock, Bill Bruton, Del Crandell, and Johnny Logan—and their starting pitching was formidable: Lew Burdette, Bob Buhl, and the great Warren Spahn.

The last time the Dodgers played in County Stadium was the day they clinched the 1955 National League pennant. They had knocked Milwau-kee's pitching rudely that afternoon, a fitting triumph for a pennant won so handily. But now good fortune came only when the weather turned foul: the heavens gave the Dodgers the gift of a rainout, and a night at the Schroeder Hotel to catch their collective breath.

They could have used a monsoon. The next afternoon was sunny but chilly and seventeen thousand people came to hoot and jeer as Bob Buhl, a perennial nemesis, shut them down on six hits. Erskine took the loss, his second in a row. His undoing began in the fourth with a walk to, of all peo-ple, Bobby Thomson, who had broken Brooklyn's heart in 1951 with his pennant-winning home run against Ralph Branca and who had found a life after the Giants in Milwaukee. Thomson went on to score on a day that felt too full of omens: Carl Furillo's five-thousandth career at-bat in the first ended with a strikeout. The Dodgers fell 3 to 1 and were now a game under .500. That night they arrived at the Conrad Hilton in Chicago to discover that the reservations made in February would not be honored. Words were exchanged, so heatedly that the staff suggested the players could sleep un-der the stars in Grant Park. They did offer to set up cots in a private dining room that had no lock on the door and only one bathroom.

They barely drew a quorum the following afternoon: a mere fifty-six hundred people came to Wrigley Field to see them play. Newcombe drew the start, which was good news; he was the only starter who'd been win-ning. That afternoon he dispatched the Cubs with such ease that he threw only seventy-eight pitches through the first eight innings—he and Cam-panella might as well have been playing a brisk game of catch, so economi-cal was his work. Newcombe, tall and broad, used intimidation as a tool. He threw fastballs mostly, mixing in a curve and a change-up, and the Cubs, the only club in the league playing worse than the Dodgers, managed six hits that produced no runs. Newcombe was an inspiration to his team-mates, or so it appeared: when he pitched they hit. They knocked out the Cubs' starter Warren (Happy) Hacker in the third, scored six runs, and evened their record at 9 and 9. It rained the next day, which was just as well. It was time to go home.

They'd slept on trains for thirteen of the thirty nights since breaking camp in Vero Beach. They rode into the night, across northern Indiana and Ohio and through Pennsylvania, which felt as if it went on forever. Some slept, but others could not; even sleeping pills did not help Duke Snider get a decent night's sleep on a Pullman foldout. Snider had once loved to travel by train. But that was when he was young and everything about the baseball life seemed fresh and exciting. Now the train travel was an irritant, like exhibition games and wise-acre writers and batting slumps and teammates who got on him for moping when he was not hitting. And then there were the fans who booed him and managers like Charlie Dressen, who had been such a small-minded martinet. Snider had once loved being a baseball player but now he sometimes stood in center field and wished he were someplace else. If his teammates had similar thoughts they kept those ideas to themselves. But not Snider. He told these things to Roger Kahn, who served as his coauthor for a story in the coming issue of *Collier's* magazine: "I Play Baseball for Money—Not Fun."

2 | ROOMIES

"The truth," wrote Snider and Kahn, "is that life in the major leagues is far from a picnic. There are youngsters who throw skate keys and marbles at my head. . . . There are older fans at other parks who bounce beer cans off my legs during dull moments in the game. There are sports writers who know just as much baseball as my four-year-old daughter." He had grown up dreaming of being a ballplayer. But now, he continued, "You're in the major leagues, and all of a sudden baseball isn't so great—and sometimes it can be a nightmare." He admitted that even during the championship World Series he was dreaming "about being a farmer."

He hated the travel. He missed his wife and children. Sleepless nights on trains only made the playing harder. He was forced to eat at odd hours; luckily he had a stomach that could handle dinner after a night game. Writers twisted his words and made him sound foolish. Charlie Dressen once berated the team for overspending on meal allowances when someone ordered a second helping of cauliflower. Snider, through Kahn, likened him to Captain Queeg in *The Caine Mutiny*.

And so it went, three full pages of lament and accusation, told in an aggrieved and plaintive voice. "Often I try to put my finger on the one thing that turned my boyhood dream around, or the one thing that happened. But

I can't. There are a lot of things, a lot of times." And though he would later insist that he was "explaining not complaining"—and had said as much in the second sentence of the fourth paragraph—he had once again succeeded in making himself the object of derision and scorn. He tried to leaven the tone: yes, he knew he made fifty thousand a year in salary and endorsements, and yes he had made some wonderful friends. But this brought him no reprieve.

The writers went to Charlie Dressen for comment. Dressen, who was now managing the Washington Senators, insisted, first off, that the offending vegetable was not cauliflower but *broccoli* and that the Duke was so childish that the joke around the clubhouse was, "Who stole Snider's candy?" In the *Herald-Tribune*, Red Smith wrote that while "sarcasm and ridicule" were not the "proper answer" to Snider's words, "chances are he hasn't more than the foggiest notion of how the other 99.99 per cent lives. Somebody should tell him, gently." So Smith did, somewhat gently, noting that traveling salesmen, too, are often on the road, but seldom sleep in Pullmans or hotels as comfortable as did the ballplayers.

Even his teammates got on him, anonymously— a particularly sensitive point with Snider who believed that if you were going to talk to a reporter you should let him use your name. Instead, they mocked him.

"When I was a kid I dreamed of being a bus driver," said one. "I guess that wouldn't seem so hot to me right now, either."

"I wanted to be a cop," said another. "They sometimes get more than marbles thrown at them, don't they. And how much does a cop make? Less than $50,000 I think."

The Dodgers and the writers were by this point well accustomed to Snider's carelessness with his words. The year before the Duke had famously ripped the Brooklyn fans, calling them "the worst in the league." He had done this in a clubhouse full of reporters, and when Reese interrupted to say, "He doesn't mean that," Snider, in a lather, cut him off. "The hell I don't." His wife, Bev, insisted upon coming to the ballpark with him the next night but he begged her to stay home. "They're liable to tar and feather me," he told her. Bev went, the fans booed, and by the end of the game were cheering him again; he had gotten a few hits. He issued an apology, the Dodgers won the World Series, and he was forgiven. Now he had done it again.

He tried to explain. He had shown advance copies of the piece to Reese and Carl Erskine, who voiced no objections. Neither, remarkably, did Walter O'Malley and Buzzie Bavasi. He was trying to show people what the player's life was like. "Naturally, I have no complaint with baseball, which has been real good to me."

IF DUKE SNIDER were a foolish man, or a simple one, his lapses in judgment might have been dismissed with a nod and a shrug and maybe a knowing smile. But Snider was no dummy. Nor was he angry, not like Jackie and not like Newk. Instead, he was cursed: at an early age he was robbed of the gift of perspective.

He had grown up near Los Angeles as that most envied and exalted of young men: the best ballplayer around. He was the only child of parents who had little money. His father worked at the Goodyear Tire Company and night after night came home with burned and blistered hands. His given name was Edwin; his father nicknamed him Duke. He played basketball, football, and baseball and by the time he was fourteen years old he was good enough to play baseball with grown men. It did not take long before he had eclipsed them, too. He was a star in grade school, at Enterprise Junior High, and at Compton High School, where he earned sixteen letters in four different sports. He had friends and girls liked him. Though he was still too shy in eleventh grade to ask out the pretty and delicate girl who would become his wife—he delegated a friend to ask Bev for him—he was still aware of the wonderful things his gifts bestowed upon him. It made the world easy. Unlike the late-bloomer Pee Wee Reese, he played the game without doubt or fear or sense of failure. "It was fun," he would later say. "I didn't know what adversity was in baseball when I was a youngster. I always got a hit."

He began playing professionally when he was seventeen, for the Dodger minor league affiliate in Newport News. He played only one full season in the minors. He spent a couple of years in the navy, bounced between Brooklyn and the minors in 1947 and 1948, and finally stuck with the big club in 1949. He was no longer getting hits every time up. That is not to say he was hitting poorly, just that things were not nearly as simple as they'd once been. This confounded him.

Branch Rickey had selected him to be one of the young men around whom he would build his great postwar club. But this merely allowed Snider, Hodges, Erskine, Furillo, and the others to be young and nervous together. Rickey had eight hundred players under contract and, Erskine would later say, "There were always rumors, always rumors of trades and releases." Snider could not understand how he could fail, which in Duke's view of the world meant not succeeding every time. He wanted to be better and tried to learn by watching Robinson, whom he had seen play football at Pasadena City College years before, and whose fire and need to win left him in awe. He watched Reese, too, just as they all did, and when Reese complimented him he felt immensely proud. The doubts and fear, however, did not abate. He needed a friend to talk with; he found one in a pitcher, Carl Erskine. That they never argued, not once in all their years together on the road, was testimony to Erskine's great equanimity.

WHEN THE BASEBALL purists speak of the game, of its lore and meaning and significance in enhancing the American Way of Life, they call to mind people like Carl Erskine, one of the most agreeable people ever to play baseball for a living. Erskine did not swear or drink or flash his spikes at a second baseman. He possessed good but not Olympian talent that he used to its fullest and which, in return, made him grateful for being able to play the game. He was a religious man but never sanctimonious, never the clubhouse holy-roller. He was bright and friendly and he could pitch—a quick overhand delivery that hurt him almost every time he threw. In the first start of his rookie season of 1948, he was pitching in the rain against the Cubs when, on a third strike, Erskine felt a sharp pain in his shoulder. The injury was diagnosed as a pulled muscle, the "cure" for which was generally keeping quiet and not losing a turn on the mound. Besides, his manager at the time, Burt Shotton, told him he was pitching well, so why sit. The injury never healed. Instead, a knot the size of a golf ball developed in his pitching shoulder, a marker so familiar to Dodger trainers that many years after he retired one of them approached Erskine, placed a hand on his shoulder, pressed in, and said, "Right there?"

Erskine did have some fine seasons. His best was 1953 when he won twenty games for the only time and struck out fourteen Yankees in a World Series game. He had pitched a no-hitter in 1952, against the Cubs at Ebbets Field. Still, he spent his career trying to find a way to pitch with a tolerable degree of pain. He did not complain, or ask to skip a turn in the rotation. He was smaller than most of the other pitchers, who marveled at how much he squeezed out of so slender a frame.

Erskine was the sort of man who would wait in line on a road trip to Cincinnati to get Fess Parker's autograph because his sons were big fans of *Davy Crockett*. He had grown up in Anderson, Indiana—the classic small-town beginnings. His father had played semipro ball, taught him to throw a curve, and on special occasions driven the family to Cincinnati to see the Reds play. They would go on Sundays, leaving so early that they'd be the first ones outside the iron gate at Crosley Field. They watched the players arrive in taxis and in their big cars. The players wore jackets and ties, which even at the age of ten struck Carl Erskine as particularly "sharp." Years later he would recall those games with wonder and excitement. It was the same way he spoke about seeing his wife and children when he pitched at Ebbets Field: "I'd see them come in, and come down the aisle behind home plate. I'd stand on the mound, look toward the batter and I was looking at Betty dressed real neat and my two little kids. She'd have them all spiffed up and I'd say, Look at me. Man, if heaven's better than this I can't believe it."

Erskine and Snider were, on the surface at least, very much alike: young men who had grown up poor, who found their place in playing ball, who married their high school sweethearts, and who were trying hard to be stoics in the face of their shared terror. They had both raced through the minors, made the big club, struggled, and been sent down. They excelled in the minors, came back, and stuck with the Dodgers. But in the first years back they remained all too mindful of how quickly the team replaced men who did not perform. Erskine was never sure how it was that he was paired with Snider, but suspected that it was Duke who asked to bunk with him.

They began rooming together in the years before they sensed their positions were, at last, secure. They talked a lot, mostly about baseball, and sometimes in the context of their shortcomings. Later they became neighbors in Bay Ridge, and better still, their wives became friends. They played bridge with the Reeses and the Walkers. They played golf and fished together on off-days. And on the road, where time could pass at a glacial pace, they talked. They talked in the clubhouse, where Reese would hold his postmortems after the games. They talked with their teammates over dinner and over beers, even as Erskine abstained. They talked late into the night, lights off, lying in their hotel room beds. Snider bemoaned his struggle to hit high fastballs. The ball would leave the pitcher's hand and be on him before he could draw a bead. This only heightened his fear; things were happening to him that were not *supposed* to happen to him. Snider doubted himself and shared his doubts with Erskine, who sensed in his roommate "a kind of inferiority complex." So Erskine listened and told Snider about his worries, too, about the poor pitches he threw that day, and about the mistakes. The two men grew so close that Erskine, who had several siblings, came to feel toward Snider like a brother. For his part, Snider told him that he hoped that when their careers ended and they returned to the places they had come from, they could still be just as close and be able to talk with each other as they did on the road.

IN TIME, THE fears of banishment to Fort Worth or Montreal abated. But for Snider, there was no end to the remorseless self-criticism and the despondence that his other teammates dismissed as childish pouting that kept him from being an even better ballplayer than he was. They got on him: Reese would feel compelled to remind him to charge every ground ball that made its way to center field—"Those guys aren't even slowing down at second, they're going on to third." Robinson would scold him for not running hard into second—"Give it a full ninety feet." They did not much care *why* he brooded, only that he did and that they had no use for it. He knew this and yet he could not help himself. "I was my own worst enemy really," he would later say. "There were times when I expected more out of myself than I got. I would get a pitch right down the middle and hit a hard shot to the second baseman. And I'd say to myself, You should have hit that ball against the right field fence. I took it out on myself and it sometimes affected my play. Some call it sulking. You can call it what you want. But I would get down on myself. I felt every time I went up there I should get a base hit. And it upset me when I didn't."

He wondered how his teammates thought about these things, how they accepted their limitations. They all seemed so contained. Then one day he watched Gil Hodges try to light a cigarette in the dugout. Hodges, in particular, revealed nothing. But Snider watched as Hodges' hands shook so badly he could not get the flame and cigarette to meet. Finally, someone grabbed Hodges' hand and lit the cigarette for him.

There was no such internal war for Snider, only the consequences of letting the world know what he was thinking. The *Collier's* piece was honest and true: that was how Duke saw the world. Almost. Because he neglected to write about driving to the ballpark, which was one of the best times of the day to be a ballplayer. He and his neighbors Erskine, Reese, and Walker took turns driving to Ebbets Field.

Each day began with no sense of the past, of yesterday's game. Whatever Snider did the day before, no matter how badly he thought he failed, the new day brought a new game, a game without a score, a game that existed in a vacuum—that is if he could succeed in putting his frustrations aside. At night he would lie in bed, close his eyes, and envision facing the next day's pitcher. He would recall the way the man had pitched him before and see himself at bat, waiting. And in the morning he would be ready to play again. "There's no such thing as yesterday," he would say of the baseball player's sense of time. "No such thing as tomorrow." In a life too cluttered with uncertainty—would he hit today, or not?—he could still be sure of this: that no matter how he might be playing, no matter how he might have sulked, no matter what he might have been unwise enough to say, he knew that when the Dodgers took the field he would stand in center field—and that he would seldom be better than he was on the days when Carl Erskine was pitching.

SNIDER HAD STARTED the season dismally, but began hitting during the otherwise disastrous trip through the west. Carl Erskine, meanwhile, struggled. His arm hurt so badly he wanted to go to Doc Wendler, the team physician, but was embarrassed because he felt he had gone to him too many times before. So in Chicago he called the Cubs' trainer, Al Scheunemann. Scheunemann, a generous man who'd once worked for the Dodger organization, came to Erskine's hotel room, examined his right arm, and told him he would give him an injection of procaine and cortisone. Erskine had never had such a shot before, and Scheunemann warned him it would hurt. Only Duke Snider knew what he had done.

That night Reese, Snider, and Don Zimmer went bowling and invited Erskine along. He tried to beg off but they told him, "C'mon, that broken arm can't hurt you." So he went and bowled, and this only made his arm hurt more.

The Dodgers returned to Brooklyn to face the Giants at Ebbets Field. Roger Craig won the first game and Erskine was scheduled to pitch the next day. His arm was so sore that he considered asking Walter Alston to give him an extra day of rest. He went to the bullpen to loosen up and was feeling so low he worried that he might not even make it through his warm-ups. So he said a prayer: "God, you must have some reason for me being here so I'll just do my best and accept the results, whatever they are."

He surprised himself when he made it through the first inning, surrendering only a base on balls to Willie Mays. He pitched without incident through the second and third but in the fourth, he walked Alvin Dark. Mays came to bat and smacked a liner to third that Jackie Robinson speared. Robinson fell to his knees but managed to hold onto the ball. Daryl Spencer followed with a drive to right that appeared destined for extra bases. But Carl Furillo chased it down for the third out. Erskine pitched on through the fifth, sixth, and seventh. The Dodgers, meanwhile, reached Al Worthington, the young Giant pitcher, for a run in the third and two more in the seventh. Duke Snider drove in two of those runs and scored the third.

In the eighth, Don Mueller pounced on a pitch over the outside part of the plate and smashed it to left—but right at Reese. Erskine retired the Giants in order and as he walked off the mound a fan screamed out what he already knew: "The Giants don't have a hit." It was a warm day and as Erskine crossed the foul line he felt a cool breeze that he took to be a gentle sign from God. In the dugout, however, he discovered that he'd ripped the webbing of his glove. Don Bessent used the same model, and while the glove did not feel quite the same, Erskine was wearing it when he walked out to the mound in the ninth.

His wife, Betty, was home, listening to the game on the radio. She had begun her ironing when the game began, and had continued through the middle innings. Now, three outs from a no-hitter, she ironed on and listened.

With one out, Whitey Lockman led off with a drive deep to right field. The ball hugged the line and was heading to the seats. Then, at the last moment of its descent, it veered right and slipped into the seats just past the foul pole. A long strike, but Lockman was not done. He hit the next pitch right back at Erskine. The ball was hit hard and low and when Erskine looked down at his mitt he could not see it. But he felt it. He raised the borrowed glove and saw that he had trapped the ball beneath it. He threw it to Hodges for the second out.

Now Alvin Dark, who with Mays had been one of only two Giants to reach base, came to bat. Dark fouled off the first pitch and the second. Erskine threw a curve for his ninety-ninth pitch of the game and Dark bounced it back to him. Erskine looked to first. Hodges seemed to be taking forever to get to the bag. Finally, Hodges held up his big mitt and said, "Throw it right here." Which Erskine did, for the final out of his second no-hitter.

Children vaulted the fence and were already pounding Erskine's back when the first of his teammates, Robinson and Campanella made it to the mound. In the clubhouse Walter O'Malley presented Erskine with a five-hundred-dollar check. Someone found a tepid bottle of champagne but Erskine begged off, and instead drank orange soda. Reporters surrounded him, of course, and Erskine was the soul of self-deprecation. No, he did not think he had terrific stuff. He didn't think he had particularly good stuff against the Cubs in 1952, when he pitched his first no-hitter. His fastball was decent and he did throw a lot of change-ups.

He went on to praise his teammates, especially Campanella, who had kept him calm and even in his pitching. In his moment of vindication, after pitching so poorly in the second half of the 1955 season, after botching his only start in the championship World Series, after struggling through the spring, he could not stop smiling.

There were almost twenty-five-thousand people at Ebbets Field that day, a good crowd for a Saturday afternoon. But as it happened, Erskine had attracted a far larger audience. CBS had made it its Game of the Week, which meant not only that millions could see what Carl Erskine had done, but that Walter O'Malley could afford to be generous with his five hundred dollars: TV money would cover the bonus, and pay for a good deal more.

3 | SKIATRON

Like his nemesis Robert Moses, Walter O'Malley was an energetic man, capable of performing several tasks at once. For O'Malley this meant being able to pursue money in several directions simultaneously. Having made up his mind to seek his fortune in the baseball business, a clever man like O'Malley recognized the need to broaden his revenue streams. He could rely on attendance, but only up to a point: for that, he had long ago decided, he needed a new ballpark. There was money in concessions, but at Ebbets Field none in parking. O'Malley, however, was not a nickel-and-dime fellow; when he thought money he thought big. Lately he'd been thinking of television. Television was big and, he believed, could get a lot bigger, in the right hands.

Television had been good to O'Malley. It earned him $600,000 a year in the rights he sold to televise and broadcast over a hundred Dodger games. This represented almost half his profits. He sold these rights, as was the practice at the time, to his sponsors, Schaefer Beer and Lucky Strike cigarettes, which were represented by BBD&O, an advertising company. He was making more money from television than his rivals, the Yankees and the Giants. Yet while the earnings from the broadcast rights were good, the current arrangement was not going to yield much more money. O'Malley wanted more.

In 1956 television was ten years old. Its growth had been meteoric. Since 1946 the number of sets across the country had ballooned from 6,400 to 40 million. The number of outlets had grown from six to 456, and the miles of television cable from 476 to 70,000. Televised sports had boomed as well. In 1946, Larry MacPhail, who by then was running the Yankees, sold the team's local broadcast rights to the DuMont Network for $75,000. A year later Gillette, the razor blade maker, paid $30,000 to cosponsor the World Series with Ford. Three million people watched the Yankees beat the Dodgers. In 1950, "Happy" Chandler, the baseball commissioner, sold the broadcast rights to the 1951 through 1956 World Series for $6 million. Those games drew an audience of 50 million viewers who in 1952, 1953, and 1955 saw the Dodgers—and the Yankees—play for the world championship. In its early years television was limited primarily to New York. But now the medium was bringing the team a national audience. Its games were broadcast from New England to Pennsylvania, which gave the Dodgers a regional following, too.

The coming of television, however, created a problem for owners like O'Malley. Watching a broadcast had once been a communal event with a limited audience; the early sets were found mostly in bars. But now the watching had moved from the tavern to the living room. How was O'Malley supposed to get people to the ballpark if they could watch the game at home for free? The answer, of course, was to make them pay. For this O'Malley needed people wise and sufficiently farsighted who understood both the workings of television and the money it might produce. As it happened, he found both these qualities in a single man, Matty Fox.

Matty Fox was one of those men who confounded other men: he was short and fat—he once said he "couldn't pass a delicatessen window without putting on weight"—but who had nonetheless married a beauty queen, Yolanda Betbeze, Miss America 1951. Matty Fox was a salesman, and this lent him a certain charm. It had worked with his wife and with Walter O'Malley, too. O'Malley believed that Matty Fox could make him a very wealthy man.

Fox's story sounded very much like that of the young Walter O'Malley, who dreamed of making a killing drilling for gold in Alaska, and who as a fledgling engineer bid to build an embassy in Lima, Peru. If anything Matty Fox thought even more audaciously about making his fortune. In 1949, when he was just twenty-six years old, he somehow managed to win the ear of the Indonesian finance minister and convinced him to grant Fox a monopoly on all Indonesian imports and exports to the United States. The scheme earned him the nickname "The Economic Godfather of Indonesia." The State Department, however, frowned on Fox's arrangement and soon the plan fizzled. But Fox was undeterred; he was, after all, a man who went into the army a private and three years later came out a major without ever having shipped out.

Fox was a man of many ideas: he had developed the pipe that children could use to blow soap bubbles; he cornered the market on 3-D movie glasses. But he was, first and foremost, a movie man. He had started humbly: a nine-year-old movie house usher in his hometown of Racine, Wisconsin. By the time he was twenty-five he had managed to become vice president of Universal Pictures and was being hailed as a "boy wonder." It had not hurt that his sister had married Universal's president.

Fox was not the first man to think that money could be made by charging people to watch television. The idea had been talked about for years in Hollywood, among producers and executives who could never quite reconcile themselves to the fact that once they sold movie rights to a television network they were dooming their creation to an eternity of being watched by millions of people for free. The Federal Communications Commission had not yet approved pay-per-view television. And the technology was still being refined—how to scramble the picture, how to run the cable, how to install all the boxes on the subscribers' sets? By the late 1940s the FCC was already fielding requests to approve such plans as Phonevision, which Zenith had developed as a way to send television signals over telephone lines. The plan was tested in Chicago in 1951, but the FCC sensed that it would face a firestorm from all those millions of TV buyers who'd purchased their new sets with the understanding that once they'd plugged them in the picture would come at no additional cost. But the FCC's resistance did not stop the dreamers, among them the California-based Skiatron Electronics and Television Corporation.

In 1953, Skiatron had come up with a scheme called "subscriber vision," a pay-to-view plan that required viewers to use computer punch cards to unscramble pictures and enable the company to charge for its shows. The program, too, had an experimental run, this time during off-peak hours over WOR in New York. The FCC balked on giving final approval. The following year Matty Fox bought Skiatron.

He already owned the rights to RKO's film library, which gave him a great programming inventory. Now he needed another inexhaustible supply of shows. Like the other pay-per-view visionaries of the time, he turned to sports. Specifically he turned to baseball, and to Walter O'Malley.

O'Malley was a believer in the separation of responsibilities: Buzzie Bavasi handled the players, Fresco Thompson the farm system. So it was that Matty Fox was almost never seen at the Dodger offices on Montague Street. He and O'Malley met instead at the Hotel Bossert. Fox had approached him bearing a gift: shares of Skiatron. O'Malley in turn championed the virtues of pay television. It was, he told *Newsweek* in April 1956, the game's financial salvation, the only way owners could compete with television's growing pull on all the fans who had stopped coming to the ballparks. "Until the government legalizes pay TV," he said, "the best any baseball man can do is to come up with a stopgap." Besides, the public was "ready to pay" to watch, he told the *Wall Street Journal*. One day, he prophesied, "we are going to have it."

The logic of charging viewers to watch Dodger games was, in

O'Malley's view, simple: the Dodgers would continue offering all road games for free. But when they were home they would charge, say, $2.50 a game, roughly the same as a grandstand ticket. But the cost to the viewer stopped there: there would be no need to pay for parking, for food. The game came at one price for the whole family.

He explained this to Tom Villante, who as BBD&O's representative to the Dodgers was in charge of the team's broadcasting. Villante, too, saw the wisdom of the plan. "It made all the sense in the world to him," he later said. "It made all the sense in the world to me."

VILLANTE, A YOUNG man of promise and ambition, recognized that O'Malley was a man from whom there was much to learn. Television, he had seen, was just one of many avenues that O'Malley was pursuing to squeeze profits from the game. Because he was not on the Dodger payroll, Villante never had to ask O'Malley for a raise. His job offered all the pleasure of being with the Dodgers and none of the pain. O'Malley even took him to lunch at Room 40 of the Bossert.

Villante was in heaven. He had graduated not long before from Lafayette College, where he had gone on a scholarship arranged, in part, by Joe McCarthy, who'd managed the Yankees. Villante, who grew up in Queens, was a Yankee batboy in the last years of the war. Now he was young and single and the envy of the office: he was traveling with the Dodgers. He ate with them, drank with them, and played putting contests with Jackie Robinson in his hotel room—*let's double that bet.*

He also watched O'Malley cultivate wealthy men who might become Dodger sponsors. O'Malley took them to Ebbets Field and sat with them in his box. He brought them to the clubhouse, too, and introduced them to his players. The players, of course, would be asked to pose for a photograph with the visitor whom O'Malley recognized would be a very big hit with the fellows at the club and with his children, too, when he came home to tell them how he'd spent his day. O'Malley flew these men to Vero Beach—the team's DC-3 was not just for the players—and made sure that they had their pictures taken there, too.

Villante saw how well O'Malley understood the power of images, and not merely those suitable for framing: rather than dismissing Willard Mullin's famous cartoon of the potbellied Dodger bum, for instance,

O'Malley, recognizing its value in cultivating a following, used it on the cover of the team's yearbook every year after he took control of the Dodgers in 1950. He also hired a team photographer, Barney Stein. Stein's job was to get Dodger pictures in the papers, because, O'Malley reasoned, the more people saw of the Dodgers the more they would think about them, and follow them at Ebbets Field. So the picture desks of the New York dailies, and the photo agencies, too, were flooded with such staged photographs as, say, of Pee Wee Reese sitting on Duke Snider's shoulders, picking a Florida grapefruit.

For Tom Villante it was a good, if sometimes nerve-racking time to be a young man working in TV: the medium was still too young for rules. The Dodger sponsors had insisted that BBD&O assign a producer to the broadcasts, and that job fell to Villante. He was winging it, like everyone else. He had to learn how to cultivate the broadcasters, to work in the commercials, to superimpose type on the screen. He also had to learn to negotiate with Walter O'Malley.

"I have in my pocket an offer from Rheingold," O'Malley would say of a rival brewery, knowing that 80 percent of Schaefer's advertising budget went to the Dodgers, and knowing, too, how to veil a threat of taking his business elsewhere. But Villante also saw how well O'Malley understood what television could do for him: he insisted, for instance, that his sponsors give the team three free minutes of commercial time during every road-game broadcast for promotions. Red Patterson, O'Malley's publicist, would write short items, Dodger commercials highlighting the team's next homestand. Television, meanwhile, was bringing the Dodgers a following that extended well beyond Brooklyn and neither the Giants nor the Yankees attracted that large a television audience: the Giants were Horace Stoneham's family project, and in Villante's view, as unaware of television's potential as were the haughty Yankees.

Villante, like O'Malley, like Matty Fox, did see the potential. And Villante, too, wanted a piece of Skiatron. So, it turned out, did the players. Together with Snider, Erskine, Reese, and Hodges, Villante formed a small syndicate. Each man anted up five hundred dollars to buy Skiatron shares. In truth, they thought it was a lark. They had a group picture taken, each man reading the *Wall Street Journal*. Whether they might ever see a return on their investment remained a mystery. Charging people to watch baseball on television was, for the moment, as much a dream as the domed stadium whose scale model Walter O'Malley kept in his office, and which he talked about with an excitement that reminded Tom Villante of a child with a new toy.

4 | THE MONEY PITCHER

Carl Erskine's no-hitter was an inspiration, or so it appeared. The Dodgers won the next day, Snider hitting two homers, including his first grand slam at Ebbets Field, and the next, sweeping their three games against the Giants and running their winning streak to four. The Cardinals came to town and the Dodgers beat them, too, at Ebbets Field and at Jersey City, where the fans were still booing them. They'd won six straight when the Reds arrived with their beefy lineup.

Cincinnati left two days later, winners of both games and reminders to the Dodgers of the powerful hitting team they themselves had been the season before: in each of their five straight wins against Brooklyn the Reds averaged three home runs. Cincinnati was generous in its cruelty to Brooklyn's pitching, spreading around the homers and extra-base hits. But they were especially hard on poor Erskine, whom they wrenched back to earth with back-to-back home runs in the second inning of his first start since the no-hitter. Luckily, the Cubs were up next and, as was customary, played their role as guests to perfection, falling twice on a Sunday doubleheader. But then they were gone, and from the visiting dugout at Ebbets Field emerged the Milwaukee Braves, who were now in first place.

Erskine, thankfully, was back on his game, and was trailing only 2 to 1 when Alston pulled him for a pinch hitter in the home sixth. Though the Dodgers did not score, Alston had no reason to worry: he called on Clem Labine, who had been just a hair's width short of brilliant all spring—twelve innings, three earned runs, twelve strikeouts, no home runs. But in a young season already littered with too many moments that defied explanation, the usually reliable Gil Hodges booted an inning ending grounder with two outs in the seventh. Johnny Logan and Eddie Mathews followed with homers, back to back. The eighth brought even more troubles for Labine—three consecutive Milwaukee doubles, which closed out the Braves' thrashing of the Dodgers, 7 to 3. Rain washed out the second game, which gave the Dodgers another day at home to brood before heading to Philadelphia for the start of a twenty-one-game road trip.

THE PITCHING WAS failing them, that much was clear. Only Newcombe was reliable as a starter; Erskine had had his day, but had flopped, too, as had Drysdale, Craig, and Templeton. Johnny Podres was in the navy, Karl Spooner was still in Florida, and Billy Loes was in pain. Buzzie Bavasi, who always liked Loes, even if he could not always follow the younger man's curious logic, had seen enough and on May 13 sold him to the Baltimore Orioles for $25,000. Baltimore knew the state of Loes' arm, but being in sixth place, thought he might be worth the risk. Now Bavasi was an arm short. Although he had young men like Koufax, Lehman, and Roebuck in the bull pen, he was open to offers for something more when he took a call from Bill Veeck and Hank Greenberg, who ran the Cleveland Indians.

Bavasi had been with the Dodgers since the days of Larry MacPhail and had learned flesh trading at the knee of Branch Rickey. He understood, then, that Veeck and Greenberg's call was that of men who had a costly problem they needed to unload: Sal Maglie. Greenberg had cut Maglie's salary as much as he could—a 25 percent pay cut was the most the game then allowed—but was still holding a $26,900 contract for a man who had no place on his team. Bavasi knew he had the advantage over Veeck and Greenberg, who wanted to know if Buzzie was buying. Bavasi said he'd be happy to help, but needed to ask around first.

He called Alston, who liked what he'd seen of Maglie that night in Jersey City. He called Reese, too, and the captain confirmed from the batter's box what Alston had witnessed from the dugout. "He looked like the same guy to me," Reese said. "I'd like to see him on our side."

Bavasi called back Greenberg, who wanted $100,000 for the Barber.

"You've got to be out of your friggin' mind," Bavasi replied.

Greenberg dropped a zero from the price tag, but Bavasi demurred.

"Give us something for him," Greenberg begged.

Bavasi offered $100 to take Maglie and his salary off Greenberg's hands. But because he understood that Greenberg and Veeck would be roasted in the papers for such a deal, Bavasi agreed conspiratorially to announce that the Dodgers had paid $10,000 for Sal Maglie.

Unfortunately, that was what Walter O'Malley read. When he came to work the next day he was not angry. He was, Bavasi noted, "as white as a sheet." The color, however, quickly returned to his generous cheeks when Bavasi told him the truth of the deal.

Bavasi then took a long-distance call from Cleveland. This time the caller was Maglie, who was very happy and who told Bavasi, "I think I can do the job for you." He asked if he might have another day to make his way to Brooklyn; his father was sick and he wanted to stop at home, in Niagara Falls, to see him. Bavasi agreed and hung up, feeling even better about Sal Maglie: he had not called collect.

Soon afterward, Tom Villante happened to be in the Dodger clubhouse with only the batboy Charlie DiGiovanna and Carl Furillo for company. The team was already on the field for batting practice when the clubhouse door opened. There stood Sal Maglie. The room was silent.

The Brow turned to Furillo. And knowing how well he kept a grudge and how deeply he hated Maglie, cried out, "Don't do it. We're all Dagos here."

Carl Furillo rose, which in itself was not unusual when he confronted Sal Maglie. Time and again Maglie had forced him onto the seat of his pants with a fastball to the chin. Each time Furillo got up, not pleased. Furillo was not a man to rile. Now, in the deserted clubhouse, he approached Maglie. He extended a hand. Maglie shook it, and in so doing became what no one could ever have imagined: a Brooklyn Dodger.

Still, Buzzie Bavasi was taking no chances. He gave Furillo a hundred dollars to take Maglie to dinner at Toots Shor's. Bavasi then called Shor and told him to put the dinner on his tab, knowing that Furillo, a tight man with a dollar that appeared to be his, would be only to happy to pocket the hundred.

THE IDEA OF Furillo and Maglie at dinner together summons the image of long silences interrupted by the tapping of steak knives against plates. Neither man was a talker. And while Furillo was good for the occasional quote, Maglie drove the writers mad with his silence. His distance, however, only enhanced his reputation as a grim loner, mysterious and inscrutable.

Maglie's wife, Kathleen, could never be sure if her husband had won or lost because he did not talk about the games when he came home—except once, when his wife told him he had made himself look foolish when he was ejected for throwing his glove down on the mound. He never did it again. Even his roommates never claimed to know Sal Maglie well. He was pleasant. He liked a martini or two before dinner. He called his teammates "kid." He dressed well. He did, on occasion, display the rare and unexplained eccentricity: Clem Labine, who roomed with him briefly, was never quite sure what to make of the time in Chicago when he and Maglie ordered up room service dinners; his dinner done, Maglie picked up his metal tray, walked over to the window, opened it, and tossed the tray out. Labine, shocked, asked Maglie if he was trying to kill someone. Maglie pointed out the ledge several floors below where the tray had landed, thereby assuring Labine that no one was in danger but never explaining why he simply hadn't left the tray for the chambermaid.

As best as anyone could tell, two things could move Sal Maglie to words: the blond and husky infant boy he and his wife had adopted; and money. Of Sal Jr., he would say, pointing to his heart, "The little guy makes a big difference right in there." As for money, Maglie, while not given to lengthy explanations, made it clear that as a young man he understood that he could make a decent living playing baseball, but that playing baseball was only interesting when the money was on the line. Maglie hated warming up, for instance, because he found no pleasure in throwing a baseball unless a batter faced him, preferably a very good batter on a very good team whom he would greet with a fastball at the chin. Maglie did not believe in throwing at a man's head once. You had to do it twice, he explained, to keep him thinking.

HE WAS THE third child and only son of immigrant parents from the Italian province of Apulia. His father worked in a chemical plant. "We always ate," he told Sidney Fields of the *Mirror*, "but the family needed a buck." He played baseball but starred at basketball at Niagara Falls High School. He declined a basketball scholarship to Niagara University; he already had a job. He worked in the shipping room of the Cataract Bottling Co. and played baseball for the company team. He made $50 a week hauling barrels and kegs. His pitching attracted the attention of the Buffalo Bisons of the International League, who offered him $275 a month to pitch. He signed and worked in the shipping room in the off-season.

He was a bust with Buffalo. He went 3 and 15 over three seasons and later attributed his dismal beginnings to the burden of playing too close to home. Still, Elmira, of the Eastern League, signed him and there his career took off. He won twenty games, and after minor league stops with Jamestown and Jersey City and two wartime years as a steamfitter in a defense plant, he reported to the Giants in 1945. He went 5 and 4, and though three of his victories were shutouts, he recognized that he was still regarded as a "wartime" player, easily discarded when the veterans returned. As it happened, the Giants' pitching coach, Adolfo Luque, managed the Cienfuegos team in the Cuban winter league and invited Maglie and Kathleen down.

Luque had pitched in the major leagues for nineteen years and had developed certain ideas about success on the mound that he was happy to share with young men willing to listen. Maglie, recognizing that his position with the Giants was, at best, tenuous, presented himself as an eager student. Luque believed that a pitcher had to protect the strike zone—that he could not afford to cede the outside part of the plate to a batter. The pitcher who owned the strike zone, he explained to Maglie, was the pitcher who threw inside. He did not necessarily want to hit the batter, just move him back, or at the very least keep him from leaning in so that he could not hit pitches over the outside part of the plate. Luque also believed that no pitch was a "waste" pitch. This was a heretical view. A pitcher ahead in the count, say, up no balls and two strikes, would throw one well out of the strike zone to see if he might get the batter to bite at something unhittable. But Luque preached that each pitch mattered, and so when he was ahead in the count, he either came inside or "showed" the batter a pitch, say a fastball away, only to come back with the curve on the inside corner. Luque was blessed, from a pitching standpoint, with penetrating eyes, an intimidating characteristic not lost on his dark-eyed pupil.

Maglie pitched well in Cuba and attracted the attention of Bernardo Pasquel, a wealthy Mexican who, with his brother Jorge, was raiding the major leagues of players for their new league in Mexico. Maglie declined his invitation, believing that he stood a good chance of sticking with the Giants. "Besides," he later wrote in *Sports Illustrated*, "the offer wasn't that much more than what New York was paying me."

He went to spring training in Florida, pitched well, and then for reasons he did not fully appreciate found himself out of favor with the Giants' manager, Mel Ott. The raids by the Pasquel brothers were the talk of camp, and major league baseball was taking a hard line on those who even considered jumping: players who jumped would be banned from the game for life. That Maglie had spoken with Bernardo Pasquel marked him out: even though he had declined their offer, he was still being approached as a middleman for potential renegades. He did in fact intercede with two teammates, who signed with the Pasquels. And though he had struck out seven batters in five innings in his first appearance of the spring, Ott would not use him. Finally, convinced that he had no future with the Giants, he signed with the Pasquels and with Kathleen moved to Puebla, a small city high in the Sierra Madre.

IN PUEBLA, MAGLIE was reunited with Adolfo Luque, who managed the team. This was fortunate, because he quickly discovered that he had much to learn if he were to survive in Mexico. The team traveled between the highlands of Puebla and Mexico City and the coastal towns of Veracruz and Tampico, and the changes in altitude played havoc with his curve: while it broke in the humid air of the lowlands, it hung in the mountains, a fat pitch for batters to devour. Luque told him to use the fastball at home—the pitch had a natural break, hooking in on right-handers—and rely on the curve on the road. But most important, Luque, who could be a hard taskmaster, insisted that Maglie sharpen his control so that he could throw the ball wherever he wanted.

The curve itself had a marvelous provenance. Luque, who had pitched for the Giants, learned the pitch from Christy Mathewson, one of the game's immortals, and passed it on to Maglie. Maglie, in turn, refined it, tinkering with the pitch so that it broke late and just over the plate, and in time, getting it to break in any one of three directions. He pitched well, and when he won people rushed out onto the field and carried him on their shoulders. He also developed a reputation as a man not to offend: when a hitter made the mistake of laughing as he circled the bases after homering against Maglie, he was greeted the next time at bat with a fastball at the ear. If he squawked he got another.

The Mexican league was a low-budget affair—at Tampico's stadium, train tracks ran across the outfield and play was called when the locomotives rumbled through. After two years the Pasquel brothers' money ran out and the league dissolved. The renegades put together a barnstorming team—Maglie pitched and played outfield and first—that went 81 and 0 in its only season. Then Maglie went home to Niagara Falls and opened a gas station.

He was miserable. Banned from the majors and desperate to pitch, he signed on with Drummondville in the Provincial League in Quebec. Meanwhile, the major leagues had softened on the renegades and eased the ban. Maglie was in the fifth inning of a game in Canada when the call came from the Giants that he could, at last, come back.

HE WAS THIRTY-THREE years old and his manager, Leo Durocher, assumed that at best he might pitch in relief. Maglie, however, impressed Durocher with his eagerness—he asked to pitch batting practice. In truth, Maglie knew himself well enough to know that to pitch well he needed the work; he needed to pitch often to keep his control sharp. Durocher started him. Maglie won 18 games that season. He went on to win 23 games in 1951 and 18 in 1954. He got a nickname, too, but for reasons that had nothing to do with his pitching inside or with his dark stubble. One day a writer overheard Durocher say, "Look at Sal—he looks like the barber in the third chair." He became The Barber then, just for being Italian.

The Dodgers had won the pennant in 1953, but in 1954 the Giants not only beat them for the league championship but were poised to clinch the pennant against Brooklyn at Ebbets Field. Durocher approached Maglie in the visiting clubhouse before the team took the field.

"Sal, you got anything you want to tell the boys?" he asked.

"Yeah," Maglie replied. "Campanella's going down on the first pitch."

HE WAS NEVER better than he was against the Dodgers, especially when he pitched at Ebbets Field. The fans booed him, and this pleased him no end. It only raised the stakes, which made the playing that much more of a joy. He knew just what he wanted to do with the Brooklyn hitters. He threw curveballs to Furillo and Hodges and kept the ball low and away from Snider, who was so eager, as they all were, to pounce on him. Robinson kept his hands high and so Maglie brushed him back with fastballs at the elbow, especially if Robinson stepped out of the box and tried to throw him off his rhythm. And though Robinson and Furillo hated him most, Maglie was toughest on Campanella, whom he generally started with a fastball over the head.

The rivalry was all that Maglie could have asked for—two National League teams sharing the same city, seemingly taking turns winning the pennant. Even in lean years, the Polo Grounds was always full when "the Brooklyns" came to play. Years later, the men who played for the Giants in those games would recall the excitement that came from being in a ballpark filled with people whose passions, both in love and hate, were so aroused. For the Giants, in particular, who played in such a big and uninviting park—the Polo Grounds was an oval that looked best suited for football and, yes, polo—the games without the Dodgers could be gloomy affairs, especially by 1956, when the team was poor and the afternoon silences were broken only by the echo of bat against ball.

Maglie was 9 and 5 in the summer of 1955 when the Giants decided to sell him to Cleveland. The team, he was told, wanted to see what the younger men could do. Maglie was thirty-eight and had a bad back: several years earlier he discovered that because his right leg was longer than his left, his spine was twisted. He slept on a board and in the dugout slipped a magazine under one buttock to keep his back aligned.

He got little work in Cleveland. He did not know the hitters, and the American League umpires were not calling his pitches on the corners strikes as the umpires had in the National League. Still, he did not think he was done, nor did the Dodgers when they saw him in Jersey City.

They gave him his old number, 35, and introduced him to the press. And because he was not given to say more than what was necessary, he told them nothing about stopping in Niagara Falls to see his ailing father, and that in fact, his father had died that day. Instead, he posed for pictures and then went out to the park. He wanted and needed the work, and so he pitched batting practice on his first day with the team.

Pee Wee Reese, one of the few who'd hit him well, stepped in. Maglie's first pitch came inside, Reese went down, and as he got up he pointed to the name on his shirt and said, "Hey, we're on the same team now."

"It slipped," said Sal Maglie.

5 | TURNING ELSEWHERE

In early May the navy announced that the battleship *Wisconsin*, damaged in a collision with a destroyer, would be dry-docked for repairs at the naval shipyard in Norfolk, Virginia.

This was a blow to the Brooklyn Navy Yard, and to the borough's congressional delegation, whose leader, Emanuel Celler, had intervened, asking that the repair work on the *Wisconsin* be done in Brooklyn. The *Wisconsin*, wrote Celler, had been built in Brooklyn; the navy yard was its "home" and the men who worked there knew her. Repairs to the *Wisconsin* would cost an estimated $1 million, money the navy yard sorely needed. "Recently men have been laid off or forcibly retired," Celler wrote. "Great hardship has resulted."

"Amends can now be made," he continued, by bringing the *Wisconsin* to Brooklyn. The navy declined his request.

There was work coming to Brooklyn, but of a different sort: a judge threw out the Save Bay Ridge Committee's suit to stop construction of the Narrows bridge. Opponents of the bridge had moved beyond warning that the project would destroy whole blocks in Bay Ridge: the bridge, they insisted, would be a "war hazard"—all an enemy needed to do to clog the harbor was to destroy the bridge. The bridge was even denounced from the pulpit. In a sermon entitled "The Sanctity of the Home," the Reverend Frank Peer Beal of the Edgewood Reformed Church accused Robert Moses of being "a czar" and bemoaned the sad fact that the public "doesn't give a continental about men who would destroy 5,000 Brooklyn homes to build the Narrows Bridge." The Reverend Beal was himself no stranger to grand plans: in 1930 he had proposed creating a vast island in New York Harbor and building an airport on it. The plan would have been forgotten were it not revived and altered in May 1956 by a New York architect and gadfly named Vito Battista, who wanted Beal's island not for an airport but for a 150,000-seat stadium where the Dodgers, Giants, *and* Yankees would play and which the city could use to lure the 1964 Olympic Games. Battista insisted that this island would "save Brooklyn from deterioration and decay" by running tunnels beneath it to Manhattan and Staten Island, thereby eliminating the need for the Narrows bridge.

Battista was not the only man with plans for a new stadium for Brooklyn. Edward Doyle, a former state legislator, wrote to Mayor Wagner offering a site in his home district of Greenpoint, which sat on the borough's edge along the Queens border, for a stadium for the Dodgers. And while Doyle's letter was dutifully filed in the mayor's papers, the *World-Telegram* lauded Battista's plan, pointing out on its editorial page that while the price was high—$590 million—its sweep and daring removed it from "the crackpot class"; there would be no need for the Narrows bridge, and for new baseball *stadiums*. Yes, stadiums: for now the Giants wanted a new park, too, and they had an ally pushing for one.

The Manhattan borough president, Hulan Jack, one of the city's few black officials of note, announced his plan for a 110,000-seat stadium on Manhattan's West Side. Jack envisioned a stadium built over the New York Central Railroad tracks and claimed that he had put together a group of investors interested in buying the land—even as the railroad characterized news of the plan as "an interesting surprise." Jack, meanwhile, insisted that the stadium would be essential to keep the Giants from moving, perhaps to Minneapolis. And, he added, it might also become home to the army-navy football game. The mayor did do Horace Stoneham the courtesy of this time inviting him to Gracie Mansion to talk about the Giants and to look at plans for this grand stadium. But Wagner, a man who generally avoided giving offense, nonetheless felt no need to invite Hulan Jack.

Robert Moses said nothing about the stadium. He was otherwise distracted. No sooner had he sailed into New York Harbor from his three-week vacation to Spain and Portugal than reporters hurried to his stateroom on the *Cristoforo Colombo* to ask him about the group of well-connected West Side mothers who had managed to block his plan to build a parking lot for the Tavern-on-the-Green restaurant on a stretch of Central Park where their children played. Moses lit into the mothers for having the nerve to stand in his way—"those howling childless women who are howling about their non-existent children," he cried, loudly though incorrectly. He then turned his wrath on federal officials and local politicians who did not seem to understand how he did his work. No mention was made of the Brooklyn stadium. The project itself had, for all practical purposes, been loaded onto the great conveyor belt of the city's bureaucracy, which, of course, was just where Moses wanted it to be. The mayor was fielding suggestions for people who would become the three members of the sports authority, but had not settled on finalists.

Meanwhile, the future was on display at Robert Moses' New York Coliseum: a half million people were expected at the annual International Home Building Exposition. There they would see displays of prefabricated homes, all of the newest conveniences, and model homes from as far away as Belgium, Japan, Brazil, and even the Soviet Union. The Federal Home Administration and the Department of Commerce would be there, too, to tell people about how to get assistance in securing home loans.

But in the suburbs where those homes were being built, all was not going according to plan. In the Long Island town of Roosevelt, voters defeated a real estate tax increase to pay for new schools, a recreation program, and school cafeteria equipment. The plan was defeated by the town's newer residents who had moved there from the city with their school-age children, but who after buying homes that now cost between $14,000 and $24,000 were so stretched they could not afford to pay more in taxes. In Stamford, Connecticut, an established town, schools were getting so overcrowded that a group of housewives, lawyers, and businessmen established a committee to look for new school sites because the city was not doing it for them. The coming of all the people from the city was not universally well received: the tony Connecticut town of New Canaan, whose population had swelled by 4,300 people, or 40 percent, since 1950, had joined other older suburbs in "upgrading" its zoning laws—increasing the minimum acreage for new homes to ensure that they would be fewer in number and suitable for their town.

Brooklyn, too, was suffering from overcrowding, but of a different sort. While the city was shutting fast-emptying schools on Manhattan's East Side, parents in Brownsville were calling for new schools to accommodate all the children now living in the neighborhood's new housing projects.

Meanwhile, the familiar rites of Brooklyn in spring proceeded as they always had: the borough was preparing to shut down Eastern Parkway in anticipation of the thousands of people expected for the eighty-eighth annual Memorial Day parade. In Dyker Beach, a thousand people gathered in front of the Andrew Torregrossa Funeral Home to pay their final respects to Joseph Anastasia, the mobster who with his brothers Anthony, Albert, and Gerardo had for years run the New York waterfront. The thirty cars in the procession backed up traffic along Sixty-fifth Street.

And Jackie Robinson managed, with his teammates' encouragement, to offend the New York Giants and their fans by dismissing the team as "humpty"—as in "Humpty Dumpty."

"Bunch of humpties. You can't tell me they're a contending club," he said in the visiting clubhouse at the Polo Grounds after the Giants had defeated the Dodgers 6 to 5.

His teammates egged him on with mock applause, and feigned embarrassment.

"Better keep quiet or you'll have another Jersey City," warned Don Newcombe.

"I don't care," said Robinson. "Maybe 45,000 will come out to boo me but I'm still going to say what I think. They don't look like a contending club to me."

Neither did the Dodgers. And Walter Alston was growing impatient. He played with his lineup, hoping to find some runs. First he benched Carl Furillo, who was barely batting a meager .250, and moved Gil Hodges, struggling at .241, to the outfield. He sent Robinson, struggling similarly at .247, to first base and dropped his cleanup hitter, Campanella, a relative stalwart at .255, to eighth in the batting order. Only Snider and Reese were hitting over .300. The tinkering, however, did little good. The team alternated between winning and losing, going 12 and 12 for the month.

By the time they arrived in Chicago on the last day of May their record stood at 19 and 16. They were in fifth place but, in a league where no team seemed capable of an extended run, still only three games out.

Alston, however, was neither satisfied nor done. "We'll start busting loose anytime now," he said. And with that he announced that Gil Hodges would return to first base, Carl Furillo would be back in right field, and that Randy Jackson would start at third base. Campanella, his hands aching, would still catch. Jackie Robinson would sit on the bench.

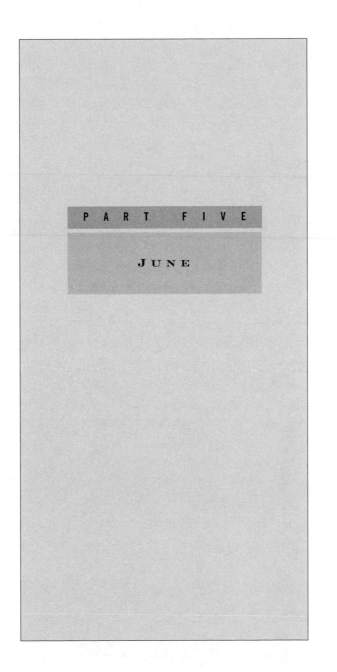

PART FIVE

JUNE

As guilty pleasures went, it was a modest one: when the Dodgers went on the road, Betty Erskine let the housework go. She ignored the cleaning and the ironing and did not worry about cutting the children's fingernails. Only when the team was heading home did she begin to get the house and the children ready for her husband Carl's return.

Betty Erskine and her family lived in a rented house on Ninety-fourth Street between Third and Fourth Avenues in Bay Ridge. It was a street of private homes in a quiet neighborhood that sat along the bay. Her neighbors were pleasant, especially the Monahans, who lived next door and whose two daughters babysat for her. She did not need a car. She could walk to the stores on Fifth Avenue, where the merchants treated her graciously, knowing that her husband pitched for the Dodgers. The butcher, Mr. Rossi, once invited them for dinner, and by the second course they were so stuffed they wondered whether they could soldier on to the entrée.

In the early years of their marriage Betty and Carl had moved from Fort Worth to Montreal to Brooklyn, back to Montreal, and finally, in 1950, back to Brooklyn to stay. They first lived in a row house in Flatbush, but moved to a two-bedroom house in Bay Ridge. A lot of the Dodger families lived in Bay Ridge. Pee Wee and Dotty Reese lived there and they were the ones the others followed.

Betty liked Dotty, whom she and the other wives regarded in much the same way their husbands thought of Pee Wee: she was older and in many ways wiser and she was, without anyone ever having to say it, the first among them. Dotty lived nearby, as did Bev Snider and Millie Walker, Rube's wife. When the baseball season ended, Betty and Carl went "home," to Anderson, Indiana, because that was where their families lived. Their parents were getting older and they had friends in Anderson. Anderson was where the children would go to school. It was the same way with Bev and Duke, who always went back to California, and for the Reeses, who went home to Louisville. They would see each other again in the spring, at Vero

Beach, where the Erskines and Sniders shared a house—who could afford to rent one on their own?

When "the boys" were traveling, their wives and children came to Dodgertown to use the pool and play golf. The team would leave Florida ahead of them, and the wives would head north, sometimes on their own and sometimes together—Bev would drive up with Norma Craig, Roger's wife, and stop along the way at her home in Durham, North Carolina. They would have the houses ready when their husbands returned. The Dodger wives were, with the exception of Dotty, young women in their mid-twenties who had married their high school sweethearts and had discovered, in ways they could not have anticipated when they left home on the arms of their young and nervous husbands, the pleasure of their own company.

Even though they sometimes stayed with each other when the team traveled—Millie Walker, who hated being alone, often stayed with Dotty Reese—they now knew that they were capable of doing a good deal without their husbands. It was only after she and Duke and their children returned to California in the off-season that Bev Snider discovered that it took her a couple of weeks to learn to be "dependent" again.

When their husbands were away the wives could do as they pleased, which was not as daring as it sounded. They all had children, and the children filled their days. Not that their husbands were necessarily around that much when the team was home: the men had their games, and on off-days they golfed at the public course at Dyker Beach. The wives did not expect them home quickly when the games at Ebbets Field were over because that was the time Pee Wee wanted them in the clubhouse to talk baseball—the wives all knew Pee Wee's refrain, "You hurry out of the clubhouse, you're hurrying out of baseball." They had been baseball wives long enough to know what was reasonable to expect from their husbands, and what sort of behavior would invite frowns from the other wives. Not that anyone *told* them how a baseball wife was supposed to behave; they just watched, Dotty mostly, and learned.

A good baseball wife did not travel with the team. She seldom, if ever, called the clubhouse. A good baseball wife did not ask her husband too many questions about the game. She sat in the stands with the other wives at home games, and if her husband was having a rough time of it she kept her feelings to herself, a measure of stoicism that would be answered by a reassuring squeeze of the arm by another Dodger wife. When her husband called from the road she was not to be, in Bev Snider's words, "a wimpy wife." In truth, they were nothing of the kind.

When the men traveled, the wives took the children out to dinner at Lundy's in Sheepshead Bay, so that the children would learn to eat nicely in public. They even got the children to eat fish. When Millie Walker decided she wanted to find a church, the other wives dressed their children in good clothes and went along with her to the Dutch Reformed Church in Bay Ridge, so that she wouldn't have to go alone. They threw baby showers. They sent their children to the same day camp—Camp Bauman, on the Island, in Oceanside. A van came around each morning to pick the children up.

Some of the Dodgers, Carl Furillo especially, thought of their husbands as the "Bay Ridge clique," and Betty sensed that some of the other Dodger wives thought that they held themselves apart. But it was not that way at all. They did play bridge together on Friday nights. Their husbands came by after games, sometimes just for a sandwich. But when new men joined the team, Betty, Dotty, or Bev called their wives to say hello, to tell them about Bay Ridge, and to offer to introduce them to the merchants on Fifth Avenue. They all used the same pediatrician, Morris Steiner, an older man whom they spoke of reverentially. They had learned about Steiner from Dotty, of course. It was Steiner who had correctly diagnosed Barbara Reese with polio so quickly that the child recovered completely and without complications. Pee Wee was on the road when Barbara fell ill, but Dotty was able to handle things. Dr. Steiner and his wife invited the Sniders, Erskines, Walkers, and Reeses to dinner, and when the team traveled the wives sensed that he was keeping an eye on them, if only by way of house calls.

The Labines lived in Bay Ridge, as did the Craigs, the Zimmers, and the Roebucks. Years later they would talk of Bay Ridge as the most inviting and welcoming place imaginable, a neighborhood reminiscent of the towns they'd left behind. Bay Ridge sat on the edge of Brooklyn, a bulge of land pushing out onto Upper New York Bay. The people who lived there were almost all white—of the 162,000 people counted in the 1957 census only 164 were black—and most of them were older. While Bay Ridge was a neighborhood where most people lived with their families, the children were getting older, and fewer young families could afford to buy there, let alone rent. Bay Ridge's population had been slowly shrinking for years. It was filled with Italian and Scandinavian immigrants and their children and, in declining numbers, their grandchildren; 40 percent of the population was over the age of forty-five.

The Dodgers lived in the exclusive section of Bay Ridge, a corner by the bay called Fort Hamilton—named for the Revolutionary War fort whose garrison was still posted in Brooklyn. The homes were modest; the Reeses lived in a small brick house that sat in a tiny cul-de-sac. Still, they were filled with people who were doing a little bit better than the families living a few blocks further inland. In 1956 the average Bay Ridge family was earning about $3,500 a year—just over the Brooklyn average. Fort Hamilton families were averaging incomes closer to $5,000. Their Dodger neighbors were earning far more: Snider was making $40,000 a year, Labine $18,000. But the money they made was not so much more as to catapult them into a different world. It is one thing to earn five times as much as the fellow next door, and quite another to earn hundreds of times as much, as ballplayers one day would; because then there is little chance of your actually being neighbors. The Dodgers could afford to rent in the Fort Hamilton section of Bay Ridge. But none of them were renting townhouses in Brooklyn Heights, where the Wall Street and white-shoe folks lived.

In Bay Ridge people knew where the Dodgers lived, and their children would ring the Dodgers' doorbells, asking for autographs. The Dodgers' sons played on the Bay Ridge Little League teams, and their wives shopped with the Bay Ridge wives. And though their names—Reese, Snider, Erskine—set them apart, they were not women inclined to put on airs.

Besides, they had the children, and the housework, and their husbands, who were not always given to handling their disappointments and fears with grace and equanimity. They tried, doing so in the belief that silence equaled stoicism. Their wives were not deceived. They knew when the men were struggling—if their husbands didn't call, they could still read the game stories in the papers—and felt it would be unfair to burden them with unpleasant news from home. And now, in June, as the season entered its third month, the dispatches from the road were often disheartening.

THE DODGERS OPENED the month in Chicago on a bitterly cold afternoon at Wrigley Field. They were tied with the Cubs at two runs apiece in the bottom of the fifteenth inning. Ed Roebuck had come on in the fourteenth with two men on and set the Cubs down on a strikeout and a double play. He had retired the first two Cubs in the bottom of the fifteenth when Eddie Miksis grounded to Pee Wee Reese, a sure game-ender. But Reese flubbed the play, and Miksis was standing on first when Gene Baker, the Cubs' stout second baseman, homered off Roebuck to give the game to Chicago.

Roebuck and Reese were not alone in their misery. The Dodgers had had ample chances to win the game, and each time botched the play—five times they got the leadoff man on, and five times they failed to score him. So woeful was their play that Tommy Holmes, the one-armed writer from the *Herald-Tribune* who'd been covering the team since he started at the *Eagle* in 1924, was now referring to them as the "once proud but now thoroughly disturbed Dodgers." Holmes, who possessed a poet's touch, did not need to stretch too far the next day when the team hit its nadir: dropping both games of a doubleheader to the worst team in the game. Their afternoon, he wrote, had been a "five hour trance" that ended only with a brief stir in the ninth inning of the second game, when they tried but failed to tie the game. The Cubs had been especially hard on Carl Erskine, whom they pounded 8 to 1 and who was now winless since his no-hitter. They beat Newcombe, too. The Dodgers were an even .500, 19 and 19. Though Sandy Koufax, making his first start of the season, saved them from a sweep by winning the last game of the series, they were, as bad luck would have it, on to Milwaukee, where the Braves were struggling but still potent.

Koufax's reprieve allowed the team to joke about "a little child leading them." But to open the two-game set against the Braves, Alston penciled in Sal Maglie, who was roughly twice Koufax's age. He had already called on Maglie twice to relieve and the Barber had been less than stellar. But this was Maglie's sort of game—his team foundering and, better still, a start against their rivals in the very stadium where he had pitched his last game for the Giants. The Braves had treated him rudely that day, and in the evening New York had sold him to Cleveland.

Almost thirty thousand people crowded County Stadium to see if the Braves could snap out of their own slump—they were in first place, but just a game ahead of the suddenly competitive Pirates. Maglie had not pitched more than four innings since the Giants had unloaded him. But now his curve was breaking over the corners, inside and out. Eddie Mathews managed two singles and only Bill Bruton made it as far as second, on a scratch single and stolen base. From the fourth inning on the Braves could not touch Maglie, and only with two out in the bottom of the ninth did they manage to produce a base runner, when Jack Dittmer reached first on an error. The Dodgers scored three on home runs by Reese and Hodges, and Sal Maglie went the distance, striking out five and walking only one.

Newcombe, embarrassed by the Cubs, shut the Braves down the next night on five hits. And though Labine failed against the Reds in Cincinnati the following day, the Dodgers trounced them the next, 8 to 5. Maglie again pitched splendidly, shutting out the Reds' muscular lineup for seven innings. The Dodgers had now beaten the Braves twice and the Reds once. But in the rubber game of the Cincinnati series both Roger Craig and Chuck Templeton could not stop the Reds. In the third inning Alston called in Ed Roebuck, who had pitched no more than four innings in a major league game and who had lost the game to Chicago.

But that afternoon, wrote Tommy Holmes, he "battled the Reds and his current stomach ulcers." He worked slowly and methodically, wiping the sweat from his brow before every pitch. Whenever he pitched himself into trouble he found a way out, as he did in the bottom of the ninth when he opened the inning by walking Gus Bell, who promptly stole second. Alston stayed with him. The Bunyonesque Ted Kluszewski stepped up but Roebuck got him to fly out. He struck out Wally Post and Smokey Burgess, and the victory was his.

THE DODGERS CAME home to their wives in the second week of June, a game out of first. They'd ended the trip west by taking two from the Cardinals. Duke Snider, who'd been hitting well, closed the trip with a lovely touch— a home run high off the clock in center field. The team was in third place, but the standings were meaningless at this stage of the season: only three games separated the top five teams in the eight-team National League. The players' return brought a temporary end to the separate world their wives had fashioned for themselves. Bev Snider's house was already clean; she did her housework as soon as Duke left, just to have it out of the way. Betty Erskine finished the laundry and ironing and, along with the other wives, waited for her husband to walk through the door.

"We had a lot of honeymoons," Bev Snider later recalled with a smile. "A lot of honeymoons," echoed Betty Erskine.

2 | LIONS IN WINTER

Roy Campanella's home, Salt Spray, faced the sea. It stood on Morgan's Island, which a stone bridge connected to the Long Island town of Glen Cove. Salt Spray was a ranch home, one level, four bedrooms and a living room with a long window that offered a sweeping view of Long Island Sound. Campanella was drawn to the sea. At Salt Spray there was a small, rocky beach and nearby was the marina where Campanella moored the forty-two-foot yacht he had christened *The Princess* after his youngest daughter. *The Princess* slept six, and Campanella liked to take her out on fishing trips with friends. He enjoyed the company of other men with whom he could spend a few days at sea, fishing for marlin, eating steaks or the day's catch, and tossing their empty beer cans into the ocean. He pampered himself. He owned a thousand tropical fish. He owned sixty model locomotives and two hundred passenger and freight cars that he ran on fifteen feet of curving track that he himself had carefully arranged. He bought *The Princess* on a whim—he had taken his family to the New York Motor Boat Show and when they saw the boat they asked him to buy it. "If my family likes it," he told Roscoe McGowan of the *Times*, "I like it." He was hoping to come to Vero Beach by sea, but the boat did not arrive in time. Instead, with the coming of the warmer weather, he took her out on Long Island Sound, then to the East River and on to the Hudson, anchoring at Jersey City when the Dodgers came to play.

He did not like sitting still. He would wake up and be in the mood to go, anywhere, and often his oldest son, Roy II, joined him. He drove a convertible and on warm days they rode with the top down. He owned a liquor store on 134th Street and Seventh Avenue in Harlem and he owned the building, too. Roy II helped order the liquor. He also did the bookkeeping and wrote the letters to tenants behind on their rent.

Campanella was the highest paid man on the team; no Dodger had ever matched his annual salary of $42,000. The liquor store was doing well. The teetotaling Branch Rickey, who had brought him to the Dodgers in 1948, had disapproved of the liquor store and asked him to consider opening a sporting goods store instead. "Mr. Rickey," Campanella told him, "you're a white man. How many businesses do you think are open to a colored man, outside of entertainment? My people drink. They'll make better customers for whiskey than for sporting goods."

He liked money, not as an end in itself as Walter O'Malley did, but for the pleasures and the life it brought him. He had grown up poor, but not desperately so; his father, the son of Sicilian immigrants, sold vegetables from a truck. On Fridays he sold fish. Roy, the youngest of his four children, helped him load the truck—after Roy had finished his milk deliveries. When Roy Campanella was twelve years old he woke at two o'clock in the morning to lead a horse-drawn wagon on his milk run. He made twenty-five cents a day that he gave to his mother. Later he went to work delivering milk with his older brother Lawrence for fifty cents a day. He also sold newspapers and carried a shoeshine kit. "I was always trying to earn some money," he wrote in his autobiography *It's Good to Be Alive*.

The Campanellas lived in Nicetown, a Philadelphia neighborhood of row houses filled mostly with Italians and Poles. Roy was husky and strong, which was fortunate not only because it helped make him a very good baseball player, but because he could acquit himself well in the many fights he had with boys both white and black who called him "half-breed." His black friends found it almost incomprehensible that his father was, in fact, white. His mother, a religious woman who attended Nazarene Baptist Church, used to drag her husband to services until he wearied of being stared at as the only white man in the sanctuary.

Roy had a room of his own, plastered with cut out pictures of baseball players. He thought of little but playing baseball. He was not a student, although he did enjoy the order and cleanliness of mechanical drawing. His parents did not approve of his playing baseball, and he swore, time and again, that he would give up the game. He ditched school to play. He played softball, hardball, and stickball in the school yard with friends, then in the Philadelphia sandlot league, the American Legion League, and finally, at fifteen, with the Bachrach Giants, a Negro League semipro team. His parents may have thought of baseball players as "bums" but they could not ignore the fact that their less-than-studious son stood to make a reasonable living playing ball. Grudgingly, they allowed him to play for the Giants, who paid him $15 a game, but insisted that he be in school the morning after road trips to New Jersey and New York. When he came home at dawn his mother would be waiting for him with the strap.

His reputation grew quickly. When he turned sixteen and no longer needed his parents' permission to work, he signed for $60 a month with the Baltimore Elite Giants, one of the better Negro League teams. His parents insisted that the team send them his paycheck. His mother gave him $7 a month for pocket money. This was 1937. He would spend the next twenty years of his life playing baseball for a living.

He was stocky, powerful, and surprisingly agile behind the plate. But it was his temperament that truly made him a catcher. He was a student of the position, gleaning what he could from a succession of aging mentors who were wise and generous enough to recognize that his skills now surpassed their own. He learned from people like Tom Dixon of the Bachrach Giants and then from Biz Mackey of the Baltimore Elite Giants, who was second only to the great Josh Gibson as the best catcher in the Negro Leagues. The spitball was legal in the Negro Leagues, as was the emery ball and the shine ball—doctored pitches that danced, dove, and tested the reflexes of any catcher. Mackey taught him to throw; Campanella had a strong but erratic arm and rushed his throws to second. Mackey, who hounded him and reduced him to tears, also taught him to spot and catalog each batter's weakness. And most important, he taught him how to make pitchers do what he wanted them to do—"You gotta scold some, you gotta flatter some, you gotta bribe some, you gotta think for some, and you gotta mother them all!"

The position came to define Campanella. "I thought of myself as a catcher first, not as a Negro," he later said. "A catcher has to make everyone like him, no matter what."

HE LOVED THE baseball life: the Giants played by day and traveled at night, by bus. In the Negro Leagues players ate on the bus, slept on the bus, and changed on the bus. Road trips were like voyages at sea, lasting months at a time. The team played as many as four games a day—two doubleheaders, with Campanella catching every inning. He learned to smoke cigars and play poker and by the time he was eighteen he was married and the father of two daughters. His wife, however, stayed at home in Philadelphia with her parents, and though he tried to see his daughters when he could, the marriage fizzled. He spent his winters in Puerto Rico playing baseball, and when he and Mackey got into an argument over a $250 fine that Campanella refused to pay, he took his mitt and spikes and little more than a change of socks and underwear and accepted the Pasquel brothers' offer to play for Monterrey in the Mexican League. He may have dreamed of playing in the major leagues, but thought it foolish to get his hopes up. No matter. "Sombreros and hot tamales—and that hundred bucks a week most of all," he wrote. "Campy was fixin' to do all right."

The war barely touched him. He spent some time in a defense plant, but his draft board was lenient and allowed him to keep playing ball. He returned to Mackey and the Giants. He married a second time, this time to a basketball player named Ruthe who already had a son. There was talk of major league baseball allowing black people to play, but every time he allowed himself to believe this might happen, the talk led to nothing but disappointment. He thought integration of the game so unlikely that even when Branch Rickey brought him to Brooklyn for a chat in 1946, he assumed that their interminable meeting—Rickey, who did most of the talking, went on for four hours—was about Campanella's joining the Brown Dodgers, a team in Rickey's own proposed Negro League. Campanella made no promises and thought little of Rickey's interest in him until he was in Chicago a week later for a Negro League all-star game and ran into the first-year shortstop for the Kansas City Monarchs, Jackie Robinson.

Robinson invited him up to his room to play gin rummy. They played for half a penny a point, wrote Campanella. He lit a cigar. Robinson abstained. But then he surprised Campanella when he said, "I hear you went over to see Mr. Rickey last week." Robinson went on, "I was over there myself. What happened with you?"

Campanella told him about Rickey's long talk.

"Did you sign?" Robinson asked.

"No, I didn't," replied Campanella. "I let him know right quick that I didn't want to play for no Brown Dodgers." He explained to Robinson that he was already a star in the Negro Leagues and had no interest in a new venture that might fail.

"Did Mr. Rickey tell you that he wanted you for the Brown Dodgers?" Robinson asked.

"No, come to think of it, he didn't even mention them," Campanella replied. "I told him I wasn't interested in signing. I told him I was making three thousand for six months with Baltimore and two thousand more playing winter league ball. I told him I got a bonus of two or three hundred at the end of each season, too. And Mr. Rickey said, 'that's good money.' And I told him, 'darned right it is.' How about you?"

"I signed," Robinson said. "But it's a secret."

Campanella told him that that was all well and good for Robinson, but he had children and a reputation to think of.

"I didn't sign with the Brown Dodgers," said Robinson. "I'm going to play for Montreal."

"What do you mean Montreal?" Campanella asked.

"I'm going to be the first Negro in organized ball," said Jackie Robinson.

Campanella fell silent. He puffed on his unlit cigar, stared at Robinson, and felt like a fool.

"I'm really happy for you, Jackie," he said at last. "I know you'll make it and I wish you all the luck in the world. Now take a good look at yours truly. You're looking at a dumb boy. Man, you're looking at the all-time prize."

The Brown Dodgers and the new Negro League, he now saw, were phantoms, a Rickey ploy designed to distract from his true intention, which was to scout the best black players. Campanella knew he could not call Rickey without violating Robinson's confidence. And he could not be sure that Rickey would ever call again. He was preparing to leave for an exhibition series in Venezuela with, among others, Robinson. The signing was now official and had become the talk of the Negro Leagues, with players speculating on his prospects, and any black man's prospects, for success in the major leagues. Campanella sent Rickey a note with his address in Venezuela, and that was where Rickey tracked him down to summon him back to Brooklyn.

This time he was ready to sign. But the news of Robinson's signing had not gone smoothly and now the Dodger farm teams were reluctant to field any black men. Danville, the Class-B affiliate did not want them. But Nashua of the New England League did. Buzzie Bavasi then ran the

Nashua franchise and agreed to take both Campanella and the young pitcher, Don Newcombe. Campanella would be making $185 a month in Nashua, which translated into an annual cut in pay of $4,000. He calculated the loss, and hesitated to go until his wife told him that he was passing on the opportunity he dreamed of. So he moved to New Hampshire. He spent two years in the minor leagues before Rickey brought him to the Dodgers in 1948, a year after Jackie Robinson's debut.

NOW, TEN YEARS after their talk in Chicago, and after eight years as teammates, the two men had little use for one another. They were cordial in public and took pains to be complimentary of the other's skills on the field. But their teammates and the beat writers were well aware of their mutual disdain. The people who liked Robinson would, on occasion, roll their eyes when Campanella launched into another yarn; it was all too folksy. The people who liked Campanella would grow equally weary when Robinson insisted on turning the conversation to race and justice.

There were Robinson people on the team—of the black players he was closest with Jim Gilliam—and Campanella people—his roommate and close friend was Don Newcombe. This is not to suggest that the two men polarized the Dodgers: they both wanted the team to win too much to allow that. But nor was this akin to Carl Furillo's resentment of the Bay Ridge "clique"—the inevitable tension that comes when twenty-five men of such different backgrounds and temperaments are shut away together, day after day, month after month, in the hothouse of a baseball team.

Robinson and Campanella were two big personalities central to the team's fortunes. They were also two black men who'd triumphed in a world once exclusively white. Unlike almost everyone else on the team they had been observed from the moment of their arrivals, Robinson especially. White players may have been watched to see if they had the talent to stick. But people watched the black men as much to see if they would crack as to see if they could play. It was hardly surprising then, that when people started thinking of Robinson and Campanella as individuals, as white people began to realize that black people did not all know and like each other, the tension between them was magnified. And because one of them was Jackie Robinson, who never let the topic go, the gossip and speculation turned, inevitably, to race. This meant that while many among the Dodgers had no interest in taking sides, others did, in the press and in the Dodger offices on Montague Street.

THE RIFT SHOULD not have been surprising: they had nothing in common but baseball and race. Robinson was a college man, an army officer who'd almost been court-martialed for refusing to move to the back of a bus. He'd been a four-letter man at UCLA; baseball, it was said, was his third-best sport, after track and football, and he'd also starred at basketball. Robinson had grown up in Pasadena, the son of a working mother and a father who'd abandoned the family when he was three years old. He was the sort of person for whom everything mattered—every slight, every pleasure, and every game. Like Campanella, he wrote an autobiography, a book as revealing in its title—*I Never Had It Made*—as was Campanella's. The books reflected much of what people came to think and say about them: *It's Good to Be Alive* is a storyteller's personal history, a succession of anecdotes rich in detail and dialogue. Robinson's story reads, in comparison, like a disquisition. Not that his story lacks drama; rather it is that Robinson seeks the larger point in every encounter. His is a story of struggle and triumph, followed by yet another struggle, always about race. It is an angry man's book, understandably and justifiably, but angry just the same. Campanella, even in his despair after the 1958 car accident that would leave him a quadriplegic, remains a man who wonders when he will be able to smile again.

They had both become hugely successful in the game. Campanella had won his third Most Valuable Player Award in 1955. Robinson, who'd won the award in 1949, was so daring and explosive that he could take over a game like no other player. Years later his teammates would still talk of the photograph of him that hangs at Dodgertown—Robinson in a rundown between third and home, chased by *five* opposing players; and, his teammates would say, he scored.

But now their skills were vastly diminished. Catching had ruined Campanella's hands. He'd had two operations on the left, and in the spring at Dodgertown he was again feeling the numbness that had plagued him in 1954. He broke his right hand in June, in Chicago, when he tried picking a runner off first. He smacked his hand on the hitter's bat, breaking the thumb and two fingers. The thumb swelled to twice its size. Bone chips cut into the meat of his hand every time he swung a bat. He tried to play through the pain, but he was not the same player at bat, or behind the plate.

The Dodger pitchers had always relied on him to carry them through difficult innings. Labine had loved pitching to Campanella. Campanella did not lose his temper. He did not come out to the mound, screaming about a poorly thrown pitch. Instead, he'd take off his mask and approach the mound and say, "C'mon, that's not the way you learned to pitch. You can do better than that." He offered a splendid target: he did not say, Throw to my shinguards, as some catchers did (Labine hated this; legs moved and the target moved with them) but to his big, unwavering mitt. But now, Labine found throwing to Campanella "exasperating." Campanella's left hand was simply too weak to squeeze a ball in his thick catcher's mitt, and he was resorting to the trick of "blocking" the ball, allowing it to hit the target of his mitt, but then letting it drop to the ground. The pitchers were losing too many called strikes that umpires took to be balls when they did not stay in Campanella's mitt.

Robinson was now Randy Jackson's substitute at third. He could not abide it. Yet he now enjoyed a reputation that transcended the game: he had become an important man. He served on the National Conference of Christians and Jews and on the New York chapter of the United Negro College Fund. He was invited to speak and appear at significant events: the "Negro golf tournament" that the writers cited for his delay in coming to Vero Beach was, in fact, a celebrity tournament that marked the first time black people were permitted to play for more than a day at a time at the Miami Springs Golf Course. He did not define himself exclusively as a baseball player, and this alone set him apart from Campanella, and from most of his other teammates. It was also what made him interesting company for some of the writers, and for such Dodgers as Clem Labine.

"When you're a ballplayer, that's what you are—a ballplayer," Labine would later say. "This is what you do, that's all there is." But with Robinson "there were other things to talk about aside from baseball. It was interesting to hear about his life, about his joys and fears." What he feared, Labine learned, was not being accepted on his own terms. "I want to be accepted for who I am," he told Labine, "and not what I stand for."

Robinson had become a man with opinions that people solicited. In June, for instance, *The Sporting News* reprinted an essay he'd written for the *Pittsburgh Courier*, a black-owned paper, on his views of the South, ten years after he'd signed with the Dodgers. This in itself reflected Robinson's stature in the game: *The Sporting News*, the journal of the baseball establishment, had not always been kind about his coming to the game, and about the way he had carried himself. Now it devoted space to a piece in which Robinson wrote both of still being refused rooms at the hotels where his white teammates stayed, and also of the growing willingness of black people to make plain their resentment and rage: "When we played in New Orleans during spring training the Negroes in the stands booed every time they announced anything about the New Orleans Pelicans"—the local, whites-only minor league team. Southern players, he wrote, were now more willing to talk about race: unlike northerners, who were used to living with black people, the southerners he admired, like Pee Wee Reese, were forced to confront bigotry. He had seen change in the South, but not enough. "Traveling in the south," he wrote, "I don't think the advances there have been fast enough."

THAT WAS NOT how Roy Campanella saw things. "I tried not to notice the things that bothered Jackie," he wrote. "Not that I didn't mind them. It's just that some men can have the same problems and yet face them differently." The two men, for instance, had disagreed in 1955 on whether they should stay at the Chase Hotel in St. Louis. After years of denying rooms to black people, the Chase had relented, even though it would still not allow them to eat in the dining room or sit in the lobby. Campanella refused the invitation—"It's got to be the whole hog or nothing for me," he told Lee Scott, the traveling secretary. "If they didn't want me all this time, then I don't want them now." But Robinson believed they should stay. "Now that we had broken the barriers at the Chase," he wrote of his reply to Campanella, "other blacks, not in baseball, who wanted to stay at a decent hotel would begin to find acceptance."

He went on. "I'll never forget Campy's answer to that. 'I'm no crusader,' he said." Years later, when his son Roy II began asking his father about his relationship with Robinson, Roy Campanella, as always, told a story: The Dodgers were in Miami, and after an exhibition game he and Robinson called for a cab to take them back to the Lord Calvert Hotel, where the black players stayed. The cab arrived and when the driver saw who was about to get in, he said, "I can't take you." Robinson told him that they had called for a cab. The driver told them they'd have to call the black cab company. Robinson, Campanella told his son, was enraged. He screamed at the driver and lectured him about how he was doing something wrong. Campanella was angry, too. But he told Robinson that they should just call for a black cab. Robinson was still furious at the driver. And finally, Campanella told his son, he said to Robinson, "There's nothing you can say that will change this guy's mind."

There was a postscript to this story for Roy II. While his father was never a reader, Roy II was—he went to college at Harvard. His father, noting his interest in literature and being a spender by nature, gave him a four-hundred-dollar collection of great books that included works by Dickens, Melville, and Hemingway. And only when his son had finished the series did Campanella tell him his Ernest Hemingway story. The team was playing in Cuba and Hemingway came to see them play. Because he thought of himself as a sporting man who liked the company of other sporting men, Hemingway invited the Dodgers to his home. That is, all the *white* Dodgers. What struck Roy II was less Hemingway's bigotry than the fact that his father had waited to tell him the story until after he'd had the chance to read him.

ROBINSON FOUND MORE to dislike about Campanella than his views on race. He believed he lacked depth and moral fiber. He disapproved of his habits. Robinson, who did not drink or smoke, dismissed him as a libertine, a womanizer—hypocritical considering Robinson's wartime bout of gonorrhea, contracted after his fiancée, Rachel, briefly broke off their engagement. "The more you see of Camp the less you like him," he wrote in a letter to his wife, published many years later. "To me he's like a snake ready to strike at the best possible moment."

He also recognized, angrily, how much more popular Campanella was among the beat writers. Robinson may have been good for a quote and an angle. But Campanella was so much easier to take. While the New York writers had been generally accepting of Robinson's coming to the major leagues, and while several were sensitive to the struggle of black people in America, others found Robinson grating, none more so than Dick Young of the *Daily News*. Young was a sportswriter the likes of which no player had

Roy Campanella (*left*)
shows Walter Alston his
battered catching hand.
(*The Baseball Hall of
Fame Library*)

Sal (The Barber) Maglie
(*The Baseball Hall of
Fame Library*)

Carl and Betty Erskine
(*The Brooklyn Public
Library*)

An island in Brooklyn: Ebbets Field (*The Baseball Hall of Fame Library*)

Robert Moses (*left*) receiving a plaque from Mayor Robert Wagner at the Amateur Sports Dinner (*The Brooklyn Public Library*)

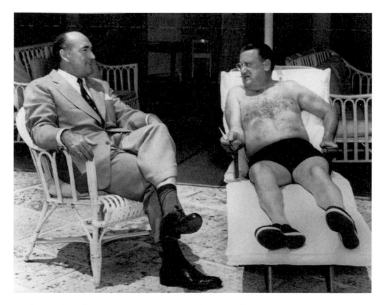

Walter O'Malley, cigar in hand, at the Hotel Nacional de Cuba, with the hotel's general manager, T. James Ennis (1954) (*The Brooklyn Public Library*)

Clem Labine *(Bettman/ CORBIS; The Baseball Hall of Fame Library)*

September 1955. The Dodgers have just clinched the National League pennant. *(The Baseball Hall of Fame Library)*

October 1955 *(The Baseball Hall of Fame Library)*

Don Newcombe
(The Brooklyn Public Library)

"O'Malley's Tammany":
Walter O'Malley graduating
from Penn (1926)
(*The Sporting News*)

Jubilation: Alston (*left*), O'Malley, and Reese. September 30, 1956
(*The Sporting News*)

Buzzie Bavasi, O'Malley, and Fresco Thompson (*The Brooklyn Public Library*)

The cover of the 1956 Dodgers Yearbook with cartoonist Willard Mullins's immortal bum (Courtesy of the Ron Schweiger Collection)

Duke Snider (*left*), Pee Wee Reese, Carl Erskine, and Carl Furillo celebrating the 1953 pennant. The dancer is Loma Duke. (*The Baseball Hall of Fame Library*)

Distance: Jackie Robinson (*left*) with Roy Campanella (*Bettman/CORBIS; The Baseball Hall of Fame Library*)

Endgame in Brooklyn: O'Malley (*left*), Wagner, Giants owner Horace Stoneham, and Brooklyn Borough President John Cashmore in June 1957. Wagner announced that both owners assured him they had not committed to moving to the West Coast. (*The Baseball Hall of Fame Library*)

ever seen. He was interested in the games, but only up to a point. He was more interested in getting stories because stories got a man noticed. Young chased stories with a passion and relentlessness never seen among the older fellows, who saw their work as describing what they had witnessed on the field of play, and, if they were given to puffery, celebrating the heroics of the men with whom they drank and ate and played cards on the road. Young descended from the press box to the clubhouse after games and, in a break from tradition, asked questions that made people uncomfortable. He nosed around, listening for anything that might make a piece apart from the game story. The players feared him and some hated him: he aired their differences and secrets and printed items they regarded as no one's business. Labine once challenged him to a fight—with one arm taped behind his back—after Young ran a piece questioning his guts. Dick Young was a man capable of great generosity, especially to young writers, and profound vulgarity: the father of eight girls, he once handed out cigars in the press box when his wife got her period. He boasted, loudly, of his dalliances. Young had been covering the team for ten years and there were few men on the team he liked better than Roy Campanella. He had coauthored Campanella's first autobiographical book in 1953. So it was that Young believed he might have been helping Robinson when he advised him how best to approach the press.

"I'm telling you as a friend," Robinson later wrote of a talk they had, "that a lot of newspapermen are saying that Campy's the kind of guy they can like but that your aggressiveness, your wearing your race on your sleeve, makes enemies."

Robinson replied that he was more interested in having people respect him than like him. "I know that a lot of them don't like me because I discuss things that get in the way of their guilt complexes, but I'll bet you they respect me."

"Personally, Jackie," said Young, "when I talk to Campy, I almost never think of him as a Negro. Anytime I talk to you, I'm acutely aware of the fact that you're a Negro."

"If you tell me that when you think of me, you think of a whining, cringing, handkerchief-head standing before you with his hat in his hand expressing eternal gratitude for the fact that you only had nine little digs in yesterday's story when you could have had ten, that's one thing. If you think of me as the kind of Negro who's come to the conclusion that he isn't going to beg for anything, that he will be reasonable but he damned well is tired of being patient, that's another thing. I want to be thought of as the latter kind of Negro and if it makes some people uncomfortable, if it makes me the kind of guy they can't like, that's tough. That's the way the ball bounces."

Robinson wrote that he assumed Young either did not understand what he meant, or did not care. Besides, he added, the black writers liked him, and understood him. They also understood the way black people looked at him, and at Roy Campanella, and why Campanella, so favored by men like Dick Young, was seen differently by black people. Sam Lacy, who had covered baseball for the *Baltimore Afro-American*, believed that Campanella envied Robinson. The two had barnstormed together after the 1949 season and years later their teammates wondered whether the rift had not begun then—when Campanella, who always kept one eye on his personal payroll, noticed that Robinson was making more money than he was. But it was not money, Lacy said years later. It was the adoration that black people felt toward Robinson. The autograph seekers, he said, "all ran to Jackie and very few went to Roy. It was a psychological thing. Being of swarthy complexion and having an Italian name was not the symbol that Jackie was. That was the initial rift. From that point on there was an estrangement."

Robinson looked like a movie star; and he could boast that, up to a point, he was. He had starred in the 1950 film version of his life story. *The Jackie Robinson Story* looks like a movie made on the fly, and Robinson was no actor. Yet on the screen he is magnetic—muscular, handsome, and dark. Campanella was, in comparison, cherubic. The film manages to capture, because it is Robinson himself on the screen, the sense of humiliation and degradation heaped upon him first in Montreal, when he played his first season of minor league ball, and then with the Dodgers. So many of the words are there, the taunts and the slights and the threats. There are moments when the film captures Robinson in close-up, restraining himself, as he'd promised Branch Rickey he would: his eyes betray his impotent rage. The cheapness of the film cannot dilute the brooding power of his presence, charisma no one has ever associated with the joyful Roy Campanella.

Jackie Robinson could be priggish and sanctimonious, and when it came to his teammates he could be a snob. "The fellows are all very nice," he wrote to his wife. "Actually there are only a very few I would like to socialize with." He liked Reese, Hodges, Erskine, and Clem Labine. He thought some of the others, whom he did not name, were boorish. They spat on the clubhouse floor. They spoke poorly. They availed themselves of the favors of the team's two camp followers, the women known as "the hook" and "the nook." But his teammates' habits were a minor irritant compared to his views of Walter O'Malley.

Robinson detested him. He hated him for forcing out Branch Rickey, whom he had so admired. Robinson believed that O'Malley regarded him as a Rickey man, and therefore guilty by association with a man he disliked. He and O'Malley had clashed: in 1952, O'Malley lit into him for using injuries as an excuse for missing exhibition games and for complaining about the black players being forced to stay in separate hotels. O'Malley had done this in front of Robinson's wife, assuming, incorrectly, that she would take his side against her husband.

But more than the bullying and the barbs about being Branch Rickey's "prima donna," Robinson also hated him for being, in his view, a bigot. "I was," he wrote, "one of those 'uppity niggers' in O'Malley's book."

WALTER O'MALLEY DID not speak ill of Jackie Robinson in front of his own family, although his daughter, Terry, did sense that her father had had a difficult time trying to get close to Robinson. It had not been that way with Roy Campanella, whose stories he liked to repeat at the dinner table. O'Malley thought well of Campanella, so much so that in 1953 he told Campanella that he wanted him to stay with the Dodgers as a coach when his playing days ended.

Campanella wrote that he was surprised and thrilled. "A coach?" he asked.

"Why not? You're intelligent, level-headed," O'Malley replied. "Besides, you have a way about you. You're popular with the players. There's no question in my mind you'll make a fine teacher. And I'd like to have you working with me for as long as you care to."

"But me, a coach in the major leagues?" said Campanella.

"You mean, you're wondering how it would be for you, a Negro, coaching white players? I don't think you need to worry about that. No, I see no problem in the first Negro coach in baseball, except for one thing."

"What's that, Mr. O'Malley?" asked Campanella.

"Your weight," replied O'Malley, who reminded Campanella that he tended to put on weight in the off-season. "Now, if you want to coach, you have to set an example for others. If you want to handle men, you first have to handle yourself. You think you can do that?"

Campanella assured him that he could, and, in telling the story, did not suggest that perhaps O'Malley ask Clem Labine and the other pitchers whether, husky or not, he was capable of "handling" men.

O'MALLEY MADE NO such offers to Jackie Robinson. He did, however, once allow Robinson to play the role of consultant. In 1954 the Dodgers had signed to a minor league contract a young, thin Puerto Rican outfielder named Roberto Clemente. Bavasi thought he would be a star. Whatever O'Malley might have thought of Clemente's talent, however, did not matter as much as the matter of his color.

He made it clear to Bavasi that bringing Clemente to Brooklyn would be a problem—less for the fans, he explained, than for the players, who might think that too many black men were taking jobs. Bavasi suggested they put the question to one of the players—Jackie Robinson.

Bavasi explained the situation to Robinson, who asked who the team would trade or sell to make room to bring Clemente up to the Dodgers. Bavasi thought George Shuba, a white player, would be the one to go. Shuba was an outfielder, a good, though not in Bavasi's estimation, great player. He was, however, a popular one. Dropping him to bring up Clemente, who might not even be ready to start, Robinson suggested, would not be wise—to bring up Clemente now, he advised Bavasi, would set back by five years the effort to truly integrate the game.

Bavasi accepted Robinson's advice, but did not want to lose Clemente. But as it happened, Clemente was vulnerable to being drafted from Montreal by other teams. Bavasi heard that Branch Rickey, now president of the Pittsburgh Pirates, was interested. Rickey had offered Bavasi a job with the Pirates when he was forced out in Brooklyn. Bavasi had declined but Rickey, who liked him nonetheless, told him that if he could ever do him a favor all he needed to do was ask. Bavasi got on a plane, flew to Pittsburgh, and asked Branch Rickey not to move on Roberto Clemente.

"Judas Priest," Rickey replied. "That's asking a lot."

Bavasi offered him a right-handed pitching prospect. Rickey agreed and

Bavasi returned to Brooklyn, believing that one day Roberto Clemente would be playing left field for the Dodgers.

Three days later he got a call alerting him that the Pirates were drafting Clemente at the owners' meeting in Chicago.

What happened to the deal with Rickey? he asked.

It seemed that Walter O'Malley, who had never forgiven Rickey for squeezing him for an extra fifty thousand dollars on his sale of Dodger shares, had harsh things to say about Rickey in front of the other baseball executives. Rickey heard what O'Malley had said. In retribution, he plucked and signed Clemente, who would one day be inducted into the Hall of Fame.

IN 1956, WALTER O'Malley had five black men on his payroll and was very eager to rid himself of one of them. Three times that season he told Bavasi to see what he could get for Jackie Robinson.

One of the pleasures of Bavasi's job was the freedom O'Malley granted him to run the team. He did not interfere with signings and trades. That is, he did not interfere except on four occasions: with Roberto Clemente, Joe Black, Jackie Robinson, and, later, with Maury Wills. With the exception of Clemente, who had merely represented to him one black man too many, the other three were black men who had offended his sensibilities. O'Malley had told Bavasi to get rid of Joe Black, a pitcher of great talent, after Black had sent a case of champagne to the press box to thank the writers after they'd voted him Rookie of the Year in 1952. "Walter thought he was getting too big for his britches," Bavasi later said. He had Wills, the best base-stealer of his time, traded to Pittsburgh in 1966 after Wills had left a goodwill tour to Japan early to appear at a banjo concert in Hawaii. O'Malley regarded this as insulting the Japanese. Of Wills and Black, Bavasi said, "They didn't act the way he thought they should act."

Bavasi did not underestimate the degree of O'Malley's dislike for Robinson. Nor did he doubt O'Malley's resentment of anyone on the team being more prominent than him: "Walter didn't like people taking any thunder away from him."

Still, Bavasi resisted O'Malley's entreaties to see what he might get for Jackie Robinson. "Without him we lose," he told O'Malley. "With him we win."

———

SO ROBINSON WAS left to try to prove that he still had worth to Walter Alston, a manager with whom he shared a mutual disregard. Robinson had thought little of Alston when he was hired to replace Charlie Dressen in 1954, and, as was his habit, made his disdain all too clear. Alston, for his part, regarded the aging Robinson as a part-time player. And by 1955, as Robinson's hitting dipped well below .300, that is what Alston made him.

With Randy Jackson hitting and playing well at third, Robinson started working out at second base. Charley Neal and Jim Gilliam had been playing Robinson's old position: both struggled to turn the double play. Robinson had not played second in four years.

"I'm being realistic," he told Bill Roeder of the *World-Telegram*. "Second base is the only place where I can break in, so I'm going to let them see me there."

He insisted that although he had moved to third years earlier as he began slowing down, he could still play second base. "I know this much: I'm a step faster than I have been for a couple of years, and I'll still make the double play," he said, sounding very much like a man trying to convince himself and everyone else that he was not yet done. "You never lose that."

So he fielded ground balls hit by Billy Herman, a Dodger coach. And when Roeder asked if Alston had been watching him, he replied, "I don't know. But I got Herman hitting to me, and if I look good Billy will say something."

If he did, Alston paid him little mind. Charley Neal and Jim Gilliam took turns at second base, and Jackie Robinson still sat.

3 | GAINS AND LOSSES

The Milwaukee Braves arrived in Brooklyn on Friday, June 15, with one manager, and at the end of the weekend left town with another. They had opened their season of lofty expectations managed by Charlie Grimm. Grimm liked to joke and laugh and play the guitar left-handed. Not for nothing was he dubbed "Jolly Charlie." In spring training, however, he was anything but. He had come to Florida under the cloud of a bold prediction: in October 1955, after the Braves finished second to the Dodgers, Milton

Richman of the United Press wrote that if Milwaukee was not in first place on June 15, 1956, Grimm would be out of a job. Though it might have been easy to dismiss Richman's prediction as too distant to be taken seriously, Grimm acted as if the words had come from the Temple at Delphi.

He was not himself in Florida. He was not funny anymore. He was tense and his tension spread to his players, who had always liked him. He was quick to pull a pitcher who appeared to be faltering. This, in turn, so rattled the pitchers that as soon as they surrendered a couple of hits they looked toward the dugout, assuming that their once-buoyant manager was on his way. The Braves had opened well and spent the early weeks close to the top of the standings in a race many believed they could win. But they were an anxious club, and by the time the Dodgers arrived at County Stadium in early June they were in the midst of a home stand of mythic failure. The Dodger victories were but two in a fifteen-game stretch in which the Braves lost ten. The Braves lost to good teams and weak teams, and the day after the Dodgers beat them for the second time, the team's general manager, John Quinn, arrived at the clubhouse door and told Grimm that he wished to address the team. Quinn was seldom seen in the clubhouse.

He lit into his team, berating them for failing the fans and for failing themselves, as well. But Charlie Grimm found this unacceptable. When Quinn was gone he told the players that the boss was wrong: they were not quitting; they were trying *too hard*. He believed in them. And while Grimm's kind words resonated—the Braves won the next day—their impact was short-lived. The Braves were sinking when they arrived in Brooklyn. They had left Milwaukee besieged by their heckling and disappointed fans, and they were left to wonder how much time Grimm had left.

Grimm, meanwhile, went to his superiors and asked where he stood. They made no commitments. The Braves dropped the Friday night opener at a crowded Ebbets Field, 5 to 4, when the Dodgers, who'd been trailing, scored in the seventh and eighth and won with two out in the bottom of the ninth on Rube Walker's single with the bases loaded. Ed Roebuck won in relief of Sal Maglie. The Dodgers took them on Saturday, too, 3 to 2, on Duke Snider's fifteenth home run of the season. Brooklyn had now won six in a row. And with the Saturday loss, Charlie Grimm was granted the nicety of announcing his resignation.

Sunday dawned with Fred Haney managing the Braves. Where Grimm was pleasant and doughy-faced, Fred Haney, a Braves' coach, looked like Harry Truman in a baseball uniform. He was a man of rules and quick reprimands for sloppy play; he was the sort of person of whom people were quick to say that, really, when you got to know him you saw that he *did* have a sense of humor. But now, at the close of a weekend that began with the Braves ready for the plucking, the Dodgers let them slip away.

Milwaukee won twice on Father's Day, before the biggest crowd of the season, 34,394. The Braves took the first game 5 to 4, when Joe Adcock did what no man had done before—hit a home run over the 83-foot left field roof at Ebbets Field. The blow came against Ed Roebuck, who'd retired ten Braves in a row but who then surrendered the game winner in the top of the ninth. While the press box wags tried to calculate the length of Adcock's shot, eleven-year-old Fred Gordon found the ball under a car. Fred was one of the boys who congregated by the hot dog stand on the corner of McKeever Place, waiting to catch foul balls that made their way over the fence. The hot dog peddler kept the game on the radio, and the boys would listen for word of balls coming their way. Fred found the ball after a ten-minute search. A policeman escorted him to the Milwaukee clubhouse between games. Fred gave the ball to Adcock, who gave him in return two new ones and a Braves' cap. The Dodgers, learning that young Fred was a Brooklyn fan, gave him a cap, too.

Walter Alston, meanwhile, called on the reliable Don Newcombe to pitch the second game. Adcock homered against him, too. The Braves took the nightcap 3 to 1. They departed for Pittsburgh, leaving the Dodgers and the beat writers to contemplate what the Braves had just done.

TALK TURNED, INEVITABLY, to 1955. Roscoe McGowan of the *Times* had already broken out his adding machine in late May and produced numbers that might not have been discouraging had they not been compared to data from the championship season. The Dodgers were running eight games behind their breathtaking pace of a year before, when they'd won 24 out of their first 27 games and stood well in front of the rest of the league. The beat fellows took stabs at philosophy—"What's wrong with the Dodgers?"—and at attempting to read the opaque mind of Walter Alston. McGowan called Alston at home one morning. It was ten o'clock, but McGowan was pretty sure he'd woken him. Still, he wanted the manager's assessment of what ailed his team.

Alston was a man who spoke as if he would rather visit a periodontist than offer a pungent quote. He did tell McGowan what everyone already knew: that the hitters the team relied on were not hitting; that the starting pitching was faltering—time and again Alston was compelled to call on Labine, Roebuck, and Don Bessent to bail out his starters. But he was seeing some pleasant surprises: Randy Jackson excelling at third base and Roger Craig performing well on the mound. Sal Maglie was as good as any pitcher on the team.

Yet there was talk of relegating Carl Erskine to the bull pen until he could rediscover what got men out. Erskine was so desperate that he even got Irving Rudd to come out with a movie camera and film him pitching, so he could see what he might be doing wrong. Dodgers were also getting hurt. Newcombe was complaining of a sore shoulder. Sandy Koufax, who'd pitched well, had hurt his arm and was out for ten days. Duke Snider had a sore leg and his hitting was not the same.

Buzzie Bavasi did what he could to supply Alston with fresh bodies: he called up Rocky Nelson from Montreal in the hope that Nelson, who'd been crushing minor league pitching, might at last fulfill his great promise and hit home runs in the majors. The trading deadline, however, came and went, and the team, for better or worse, was much as it had been for years. This, in turn, allowed speculation to return to the theme that had haunted the Dodgers since Vero Beach: age.

That they were only a year older than the team that had beaten the Yankees seemed not to matter at all. They were no longer playing as they had when they were young men. And because the core players had been around so long, their fans had little trouble recalling what they had looked like when they were pushing twenty-five, not thirty-five. "Sure they're older," Alston told Roscoe McGowan. "But they're not that old."

McGowan wrote for *The Sporting News* as well as for the *Times* because, he confided to Frank Graham, Jr., *The Sporting News* gave him license to create that the staid *Times* sports section denied him. The question of age was a poet's dream, an opportunity McGowan did not let slip by.

"Probably these old Dodgers do not need any special urging," he wrote. "They've been to the wars and they know what the battle toward triumph entails."

Perhaps, he went on, Alston might do well to call his troops together and address them as Ulysses had spoken to his mariners. And here he let Homer do the talking for him: "Some work of noble men may yet be done, Not unbecoming men that strove with Gods." Okay, maybe the Yankees weren't "gods," McGowan felt compelled to add, but they were still the champions the Dodgers had vanquished—"a thrill the 'old pros,' especially Captain Reese, will never forget."

Meanwhile, for the older fellows, rest was a commodity in short supply: even if Reese wanted to sit out a game, he was now without the luxury of a backup: On June 23, Hal Jeffcoat of the Reds hit Don Zimmer, the second-string shortstop, in the face with a fastball. The pitch left him with a concussion and a broken cheekbone and he was done for the season. Reese came to visit him at Long Island College Hospital, where surgeons put Zimmer's sunken cheekbone back into place. "Getting yourself hit just before a double-header," Reese teased him, "just when I figured I was going to take it easy."

ON MONTAGUE STREET, Buzzie Bavasi sensed a turn toward despair. A door connected his office to Walter O'Malley's. O'Malley almost always left the door open. But for a week he'd kept it closed.

It did not take a man of O'Malley's political wisdom to recognize what was happening with his stadium project. On the surface things were proceeding: the mayor's office announced, once again, that it was close to naming the three members of the Brooklyn Sports Authority. The engineers had submitted their report to John Cashmore's office. The report confirmed that a stadium indeed could be built on the meat market site. Traffic could be rerouted and the railroad tracks moved. They estimated the cost of the land at $2.4 million. The stadium itself would cost $9 million with a dome, or $7 million without one.

But in truth the plan was stalled. The mayor was having a difficult time getting people to serve on the authority. And Robert Moses applied yet another dagger in the side. Asked whether the project was economically feasible, he replied, simply and cryptically, "I don't know." It was a discouraging prognosis for a project whose success rested on finding buyers willing to risk buying the millions of dollars in bonds that the sports authority could issue. Moses, meanwhile, had made sure that he was not going to allow Cashmore to once again cut him out of the loop: the engineers submitted their study to the borough president's planning consultant, Edwin Salmon. Salmon, however, owed his job not to John Cashmore but to Robert Moses, who had pressed Cashmore to hire him after he was forced out as chairman of the city's planning commission.

Walter O'Malley now found himself in the position he most disliked: he was no longer a player in shaping his future. Moses had skillfully rendered his project a bureaucratic orphan, lost, without a powerful hand to shepherd it along. Worse still, O'Malley could not argue, and could not convince his well-placed friends, that Moses had undermined him. Robert Moses was no longer being flooded with letters on O'Malley's behalf; what was the point in writing, after all? There was a growing pile of engineering reports, fiscal documents, and billing statements to prove that the plan was being taken seriously. And so it was that in June 1956, Walter O'Malley closed himself off in his office and weighed his limited options.

Buzzie Bavasi now saw an O'Malley he did not recognize. Bavasi was a shrewd judge of people, a necessary skill in getting a man to accept less money than he wanted, but to leave feeling good about it. He had seen many looks in O'Malley, but he had never seen him defeated.

Then, a week after he shut the door, O'Malley opened it and stepped into Bavasi's office. He was smiling.

"I just got a call from Los Angeles," he said. "They say they'll have a proposition for us in six months. We've got something going for us. Now we have something to work with. I think we're going to get what we want."

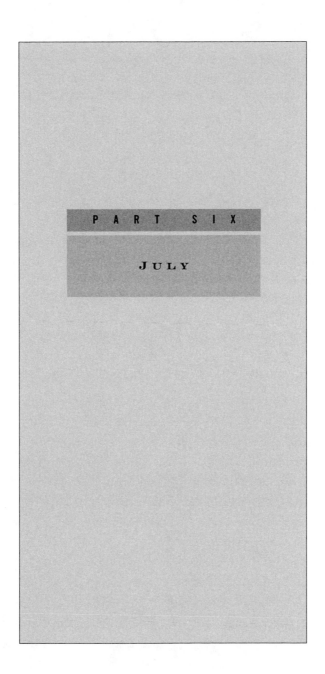

PART SIX

JULY

1 | THE SECRET SPEECH

Had Charlie Dressen or Leo Durocher still managed the Dodgers, the events in the visiting clubhouse at Milwaukee's County Stadium on Friday night, July 13, might have transpired without comment, or perhaps any attention at all. But Walter Alston managed the team, which meant that incidents or words that shifted attention away from his players and onto him were extraordinary. This is not to say that Alston's name did not appear in the papers: he was cited for his benchings, lineup shifts, and pitching changes, and did provide the occasional, enervating quote. But these tasks came with the job, and Alston went about them in his distant and phlegmatic way.

Walter Alston was forty-five years old and now, in his third year as a major league manager, had succeeded in gaining the respect of most of his players. This had not come easily, in good measure because he had come to managing after a notably unsuccessful career as a player. His life as a player had begun with promise; in 1936, his second season in organized ball, he led the Mid-Atlantic League with thirty-five home runs. The Cardinals summoned him to St. Louis. He came to bat once, to pinch hit for Johnny Mize, a fearsome hitter. He struck out. He never again batted in the majors. Instead, the Cardinals sent him down and Alston joined the saddest of baseball fraternities: the career minor leaguer. He shifted from position to position, never making enough of an impression to prompt a call to return him to the big leagues. He was big and strong and hit for power in the minor league mid-levels; but even in the war years he did not warrant a call-up. Finally, in 1944, even with the good players still in the military, Rochester of the International League released him. He was thirty-three years old.

His career with the Cardinal organization, however, had provided one bit of luck: Branch Rickey got to know him, and thought well enough of Alston to offer him the managing job in Trenton, of the International League. He managed—and played—in New Jersey for two years, before moving on and up in the Dodger organization, to Nashua, New Hampshire; Pueblo, Colorado; St. Paul, Minnesota; and finally to Brooklyn's top farm team, Montreal, after his St. Paul team won the "Junior" World Series—the championship of the bush leagues. At Nashua, where he worked for Buzzie Bavasi, he did accomplish what no man had done before: he made a black man a manager, if only briefly. Sensing that he was about to be tossed from a game, he turned to his catcher, Roy Campanella, and told him that if the umpire ejected him, Campy was to run the team. "Anybody got a problem with that?" Alston asked his players. No one said he did. The umpire gave Alston the thumb, and, to the delight of his teammate Don Newcombe, Roy Campanella—whom Walter O'Malley later believed might one day make a fine *coach*—managed a team of white men without comment or incident.

The men who had played for him in the minors, Labine among them, thought well of Alston. Others, Robinson in particular, did not. They tested him that first year, intentionally arriving late for practice and treating him like a man not worthy of their company. The Giants won the pennant that season. But in 1955, after the acrimonious spring capped by Newcombe's refusal to pitch batting practice, the Dodgers won their championship and Alston's job was safe.

While no one was now suggesting that his job was anything but secure, Alston was wearying of the inconsistent play of his champions. He tried cajoling them, and when that did not work he brought to his side Joe Becker, the pitching coach, hoping that Becker, a "holler guy," might give the team a spark. He shifted his lineup and sat his stars, and while the team might win a few in a row, they were just as prone to even things out with a series of dispiriting losses. Only one Dodger had been selected by the other managers to the National League All-Star Team, Clem Labine, whom Alston had called on to relieve in nearly half of the team's games. The Dodgers had gone 18 and 12 in June, good enough to move them to eight games over the mediocrity line of .500. They were in third place, a game behind the first-place Braves in what the adding machine men now declared one of the four closest pennant races in the history of the National League—five teams separated by a mere three and a half games.

The Dodgers were beating the weak teams, the Cubs, Phillies, and crosstown Giants, but not the Reds and Braves. Don Newcombe was nursing a sore shoulder and had not pitched since June 21, or won since the eleventh. Erskine finally won in relief, and then again in a game he could not finish. Time and again Alston felt compelled to call to the bull pen; the starters were fading well before the ninth inning. Milwaukee had won eleven in a row under Fred Haney, but the Reds were playing just as well and were now in first place, a game and a half ahead of the Braves and two in front of the Dodgers.

Walter Alston managed the National League All-Stars, an honor that came with Brooklyn's winning the 1955 pennant. He offered, as was his privilege, slots as reserves to Snider, Campanella, and Jim Gilliam, and then enjoyed a brief respite from his team's confounding play: the National League trounced the American 7 to 3 at Griffith Stadium in Washington, a park so cramped—it sat twenty-nine thousand—it made Ebbets Field feel spacious.

With the end of the three-day All-Star break, the Dodgers reconvened in Milwaukee. As their prevailing luck would have it they would open the second half of the season with a doubleheader against the Braves.

They faced Bob Buhl in the opener, and Buhl, who always pitched well against them, shut the Dodgers out on six hits. Rain washed out the night-cap. So the teams played two on Friday, the thirteenth.

IT WAS DICK Young who broke the story of what took place in the visiting club-house after the Braves scored six runs against Don Newcombe in the first inning of the first game, then surrendered the lead, but still rallied to beat the Dodgers 8 to 6.

Young opened his column, "Clubhouse Confidential," by first citing the manifesto tacked by the Milwaukee clubhouse door: "What You See In Here, What You Say In Here, What You Hear In Here, Let It Stay In Here, When You Leave Here." With that little nod to baseball's code of *omerta*, he proceeded, snarkily, to tell what, in fact, had not stayed "in here." "Every so often," Young wrote, in his bard-of-the-sidewalks voice, "something hap-pens, or is said, that is so hot it boils over and runs out of the clubhouse."

The Dodgers had just botched the opener—Furillo misplayed a Hank Aaron fly ball into a double, Labine dropped a throw to first, and the lead they'd built was gone. Now the clubhouse door was closed. The players sat at their cubicles. And Walter Alston started ranting. He walked up and down in the clubhouse. And as he did, Young wrote, he bellowed—"I don't think you can play under pressure. If this doesn't stop, I'm going to call up a bunch of kids and play them, and sit down all the stars."

Or words to that effect. Young's tip and the re-creation of Alston's tirade came from that most despised of baseball sources (at least from the players' perspective)—the anonymous tipster. The source provided Young with player reaction, too: they either ignored Alston or walked away. No matter. Alston had not only berated his veteran players but, Young reported, had called them "gutless." "Gutless" is a bad thing to call a baseball player; it questions his manhood. To level the charge, Young noted, meant the accuser would do well to ball his fists and be ready to fight. In the days to come the question of whether Alston had, in fact, used the word "gutless," the implications of its use, and the explosion itself were analyzed and considered, over and over again. Leonard Koppett of the *Post*, for instance, had it differently: Alston had called the Dodgers "a bunch of choke-up guys with their tails flying out at home plate who couldn't win under pressure." If this was so, the charge was still bad, though not quite as bad as "gutless." Alston told Roscoe McGowan of the *Times* that he hadn't used the word "gutless," but admitted that he had "told them off." "If I did say it I shouldn't have," Alston said, recognizing the enduring damage that using "gutless" might have brought him. "I've tried everything—I tried encouraging them and I tried being tough."

He went on. "I thought I'd stir them up. If they're mad, that's all right, in fact, that's the idea. I just hope they stay mad enough to go out and win some games."

Things, however, did not go according to plan. The Dodgers dropped the second game of the bad-luck doubleheader: they did emerge from the clubhouse after Alston had calmed down and scored four runs in the top of the first inning, but then were undone by a Joe Adcock grand slam. They lost on Saturday and again Sunday, before big and noisy crowds in what Tommy Holmes, unable to resist some big city snobbery, liked to call "the Great American Cheeselands." For their part, the Milwaukee faithful who jammed County Stadium were taking great pleasure in beating the New Yorkers: it did not matter that the Dodgers represented an *outer borough*; they were from "back east" and were perennial winners whom people in the smaller cities were ever more eager to see lose.

Swept in Milwaukee, the Dodgers were now losers of five in a row. They were sinking in the standings: they stood five games behind the Braves. The losing streak and clubhouse acrimony were providing grist for those who enjoyed some anti–New York schadenfreude. The Dodgers arrived in Chicago a team divided between Alston backers and Alston detractors. The beat fellows, seizing on Young's scoop, began turning over rocks for a peek of their own.

The view was not pretty. "Alston is dissatisfied with his Dodger ballclub," Koppett wrote, "and his players are even more bitterly dissatisfied with him." Players whispered, sotto voce, that they did not like his lineups, or his pitching changes, or the plays he called from the bench. He was, said the critics among them, indecisive. "Getting us mad isn't going to win games," another unnamed player told Bill Roeder of the *World-Telegram*. "It's true we haven't been doing very well but neither has he. We all think he pulls too many rocks."

That all this was said anonymously did not sit well with such players as Duke Snider, who took pride in not ducking even from his most ill-advised comments. Snider defended Alston, as did Erskine. But the voice that mattered most was that of Pee Wee Reese. And when the time came for him to speak, the captain made it clear that he wanted the sniping over.

"If Alston used the term 'gutless' I never heard him say it," Reese told Roscoe McGowan. Then, choosing his words with a lawyer's precision, he added, "If he did say we couldn't play under pressure—which I don't recall him saying—I'm sure he didn't mean it. He knows we won the last World Series and you certainly play under pressure in the Series. Even if he did say it, under such circumstances a manager will say things he doesn't necessarily mean."

It was a masterful piece of rhetoric. Reese offered his manager not a fig leaf but a sequoia: we all know what he said and we are not going to take his words to heart; besides, we've been lousy. Reese, never one to shy from the burdens of his office, even took a bullet for Walter Alston, and knew his friend Erskine would be willing to take one, too: "Is he responsible for my hitting .240," Reese asked, "or for Erskine's 6 and 6 record?"

The front office was pleased. O'Malley, insisting that Alston was his manager—"He's my man, he always has been"—was saddened by the mess the leak had caused: "What goes on in the privacy of the clubhouse should remain there, like an argument between a father and son at home." He sent Reese a telegram, and one to Erskine, too, thanking them for supporting Alston. "Captain," he wrote, his written prose as orotund as his spoken words, "I had an idea that you would be present when the roll was called to defend the manager and resent recent anonymous quotes."

But just to keep things boiling at an uncomfortable temperature, Don Newcombe opened a series against the Cubs by getting himself locked in a nasty game of "beanball" at Wrigley Field. This unwise competition with the former Dodger pitcher, Jim Hughes, began when Gene Baker hit the first grand slam that Newcombe had ever surrendered in the major leagues. Taken aback, Newcombe knocked down Baker with a pitch when he came to bat in the fifth. And just to make his point clear, he knocked down Dee Fondy, Jim King, and Walter Moryn, too. For his part, Hughes hit Newcombe in the leg as punishment for Gil Hodges' home run. He also knocked Campanella to the ground, which seemed doubly unfair considering that Campy's broken right hand hurt so much he was striking out time and again. Finally, with Newcombe back on the mound, the umpires summoned both managers and advised them that the brushbacks were over.

Newcombe, whose temper was explosive, stomped over and, his broad shoulders shaking, insisted, less than politely, that he had no intention of curbing himself. Artie Gore, the umpire crew chief, advised him to desist or face a ten-day ejection, at which point Alston, seeing how Newcombe was mumbling to himself and kicking at the dirt like a bull preparing to charge, pulled him from the game. Now Newcombe was indeed upset. He took off his mitt, tossed it over the foul line, and threw the ball to the ground. "In the mood he was in, I couldn't risk letting him continue," Alston said.

Newcombe smoldered all through the afternoon and well into the night, but by the morning appeared calm. "Don't worry about my roomie," said Roy Campanella. "He's okay now but it took me most of the evening to convince him that Alston isn't against him."

Newcombe may have been fine with his manager but not with the umpires. In his wrath he had committed professional blasphemy: he called them "gutless." And this time the word was confirmed. When the team reached Cincinnati, he was summoned to the office of the National League commissioner, Warren Giles. Facing a stiff fine and suspension, Newcombe prudently signed a statement insisting that he never said it.

The Dodgers, meanwhile, dropped two to the Reds—the second, a heartbreaker for Sandy Koufax, who'd pitched well, but saw his victory vanish when Ted Kluszewski singled with the bases loaded off Clem Labine in the bottom of the ninth. And, as if the Fates had voted unanimously to tip the cosmic scales to Brooklyn's disadvantage, Duke Snider was accosted on his way to the clubhouse by Ralph Baumel, a tall and broad Reds fan from Mason, Ohio.

"What's the matter, Duke, ain't you got no guts?" he yelled. The word now seemed to be on the tip of every tongue.

The two exchanged words. Then they exchanged blows. Baumel emerged from the encounter with a bloody face and two missing teeth.

The following morning the two men appeared before Municipal Court Judge Clarence Denning, who suggested they shake hands and make up. Baumel hesitated.

"What do you want?" the judge asked. "Your Redlegs won the game last night, didn't they?"

Even with his missing teeth, Ralph Baumel could not resist a Brooklyn-hater's smile.

2 | THE RAINY SEASON

July that year was a rotten month to be off from school, to be in day camp, to have a cabana at Brighton Beach. It rained every day but a handful for the first three weeks of the month. If it did not rain on Saturday it rained on Sunday, and there was little point in planning a trip to Jones Beach, or a picnic at Prospect Park, or an afternoon at the ballpark, where if the Dodgers were not on the road the umpires were likely to look at the sky and suggest that everyone come back and try again tomorrow. July was warm and steamy, and in Canarsie people were begging the city to spray for mosquitoes.

It was a month when little seemed as appealing as an afternoon at the Albee, Alpine, or Oriental Theaters, which offered a good four hours of air-conditioned diversion with such double features as *Forbidden Planet* and *Thunder over Arizona*, or *The Man Who Knew Too Much* and Randolph Scott in *A Lawless Street*. The second-run houses like the Kenmore and

Dyker had Joel McCrae in *The First Texan,* a picture that came with a price: topping the bill was *Crime in the Streets*, with Sal Mineo and John Cassavetes. *Crime in the Streets* was a parents' nightmare, a tale of juvenile delinquency that made the winter's hit, James Dean's *Rebel Without a Cause*, look like an Andy Hardy comedy. In *Crime in the Streets* the young people said things like "Go, man" and "Crazy," fought rival gangs with knives and broken beer bottles, beat their rivals mercilessly, and even planned a murder. The young men wanted only to be tough. Never mind that they wore white sweaters and plaid shirts; they were very bad and hopelessly misunderstood—what mother had time for her villainous son, Frankie Dane, when she was single and had to work in a *diner*? Luckily, a social worker appeared in the end to explain to Frankie that all he really wanted to be was loved.

The critics dismissed *Crime in the Streets*; it looks, wrote Bosley Crowther in the *Times*, "like one of those B-grade agonies of yore." But they failed to grasp its success in capturing the zeitgeist: because even if parents were forbidding their children from seeing *Crime in the Streets* and even if they were reluctant to see it for themselves, they were still afraid for their children and about the perils that awaited them on the streets. Even when the skies cleared and the children were out and occupied there appeared to be ample reason for concern. Young people sat in the park and listened to the radio, and while there were still good and pleasant tunes—Nelson Riddle's "Lisbon Antigua" was a hit—the charts were littered with discomfiting songs by the Platters, Frankie Lymon, Carl Perkins, and, in the Top 10, no less than three songs by Elvis Presley. And now Ed Sullivan himself, the arbiter of acceptable entertainment, was paying Presley fifty thousand dollars to appear on his Sunday night show *three times*. Brooklyn's parks, which the *World-Telegram* reported were now eerily deserted at night, were reportedly littered with teenagers engaged in "necking parties." So disturbing was this development that one local judge—a former Brooklyn district attorney named Miles McDonald—called for a police crackdown in the parks' secluded places, lest Brooklyn's youth fall prey to such "serious social problems as illegitimate children."

Even if the canoodling did not lead to unwanted pregnancies, it was triggering a surge of syphilis and gonorrhea among teenagers. The United States Public Health Service was now estimating that 200,000 American teenagers would contract a venereal disease in 1956 alone. While the health service was trying to calculate the potential infection rates—one in every 200 teenagers could be infected by the year's end—police department statisticians were preparing a report that was sure to make parents long for the first day back at school: while crime in general was down, it was surging among teenagers.

In late July the police department reported a 40 percent surge since 1955 in arrests of minors for such crimes as murder, rape, burglary, and robbery. In the first six months of 1956 alone the department had arrested 4,826 boys and girls under age sixteen—among them five for murder, 82 for rape, 362 for assault, and 533 for car theft. The papers were filled with news of crimes of the most troubling sort—"3 Boy Vandals Admit Setting 8 Boro Fires" and "Armed Girls Help Youths Terrorize Church Group"—as well as data that confirmed all of the worst suspicions about the horrific things that teenagers were doing with themselves—"Teen Crime on Rise; Parents Are Warned."

Theories of causes abounded. Perhaps, some suggested, the young people were suffering from a collective case of teenage anomie. This emptiness and despair came with the terrible knowledge that the good and prosperous life their parents were working so hard to provide—lives so much richer than their parents had known as children of the Great Depression—could be incinerated in an instant by one of those Soviet nuclear missiles pointed America's way. And lest they try to ignore the perilous state of their existences, their parents' generation provided chilling reminders. On the afternoon of July 20, in fact, the entire nation, President Eisenhower included, dropped everything for fifteen minutes for a national "civil defense drill." At 4:10 P.M. air-raid signals sounded and across the city people hurried to underground shelters. Times Square was evacuated. Twenty-four doctors and nurses at Bellevue Hospital stood on alert in anticipation of the many "casualties" from the five hydrogen bombs "dropped" on New York alone—including the one that "hit" the intersection of Linden Boulevard and New York Avenue in Brooklyn, about a mile from Ebbets Field.

It was in the midst of this panic about the fate of the urban teenager that Lawrence Williams returned to his parents' home in Bedford-Stuyvesant and set about trying to establish his place in the world. Lawrence was fifteen. He had been living for several months with his aunt, uncle, and cousin Fred in nearby Williamsburg. Lawrence was one of five children, and because Fred was an only child Lawrence's aunt had prevailed upon his mother to let Lawrence live with them so that Fred might have a companion close to his own age. The time with Fred was useful for Lawrence because Fred was not only five years older but was, in Lawrence's estimation, the coolest person he had ever met. It was from Fred that Lawrence learned the importance of bathing, of changing his underwear every day, and the social advantages that came to those who knew how to dress well. Fred affected the look of a jazz musician: chino slacks with buckles in the back, a stingy brimmed hat, argyle socks. His hair was processed with "Tony Curtis" curls. Fred was a "coolie," which meant he had no gang affiliation. Some "coolies" were "turkeys" and "creeps," but not Fred, who possessed the air of a young man who did not need to be a member of a gang to know where he fit in. Lawrence was not quite so assured.

In the spring of 1956, Lawrence started missing his brothers and sisters, so he came home. But Lawrence found Bedford-Stuyvesant a confounding place. He noticed, for instance, that white people were moving out and that many black people took this as an insult, evidence that the white people did not want to be near them anymore. But others in Bedford-Stuyvesant delighted in the white exodus because, they felt, the neighborhood was truly becoming theirs. Lawrence's father owned a bar and his mother a hairdressing salon. This meant that while they were by no means rich they had enough money for such weekend diversions as a trip to Ebbets Field. Lawrence had been going to Ebbets Field since he was eleven years old and understood that a trip to the ballpark meant dressing appropriately: a suit, a hat, pressed slacks. The ballpark was an affordable outing, but an outing nonetheless which meant that in Lawrence's family, like so many others in Bedford-Stuyvesant, there was the understanding that they "would be seen." Lawrence's mother was not about to let her family be seen in anything but their best.

Just as the Dodgers had helped Sam Qualiarini order his universe, so too did the team help Lawrence make sense of himself and his place. As it happened, Lawrence's teachers at Junior High School 248 had made it clear to him that they regarded black people as inferior; none of them, he later recalled, ever mentioned the accomplishments of such men as Booker

T. Washington and George Washington Carver. Worse still, his biology teacher insisted that members of the Negro race possessed a brain smaller than those of the Caucasian, Mongol, or Indian.

The Dodgers, Lawrence believed, proved this myth of racial inferiority false. The Dodgers had Jackie Robinson and Robinson had proven all the white bigots and skeptics wrong when he became a star in a game that had excluded black people. Now the Dodgers had Don Newcombe, too, whose menacing edge appealed to Lawrence. And though Lawrence liked Roy Campanella he was drawn to Robinson, especially because Robinson was dark-skinned. Lawrence had noticed that the girls in Bedford-Stuyvesant preferred lighter-skinned boys. Lawrence had dark skin, like Robinson. Robinson made Lawrence believe that a dark-skinned teenager could be popular, too. He was right. But this popularity would only make life more complicated for Lawrence.

Bedford-Stuyvesant was a balkanized neighborhood where turf was divided and claimed by rival gangs. There were gangs elsewhere in Brooklyn. Lawrence had learned in Williamsburg, for instance, that if he swam at the McCarren Park pool he risked being stomped by the white gangs like the El Rebops and Vikings. When Lawrence returned to Bedford-Stuyvesant he recognized the perils awaiting those who were not joiners; his cousin Fred could get away with it, but then his cousin was so cool that people left him alone. But Lawrence's older brother, Frank, was a member of the Buccaneers. Frank was a quiet young man, so quiet, in fact, that he was nicknamed "Undertaker." Frank was now close to graduating from the Buccaneers, which like many of the other Bedford-Stuyvesant gangs—the Bishops, the Chaplains, the El Quintos—was going through a generational change: the older members were leaving for work, and marriage. Though some lingered a little too long, the gangs were giving way to a new generation of members, who understood the values of loyalty and bravery. They also knew that if they wanted to chase girls, if they wanted to go to parties, and if they just wanted to feel safe they needed a gang behind them. Lawrence learned this one night when, in what was becoming a relentless pursuit of girls, he went to a party at the Marcy Avenue projects, but failed to take into account that the party was taking place on the Chaplains' turf. The Chaplains did not want Lawrence at a party with their girls on their turf. They called for him to come downstairs and Lawrence, believing it was wiser to take his blows outside than being trapped inside, complied. The Chaplains surrounded him, and as Lawrence started taking off his coat they began pummeling him. Somehow, amidst the fists, Lawrence spotted a gap in the Chaplains' ranks. He broke and ran as fast as he could. The Chaplains chased him but soon gave up. Lawrence, however, had seen enough. "A lot of the problems," he later said, "came from the young girls."

So Lawrence became a Buccaneer. Not long afterward he was in school at Brooklyn Automotive High School and staring down at a desk scarred with nicknames. He still needed one. There, dug into the desk, was a name that struck him as just right: Keno. In time his new friends in the Buccaneers took names that sounded a lot like his: Dino, Reno, Chino. And because they represented the new and eager members of the Buccaneers, the gang became ever more theirs. In time they were brawling with the Chaplains. They had concocted such initiation rituals as holding new members upside down from a roof to see if they would scream; crying was evidence of being a "punk" and no punks could join the Buccaneers. They shook down "coolies" for change, making them jump up and down to see if anything was rattling in their pockets. They would soon start studying and refining techniques of street combat, such as drawing their rivals into an ambush by having them first chase a group of fifteen Buccaneers, only to have a larger force ready and waiting with chains, belts, pipes, car antennas, knives, and that most lethal though imprecise gang war weapon, the zip gun—a metal pipe rigged with rubber bands and a nail and capable of firing a single bullet at a time, like a musket.

The battles were organized and ritualized which meant that even the violence in Lawrence's world felt ordered and clear. He had found a safe place among the members of the Buccaneers. He also began noticing that he possessed the qualities that made the other young men follow him and the girls seek his company. He was not as cool as his cousin Fred. He was different. "I was a little more meaner," he later said. "I became a real bad guy." So bad, in fact, that soon his mother would be warning him to stay clear of the young man people called Keno. Keno, she told him gravely and innocently, would only bring him harm.

3 | THE SHAPE OF THINGS TO COME

In the last week of July, on the front page of the *World-Telegram*, the paper whose Brooklyn edition had assumed the mantle of the borough's own since the *Eagle* folded in 1955, there appeared a photograph of a baseball stadium the likes of which few had ever seen. It looked like a great, round fruit bowl suspended by seventeen buttresses that, with a squint and some imagination, might have been a band of soldiers supporting the bowl's weight on their shoulders. On top of the bowl sat a dome covered in mesh. The dome was off in a second photograph, which revealed, at the bottom of the bowl, a baseball diamond. By 1958, predicted sports columnist Dan Daniels, the Brooklyn Dodgers would be playing baseball there.

Daniels had good reason to believe this would really happen. The public debate that came with the unveiling of Walter O'Malley's stadium model focused on *which* corner of Flatbush and Atlantic Avenues the stadium would stand—*not* whether it would rise at all. While Robert Moses and the always-prudent O'Malley favored building the park over the Long Island Railroad tracks, the borough president, John Cashmore, wanted to see it across the street.

Mayor Wagner meanwhile had finally settled on the three members of the Brooklyn Sports Authority—a banker, a realtor, and a department store executive, who would all work without pay for the greater good of Brooklyn. Publicly, at least, Moses praised the three men and insisted that they be given the freedom to do their work. "Let the critics with their ever sharp harpoons lay off," he proclaimed in a written statement. "Let the Dodger fans refrain from throwing bottles and moaning that the Bums are being driven from Brooklyn to Cripple Creek. Let the inventors of plastic bubble roofs . . . atomic meat freezers, four-deck highway bridges and automatic parking hold their fire. Give the members a break. They will, I am sure, turn in a good score."

He closed this bit of Zeusian rhetoric with "Amen."

But privately Moses regarded the men as stooges, which together made them just the sort of sports authority he needed. The chairman, realtor Charles Mylod, was "slow, ponderous, believes successful businessmen can ipso facto solve all public problems, is actually a babe in the woods on City government," he wrote several months later to Jack Flynn. Moses did acknowledge charitably that Mylod was "no fool." Robert Blum, of Abraham & Straus, was "a wonderful fellow but lacks force." The third member, the banker Chester Allen, was, Moses wrote, "nothing."

Moses, of course, allowed himself to be prevailed upon by Robert Blum to offer his "advice." With that he drew up the agenda for the authority's first meeting. This he did with all the predatory skill of the fox in the hen-house. He advised, for instance, that the authority appoint an architect *other* than the acclaimed Gilmore Clarke. Clarke had angered Moses with his encouraging report on the viability of the stadium. He recommended that an attorney he knew, John McGrath, serve as the authority's counsel. He advised that a new study be conducted because, he suggested, the study commissioned by John Cashmore "magnified" the stadium, eliminated the "public improvements," and doomed the entire project to "failure."

He made sure to cut out Cashmore, who had used the little power he had to give the stadium plan its initial ballast in 1955: Moses wanted money that had been allocated to the borough president's office to be directed through the authority board. He gave the board a timetable. He wanted a report by November. His agenda had eleven items and was so comprehensive that he made it impossible to see that he was doing his best to make sure the stadium was never built.

THE DAY THE photograph of the stadium model ran was, for all appearances, the best day Walter O'Malley had had in a long time. But then O'Malley had said nothing publicly about the overture from Los Angeles, and the leverage it might yet bring him. In Brooklyn people were talking about his ballpark, noting its dimensions and such features as the "giant motors" capable of moving entire seating sections depending on whether the day's event was football, boxing, or, of course, baseball. The park could be converted into a vast conventional hall, too. "The Brooklyn stadium would cater to all sports and would be in use year round instead of being just a 77-game luxury arena for the baseball season," he said. He went on to cite the good work turned in on the project by his old engineering friend, Emil Praeger. There was no mention of the work of the young Princeton architecture student, Billy Kleinsasser, or of his mentor, J. Buckminster Fuller. Instead, O'Malley looked to the future, to a place and time where wise men would find new profits in the game.

Dan Daniels came by his office for a chat, and O'Malley, seizing on the attention and momentum of the stadium plan's unveiling, offered his views on the perils of dwelling in the past. As it happened, Ringling Brothers had just announced that its circus would no longer perform under the big top: the tent was folded for the last time in Pittsburgh; the circus was moving its 1957 season to air-conditioned indoor arenas. O'Malley, with an eye for a useful metaphor, seized upon the connection. "It's up to baseball to profit by the sad experience of the Greatest Show on Earth and to hasten to do something about the comfort and well being of the fans." Baseball stadiums, he explained, were uncomfortable places: there were too many ramps and stairs and older people had to exert themselves just to get to their seats. "How much longer can baseball hope to get away with it? Your motion picture theater has comfortable, wide seats. It is cool in summer, warm in winter. There is no standstill policy. Let baseball take all this to heart."

Baseball, he concluded, "must spruce up, clean up, attract the family. It has got to stop crying into its coke, and must fight the counterattractions with their own weapons. All of the considerations I have now enumerated enter into our planning for the new Brooklyn stadium. We have got to stop defying the people to come to our ball games."

He was not the agent of change. He was merely keeping up with the race to the future. He did not want to be left out. And it did not necessitate a Pollyanaish view of the world to believe that the future would bring good things to Brooklyn. The navy yard, which lost the repair job on the *Wisconsin* in May, did win the contract to build a new, cutting-edge aircraft carrier. People at the navy yard cheered when they heard the news, which like the weather was now so much more encouraging than it had been for a while.

The same, however, could not be said for the Dodgers.

4 | RESURRECTION

In the last week of July, the team returned home from St. Louis six games out of first place. They had not been this far back in the standings since 1954. Though they'd closed their thirteen-game road trip with doubleheader victories against the Cardinals, Tommy Holmes of the *Tribune* was not sanguine about their play or their prospects. The pleasant conclusion to the trip, he wrote, merely gave it "the look of deceptive mediocrity." The Dodgers had won six and lost seven, and six of those losses had come against the Braves and Reds. The Dodgers won where they could, which almost always meant in Chicago, where the Cubs could be relied upon to give the odd game away. One afternoon at Wrigley Field, for instance, Gene Baker, the Cub second baseman, elected to try his luck running down Sandy Amoros between first base and second, all the while ignoring Gil Hodges, who seized upon the blunder to jog home from third, giving the game to the Dodgers. "It was," Baker said, "just a mental lapse," one that Bill Roeder wrote would be forgotten—unless, of course, the Dodgers somehow managed to win the pennant by a single game.

The Dodgers were joined in St. Louis by Walter O'Malley, who seldom traveled with the team. Though his players were struggling, O'Malley found reason to be pleased: the visit to Busch Stadium had pushed the Dodgers' road attendance over one million, an indication not only of the team's popularity, if only to see the home team beat them, but of the handsome returns to the team's coffers for its share of the road revenue.

Fortune, at last, smiled the Dodgers' way: the team would be home for its next twenty-two games. But, as was fitting in this season of promise and aggravation, waiting for them at Ebbets Field were the Cincinnati Reds. The Reds stood in second place and the Dodgers had been as woeful against them as they'd been against the Braves. The pennant race, which had been so close only weeks before, had now righted itself into a three-team contest: Milwaukee, Cincinnati, which was two and a half games back; and, in distant third, the Dodgers. St. Louis, which led the pack of also-rans, had slipped to thirteen games out of first.

TWENTY-TWO THOUSAND people came to Ebbets Field for the opener to see what the Dodgers had left. They left happy. The Dodgers mauled the Reds, 10 to 5. Duke Snider hit two home runs, Sandy Amoros tripled twice, and Sal Maglie won his fourth game of the season. They won the next night, too, in Jersey City, when Snider, his hitting woes and court date now behind him, homered in the bottom of the ninth to win the game, 2 to 1. They completed the sweep on Thursday, at Ebbets Field, 5 to 3, and had now run their winning streak to five. The Braves, however, were in town, too, feasting on the woeful Giants, and keeping the Dodgers stuck at six back. So horrid was the Giants' play that their manager, Bill Rigney, locked the club-house door after an 11 to 0 drubbing and lit into his men. But then Rigney was a passionate man and the beat fellows felt compelled to note the tirade in the context of Alston's outburst in Milwaukee.

The Cubs were up next, and graciously allowed the Dodgers to run their winning streak to eight. Carl Erskine, who had struggled for weeks after his no-hitter, won his seventh straight. Maglie followed him, pitching his second complete game victory of the week. The streak might have reached nine, but the Dodgers slipped in the second game of a double-header on the last Sunday of the month. Milwaukee, however, conveniently lost in Philadelphia and, with the split, the Dodgers moved to four games back. The Braves boarded their train in Philadelphia and headed north through New Jersey, leaving the anxious writers who followed them to won-der whether they had what it took to win the pennant. The Dodgers, they reported, were surging. The Reds, though losers in Brooklyn, were still just two and a half games back in second place. And now the Braves, who had been playing so well, had just handed one to the woeful Phillies. So con-founding was the loss, that R. G. Lynch, the *Milwaukee Journal's* sports ed-itor and columnist—his daily rumination bore the decidedly un–Dick Youngish title, "Maybe I'm Wrong"—suggested that perhaps the Milwaukee catchers were calling for the *wrong pitches*. How else to explain the Braves' wonderful pitching staff losing nine games out of fifteen to a Phillies team collectively batting .246?

"Things like these," Lynch wrote, "make a man wonder if the Milwau-kee team is a smart one."

The Braves, however, were still in first place. They had beaten the Dodgers seven straight, in Milwaukee and at Ebbets Field. A sweep, or even three victories in their four-game series would open a gap between the Braves and the Dodgers that Brooklyn might never be able to overcome. Of course, if the Dodgers somehow managed to reverse their fortunes, the race would grow unnervingly tight—unnerving, that is, for the Braves, who un-like the Dodgers were not used to playing two months of baseball in which every game mattered.

WHILE THE YOUNGER Braves were not necessarily aware of what was happening to them, their veteran left fielder, Andy Pafko, understood the burden of trying to win a first championship. Pafko had played for the Dodgers in 1951 and 1952 and recognized the benefit Brooklyn enjoyed of having been through difficult times together: he had been with the Dodgers when Bobby Thomson, now a teammate with the Braves, hit the home run that gave the Giants the pennant; Pafko was playing left field that afternoon and watched the ball and the pennant sail out of the park. For the Dodgers, the novelty of winning had been replaced by a deeper need to do so, again and again. (Randy Jackson, who'd known nothing but losing with the Cubs, had seen the same thing: the Dodgers had won so often and had played in so many important games that they *expected* to win.) Forgotten in the wake of many World Series losses to the Yankees was the fact that the core of the Brooklyn team now chasing the Braves had been in every National League pennant race since 1947, and had won half of them.

Milwaukee, meanwhile, was still so excited by the newness of it all, Pafko saw, that every day at County Stadium had the carnival feel of the World Series. Fans came out early just to watch batting practice. Pafko, who had come to the Braves the year they moved from Boston, understood the city's enchantment with their team: until 1953 many of the Braves' fans had never seen a major league game. But there was more to the city's collective good feeling than baseball alone. Milwaukee that summer was a Chamber of Commerce booster's dream: the Braves were winning, and business was so good that the downtown merchants were taking it upon themselves to spruce up and remodel their stores. This was a wise investment of $3 million considering that even with the coming of the malls, people were still heading downtown to shop. Commerce was so good, employment so robust, payrolls so high that people were now saying that 1956 could well become Milwaukee's most prosperous year. The optimism was so infectious that Bill Eberly, the Braves' ticket manager, had already gotten five hundred requests for World Series tickets, even though the team was still in no position to put any on sale. The Braves were the hot ticket in town—the Braves-Dodgers game at County Stadium a month away on August 26 was already all but sold out. The Braves Booster Club boasted 27,000 members in 48 states and 17 different countries. A hundred of its members even made the trip east to follow the team. They'd each paid $189 for the trip and were having a wonderful time. They sat together and performed a snake dance in the aisles of the enemy ballparks, led by Jim Bird, a retired car salesman who carried a six-foot baseball bat. A cowbell followed and then came a banner proclaiming the unconditional love of those not yet bruised or tormented by affection: "Win or Lose, We Love Our Braves."

The Milwaukee Braves, too, were young and, in a baseball sense, innocents in need of a steady hand. Unfortunately, their veteran, Warren Spahn, although a marvelous pitcher, played only every fourth day: he could not be with the players on the field, talking and aligning them defensively, the way Pee Wee Reese did for the Dodgers. Spahn was at a further disadvantage: he could not beat the Dodgers. Brooklyn's right-handed hitting lineup feasted on the lefty Spahn, whose record against most everyone else was so remarkable that he would later be inducted into the Hall of Fame. He had stopped pitching regularly against the Dodgers in 1951 and was not given another chance until 1953. The Dodgers knocked him out in the second inning and he never faced them again.

Still, Fred Haney had a pitching staff to rival, and perhaps even surpass, Brooklyn's. And no one in the league was more reliable in stopping the Dodgers than Bob Buhl, to whom Haney handed the ball for the opener at Ebbets Field.

BY THE SEVENTH inning the Dodgers' season appeared in jeopardy. They were down 7 to 1 and for the first time in their many losses to the Braves, the contest was turning into a rout: every other Brooklyn-Milwaukee game had been decided by a margin of a run or two. But Roger Craig, who'd won ten straight at Ebbets Field, surrendered five runs—including the inevitable Joe Adcock homer—before giving way to Ed Roebuck, who gave up two more runs. Buhl, meanwhile, had retired nine batters in a row before walking the first two men he faced in the eighth. He struck out Duke Snider, but Carl Furillo drove in a run with a single, and Gil Hodges doubled in two more. The Braves bolstered their lead by a run in the ninth, but in their last at-bats, the Dodgers came back again. The ballpark was alive and noisy, even if, the Milwaukee writers noted, there were ten thousand empty seats (they were spoiled, knowing only packed houses at home). Reese homered just over the outstretched glove of Bobby Thomson and now the Dodgers were down 8 to 6. Snider came to bat, with two down and the chance to pull the Dodgers even closer. But he grounded to first, ending the game. Brooklyn was five games back, and in the visiting clubhouse the Milwaukee writers surrounded Joe Adcock, eager to know why he hit so well at Ebbets Field. "Maybe I unconsciously bear down harder against the Dodgers," Adcock said. "I figure they're the team to beat."

THE PEOPLE OF Jersey City had not forgiven Jackie Robinson for the dismissive things he had said about their town in April. If Walter Alston, too, had no reason to give Robinson the benefit of the doubt in selecting his lineup, he now found himself stuck with having to use him. Randy Jackson, who'd been batting cleanup and hitting well, somehow managed to cut his hand on a porcelain shower faucet. It would be a month before he could pain-lessly grip a bat.

Alston knew that Robinson's teammates wanted him. And if he did not want to hear it, he would have been hard pressed not to read it: Bill Roeder reported that the players were fairly beseeching their manager to use Robin-son, whom they still believed possessed the skill and fire to help them win.

And so it was that Robinson was crouching at third base when the Braves came to bat in the top of the first at Roosevelt Stadium. The Jersey fans booed him. Carl Erskine, following the script, surrendered a home run to Joe Adcock in the top of the second. The Braves led 1 to 0 when Robin-son came to bat in the bottom of the inning with Carl Furillo on first. The booing did not stop, even when Robinson homered against Gene Conley, giving Brooklyn a 2 to 1 lead. The Dodgers stayed a run ahead until the top of the ninth, when Eddie Mathews homered against Erskine. Milwaukee might have taken the lead had Adcock not committed a woeful baserunning blunder: he was standing on second when Rube Walker, substituting at catcher for the aching Roy Campanella, pounced on Johnny Logan's weak grounder. Adcock guessed he would throw to first, and so broke for third and then for home. But Reese had called out to Walker that the big man was heading his way, and Rube held his throw and the ball and was waiting at home to apply the tag when Adcock came lumbering his way.

Pee Wee Reese led off the bottom of the ninth with a single. Snider sacrificed him to second. Fred Haney ordered Furillo walked intentionally, so that Dave Jolly could pitch to Jackie Robinson.

He took Jolly's first two pitches for balls. He jumped on the third. His line drive to center was headed to the low outfield wall toward Bill Bruton, the Braves' center fielder. Bruton had a powerful arm. Reese, who carried the winning run, could not be sure he'd make it home if Bruton failed to make the catch and had to field the ball on a bounce. Reese started toward third, stopped, and was heading back toward second when Bruton lunged for the ball, missed, and crashed into the wall. The ball trickled away.

Now Reese rounded third and headed for home. Tommy Holmes, reminding everyone that the captain, like Robinson, was running on thirty-seven-year-old legs, watched him from the press box and after so many years of seeing him play wrote that "never did he travel faster as he tore around third and gambled with fate in a dash for a plate."

A perfect throw might have nailed him. It did not come. Del Crandell, the Braves' catcher, never laid a glove on Reese as he scored the winning run. The Dodgers, who had looked dead in the water in Milwaukee only two weeks before, were four games back. August would begin with two more against Milwaukee at Ebbets Field.

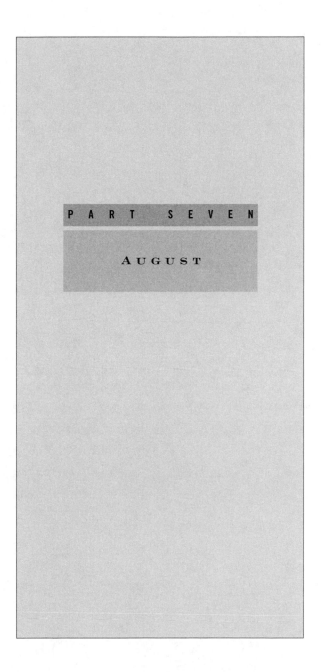

PART SEVEN

AUGUST

Maybe Lew Burdette threw a spitball, or maybe he just had a terrific sinker. If Burdette threw a spitter no one had ever been able to spot the precise moment when he "loaded up." Burdette was a fidgeter on the mound. He wiped the ball on his Milwaukee Braves uniform, rubbed the back of his neck, tugged on the bill of his cap, took off his mitt to rub the ball, rubbed his forehead, rubbed his fingers on his uniform, smoothed the dirt in front of the mound, kicked at the dirt in front of the mound, turned from the plate and looked to the outfield, rubbed the ball inside his mitt, and picked up the rosin bag. There was no way of knowing when in the course of these many gestures he might actually have applied his spittle to the ball. The prevailing wisdom had it that he chose the most deceptive moment of all: the rosin bag. The cognoscenti noted that Burdette picked up the rosin bag *only* with his fingertips, thereby giving the appearance that he was drying the sweat from his pitching hand, all the while possibly hiding the wad of expectorant in his *palm*. Clever man.

Spitballs were a pitcher's attempt to turn nature to his advantage: a slight, damp deviation in the ball's surface that allowed the air currents to work some magic. The pitch had been illegal since 1931, and Burdette insisted he was no lawbreaker. But then others had made the same claim and once they'd retired would admit that they'd been miscreants all along. Preacher Roe confessed to a magazine writer that he'd thrown spitters for Brooklyn. Lew Burdette was a fine pitcher who possessed an adolescent sense of humor—he liked to set newspapers on fire, tie his teammates shoelaces together, and lean out of bus windows to see if he could stop passing motorists with his shrill whistle that sounded like a traffic cop's. But he was also wise enough to understand the key to success as an alleged spitballer: letting the batters *think* he threw a wet one was just as effective as actually throwing one because it kept the hitters guessing. Batters around the National League stepped in against Lew Burdette, sure that every pitch that dipped and danced did so because Burdette had doctored the ball.

Burdette was not the game's only accused man. The handful of alleged spitballers also included Sal Maglie, who like Burdette insisted that he was as innocent as a babe. That they were now facing each other at Ebbets Field on the first night in August made the showdown even more compelling. Burdette, spitter or no, was enjoying a wonderful season, having won twelve and lost only three. Maglie had made Buzzie Bavasi look like the wisest horse trader alive: his record stood at four and three, but that was deceptive. He had only been getting better, and stronger—just as he believed he would with regular work. Walter Alston had come to rely on him and had seldom been disappointed.

Almost thirty thousand fans came to Ebbets Field, and though they fell short of a sellout they kept the evening loud and edgy as they waited to see if the Dodgers could pull within three of the Braves. It was a hot and humid night, with so little breeze that the outfield flags hung like damp laundry.

After Maglie dispatched Milwaukee easily in the first, Lew Burdette walked to the mound, and the Dodgers were ready for him. Alston had instructed his men to step out of the batter's box every time they suspected he was going to his mouth. But Burdette was a crafty man, and even when the umpire asked to inspect the ball, he smiled and obliged and made sure to wipe it on his uniform before tossing it over. Jim Gilliam led off and Burdette struck him out, and then fanned Sandy Amoros and Duke Snider.

There are pitchers' duels that please only purists and insomniacs. These are the games that are made compelling only in the retelling, when two hours of batters up and batters down are telescoped into a snappy read. And then there are pitchers' duels in which only a fool turns from the field. These are games when the stakes are high for both teams, when the season is well along, and when each pitcher spends the evening teetering on disaster. This was the kind of game unfolding between the Braves and Dodgers at Ebbets Field.

Both pitchers breezed through the second inning. But in the top of the third with one man out Maglie walked Bill Bruton. Henry Aaron singled. Eddie Mathews flied to left, and Amoros tried to catch Aaron tagging up at second for a double play. The throw was late, Aaron was on second, and Bruton took third. Up came Joe Adcock, who had hit ten home runs in his last nine games against Brooklyn. The noisy crowd was suddenly quiet.

Maglie delivered and Adcock lit into his pitch. His fly ball out ended the inning without a score for Milwaukee.

Burdette, meanwhile, was accumulating strikeouts and, like Maglie, sidestepping perils. Jim Gilliam came to bat with a man on in the bottom of the third and might have opened things up for the big hitters who followed him, when he lined a sinking shot to left, only to have Bobby Thomson make a splendid catch. Maglie retired the Braves in order in the fourth and when Burdette opened the bottom of the inning he had reason for confidence. Duke Snider came to bat and he had been awful. Hitless in his last thirteen-at-bats, Snider, who was tied for the league lead in home runs, had come to the park early for an extra twenty minutes of batting practice. But now Burdette could only look on in sadness as Snider homered to left, giving the Dodgers the skimpiest of leads, 1 to 0. Carl Furillo followed with a single, as did Jackie Robinson. Robinson on first was a pitcher's equivalent of an itch that never subsides: he danced off the bag; he yelled to Burdette; he called time to chat with Furillo. When Burdette was pitching well he was a quick worker, twitching and all. But when he struggled he slowed his pace to a crawl. Gil Hodges was up next and Burdette started to fidget. He wiped his face. He kicked at the dirt in front of the mound.

Hodges stepped in and Burdette struck him out. Then he fanned Amoros. When he struck out Roy Campanella to end the inning, the Dodger bench rose in such loud and angry protest at the spitters they believed Burdette had thrown that Don Newcombe, a bystander, was ejected for his commentary to the umpire.

Burdette led off the fifth, an advantage to Brooklyn: the law of averages overwhelmingly favored an out when the pitcher batted. But Burdette doubled. Then he got greedy. Danny O'Connell flied to Furillo in right and Burdette, in an act of baserunning hubris, attempted to take third. It was common knowledge that Furillo possessed the strongest arm of any outfielder in the game—not for nothing did the writers dub him "the Reading Rifle." Burdette broke. Furillo threw across the field and Robinson was waiting with the ball to tag Burdette out.

The Dodgers got two on in the bottom of the fifth, but did not score. Nor did Milwaukee score their two runners in the top of the sixth. Brooklyn still led by a run in the top of the seventh when Chuck Tanner singled against a tiring Maglie. So did Wes Covington and Bill Bruton. The bases loaded and only one man out, Alston turned to Clem Labine.

This was Labine's kind of moment, a situation made better still by his opponent, Henry Aaron, who was competing for the league's batting title. Labine was a master at keeping the ball low, and got Aaron to ground hard to first. Hodges snagged it and threw to home where Campanella stepped on the plate, forcing out Tanner. Then Campanella cocked his arm to throw to first to complete the double play and end the inning. Maybe the ball slipped from his grip because his right hand was broken and still aching, or maybe he just botched the throw. But Campanella could only chase the slithering ball to the pitcher's mound as Covington came home to even the score at a run apiece.

Brooklyn again had two men on in the bottom of the inning, only to fade when Burdette struck out his tenth batter of the evening. Milwaukee could do nothing against Labine in the eighth.

The crowd was growing ever louder and Lew Burdette's gray shirt was getting dark with sweat as Jackie Robinson led off the Brooklyn eighth. Ever since Randy Jackson had lacerated his hand and Alston was compelled to put him back in the lineup, Robinson had been hitting as well as any man on the team and had brought his average close to .280.

He opened the inning with a single to left. Bobby Thomson bobbled the ball, a fielding mistake that Robinson thrived on. He took second.

Hodges sacrificed him to third and the infielders moved in for a play at the plate. Milwaukee's strategy almost backfired when Sandy Amoros chopped a high bouncer to second. But Jack Dittmer timed his leap well and came down with the ball perched on the fingertips of his glove. Amoros was out at first. Robinson was still on third.

Next came Campanella, who was still hitting eighth and whom Fred Haney feared less for his recent performance than for his reputation. He ordered Campy walked intentionally, forcing Alston's hand: he could send Labine up to bat, keeping him in the game to pitch the ninth. Or he could send up a pinch hitter. Bavasi had just bought Dale Mitchell from Cleveland, and Mitchell hit well off the bench.

Alston decided to take his chances with the ninth and sent Dale Mitchell to bat. He fouled off the first two pitches and Burdette had him down by two strikes. But Mitchell bounced Burdette's third pitch toward short. The ball arched high and Mitchell, never a speedy runner, pounded to first. Eddie Mathews, the third baseman, and shortstop Johnny Logan both waited a lifetime or two for the ball to come down. And when it finally did Mathews grabbed it and threw to first, a heartbeat too late to catch Mitchell. Robinson came home and the Dodgers took a 2 to 1 lead into the ninth.

Alston called on Roger Craig to finish. This was a risk. Craig had been unbeaten at home until the Braves throttled him in the series opener. He had not pitched in relief all season. Still, Craig possessed a wicked fastball, and he used it to set the Braves down in order and clinch the game for Brooklyn.

In the Dodger clubhouse the talk was not of pennants, and victory, and the thrill of playing in such a game. Such talk would have been tired and familiar; hadn't they done this so many times before? Instead, the Dodgers wanted to talk about Lew Burdette—not with generosity about his ten strikeouts and his gritty performance. They wanted to talk about all the spitballs they were sure he'd thrown. Jackie Robinson, typically, had the most to say. "I don't know if Burdette is throwing a spitter, and I can't accuse him, all I know is that he's going to his forehead quite a bit and he's getting his glove wet by rubbing the sweat off his arm."

Reese joined in. "I'd like to see how he holds that sinker of his."

They went on a while longer and when they were done the writers sought out Burdette for a rebuttal, which he offered with a grin: "They think about it all the time and it's bound to bother 'em."

Which it did, but only up to a point. Brooklyn now stood three games out of first, with the series finale the following afternoon. The Milwaukee Braves Booster Club headed to Lower Manhattan, to Sammy's Bowery Follies, where they put on a display of good cheer: "So we lost tonight. We'll get 'em tomorrow."

EBBETS FIELD WAS packed as Alston was prepared to press his advantage: it was Don Newcombe's turn to pitch and in the last two weeks Newcombe had been close to unhittable. He'd pitched fifteen consecutive scoreless innings, running his record to 15 and 5.

He fed the Braves the odd curve and change-up, but offered them mostly fastballs with which they could barely keep up. The Braves managed only four hits against him while Brooklyn performed an efficient execution of Milwaukee pitcher Ray Crone: home runs by Furillo and Campanella. Brooklyn took a tidy 3 to 0 victory and now was just two games out of first. Worse still for Milwaukee, the Reds were also in town, and had spent the afternoon punishing the Giants at the Polo Grounds, 10 to 2. Second-place Cincinnati was a game out.

The Dodgers, who had taken a while the night before to ease themselves back from their competitive edginess, had the luxury of an easier win in which to reflect on their reversal of fortunes. They'd won fifteen out of the twenty games they'd played since Alston's tirade in Milwaukee. And even an Alston critic like Jackie Robinson was quick with indirect praise.

"I'll always believe that the clubhouse fuss in Milwaukee was a good thing," he said. "Players who had something on their chest brought it out in the open. With that out of the way, they were ready to play ball and prove that they don't choke up in important games."

Tommy Holmes, who had visited so many Dodger clubhouses in lean years and in good, sensed confidence and ease in this one. The Dodgers, he reported, were "sedately confident," a sensation enhanced by experience, and by the knowledge that the Braves were neophytes at this sort of game. "No matter what anybody says, they're starting to feel the pressure on their club," Reese said. "When you're in front and that lead begins to dwindle, you start thinking about it. You can't help it. If anybody asks you shrug it off and say there's nothing to worry about, but deep inside you begin to wonder, how are we going to lose today?"

If Reese was trying to make the Braves doubt themselves, Jackie Robinson wanted to apply a final knee to the groin. "I would say that there is nothing wrong with that Milwaukee club except this is all new to them and they have begun to taste that pennant," he said. "And it looks like they are beginning to choke up on it a little, too."

2 | A BAD GAME AWAY FROM THE MINORS

Roger Craig knew that he had arrived as a member of the Brooklyn Dodgers not when he won his first game as a midseason call-up in 1955, and not when he struck out eleven in his second, and not when he won a game in the World Series. His moment came when he passed the Carl Furillo Test.

Because the Dodgers had played in so many World Series, they were well accustomed to the ritual of dividing their spoils—even though this had always meant divvying up portions of the loser's share for the players who hadn't been with the team all year. While some Dodgers were inclined to be generous, Furillo was not. He generally was the last to speak, and could be relied upon to veto any suggestion of a full share to a man who'd not spent all season with the club. Only those with a full season's tenure were permitted in the meeting room, which explained the wording of Furillo's blackball: "If they ain't in this room, fuck 'em."

But when the Dodgers met at last to divide the winners' pot, Furillo agreed to vote Roger Craig a full share—eight thousand dollars. He was a Dodger now, which in the short term meant he would not have to spend the off-season at home in North Carolina working with his brother at the post office during the Christmas rush.

While the core of the Dodgers had remained virtually unchanged, Buzzie Bavasi was always replacing aging or less than stellar players with young men who might be of use. Coming to the Dodgers could be intimidating, not only for the burden of finally playing in the major leagues, but for joining the company of men who had been stars since Roger Craig was playing sandlot ball at Durham. Craig was so new to the big-league world that he had never even seen a major league game until he pitched in one. Still, whatever fears he harbored about acceptance by his new teammates evaporated immediately after his first game. Walter Alston approached him in the clubhouse and asked, "Kid, where's your family?"

Craig replied that his wife and child were still in Montreal.

Alston suggested that because his turn to pitch would not come for another few days, that he go north and fetch them. Craig was asking around for directions to the airport when Jackie Robinson approached and said, "C'mon, kid, I'll take you to the airport."

As they drove to Queens, Robinson took it upon himself to offer words of encouragement and warning. "You made your first step," he said. "You pitched a real good ballgame. You have the natural ability from what I've seen. You have a great future ahead of you."

Then he added, "You represent the Brooklyn Dodgers and major league baseball. Take care of yourself. Don't hang around with the wrong crowd." Craig suspected that Robinson had driven out of his way just to take him to the airport. Craig was twenty-five years old, tall, skinny, friendly, and observant. He watched his new teammates, the better to learn where and how he might fit in. The clubhouse floor plan at Ebbets Field was his map.

The pecking order of lockers began in the corner where Pee Wee Reese dressed. A rocking chair sat in front of Reese's locker, and because the locker next to his was kept vacant, the captain had a large corner office. Jackie Robinson's locker came next, and after his was Gil Hodges'. Roy Campanella and Duke Snider sat across from them. Carl Furillo, fittingly, was off in a corner. The new men got hooks and hangers. This arrangement afforded Reese and Robinson good views of their teammates, perches from which they could watch, listen, and, if necessary, intercede. Craig noted how Reese "agitated" the sulking Snider, and how Robinson lit into Don Newcombe, when he felt Newcombe's brooding might hurt the team: "You don't want to pitch, take your uniform off. We'll beat them without you." Craig, who'd grown up in the South, noticed that there was no tension between the black and white players, who ate and drank together on the road. Still, it was Robinson and Campanella who rode Newcombe, not Reese.

Craig and the other new men understood that they were a poor outing away from being sent back to the minors. They recognized, too, that they were sometimes competing with each other for jobs and playing time. Yet the veterans were generous men, who were not about to let them founder and fail; there was too much riding on their success, primarily a World Series check. The help began, of course, with Reese, a frequent and, for Roger Craig, always welcome visitor to the mound. Reese stopped by between batters. He would pick up the rosin bag and remind Craig of the game situation—left-handed batter, say, and a man on first—and then remind him to be sure to cover first on a ground ball to the right side of the infield. Craig appreciated the advice, especially because Reese phrased it in a way that suggested he believed that Craig knew what he was doing: it was never, "Don't hang this guy a curve," Craig recalled years later, but rather, "You pitch him low and away, we'll get you a double play."

Hodges, too, stopped by. He would amble over from first base, take the ball, rub it once in his big hands, hand back a ball now so soft and pliable that it felt like a kitten, and say, "Hey Roger, I got you a good pitch right there. Throw it."

Roger Craig was not ashamed to ask for help. He approached Sal Maglie, with whom he briefly roomed, who explained the wisdom of working contrary to the conventional wisdom: when the expected pitch was a slider over the outside corner, for instance, Maglie advised a fastball inside, believing that a hitter who knew "the book" would be looking for a pitch away. Maglie needed to be asked for counsel, and was happy to offer it except on the days he pitched. Then he would retire to his room, eat a steak, and avoid all company. Carl Erksine, however, was always available for a chat.

Erskine, in fact, approached the younger men, and Craig, in particular, enjoyed the attention. Craig knew he was not about to get much help from Joe Becker, the pitching coach who, as was typical of the time, was of little use in instructing his charges: Becker believed that running solved all mound woes. It was Erskine who had approached Craig just after his first game, a three-hit complete game shutout. Craig was in the outfield at Ebbets Field when he heard a fan call out, "Hey, Craig, ya bum, you'll be back in Triple-A in a week."

"That means they like you," said Erskine, serving as an interpreter. "Don't say anything to them."

Craig, in turn, recognized in Erskine a wise man whom he could ask vague and difficult questions. "Carl, what do you see in my pitching?" he'd ask. "What do I need to do better? Throw more fastballs, or work on my curve?"

Erskine first offered encouragment—"You've got good major league pitches"—and then explained the importance of making each pitch count. This sounds laughably obvious. But for a young pitcher like Craig it was a point he never before needed to consider. He possessed a fastball and curve and had succeeded in the minors simply by rearing back and throwing. He lacked finesse and gamesmanship, qualities he would need as the hitters became familiar with his pitches. So Erskine talked with him about control, about hitting his spots, doing so in a way that Craig, who later became a successful pitching coach and manager, appreciated for its recognition of his particular strengths and needs. Erskine made him believe that he could get big-league hitters out. And while Craig was a confident young man, he needed the boosting. He did not have Clem Labine's swagger, a quality he observed in wonder and amusement.

One of the highlights each day came for Craig and fellow newcomer Ed Roebuck in the seventh inning when Clem Labine prepared to enter the game. Labine rose from his seat on the bench, folded his mitt, tucked it in the back pocket of his baggy uniform pants, and slowly walked through the dugout. Each time he passed them, Craig and Roebuck would snicker, "The cocky son of a bitch."

Labine, they sensed, *knew* he could get batters out. Craig enjoyed the sensation occasionally. But Ed Roebuck hardly felt it at all. Roebuck was Craig's best friend and roommate, and Craig worried about him. Roebuck, too, had come up in 1955, and while he'd pitched well he did not match Craig's stellar beginning. Roebuck pitched exclusively in relief, and was seldom Walter Alston's first option. More than Craig, who had secured a place in the rotation, Roebuck was a man on the periphery, a young pitcher of great skill who had little belief in his ability to get men out. "It is such a struggle for survival," he would later say, "when you're on the fringe."

Roebuck struck Craig as a man who could not take pleasure in the game, and in the moments of his success. Roebuck was bright and sought his own counsel. He did not seek pitching tips, as Craig did, and was not much interested in the things people wanted to tell him. "Eddie was not hard headed," Craig later said. "But he had his own thoughts." He shared these thoughts with Craig, and sometimes Labine. They talked on the road, after games and dinner and beers. "He'd say, 'when I'm out there I want to get this over with and get out of there,'" Craig later said. "Even when he'd win he'd still get depressed. On the road he couldn't sleep if he didn't have a few drinks. He'd just stay up all night long."

Roebuck did not share these thoughts with his wife, Jan, a wise and perceptive woman who was not deluded into thinking that his silences suggested contentment. Jan Roebuck knew her place well enough to recognize that while her husband would not share his worries, they were her worries just the same. "There was no 'I,'" she would later say. "It was 'we.'" She had known Ed since high school in Brownsville, a town outside of Pittsburgh, and married him in a manner that passed for romantic in a baseball view of things: one day, when Ed was pitching in the minors at Elmira, he called to say that his roommate, Don Zimmer, was getting married. Zimmer suggested that as long as he was getting married, Ed should get married, too. So Ed called and Jan accepted his hasty proposal. They had arrived in Brooklyn in the midst of the team's march to the pennant and World Series, having never before been in a big city. They drove over the Manhattan Bridge, not knowing where they were going. A policeman directed them to the Dodger offices on Montague Street. They found a place in Bay Ridge. The Bay Ridge merchants were solicitous to her, even though Ed had insisted she not make too much of a fuss about his playing for the Dodgers.

But now, a year later, the excitement of that arrival was long over, and in its place came days at the ballpark, watching the other wives cross their legs for good luck, and then, when the games were done, waiting to drive home with her tall, young, and remote husband. "For him," she would later say, "it all felt temporary."

On the road Ed Roebuck had the company of his teammates, to play bridge and pinochle and to drink. He, along with Zimmer, Craig, Don Bessent, and Chuck Templeton, were part of what Roebuck called "the hard core of guys who are not stars." They did not think it their place to invite themselves to join their famous teammates—"We felt we had to be invited," said Roger Craig, "and if we weren't invited we were not going." The Dodgers drank at The Rendezvous Room in Cincinnati and The Cottage in Chicago, the same bars in the same cities where the team stopped, time and again. They talked baseball, of course, but more in the vain of shoptalk and bitching: "I'm not pitching enough" and "How do I get him out?" No one admitted to fears or weaknesses, at least not directly.

Roebuck would not confess to his teammates what he was sure they all thought—that they did not think he was as good as Clem Labine, which meant that where Labine was so reliable, he was not, that where Labine's appearance all but assured a win, the call to the bull pen for Ed Roebuck did not. He would stand on the mound and think, I just hope he hits it at someone.

There was no shortage of liquor for the Dodgers. The team's sponsor, Schaefer Beer, kept the players well stocked. And on the road, Campanella could be relied upon to have a bottle of V&O scotch in his room. The road offered little but movies and hotel lobbies and bars that were, in the end, not so much places to talk but, as Ed Roebuck would later say, "just an excuse to drink. Then you wonder how you became an alcoholic."

ROGER CRAIG BEGAN the month with a record of 10 and 6 and the confidence of his manager. Ed Roebuck, meanwhile, had won three and lost four, and along with Don Bessent was generally called in when a starter faltered early and badly. He had had some rough appearances, but had also pitched well, though never longer than five innings. The Dodgers carried ten pitchers going into August and all were starters with the exception of Labine, Bessent, Ken Lehman, and Ed Roebuck. While Alston did call on his starters to pitch from time to time in relief, he relied on his relievers to keep his team in games the starters were giving away—as Sandy Koufax seemed destined to do against the Cardinals in early August as the Dodgers, who'd slipped past Cincinnati into second place, were trying to stay two games behind Milwaukee. While Sal Maglie, as was becoming almost habitual, won the opener of the Sunday doubleheader at Ebbets Field, shutting St. Louis out on four hits, Koufax could get no further than the second inning in the nightcap.

Alston signaled for Roebuck. The park was only half full as Roebuck took the ball and completed his warm-ups. Koufax had left after surrendering two singles and a walk, and though St. Louis picked up a run in the inning, Roebuck shut them out until the seventh. Brooklyn was ahead 4 to 1 when Roebuck surrendered a pinch hit homer to Rocky Nelson, the former Dodger prospect. Though St. Louis now trailed only by a run, Alston did not call on Labine, and instead allowed Roebuck to complete his longest outing in the big leagues.

This time it was Ed Roebuck whom the writers sought out. And though he was not one for sharing his thoughts, Roebuck did admit that he began tiring after his first two innings. "But then I sort of got my second wind and at the end I felt strong," he said. "It felt like starting a game."

It mattered little how Ed Roebuck regarded himself in the hierarchy of the Dodgers. His teammates and his manager needed him. And that need would only become more urgent in the third week of August when Larry Jackson of the Cardinals hit Clem Labine on the right wrist with a pitch. Labine closed his forty-second game of the season, but his pitching arm ached. He went to the hospital, where x-rays revealed a chip fracture of the hamate bone. Doctors placed his arm in a cast and announced that he would be out for ten days. Maybe longer.

3 | A MAJOR LEAGUE TOWN

The Brooklyn Academy of Music stood across the street from the corner where Walter O'Malley envisioned his great domed stadium rising. The academy was a heavy, red brick building where Caruso coughed blood into his handkerchief as he sang *L'Elisir d'Amore*, where Isadora Duncan stood frozen onstage unable to dance after a backstage row with her husband, and where so few people now came that the board of trustees was threatening to shut the place down.

The academy had been running at a loss for twenty years, and while the trustees were willing to tolerate a modest deficit, they warned that unless the membership rolls grew from 3,000 to 9,000 they could see no way to go on. The academy, they announced, would be "on trial" for the coming season, and with that John Cashmore dispatched volunteers across the borough to sell fifteen-dollar memberships. The academy had been part of Brooklyn's cultural life since 1891, when 100 people gathered for an "illustrated lecture" on Chinese music. The hall itself opened in 1908. The Metropolitan Opera played the academy, as did the Boston Symphony. But this history, and the ongoing films, lectures, dance, theater, and "discussion groups," did not represent a sufficient draw for what the trustees called the "new" Brooklyn people. Perhaps, they suggested, the "new" people—and here they did not elaborate on who those people were—did not know what the academy offered, but surely the "old" Brooklyn people would rush to its rescue.

Others, however, were not so sanguine. Jean Dalrymple, director of the New York City Center, did not believe Brooklyn people possessed the cultural enlightenment to keep an institution like the academy afloat. "Brooklyn has no civic pride," she said. "If the academy were in a Midwestern city it would be successful. . . . The only thing Brooklynites pride themselves on are the Dodgers and their own accents. They would rather come to Manhattan to Carnegie Hall or the City Center, so they can talk about where they've been."

The words were unkind, but not without some truth. The academy sat in an uninviting location. The meat market that both Robert Moses and Walter O'Malley were eager to raze stood across the street, and there was little in way of fine dining in the neighborhood. The academy was not Carnegie Hall, and Brooklyn, alas, was not Manhattan. Hard as Jean Dalrymple's words were to take, she was not wrong in her assessment of the lure of "the city." For all the boasting about Brooklyn as the nation's "fourth largest city," it had for over fifty years been an appendage to the country's biggest metropolis. It did not seem fair to expect Brooklyn to compete with Manhattan when it came to choosing a destination for an evening out. There was nothing *wrong* with the Academy of Music, just as there was nothing wrong with the Botanic Gardens, Prospect Park, and the famous Brooklyn restaurants like Gage & Tollner, F.W.I.L. Lundy Bros. and Peter Lugar's Steak House, which had been around since 1887, when Brooklyn was still a city in its own right. They were nice places. But Manhattan was more than nice. Manhattan had more than *one* of everything. Brooklyn, like so many other "cities," had one great museum, one symphony hall, one ball club.

And that was enough for the people who believed that Brooklyn offered all they needed. It was especially so for the men and women who had made something of themselves in Brooklyn, who by dint of their enterprise and connections had established themselves as members in good standing of the borough's gentry. These were not Brooklyn's wealthiest or most powerful. They existed at a tier or two below men like Walter O'Malley, who moved among Brooklyn's most useful men. Rather these were the people who filled the ballroom of the Hotel St. George in Brooklyn Heights for the Brooklyn Board of Realtors dinner, an event so popular that the dais was constructed on three decks. They were not necessarily rich men: a fledgling realtor in Brooklyn would be lucky in 1956 to be subsisting on as many $200 commissions for sales of $12,500 houses as he could amass. And even if the money was not much better for the established men, they had nonetheless staked their careers on the belief that there would always be a place for them in Brooklyn.

George Clark was such a man. He sold real estate in Gravesend, a largely Italian neighborhood out near Coney Island. His father had sold real estate, as had his grandfather. His grandfather was an Irish immigrant who had come to America in 1870 and started selling real estate in, of all places, Long Island. He moved to Brooklyn in 1903 and four years later opened the office on Avenue N, the commercial strip where his grandson George Clark was grooming *his* son, George, to one day take over the family business. Young George admired his father and enjoyed his company, which was fortunate because his father did not believe it was too soon to begin introducing his teenage son to the people with whom he did business. There were many people and, it seemed, many meetings, dinners, and parties. There was the Flatbush Real Estate Board, the Bay Ridge Real Estate Board, and the members of the Bensonhurst Multiple Listing Service. His father seemed to know everyone, and everyone seemed to like him. His father sold one- and two-family homes to Jews and Italians, and while there were other realtors who worked, it seemed, without pause, scrambling for the nickels and dimes they could squeeze from finder's fees for the title companies, the elder George Clark most enjoyed the time that he could spend in the company of friends and associates.

He took them fishing on his boat *The Mickey*, named for the cartoon mouse. He met them in downtown Brooklyn for lunch, at the exclusive Brooklyn Club. The elder George Clark had two brothers, John and Tom. John worked in the family's business. Tom had struck out on his own. He had reversed his grandfather's journey, leaving Brooklyn for Long Island, and there he had become a very wealthy man. He owned land and at any one time might be holding over a thousand mortgages on properties. He tried to get his brother George to join him. George Clark visited his brother and saw what he had amassed and then declined his invitation. Wealth was not enough of an incentive to lure him away from Brooklyn, which was surprising because during the Great Depression business was so bad for Clark Realty that George lined his worn shoes with cardboard.

But he had survived the Depression. He owned his own home in Flatbush. He was cultivating his son to succeed him. He had no desire to leave Brooklyn because, he explained to his son, he would have to leave his friends, and their world, behind. "When I die," George Clark told his son, "the church will be so filled with friends. It will be packed."

Predictability mattered in Brooklyn, and this sometimes bred a lack of curiosity and adventure. It meant that if you lived on, say, on the Jewish side of Bedford Avenue in Flatbush, there was little reason to know or much care about what was taking place on the Catholic side. It meant that it was possible to take the family for seafood at Lundy's every Sunday night and always have the same waiter. Yet Manhattan still sparkled and beckoned with so much promise of glamour and diversion that even short-term renters like the Brooklyn Dodgers would take the subway into town with their wives on Saturday nights to eat and take in a show. Manhattan had too much, a view confirmed from such vantage points as the Brooklyn Heights promenade and Robert Moses' Gowanus Expressway: There were no such alluring views of Brooklyn from the Manhattan side of the East River, except perhaps for the Brooklyn Bridge. The only break in a panoramic view of the great, flat expanse of Brooklyn was 512-foot-tall Williamsburg Savings Bank, the borough's tallest building, which sat between the corner where Walter O'Malley's stadium might stand and the Brooklyn Academy of Music.

The president of the academy's board of trustees was left to hope that the volunteers John Cashmore had combing the borough might yet find six thousand people who were still interested in seeking the high life locally. "There are three million people in Brooklyn," lamented Robert Blum of Abraham & Straus and the Brooklyn Sports Authority, "and you can't tell me there are no wealthy or cultured people still living here."

THE ACADEMY'S FATE did not appear to consume the men at the center of the borough's political life. Nor did the question of the Dodgers, of their future, of the domed stadium, of O'Malley's Jersey City ploy appear to trouble them at all. That, at least, was how it appeared to Frank Lynn, who covered Brooklyn politics for the *World-Telegram*. Lynn wrote a column filled with the minutiae of political life: "Mario DeOpitatis denied 11th AD Democratic leader Ross DiLorenzo's charges that he and Borough Democratic chieftain Philip J. Schupler encouraged Vincent LaBella to run as an insurgent. . . ." or "Richard G. Hickey, one of the dissident aspirants for the sixth district Municipal Court berth also will not be challenged by the county organization. . . ."

There was a delightfully small-town quality to Lynn's column, just as there was in Jimmy Murphy's paeans to the borough's best high school athletes and to Ruth G. Davis's chronicles of Brooklyn "society": " 'A Night in Vienna' will be the theme of the annual scholarship fund celebration of the

Women's Faculty Club of Polytechnic Institute of Brooklyn." Brooklyn was just as parochial when it came to power, which did not disappoint Frank Lynn. He loved the clubhouse and the machinations, and, most of all, the players—men like Joseph Sharkey, who had succeeded Irwin Steingut in running the borough's Democratic machine. The men Lynn covered spent their days deciding whose turn it was to become a judge, whose cousin needed a job, and who, inevitably, needed a little political slapping around. Vision was a word never uttered; the future extended no further than the next municipal election. Years later Lynn would recall that all through the spring and summer of 1956 he never once heard a Brooklyn politician talk about the fate of the Dodgers. Which meant that for all his careful cultivation of men of use, Walter O'Malley was on his own in his battle with Robert Moses.

Moses knew it, too. He knew that for all the letter writing and luncheon meetings and beseeching phone calls, the men who had petitioned him on O'Malley's behalf had no stomach for a fight, nor any understanding of when a fight was essential. Any doubts he had about their will were dispelled the year before, when the *Eagle* folded. The paper had been in business for 114 years. It had won four Pulitzer Prizes, most recently in 1951 for its reporting on crime. It had a circulation of 130,000. But in January 1955 its reporters and editors went on strike, demanding that they be paid as well as journalists in Manhattan. The publisher Frank Schroth offered a raise that was rejected. He threatened to shut the paper down. This was dismissed as a bluff. Then, citing the impossibility of staying in business, Schroth made good on his promise. He folded the *Eagle*.

Robert Moses, whose regard for newspapers was enhanced by their endless tributes to him, was dismayed. And in May 1955 he wrote to Walter Rothschild of Abraham & Straus, bemoaning the inability of Brooklyn's prominent men to rally to save the *Eagle*. Moses was writing to push those same men to support his grand plans for the Brooklyn Civic Center. He sensed that they needed a swift kick.

"It seems to me absolutely incredible that there are not enough prominent, forceful, intelligent leaders in Brooklyn, in business and civic affairs, to save this newspaper," he wrote. The important men in places smaller than Brooklyn had saved their town's papers, he wrote. Even with the *Eagle*'s doors shut, Moses still wanted Rothschild and his peers to band together to buy advertising, to find new subscribers, to underwrite subscriptions for their employees. "If there isn't enough leadership in Brooklyn to do something as simple as this I think you had all better prepare for further retrogression ending God knows where."

But the *Eagle* died. And Robert Moses had the measure of Walter O'Malley's friends.

4 | A Team to Beat

In July the Dodgers had needed a winning streak to put them back in contention. Then they'd needed to defeat the Braves and the Reds, if only to remind them that they could. Now they needed to beat the weak teams to keep pace with their challengers.

They had had their streak. They had beaten Milwaukee and Cincinnati and had earned a reprieve, of sorts—three weeks to feast on the Phillies, Pirates, Cardinals, and Giants before they had to face the Reds and Braves again. Tempting as it might have been to forecast a seventeen-game winning streak, only a child or a fool would have thought that possible, or reasonable. The nature of the game—154 contests played day-after-day between men of roughly similar abilities—ensured that no baseball team could win all the time. The best record ever compiled was that of the 1906 Chicago Cubs, who won 116 of the 152 games they played. The Cubs, however, lost not only the World Series to their crosstown rival White Sox, but thirty-six regular season games, too—roughly one in every four games they played.

That level of success, winning three out of every four games, defined the Dodgers' relationship with Jim Brosnan's team, the hapless latter-day Cubs. Brosnan, a bespectacled pitcher and an erudite man, later went on to become an author; his books include *The Long Season* and *The Pennant Race*. Brosnan spent several seasons watching the Dodgers from the sorry vantage point of the Chicago bull pen. He recognized that while the Cubs could still win the odd game against Brooklyn, they were not going to take two out of three. Ernie Banks might hit a home run against, say, Don Newcombe, and Brosnan himself might strike out Duke Snider with men on base. But those moments, he believed, came only by chance, like hitting a jackpot with the first nickel dropped in the slot machine. The wise baseball bettor would still have his money on Newcombe getting Banks to fly out with the bases empty and on Snider banging Brosnan's curveball off the wall. A season of baseball successes, Brosnan concluded, came not with the grand moments, but with consistent performances in the endless smaller ones.

He would sit in the cramped visiting bull pen at Ebbets Field, the Dodger fans howling in his ear—"Hey, four eyes, aren't you glad you're not out there?"—and watch with admiration as the Dodgers executed the game to near-perfection. Reese and Gilliam were always positioned in precisely the right spots to take cutoff throws from the outfield, and Snider and Furillo's throws seldom failed to hit them. Hitting the cutoff man was a metaphor, a significant event that lacked glamour and drama. It succeeded in keeping a runner on first base from advancing to second, denying him the chance to score on a base hit. Hitting the cutoff man could save a run, and maybe a game, and in the course of so many games the team that could hit the cutoff man generally won. It was baseball's equivalent of "for want of a horse, my kingdom was lost"—the small event that came to loom large. Brosnan had pitched against Dodger teams at every rung in the minor leagues. And while some might not notice what he called "the cognitive part" of the game, and others might be jealous, Brosnan found himself looking on in wonder and admiration. "If you didn't say, 'God, I wish I played for that ballclub,' " he later said, "you'd say, 'It's hard to play them.' "

He wished he played for them. He knew, for instance, how much time the Dodgers spent dissecting each game in the clubhouse, and how much they talked about the things they did *wrong*. The Cubs did not engage in such conversation—they had no tradition for it, and no leader, like Reese, who insisted on it. In the most essential way, the Dodgers were a *team*, a collection of individuals with a common purpose, a collective confidence, and an ability to understand how each of them fit with the others—regardless of their feelings for one another. "The more you're willing to share with someone asking questions," Brosnan later said, "the closer you feel to that player." The Cubs were not a team. They were a collection of skilled baseball players who possessed the potential to beat the Dodgers, but not the appreciation of what it took to do so, day after day.

Years later, Brosnan was researching a story and spent some time talking with a retired Pee Wee Reese. They talked baseball, a subject at which

Reese excelled. Brosnan asked how the Dodgers were able to maintain a psychological advantage against teams like the Cubs. Reese's reply was simple, which was fitting for a man never much given to speeches. "We were a team," he said. "T-E-A-M. No one thought of anything but making the team win." His words may have been among the most hackneyed in sports. But Reese was talking not to a mere writer, but to a former opponent—a man who understood their significance.

The Dodgers began their baseball educations in D-Ball, the minor league entry point. There they learned Branch Rickey's "Dodger way," an approach to fundamentals that was drilled into them so relentlessly that hitting the cutoff man became as habitual as swearing. And those men talented and lucky enough to make the big club, and perhaps to star with Brooklyn, would *still* be reminded of what they needed to do at any given juncture of the game. Roger Craig would recall how Reese approached the generally unapproachable Carl Furillo before a crucial at-bat and reminded him that the team did not need a home run—just a hit, or maybe just a fly ball, a productive out to move the runners over. Furillo, he noted, did not take offense.

Jim Brosnan always wanted to pitch for the Dodgers. Because then, he reasoned, he would have been in the company of men who embraced, celebrated, and performed the myriad small tasks of the game, a collective habit that transformed them into a team. "I would have finally found out," he said, "how to learn how to pitch."

ON FRIDAY NIGHT, August 3, the day after Don Newcombe shut out the Braves to bring Brooklyn to within two games of first, the Dodgers lost at Ebbets Field to the Cardinals. They did win the next day, and the next. Don Newcombe shut the Pirates out at Jersey City, his third straight shutout. The Dodgers lost in Pittsburgh the following day, when a ninth inning rally fell short.

And so it went, on the road and at Ebbets Field, two wins, followed by a loss, followed by a win, followed by two losses—ugly, doubleheader defeats to the Giants. The Dodgers lost no more than two in a row, and won no more than four straight. The losses were disappointing but, taken together, represented baseball's equivalent of life's inherent unfairness: a Jackie Robinson error in the ninth, Duke Snider striking out with the bases loaded, Clem Labine walking in a winning run. Willie Mays homered twice to spark the sweep at the Polo Grounds. The Braves and Reds, meanwhile, maintained similar paces. By the time the Dodgers reached Cincinnati on August 23, they'd won eleven of the seventeen games they played against the lesser teams, which was just what they'd needed to do.

None of the contenders had put together a streak, and none had slipped behind the pack. The Dodgers inched as close as a game and a half out, only to slip to three back. Roy Campanella was hurting and not hitting. Newcombe's scoreless streak extended into his fourth game in succession before he finally surrendered a run. Don Bessent assumed the closer's role and pitched twenty scoreless innings. Ed Roebuck appeared often in the middle innings.

The three games the Dodgers and Reds played at Crosley Field resembled a showdown between heavyweight club fighters: finesse was not much in evidence. Instead, both teams took turns hitting home runs and knocking out each other's pitchers. The style of play was Cincinnati's, whose pitching did not equal Brooklyn's. But for three days the Dodgers showed that they could pound with the Reds. Furillo and Snider did the grunt work, driving in twelve runs between them in the first two games, offsetting the damage Cincinnati inflicted on Newcombe and Maglie. The Dodgers took the first two, and though Cincinnati salvaged the third, they now stood in third place, four games back. The Dodgers boarded their train and traveled west, bypassing Chicago and heading straight to Milwaukee.

5 | JIMMY CANNON'S ELEGY

The Brooklyn Dodgers arrived in Milwaukee in the last week of August two games out of first place, with two to play against the Braves. A sweep would tie them for first place. But Bob Buhl was waiting on the mound when they came to bat in the first, a pleasing sight for the nearly forty-four thousand people who packed County Stadium.

Buhl had beaten Brooklyn in each of the six games he'd pitched against them. The skies over Milwaukee were dark and threatening. More ominous still, in the bottom of the first Roger Craig allowed Danny O'Connell to steal third when he took too long a wind-up. For this transgression, Craig was punished when Roy Campanella's throw to third sailed into left field and O'Connell scored.

In the sixth, Duke Snider misplayed a Joe Adcock line drive into a double, a gaffe that brought home another Milwaukee run when Bobby Thomson singled. The Braves and Buhl appreciated the help, but did not need it: Henry Aaron homered, as did Johnny Logan. Buhl was wild, walking seven, but the Dodgers could not take advantage of his mistakes as the Braves had done with theirs. The Dodgers scored twice, and that was not enough. Milwaukee stood poised to extend its lead to four.

The Braves were so eager to inflict the mortal blow the following afternoon that they started taunting the Dodgers during warm-ups. Lew Burdette led them. Gene Conley was scheduled to pitch but Burdette was prepared to do his part in rattling the champions. He aimed his invective at Robinson, who was more familiar with slurs and epithets than any man in the game. But it had been years since Branch Rickey lifted the prohibition on fighting back that he'd placed on Robinson in his rookie year. Robinson was at third base, fielding ground balls when he heard Lew Burdette, or thought he heard Burdette, resort to the kind of barb that had so plagued him in the early years of his career. Robinson heard the word "watermelon" and was not about to let it pass.

He fielded a grounder, turned to throw to Gil Hodges at first and instead hurled the ball into the Milwaukee dugout, barely missing Burdette. It was a rash and stupid act. Not only could he have ended Burdette's career and possibly his life, but a throw that found its unfortunate mark would have done Robinson's reputation lasting damage. At the very least he risked being suspended when his teammates needed him. The players noticed, as did the writers, who would wait to take up when the game was over.

It was Don Newcombe's turn to pitch the second game, and Newcombe had been masterful. Nature, however, conspired against him. In the fourth inning Newk began complaining of a stomachache so severe that Doc Wendler, the team trainer, felt compelled to medicate him. But the treatment was to no avail. Newk was gone in the fifth, down 3 to 0 on home runs by Adcock and Thomson.

The season's fortunes were in peril when Dale Mitchell came to bat for him in the sixth. Mitchell, as was becoming his habit against Milwaukee, squeezed out an infield hit. But Jim Gilliam popped up and Reese forced

Mitchell at second. Gene Conley, the six-foot-eight-inch-tall Milwaukee pitcher—he played basketball for a living, too—had stymied Brooklyn all afternoon and there was little reason for hope when Snider came to bat with two out and Reese on first. But Conley offered a pitch with which Snider could work, and he parked the ball over the left field fence, bringing the Dodgers to within one. They tied the game in the seventh, when Robinson doubled and Amoros singled him home.

Don Bessent, meanwhile, was keeping the Braves from inflicting further damage, and the score was knotted at three apiece when Gilliam doubled in the eighth. Reese sacrificed him to third. Fred Haney, fearful that Gilliam could tag up and score on a Snider fly ball, ordered Duke walked and took his chances with Furillo. This was the sort of moment in which Brooklyn had made its reputation: with a runner on third and less than two out, they would, as likely as not, bring him home on a hit or a shot to the outfield. But Furillo botched it, driving the ball back toward the mound. Conley fielded it and threw home, and Gilliam might have been an easy out. But he stopped, headed back to third, and then toward home, keeping the rundown going long enough for Snider to reach third and Furillo second, a thinking man's play. Now there were two out. First base was open and Robinson came to bat. Haney, looking for a force-out at any base, had him walked. Campanella was up next and he had been dreadful, two hits in his last twenty-two at-bats. His broken right hand was so mangled he could only shake hands with two fingers. His thumb was bruised and swollen.

But Campanella somehow caught up with Conley's pitch and held the bat in his hands long enough to smack the ball over Johnny Logan's head at shortstop. Snider scored and Furillo followed. Robinson was sprinting from first. Billy Herman, the third base coach, signaled him to stop. But now Robinson looked over his shoulder and saw that Bill Bruton, who fielded the single in left, had committed the sin of *missing the cutoff man*. Instead, he tossed the ball lazily to second and Robinson, sensing the moment's advantage and greedy for another run, ran through Herman's sign and raced home to give Brooklyn a 6 to 3 lead.

Bessent shut out Milwaukee in the eighth. But with two out in the ninth he walked two men. Johnny Logan came to bat with the chance to tie. Logan, however, made a tactical mistake: rather than seeing if he could induce another walk from the suddenly wild Bessent, or work him well enough to force him to throw a fat pitch, Logan swung at the first pitch, grounding out to end the game. While the Braves could only lament what they had frittered away, Roy Campanella, so seldom a hero all season long, accepted handshakes like a nervous pianist.

"I ain't gonna miss many more of these games," he said, "not unless all of these fingers got banged up."

Meanwhile, Jackie Robinson wanted to fight Lew Burdette and in the Dodger clubhouse challenged Burdette to meet him outside. Burdette declined. He smiled and told the beat writers that "any moron" could get himself suspended. He could not understand why Robinson was so upset. He swore he never said "watermelon."

The Dodgers left for Chicago in precisely the same position they were in the night before: two games out and in contention. They did as they were supposed to do at Wrigley Field, winning twice, losing once, and then they headed home.

NEW YORK WAS hot and rainy, and from the room that was his home at the Edison Hotel in the heart of Times Square, Jimmy Cannon looked out at the lights of Broadway and at the people hurrying home in a downpour. He could hear the noise of a nearby shooting gallery. He had the radio on low, so he could work.

Cannon wrote a sports column for the *Post* and approached his work with a poet's sensibility. He was a single man whose writing reflected a place and a time that was beginning to vanish, a time when he could still leave his room and walk out onto Times Square at night to buy his paper and several others. Cannon loved the men he wrote of: Joe Louis, Rocky Marciano, and most especially Joe DiMaggio, whom he elevated to Olympian proportions. Cannon was a celebrant of Damon Runyon's New York, the wisecracking-heart-of-gold-world-weary New York of touts, shills, fight nights at the Garden, and drinks at Toots Shor's saloon.

The Dodgers fit his worldview handsomely. He saw in them virtue and nobility. He admired the way Carl Furillo played the game. He thought Duke Snider was a wonderful player and insisted that he be treated with respect and tolerance. He had liked the Dodgers for years, when they were the team of Preacher Roe, Billy Cox, Cookie Lavagetto, Pete Reiser, and Joe Medwick. Now, as he sat in his room and wrote, he invoked their names and lamented that they were all gone from the game, save for one, Reese, he of the "alert serenity." He adored Roy Campanella, and while he would have trouble in the years to come with black athletes who were bold and vocal, particularly the young Cassius Clay, he admired Robinson, of whom he wrote: "There is no one I respect more in sports."

That night Jimmy Cannon, however, wrote about growing old, a fact that he cautioned his many readers to consider when they watched these Dodgers play.

"It is the last time you will see them as they were on the good days this year," he wrote. Time, he went on, sapped a team gradually, a step-to-first-base slower at a time. "There is about them the frantic haste of the pedestrians who move quickly through the Broadway night. They can win this year but it's the last time and a lot of them will be gone when spring comes again."

Milwaukee, he sensed, was poised to become the club that Brooklyn had been—the National League's dominant team. He faulted the writers who still foolishly associated these Dodgers with the sorry teams of the past, the team that on an August afternoon thirty years before somehow ended with three base runners stranding on third. If anything truly ridiculed them, he wrote, it was age, and the erosion it wrecked on their skills.

"It's not over yet and I don't think it will be decided until the last week of the season," Jimmy Cannon told his readers. "But when you watch them remember this may be the last time a lot of them pass your way as players. You'll be talking about them a long time after they're gone, too."

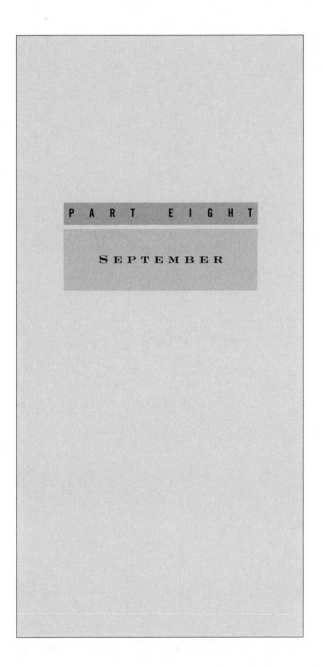

PART EIGHT

SEPTEMBER

On Labor Day, as Egyptian president Gamal Abdel Nasser threatened to nationalize the Suez Canal, as hundreds of white men stormed a Tennessee courthouse to protest the integration of a high school, as a New Hampshire grammar school principal was fired after his wife published her small-town-tell-all novel *Peyton Place*, and as the New York Police Department reported that no Brooklynites had died in any of the borough's 363 holiday weekend car accidents, the Dodgers left Ebbets Field trailing the Milwaukee Braves by three and a half games. They were exhausted.

They had just split a doubleheader with the Pittsburgh Pirates and had looked weary in the process. It would have been cruel to fault them for their fatigue. They had played six games in four days, a week's worth of games in about half the time. They had beaten the Giants on Friday, split their Saturday doubleheader, taken both games with New York on Sunday, and dropped the Monday nightcap against Pittsburgh when they did not seem to have the energy to score the tying run against the Pirates' Bob Friend. For the first time in two years they failed to hit a single home run in an Ebbets Field doubleheader. "You can overpower a tired man," Friend said. "You can fool him because he's not aggressive at the plate."

The Dodgers did not dispute this. Jackie Robinson emerged from the shower, sounding like a marathon runner. "I made it," he said. "I don't know how, but I made it."

Mercifully, they had Tuesday off. "I'm going to sleep all day," said Pee Wee Reese.

THE BRAVES, REDS, and Dodgers each had just over twenty games left to play and the pennant was Milwaukee's to lose, just as it had been all season long. The Dodgers and Reds had had their runs at Milwaukee, and the Braves had had their droughts. Their season had looked lost when Charlie Grimm was fired. But Fred Haney had kept his team in first place, if only barely at times. Now, with the Reds in town, the Dodgers gasping, and with a welcome visit to Wrigley Field to follow, the Braves were poised to open a gap their rivals would be hard pressed to overcome. Over 47,000 people jammed Milwaukee's County Stadium on Labor Day, the largest crowd ever squeezed into the park. They filled the parking lot with 12,000 cars and approached the stadium in such numbers that the hill leading to the gates was black with people. Inside their clubhouse, the Braves played cards, listened to a loud radio, and allowed themselves some chest puffing. "They keep calling 'em the old pros," Johnny Logan said when someone mentioned the Dodgers. "Well, we're the young pros."

Perhaps. Henry Aaron carried them in the first game, hitting two home runs and scoring the game winner in the ninth. But Frank Robinson beat them in the second, on a homer in the tenth. For the rubber game Haney called on Warren Spahn. But Spahn was gone after twenty-seven pitches, with the Reds leading for good, 5 to 0. The tens of thousands who had come to County Stadium filed out so quietly that in the silence all could hear the lone voice of an older woman intoning the sad words, "The Braves is dead."

But the Reds' manager, Birdie Tebbetts, was not so sure. "You know what it does?" he said. "It makes this a three-team race for the last three weeks and for the first time it proves to everybody that this is a three-team race. Now we're in it all the way. The Braves had a chance to knock us out in this series, and they didn't."

THE DODGERS, MEANWHILE, had made the most, or more precisely the least of their one-day holiday. Reese slept late and in the afternoon took his daughter to see Dr. Steiner for a checkup. Roy Campanella loaded his family onto the *Princess* for a day trip on Long Island Sound. Carl Furillo fished off Sheepshead Bay. Jackie Robinson took his wife and children into the city to see *Moby Dick*. The Erskines, too, went into town, to shop on Fifth Avenue, to see friends, and to eat dinner. Duke Snider visited friends on Long Island. Sal Maglie took his son to the park and pushed him on the swings.

The day's reprieve, however, brought no end to the questions about the fate of a team that was not hitting. In 1955 the Dodger batters had torn through the league. And while each man was now taking turns hitting, the team seemed incapable of doing so collectively. Worse still, two of the team's best hitters, and most popular men, Hodges and Campanella, had hit poorly all season. Hodges' batting average hovered at an unacceptable .250, and even more troubling was his penchant for going games on end without driving in a run.

A Hodges slump was the stuff of legend in Brooklyn. He was a popular man, with his teammates and with the fans, even though he displayed none of Robinson's fire, Campanella's ebullience, or Reese's sense of command. Gil Hodges was simply a decent man whom people liked. Like Erskine, he was from Indiana. He'd started out as a catcher, but Rickey, seeing Campanella behind the plate for years to come, switched him to first base in 1948. He became a marvelous fielder, graceful and dependable. He was also remarkably strong, capable of stepping between two brawling players and lifting each man with one arm. Hodges was a quiet man. He was restrained in his emotions, perhaps too much, as Duke Snider had noticed when he watched him try to light a cigarette with shaking hands. Ironically, it was in a time of despair that he made a name for himself in Brooklyn.

In the late days of the 1952 season, as the Dodgers were surging toward a pennant, Hodges stopped hitting. He ended the season in a slump and found no relief in the World Series against the Yankees. He was hitless in his first seventeen times at bat. So desperate were the fans to lift Hodges out of his slump that they began to pray for him. Hodges was a devout Catholic and the priests rallied to him. All across the borough they called on their parishioners to pray that Gil Hodges might be freed from the burden of his slump. Instead of turning against Hodges, Brooklyn embraced him. The prayers, however, did no good. The Dodgers lost the World Series. Hodges never got a hit. No matter. He may have been a failure at bat. But he was Brooklyn's failure, and for that he was rewarded with kindness and admiration.

WHILE HODGES HAD now simply stopped hitting, Campanella's hands looked as if they'd been bludgeoned with a meat tenderizer. The right thumb was swollen to twice the size of the left. The fingers on each hand pointed in several different directions. His catching palm, the left, looked like a bouncer had stomped on it. The fourth finger and pinky of his right hand were broken and the nail was almost gone from the pinky. His fingers, he admitted to Milton Gross of the *Post*, were all but paralyzed.

Gross asked the obvious question: "Why don't you ask out?"

"Why?" Campanella replied. "There's no answer to that question. They want me in there. We're trying to win something."

He did admit, however, that several weeks before a doctor had recommended surgery. The recuperation would have lasted six weeks. Campanella explained this to Buzzie Bavasi who told him, "We can't afford to lose you for six weeks. You just got to play if you can."

So, Campy went on, "I'm playing." Runners were stealing on him. Balls were getting past him. He had switched from his preferred thin-handled bat to one with a thick handle. It barely helped. He was left to let the bat rest on his all but useless right hand while his left hand did the work. Gross, a sensitive and perceptive man, recognized that Campanella was not complaining. Rather, his capacity to endure pain so intense that his saying that a simple swing made his right hand "feel like it's coming off" was a declaration of pride, just as it was in 1954, when he played in misery and still came back to win the 1955 Most Valuable Player Award. "I ain't through yet," he said. "A lot of people think I'm through but I fooled them last year and I'll fool them again once I get that thumb operated on and that bone pushed back to where it belongs."

But first there was the pennant race, and maybe another World Series, and then the postseason trip to Japan. He would hate to miss that one. "They say people over there want to see me."

HE WAS DOWN to one working finger on his right hand when the Dodgers closed out their series with the Pirates after Tuesday's day of rest. A foul tip caught Campanella's index finger and he was forced to leave the game for x-rays, which proved negative. The Dodgers, meanwhile, edged Pittsburgh 4 to 3, and took particular delight in watching Gil Hodges send one into the left field seats. Snider homered, too, and in a handsome display of finesse, Jackie Robinson bunted Reese home on a squeeze play. Sal Maglie pitched into the ninth with such efficiency that 18 of the Pirates' 27 outs came on ground balls. The numbers confirmed that Maglie was growing stronger as the season wore on: he was averaging just under two earned runs for every nine innings over his last ten starts. And when he faltered in the ninth, Alston called on Don Bessent to finish the job, as he had done time and again since Clem Labine broke his wrist. Bessent, who threw very hard, said very little, and bore the unfortunate nickname "Weasel," had not given up a run in weeks. He had been as steady as Labine, which meant that Alston now had two reliable closers, because now Labine was back. He had gone home to Rhode Island to convalesce and immediately started fidgeting with his cast to see if he could somehow grip a baseball. Once he got his fingers around the ball, he tried to throw. And once he saw that he could throw he began doing so in earnest. The cast came off. He was gone only a week.

THE REDS, NOW a game and a half out of first, boarded an overnight train to St. Louis, preparing to unload on the soft Cardinal pitching. The Braves slipped out of town and headed for Chicago, seeking asylum. Milwaukee's city fathers, meanwhile, unveiled plans for a thirty-five-foot plywood "Milwaukee Brave" cutout that would grace the city's skyline—contingent, of course, on the Braves winning the pennant.

The Cubs, typically such hospitable hosts, offered the Braves the backs of their hands. Sad Sam Jones, a skinny pitcher capable of the occasional dazzling performance, chose the opener for just such an occasion, shutting out the Braves, 5 to 0. Haney closed the clubhouse for ten minutes to expound on the virtues of hitting. Lew Burdette opened a beer and tried to cheer up his teammates. Things were no better for the Reds in St. Louis, who were shut out on two hits by Vinegar Bend Mizell.

Rain washed out the Dodgers' opener against the visiting Giants, which meant yet another doubleheader on Friday, and with it the risk of a split. The Giants sat in seventh place, barely ahead of the Cubs, yet playing the Dodgers gave meaning to games long ago rendered insignificant. The Giants took special delight in playing and beating "the Brooklyns," as their manager Bill Rigney later said, if only because the Dodger games were the only ones his team played before large audiences. New York now had little with which to challenge the Dodgers, except for Willie Mays' hitting and the pitching of Johnny Antonelli, who might well have been considered the best pitcher in the league had he been with a team that could hit. Still, the two of them were all the Giants needed to take the opener, 6 to 2 on two homers by Mays, and shutout pitching by Antonelli into the eighth.

The game, however, provided a more interesting coda. The Giants may have disintegrated from their 1954 World Championship team, but were still reminders to the Dodgers and their fans that the great cosmic scales had too seldom tipped Brooklyn's way. Now the Dodgers' passive batting was being analyzed, inevitably, in the context of the Great Collapse of 1951, when the Dodgers squandered their thirteen-and-a-half-game lead, setting up the playoff game that ended with Bobby Thomson's terrible home run against Ralph Branca. And as if the twenty-two thousand souls who came to Ebbets Field needed living proof of life's capricious cruelties, trudging in from the Dodger bull pen in the top of the seventh to sift through the wreckage left by Carl Erskine and Ed Roebuck was none other than the most snakebitten of all Dodgers, Ralph Branca himself.

He had been gone from the majors for three seasons, and had, most believed, ended his baseball career with his release by a minor league franchise in Minnesota. But over the summer he had begun tossing batting practice to his brother's high school team in Westchester and discovered that the bad back that had cut short his career now felt better. He started pitching batting practice for the Dodgers, and when Hodges and Rube Walker told him how good he looked he began wondering whether he might not have something left. He threw to Joe Becker, the pitching coach, who was pleased. Alston asked if he might be interested in giving the game another try. Buzzie Bavasi, short on arms, offered him a spot in the bull pen. Branca arrived at Ebbets Field not at all sure how the Brooklyn fans, whose memories were long, might receive him. "I wonder how it will be to walk out there again," he confided to Milton Gross. "Don't press. Try to relax. Get the ball over . . . if they hit it, they hit it."

He came on to face Willie Mays with two on, an immediate and difficult test. Branca struck him out. He pitched two innings. He gave up one hit, two walks, and struck out two. The fates had granted Ralph Branca an unexpected chance at redemption. And now Branca, once again in a Brooklyn uniform, was facing the New York Giants. This time, however, he did not give up a run.

Bavasi had signed him for the rest of the season. But he never pitched again.

His work done, Branca was left to look on at the nightcap as Don Newcombe, the man he had relieved to face Bobby Thomson, pitched into the eleventh inning while holding the Giants to a single run. The Dodgers appeared poised to salvage the game when Jackie Robinson, of all people, got himself picked off in a rundown between first and second. But Carl Furillo saved him from humiliation when he ended the game with a home run into the left field seats.

"Carl *Furillio*, [*sic*] you baseball hitting son of a bitch," Robinson shouted to him in the clubhouse. "I can sleep tonight now." For when Robinson's head hit the pillow, Brooklyn was tied for second place with Cincinnati, a game and a half out.

The Braves sent Lew Burdette to face the Cubs on Saturday afternoon and he, too, walked away defeated. Milwaukee, now officially the weakest hitting team in the league, had lost five in a row and was sagging so badly that a flattened Burdette, the team booster, took three puffs from a cigarette, tossed it away, and muttered, "Fuck 'em all." The Reds, meanwhile, could not press their advantage, again losing to the Cardinals and dropping to third. Less than a week after their interminable Labor Day weekend, the Dodgers, who edged the Giants 4 to 3, were in second place, a mere half game back. "Seems as if they can't score any runs," Duke Snider said of the Braves. "Doesn't it."

The Braves salvaged the rest of their series in Chicago and headed to Brooklyn for two games at Ebbets Field, their final games of the season against the Dodgers. Brooklyn could take first place with a sweep. "I don't know if we're going to win—our hitting is awful," said Jackie Robinson. "But I'd say we have a hell of a chance now."

For this the Dodgers could thank Carl Furillo, whose hitting had saved them against the Giants. His home run in the finale flew into a headwind so strong that an admiring Jim Gilliam came by his locker to say, "If I ever hit a ball that hard I'll do a dance on home plate." The reporters sought out Furillo after the game and found him uncharacteristically chatty and happy, allowing himself leave to express his pleasure. "I don't want this to sound like an alibi," he said, admitting that for weeks he'd been weakened by a virus he could not shake. "But since we came home I've gotten plenty of my wife's good cooking, and I'm just beginning to feel like myself."

2 | A MAN APART

Carl Furillo was a man so ordered and predictable in his ways that young boys in search of autographs knew precisely where to ambush him after games. Furillo parked not at the Mobil station on Bedford Avenue where the rest of the Dodgers parked, but behind a hot dog stand on the corner of McKeever Place. To get to his car, he had to leave the ballpark through the front, rather than slip out past right field. Day after day he emerged from the rotunda, and day after day the boys were waiting for him. Furillo hurried across the street. The boys chased him. Furillo ran past the hot dog stand to his car, where the boys inevitably caught up. He always signed, but did so quickly. His teammates took turns driving each other to Ebbets Field. Carl Furillo drove alone.

While those who batted before and behind him surged and slumped, Furillo hit with such remarkable consistency that if the annual batting numbers for the ten most productive seasons of his fifteen major league years were plotted out on a bar graph and then placed one on top of the next, the lines would be virtually overlapping. This meant that the Dodgers could be assured that regardless of what the other men did, they could rely on Furillo to bat at or about .300, hit 20 or so home runs, drive in roughly 95 runs, strike out only about 35 times, walk about 40, hit about 150 singles, 27 doubles, and a handful of triples.

He earned the same salary every year—$33,000; he had suggested the arrangement to Bavasi after winning the National League batting title in 1953. He preferred a steady paycheck without fear of a cut, to the possibility of raise that was not guaranteed.

Furillo was thirty-four years old. His teammates called him "Skoonj," short from scungilli, the Italian snail dish. The nickname came with a risk, because Furillo did not possess a sense of humor about himself. He enjoyed the company of a few of his teammates, Gil Hodges among them. But he kept his distance from the others. His roommate was Sandy Koufax, which was just as well because Koufax was not a talker. He did not spend much time with Koufax and the other younger men on the road. He did not like going out, or drinking or, as he later said, "living it big." He had enjoyed the road company of the men he had played with when he first came up, if only because they did little but talk about baseball. Furillo had an eighth grade education and suspected his teammates did not think him very bright. He liked to be with his wife and his two sons. In the off-season they returned to Stony Creek, Pennsylvania, the town outside of Reading where he had grown up. There he worked on his farm, hunted, and fished. His wife called him "dago."

"I'm a family man. I enjoy just hanging around the house, walking around in my shorts, working around the garden," he later told a reporter from *Time*. "I never ignored the other fellows. I just felt like I liked my personal life and I wanted to keep it personal. I never really wanted my left hand to know what my right hand was doing."

It had taken him almost ten years to feel that his job was secure, a degree of self-doubt that bore no relation to his skills. No one, it was said, played Ebbets Field's maddening right field, with its uneven walls and haphazard caroms, better than Furillo, and no outfielder possessed a stronger throwing arm. Tales of his throwing, in fact, had assumed legendary proportions—a reputation that came when he performed the all but unheard-of feat of throwing a runner out at first base from the outfield. He did it only once, to Mel Queen, a Cincinnati pitcher. But that was enough to transform the feat into myth: Dodger fans were sure he did it all the time.

Furillo had grown up poor and started working when he was a child, doing an after-school shift on a vegetable wagon for fifty cents a week. He gave forty cents to his mother. Money came later, with baseball. Pocomoke City, a tiny minor league town 150 miles from home in Maryland, paid him eighty dollars a month and while the money was good Furillo was so homesick he was not sure he could last. Luckily, Reading's team needed an outfielder. "Living at home I found myself," he told Michael Gaven of the *Journal-American*. Luckier still, the Dodgers bought the Reading franchise and promoted Furillo to Montreal, for whom he was hitting well when he was drafted.

He spent three years in the Pacific with the 77th Infantry Division. He landed at Guam, Leyte, Ie Shima, and Okinawa, where he was hit in the head with shrapnel. He never bothered to pick up his Purple Heart: "When I saw all the rest of the guys in the hospital with their legs and arms blown off, I was pretty embarrassed. Mine was just a scratch."

He thought little of baseball during the war, and arrived for spring training in 1946 "scared of the old major leaguers, scared of Durocher, and mostly scared of myself." The older men either ignored him or made him feel unwelcome. One day during batting practice, Durocher ordered him to take his swings before the veteran Dixie Howell had had his turn, a breach of etiquette: rookies always hit last. Furillo stepped into the batting cage. Howell stopped him. "Kid," he said, "you hit after me." Furillo gave way but Durocher ordered Howell out. "I guess," Furillo later said, "I never really got along well with Howell after that."

Nor did he get along with Durocher. He felt that Durocher wrongly branded him as a drinker after two beer bottles were spotted in his room after a party: "I was a one-beer man." He also took umbrage at Durocher's suggestion that he could not hit righties—he was a .300 hitter, he asked, so how could that be true? Their simmering feud erupted in 1953, when Durocher was managing the Giants. Furillo had gone four for four the day before and Ruben Gomez, hardly a headhunter, threw a pitch at his skull. The ball missed his head but hit his wrist. Furillo picked himself up, looked to the Giant dugout, saw Durocher giving him the finger, and took off after him. Durocher met him halfway. Furillo had Durocher's head locked in his arm and was about to smack him in the face when Durocher got hold of his pinky and bent it back until it broke. Furillo was ejected for fighting, which he did not regret. He was only upset that he never managed to get in a punch.

HE WAS NOT a tolerant man. When he made up his mind about people he did not change it. "He didn't have a lot of time for a guy who was frivolous," Carl Erskine later recalled. Erskine and Furillo would sometimes fish at night off of a dock at Vero Beach. Furillo was serious about fishing. He was serious about most things. "He was a pretty stern personality."

Furillo was equally judgmental about players who did not hustle as he was about management: he did not much care for Buzzie Bavasi. He felt that Bavasi was devious, lacking in candor, a trait Furillo disliked. As it happened, in June, when the team was foundering, the papers carried stories of possible trades, and Furillo's name was one of those mentioned. Furillo heard of the rumors from his wife, Fern, who had read of them. And while Bavasi was quick to assure all the Dodgers, and Carl Furillo in particular, that they were not going to be traded, Furillo was not satisfied. Bavasi, who was en route to Chicago to meet the team, had asked Lee Scott, the road secretary, to pass the message on for him.

Bavasi tried to play down the rumors, and the fretting. "Naturally, they all want to stay with us for that World Series money and they are pressing too hard," he said. "Why, I understand that Mrs. Furillo is so concerned that she hasn't rented an apartment in Brooklyn."

That was unacceptable to Carl Furillo. "Why couldn't he come and tell me himself?" he asked. "He blames our wives. My wife didn't call me. I called her and told her not to take an apartment until the day we returned home. I wanted to know how I stood from Bavasi. Now he passes the buck to our wives, and you can quote me on that."

When the Dodgers came home the Furillos did rent, but not in Brooklyn with the other Dodger families. They lived apart, in Queens. His teammates did not take offense. They accepted his ways, in good measure because they came with no surprises. He was not a belligerent man. He did not pick fights. He did not taunt or bait. He played his game and then he went his own way.

Still, his teammates could sometimes amuse him. Or rather that is how it seemed to the writers who noticed that when one of the Dodgers would say something a little loud or a little foolish Carl Furillo would turn from the solitude of his locker and offer a knowing and weary smile.

3 | TANTALUS

There are mysteries in baseball that defy logic and resolution. Why, for instance, could Warren Spahn defeat so many teams, yet endure a biblical plague of losses against the Dodgers? Other, lesser left-handers defeated Brooklyn. Why not the great Spahn? How could Gil Hodges hit twenty-six home runs, yet now go eleven games in a row against different teams and different pitchers and fail to drive anyone home? The long season gave baseball's metaphysicians ample latitude to ponder what lay behind the game's many ironies. The fatalists, meanwhile, could cite the same perplexing moments as proof positive that things just happen.

The coming of the Braves to Brooklyn rekindled one of the season's most vexing conundrums: If the Cincinnati Reds could beat Bob Buhl every time they faced him, why could the Dodgers not defeat him, even once? Buhl, a young man with thick eyebrows and a growing sense of confidence, threw hard. But other pitchers threw hard and the Dodger batters—at least those who happened to be hitting that day, or week—could dispatch them to early showers. Bob Buhl was not going to the Hall of Fame, as Warren Spahn would. Yet if the Dodgers were to force themselves into a first place tie with the Braves they would have to find a way to score runs against Bob Buhl. Sal Maglie would face Buhl, which meant the Dodgers would not necessarily have to score many runs. Factoring in Maglie's recent lack of generosity to the opposition, less than two runs a game, three runs should do the job. Four would give the Barber room to breathe.

TICKET SALES HAD been brisk for this one—people started lining up to buy on their way out of Ebbets Field right after the Dodgers defeated the Giants. This was not Milwaukee, where the big games sold out weeks in advance. The Brooklyn fans had waited to see where the Dodgers might be in September. And they had now seen enough to compel them to buy. Ebbets Field would at last be sold out.

The Braves, meanwhile, had boarded their train feeling immensely pleased with themselves. Now that they had defeated the Cubs twice, their funereal clubhouse was transformed into a happy place, filled with boastful young men. "I got a message for those Dodgers," Danny O'Connell called out. "Carl Furillo said that if we came out there with less than a two game lead, we'd blow the pennant. Well, we're going east with a one game lead and we'll pick up that other game right there in Brooklyn." His optimism was infectious: back in Milwaukee, the team announced that it would start selling World Series tickets the following week. And Charlie Grimm, on enforced sabbatical at home in Robertsville, Missouri, announced that "my boys" would win the pennant—although he did not for a moment believe that the race would be resolved in the next two days in Brooklyn. "There are too many games left to play," he said. "I think this race will go right down to the wire."

SAL MAGLIE SLEPT until noon on the day of the series opener, Tuesday, September 11. He ate his big pregame meal and then left his Manhattan apartment for Ebbets Field. As he drove he reviewed the Milwaukee lineup, and the mistakes he had made against them. He thought about the last time he pitched to Henry Aaron: he had thrown a strike past him on the outside corner, and when he came back with a pitch to the same spot, Aaron smacked it for a single to right.

"I made a mistake that time," he told Milton Gross. "I won't make it again." He and Gross sat in the empty Ebbets Field clubhouse while his teammates went through their warm-ups. Gross found Maglie in a rare mood: he was not only feeling chatty but philosophical, as well. "Pitching is more than throwing the ball," Maglie told him. "It's more than curves or fastballs or changeups. You got to know why you're doing everything. You're setting a hitter up with one pitch, but you need to know what the following pitch is going to be, too."

He dispatched the Braves without incident in the first. But Eddie Mathews jumped on the first pitch Maglie threw in the second and homered to left, giving Milwaukee the lead, 1 to 0. Buhl, meanwhile, could not seem to find the strike zone. The Dodger fans were on him early, loudly, and often, cheering every ball. The stand-room-only sign, which seemed destined for obsolesence all season long, was finally displayed before game time, and those who pressed their way into the park arrayed themselves along the corridors and stairwells, anywhere that offered a slice of a view.

Buhl delighted them by walking two in the first and one in the third. He had two on and two out in the fourth when he walked Campanella intentionally, loading the bases to face Maglie. But again, Buhl could not seem to throw strikes. He ran the count full and Maglie, knowing he would see something in the strike zone, lined the next pitch over second, scoring Amoros and Hodges, his first runs batted in of the season.

"We're in," came a voice from the cheering sections.

"Hey," cried out another, offering Maglie the ultimate compliment, "how ya like that bum." Two grown men danced a polka in the stands in center and strangers were seen hugging.

Jim Gilliam stepped in and Buhl walked him, too, his seventh pass of the game. The Dodgers had barely touched him. But Fred Haney had seen too much wildness and came to fetch him.

Maglie, meanwhile, flirted with trouble in the fifth, when Andy Pafko led off with a double. But the Barber struck out Bill Bruton and stranded Pafko with two ground ball outs. Milwaukee pressed again in the sixth, when Danny O'Connell and Mathews singled, bringing the mighty Joe

Adcock to bat. All night long, Maglie had worked the Braves inside and out, keeping them off stride. He started Adcock outside for a strike. But instead of coming in, he threw the next pitch to precisely the same spot for a second strike, believing that Adcock would be looking for something inside. Maglie had him at a decided disadvantage, but instead of going inside, he threw outside again, this time a little further off the plate for a ball. Now he had Adcock where he wanted him—not at all sure what he would see next. So Maglie, who had been spinning his assorted curveballs all night, threw a fastball up in the strike zone. Adcock swung, but got underneath it. His pop up sailed high over the infield and when it finally came down, Reese was waiting, mitt open, to end the inning.

The Braves kept pecking at him. In the eighth, Felix Mantilla singled and took second on O'Connell's sacrifice. Henry Aaron stepped in and Maglie, knowing what Aaron had done with him the last time they met, decided that if Aaron was going to hit anything it would be a curve. He started him with one for a ball. Then he came inside with a fastball that Aaron fouled off. He offered a curveball low, and then another away, which Aaron grounded to Gilliam for the second out.

Eddie Mathews, who had already homered and singled, was next to bat. Maglie turned toward third. Jackie Robinson was coming toward him.

"How is it?" Robinson asked.

"I'm a little tired," said Maglie.

Robinson waved Reese over. "He says he's tired," he told the captain, who needed no instructions from the dugout on what to do next.

"Let's just stand here and talk then," he said. "Take a blow, Sal."

They chatted for a while until Walter Alston came to the mound.

"What do you want to do?" he asked Maglie.

"I got to pitch to this guy," Maglie told him.

"You don't have to," Alston said. Labine and Bessent were in the bull pen, ready.

"I got to pitch to him," Maglie said again. So Alston let him, and watched as Mathews grounded hard to Gilliam to end the inning.

Robinson led off the home eighth with a single. Amoros sacrificed him to second. Ernie Johnson was now pitching for Milwaukee and Robinson, ever the rude host, decided to make him as uncomfortable as possible. He danced off of second, challenging Johnson to pick him off. Now the Ebbets

Field crowd was so loud and raucous that Billy Herman, the third base coach, jogged over to Robinson and said, "I can't make you hear me on account of the noise of the crowd, so you're on your own. Watch out for those guys you don't get picked off." Herman returned to the coaching box and Robinson took a modest lead off second. He feinted a run to third and this time Johnson turned to throw. But in his haste the ball sailed over Danny O'Connell's glove. Robinson never broke stride as he rounded third and slid into home, just ahead of the throw to the plate. Gil Hodges, so silent for so long, followed with his twenty-seventh home run of the season, and when he stepped on home plate he looked up to the stands to see his wife, Joan, blowing him a kiss.

Maglie had his three-run cushion as he took the mound in the top of the ninth. This was just as well because Joe Adcock opened things with a long home run into the upper deck in left center—his thirty-sixth of the season and twelfth against the Dodgers. His lead cut by one, Maglie dispatched the next three Braves, giving the Dodgers their first, albeit shared, glimpse of first place since April 28, when he was still a forgotten Cleveland Indian.

Afterward in the clubhouse, Maglie called out to the reporters who gathered around him, "How about that hitting? Somebody say something nice about my hitting?"

The beat fellows asked about his back, which he admitted still hurt him, and his arm, which he swore never felt better. "I'm a better pitcher now than I ever was, I think," he said. "I mean I'm doing more now. Experience, that's the difference. In 1951, for instance, I was just firing the ball."

Milton Gross asked him about Mathews' at-bat in the eighth. "I didn't want him to hit the first pitch," Maglie said. "I gave him a bad curveball. Then I tried him on a low curveball. I took a little off of it. I guess it worked."

Pee Wee Reese, meanwhile, was filled with admiration. "Lordy, Lordy," he said. "What a job that man can do."

IT WAS DON Newcombe's turn to pitch the Dodgers into sole possession of first place, just as it was Lew Burdette's to restore Milwaukee's lead. Burdette, whose taunting of Jackie Robinson had almost caused his demise in Milwaukee, had called to Robinson under the stands the night before.

Robinson approached and several minutes later walked away smiling. Burdette, he explained, had apologized for what he had said in Milwaukee, assuring Robinson that he meant the word "watermelon" not as a racial barb but as a comment on Robinson's girth. Burdette hoped he believed him. Robinson was pleased. "He said this discrimination business has gone on far enough and he wanted no part of it," Robinson said. "I'm happier about this than anything that has happened to me in a long time."

Twenty-two thousand people filtered into Ebbets Field for the Wednesday matinee, giving the aging ballpark the feel of a nightclub the morning after a party that went on too late, too loud, and too drunk. Still, those who did make it in time for Newcombe's first pitch to Felix Mantilla had every reason to anticipate a battle as tense as that of the evening before: Newcombe had already won twenty-three games; Burdette's earned run average was the lowest in the league. Milwaukee went quietly in the first and Brooklyn seemed poised to succumb to Burdette's alleged slippery pitches when he retired Gilliam to open the home first. But then Reese singled and Snider doubled him home, giving the Dodgers a quick and early lead. Robinson grounded to second, moving Snider to third, thereby precluding the need for him to sprint on his aching knee when Sandy Amoros tripled him home. Carl Furillo's single scored Amoros and Burdette was gone, trailing 3 to 0, having never given the Dodgers a chance to watch his catch-me-if-you-can shell game on the mound. No matter. First place was eight innings away, when Newk lumbered out to the mound.

Newcombe was a man of great talent, but also dark and tenuous moods. He was sensitive to slights and injustices. Eddie Mathews led off the Milwaukee second. Newcombe walked him on four pitches. When he threw two balls to Joe Adcock, Reese could see that while Newcombe had lost none of his velocity, the same could not be said for his composure: feeling his pitches too harshly judged, Newcombe appeared to Reese to be aiming the ball rather than throwing it with ease and confidence. Adcock saw it, too, and jumped on Newcombe's next offering, singling. Bobby Thomson singled Mathews home. Bill Bruton's triple scored two more and brought Walter Alston to the mound. "The way things were going for him, I thought I'd better get him out of there," he said a few hours later. Alston called for Clem Labine.

Campanella evened things at four runs apiece with his eighteenth home run of the season. But in the sixth Mathews doubled and Adcock, as if on cue, drove Labine's first pitch to center. Snider went back on the ball and stopped only when he reached the wall. There he watched the ball find the first row of seats. The Braves, who appeared destined for second place earlier in the day, had tied the score at four runs apiece, and took the lead an inning later on Del Crandell's home run.

Brooklyn was down 7 to 4 when Dale Mitchell led off the seventh with a pinch-hit single. Gilliam followed with another single, and Reese's single drove Mitchell home. The Dodgers had two on, none out, and Snider coming to bat. For all his power the Duke had been struggling, and with a left-hander, Taylor Phillips, now on for Milwaukee—Alston ordered the bunt that would move Reese to second, in position to score behind Gilliam on a base hit.

Snider took Phillips' first pitch for a ball. He squared to bunt on the second. Gilliam was breaking from second when Snider committed the Sin of Omission: he missed the ball, leaving Gilliam stranded on the base paths, a helpless out. Phillips then walked Snider. Haney pulled Phillips and called on Bob Buhl, the nemesis the Dodgers had finally beaten the night before. Used to starting, Buhl plunked Robinson with a pitch, loading the bases. Sandy Amoros was about to redeem him when he grounded to second, a sure double play. But Danny O'Connell played the ball like a croquet gate, letting it roll past him into right field. Reese and Snider scored. The Dodgers had pulled even again. And Carl Furillo was up to bat.

Buhl came inside on him. Furillo tried to check his swing but the pitch hit his bat. The ball rolled to Buhl, who saw instantly the double play that could keep the score knotted. On third base Robinson saw it, too, and wanted only to avoid it. He broke for home, slowly, hoping to draw a throw that would allow Amoros to reach second and Furillo to make it to first. But Buhl ignored him. He threw to second, starting the double play that ended the inning.

Alston now called on Roger Craig to pitch. The Braves eked out a run against him in the eighth and might have scored more had Bobby Thomson not tried to steal home with the bases loaded and two out—a play so boneheaded that Fred Haney fined him a hundred dollars. But the Dodgers could do nothing more against Bob Buhl, who got the win that, for the moment, rescued Milwaukee's fragile lead.

"We snafued it, that's for sure," said a rueful but hardly despairing Carl Furillo. "But we're not hurtin'. They're hurtin'. They got four tough games in Philadelphia in three days. They got to survive. They can't afford to split two or we're right back on their tails, a half game out."

Furillo was wrong only on the timing. The Dodgers would soon enough be "back on their tails." So would Cincinnati.

4 | AUTUMN

The National League pennant race that had begun five months and 139 games ago was down to its final two weeks. The contenders each had fifteen games to play. The Brooklyn Dodgers would play eleven of their games at home.

Children were back at school. The weather turned cooler. The Braves left town for Philadelphia. The Reds were in Pittsburgh. And a meager ninety-five hundred people came to see the Dodgers play the Chicago Cubs.

Ebbets Field was a melancholy place—a summer resort after Labor Day, a supper club where the waiters were turning up the chairs. The sell-out in the opener against the Braves a few days before was a pleasant aberration; so too was the team's announcement that it had surpassed a million patrons for the season. The number included the seven Jersey City games, where 148,000 patrons turned out, if only just to boo. The *Post*, whose editors wanted to know where all the Dodger fans had gone, dispatched reporters to Flatbush Avenue to ask. They heard complaints about seeing the best seats go to those with the best connections, about the rising price of hot dogs and beer—thirty-five cents for a beer or a ham sandwich, twenty cents for a hot dog, fifteen cents for coffee—as well as about the rotten parking and being fleeced by the local garages for three dollars a spot once the team's tiny dollar-a-spot lot was full. Taking it all together, the *Post*'s reporters heard time and again, it was better to stay home and watch the game on television.

"Why knock myself out when all I have to do is have the wife bring out the slippers, tune in the twenty-one-inch screen, and relax with some of my favorite brew," said Barry Needleman, a salesman. "It's much simpler."

"The other day I passed right by the ballpark and I was going to go in," said George Van Flet, another man in sales. "Then I decided I could enjoy the game on TV just as well in my favorite tavern, and did just that."

And Salvatore Ferretti, a designer, insisted that his passion had not waned—"Don't get me wrong, I love baseball"—so much so that he watched it on television "all the time," a situation that, he suggested, could be remedied if the Dodgers installed pari-mutuel betting machines at the park.

On and on they went, declaring their devotion to the team and their pleasure in watching them in peace at home. Milwaukee may have been drawing thirty thousand people to a day game against the Pirates. But then all this was new to Milwaukee—a major league team, and a pennant race, and the pleasure of the company of so many like-minded strangers. Milwaukee was at a further advantage: none of the Braves' games were televised.

In Brooklyn there was nothing new about the Dodgers in a pennant race. There was nothing that new about the team, and there was certainly nothing new about the ballpark. Nor was there a sense of a desire to be out there with everyone else. They had been seeing each other, so to speak, for years. And the familiarity was neither a novelty nor desirable, not when the living room and an easy chair and an ottoman beckoned.

Despite Jimmy Cannon's admonition that Dodger fans needed to go to see the old fellows in their prime this one last time, the men and women who had followed them for a decade looked on with no sense of urgency, as if to say that surely all this would go on forever. It was like the New Yorker's view on the Statue of Liberty: it has always been rare to find a New Yorker who actually made the trip to see it. Why rush? It's always going to be there.

Yet that very month, the *World-Telegram* unveiled for its Brooklyn readers a portrait of an altogether different borough in the year 2000. The paper asked urban planners, architects, and realtors to envision what Brooklyn might look like, forty-four years hence. This Brooklyn bore no relation to the Brooklyn everyone knew. In this Brooklyn people would no longer live in private houses. Instead they would live in apartment buildings, some of them thirty stories high. The buildings would be set on "superblocks"—vast tracts of land where high-rises were surrounded by bucolic, open spaces. The "superblocks" would be bounded by broad highways, eight-lane thoroughfares that cut through the borough. Six massive community centers would rise at strategic points around Brooklyn. Each would be able to accommodate one hundred thousand people who would come to see sporting events (each center would have a small stadium), go to movies (each had a half dozen or so small movie houses), and otherwise join together in the wholesome life, a life made possible by a projected fifteen-hour workweek. Families would have more time to be together. Neighbors would share in the common purpose of keeping their community grounds clean and manicured. On summer weekends everyone could go to the long stretch of beach on the borough's fringes.

It was as if Robert Moses and Josef Stalin had sat down with pencils and cocktail napkins and came up with a vision for the good life. There was, however, a caveat: this new and pristine Brooklyn could be realized only if people lived longer, if cheaper building methods were discovered, and if the world remained at peace. Otherwise, one planner cautioned, by 1975 the borough would see a drop in its population as more and more people left for the suburbs of Long Island and New Jersey.

The Brooklyn Sports Center would be just a small part of this great and new borough. And at the moment, the authority members were preparing to dip their toes in the water: they were ready to open an office, and to ask the state for money to pay for their work. That the three men were proceeding at a glacial pace may have privately infuriated Walter O'Malley. But he was still performing the charade of presenting himself as the most contented of men. He insisted that his declining attendance did not concern him. He said this to Milton Gross, and Gross believed him. "Our pitch for attendance has been made," O'Malley told him. "We're very pleased with it. I have no occasion to scold our fans."

Nor was he about to decry the rise of television, even though having two competing teams in the same market compelled him to televise Dodger home games. "If television were such a bugaboo how do you account for the fact that over the last 10 years our attendance has been as satisfactory as it has been?"

For this Gross had no answer. But as for the matter of revenue he had something to say. The Dodgers' television deal brought them $600,000 a year. Figuring the average spectator paid $1.25 for a general admission ticket, and after deducting taxes, usher and ticket-taker's fees, and 27½ cents paid to visiting teams, the Dodgers were still making 55 cents on each ticket. That $600,000, he concluded, earned the team as much as a million paying customers. And few teams were drawing that many. At the midseason all-star break, the Associated Press calculated attendance figures and reported good news: the numbers were up from 1955. The National League was averaging just over 14,000 spectators a game—up by 1,300; the American League just under at 13,864, or 694 more spectators a day. A generation later these numbers would be so unacceptable that they would occasion talk of moving the franchise to a more hospitable town. But in 1956 the Dodgers could draw an average of 15,361 fans a game—and only seven times eclipse their best night of 26,385 at Jersey City—and still be doing better than anyone in the league but the Braves, who did not have to share their baseball audience with two other teams. The Giants were barely drawing 10,000 a night (Washington did even worse, averaging under 7,000 a game for the woeful Senators). And the Yankees were doing only marginally better than the Dodgers—18,795 on average at Yankee Stadium, but 22,000 on the road, if only to see Mickey Mantle hit.

THE DODGERS STILL had their following, and the following still had its eccentricities: the fifty or so people who called the clubhouse every night—*how did they get the number?*—to bombard Walter Alston with complaints and suggestions; the middle-aged man who stole Gil Hodges' mitt and then sheepishly returned it when Hodges offered a new one in exchange. But gone were the fans whose peculiarities had given Ebbets Field a singular if somewhat cockeyed charm. Hilda Chester, the loud and batty woman who rang a cowbell and always reminded Pee Wee Reese to drink his milk, was no longer an everyday patron, and when she did come she no longer sat in the cheap seats, but in the $1.25 section in company of people she had once dismissed as "them plus-lined bums." Shorty Laurice, who led the Dodger Sym-Phony, the self-appointed and barely melodic team orchestra, with such dedication that he refused to let work get in the way of a home game, was dead, and his brother, Tony, had moved out to the Island years before. Gone, too, were Eddie Batten, a small, round man who wore a pith helmet and who used to yell "Hey, Leo, Hey, Leo," over and over again when Durocher was with the team, and Jack Pierce, who sat near third base launching balloons and calling out "Cookie, Cookie," to Cookie Lavagetto.

Bill Roeder of the *World-Telegram*, went out to the park to discover that the new oddballs were an altogether tamer lot—like the man who bought a reserved seat for every game but insisted upon standing in the runway near first base to get a better view of home, or the fellow in Bermuda shorts who had a season ticket that allowed him to move to a different seat each game: he was so loud that he was sure he bothered whomever was stuck sitting next to him.

Still, the Sym-Phony played on. A woman named Letty Allen still came to every home game, as she had for fifty years. And when the games were done she waited by the clubhouse door where the players always stopped to give her a kiss.

The Dodgers took both games against Chicago, the second on a shutout by Don Newcombe, his twenty-fourth victory of the season, best in the majors. The Braves, meanwhile, had proved Furillo wrong, but only briefly. They swept their doubleheader against the Phillies. But then they dropped the next two. On Sunday, September 16, the Dodgers came to Ebbets Field in first place, a half game up, for the first time since April. They had beaten the Cubs and Cardinals, while Milwaukee had failed in the contender's task of taking two out of three against the lesser teams. The Braves were in town to face the Giants. Cincinnati, now just two games out, was coming to Ebbets Field.

Twenty thousand people came to see them, which left ten thousand empty seats.

5 | JUST OFF THE BOAT

It had been almost a year since the October afternoon when the Dodgers beat the Yankees to become World Champions. That had been a night unlike any other in Brooklyn. People honked their horns and strangers hugged and at every bar Jose Sanchez and his friends stopped in that night the drinks were on the house. Sanchez and his friends went to the parade at Borough Hall, where the streets were so crowded that people were hanging from the lampposts to see the players. And best of all for Sanchez was the feeling that this was not merely a team's victory, but Brooklyn's redemption: "We finally won. We finally won. It was Brooklyn's day. Finally, we were the champs."

The celebration lasted for a day and then people went back to work. Sanchez returned to the factory where he made peanut brittle in a morning-after frame of mind. Now that the party was over, and with it the great surge in delight in the Dodgers' victory, the world around him once again became familiar. The view was not always a pleasing one. Sanchez was twenty-two years old and everyone called him "Tuffy." He lived in South Brooklyn, a neighborhood close to downtown. He had lived all his life in South Brooklyn and had no desire to live anyplace else. Still, the neighborhood was not as it had been when he was young, or even when he left for the service in 1951. There were so many newcomers now. And the newcomers brought new ways that were not always welcome.

Sanchez knew two kinds of Puerto Ricans: people like him and his friends whose parents had come up in the early 1920s; and the new people, the "jibaros," the hillbillies. Sanchez's father was pastor of the Antioch Pentecostal Church. The congregation was compelled to relocate from its modest home on Clinton Street in Cobble Hill, to a converted movie theater on busy Atlantic Avenue to accommodate all the new people who now came to worship. On Clinton Street the Reverend Sanchez had preached to an audience of perhaps one hundred. But now three hundred and sometimes four hundred people filled the room on Sunday mornings.

They were different. They were poorer—you could see that in the cheap clothes, and in the appeals for work. And they lacked the sophistication of city people. Those who had come to America before them dismissed them for dressing flashily and playing music too loudly and in most every way not understanding how to live in the city. They were embarrassing, especially because the Italians, Jews, and Irish among whom the long-timers had lived for a generation might now too easily associate them with the new Puerto Ricans. These were the Puerto Ricans whose ten-year-old children were stuck in second grade because they could not speak or read English. They were people who could never seem to adjust to winter. They lived crammed fifteen to a room. Jose Sanchez had five brothers and nine sisters and though the boys and girls shared rooms, the arrangement was altogether different than that of the waves of the newly arrived who came to Brooklyn only to live on a relative's couch or floor.

There were so many of them. Forty-five to fifty thousand Puerto Ricans a year were coming up from the island—a one-way ticket cost $52 on Pan

American Airlines—almost triple the number that came, by boat, in 1920. They came with the understanding that in New York they would find work—a reasonable belief: the island was being transformed through what was called Operation Bootstrap from an agrarian world to an industrial one, which meant that there would be ever less work in the countryside. There was work in New York, but not for everyone.

If the friends and neighbors of Jose Sanchez's parents had also once been farm people, they had had, often as not, a sojourn in San Juan on their way to New York, where they learned something of urban life. Besides, the earlier migrants were a self-selected group—the people ambitious enough to go. They were better educated and came with useful skills, cigar making among them. They came to Florida, and to New York and found work in the cigar making shops, where they joined similarly eager people who talked of politics and unions and events of the day. It was understood at these factories that each worker would ante up a portion of his salary to pay for the shop "reader." The "reader" was the worker chosen to sit on a high stool and read out loud as the others rolled tobacco leaves. In the mornings he read the newspapers, and in the afternoons he read translations of, say, Zola, Dickens, and Dostoyevsky. And whatever talk emerged from the readings about the oppression of the workingman was shared, in turn, with other working people of entirely different backgrounds, be they Jewish, Italian, or Irish.

Their children spoke English and went to school and played ball with the children of their Jewish, Italian, and Irish neighbors. They had black neighbors, too, though in South Brooklyn not many. There were Syrians, too, who lived near Atlantic Avenue. The children developed neighborhood rules of their own: the Syrians, for instance, threw in with the Puerto Ricans in fights against the Italians after getting beaten up by the Italians once too often. They fought with fists and nothing more and generally they got along well enough to eat in each other's homes. Their fathers worked and in the evenings came home to three-story walk-ups that had no indoor plumbing; the outhouse was in the back. The water ran cold, which made bath time an unpleasant business, especially when the bathtub was no more than a large basin that sat in the middle of the kitchen. Sanchez's mother shopped for meat every day, which was just as well because the only way to keep food cold was in a wooden box suspended outside the window. The neighbors may have differed in ethnicity, color, and religion, but they did share the affiliation of class—the genuine working class. And when their time came, as it did for Jose Sanchez in 1951, they went into the service. Jose Sanchez served three years in the army, and when he returned to South Brooklyn from Korea in 1954 he could not help but notice that while his friends were still around, and getting together at the same places to do the same things, there were a lot of new young men around, whom they did not feel compelled to invite in.

Yet even if people were no longer comfortable sleeping on their roofs on the hot nights, and if his grandmother now seemed reluctant to risk the walk to Union Street every morning to buy bread, and if his mother was now telling him "be careful" whenever he went out, there was still, in his view, every reason to believe that life as he had known it could proceed as it always had. On weekends he played softball with the same young men who had been his friends since he was a child. On weeknights, after work, they gathered at Al's, an ice cream parlor on Atlantic Avenue. They had been going to the ice cream parlor for years. The ice cream parlor had a beer license, which explained its enduring popularity with young men who had outgrown the taste for sundaes. Sometimes they went to the movies, and sometimes they went into Manhattan and sometimes they just stayed at Al's and talked. They talked a lot about the Dodgers, even if they were not going to Ebbets Field as often as they once had. It was not that they cared any less about the Dodgers. It was just that now they had discovered other things to do, most of them having to do with girls.

So instead of going to a ballgame on a Saturday they went to downtown Brooklyn to watch the girls window-shopping in front of the nice department stores like Martin's and Abraham & Straus. Or they met at the ice cream parlor and from there they went to the city to dance at the Palladium Ballroom, or they stayed in Brooklyn and went to a friend's place for a "house party." They listened to music, Tito Puente and Eddie Palmieri records, and danced and drank "sneaky pete," a lethal brew of port and muscatel that sold for thirty-five cents a pint. And if they had a girl they took her to the Manhattan Bridge, which had a pedestrian walkway. At night the walkway was dark, and lurking in the shadows of the pillars were couples, seeking love and privacy. Sanchez and his friends called the pillars the "pillows." On Sundays they had dinner with their families and afterward they went to the ice cream parlor.

The new Puerto Ricans might have thought of sitting in the booths at Al's, but Sanchez and his friends made it clear that the ice cream parlor was their place. "They couldn't sit in the booths where we were sitting or hang out at all," he later said. So the new young men hung out on the corners. Jose Sanchez was blessed with the ability to avoid reading dark tidings into circumstances that might have left others fearful and anxious. One day, for instance, a man burst into the ice cream parlor with a gun. He did not fire the gun but he waved it a lot and people ducked and hid under the tables while the man screamed about finding someone he was looking for. "I'll be back," the man shouted and then he left. For weeks afterward people at Al's talked about the man with the gun.

JOHN POWIS HAD noticed the newcomers, too, but from a more forgiving perspective. Powis was twenty-three years old and studying to be a priest. He had been spending the summer assisting the Sisters of the Most Blessed Trinity in their work in South Brooklyn. What money he made came from peddling hot dogs at Ebbets Field; years later he would still recall the way they turned from brown to green in the course of a Sunday doubleheader.

Powis now joined the Sisters in inviting families who lived in the South Brooklyn housing projects to come to church, and in welcoming their sons to the various sports leagues run by the Catholic Youth Organization. Twice a month he would take two hundred and fifty children for a day trip to Coney Island. Powis had grown up in East New York and while he was familiar with life in the row houses, he did not know many black or Puerto Rican people. He was learning a good deal from the families in the projects, enough to recognize that their needs were not nearly as pressing as those of the people who lived on South Brooklyn's side streets. There, in the three-story walk-ups vacated by the people who now lived in the projects, were the homes of the new arrivals. The newcomers came to church. They packed the Spanish-language Mass at St. James Roman Catholic Church with perhaps eight hundred people.

Powis began to visit them. He climbed the steps and knocked on doors and when people found out he was going to be a priest they invited him inside. What he saw was nothing like life in the projects. Several families would share an apartment. They hung blankets from the ceilings to divide the rooms. The apartments were so cold in winter that the burners on the range were kept burning all day and night. Children were often naked, which Powis learned had made perfect sense in the world that the newcomers had just left—the countryside, where it was hot and humid and where children did not need to wear clothes. "And," he later recalled, "they always had a lot of kids." People were always home. Fathers were out working, some of them at two jobs, maybe at a factory, or bussing restaurant tables, or making deliveries. Sometimes the fathers were no longer around, leaving the responsibility for raising the family to their eldest sons. There were sons who worked and who took their responsibilities seriously, making sure that their sisters were going to school. Others were hectored by their mothers for sleeping late and never finding jobs. Some of the young men, lost and hurt and with no sense of their place in the world, joined the gangs. The gangs were not necessarily large and formal organizations; often as not, they were no more than a group of teenage boys who lived in adjoining buildings and who formed an alliance for protection. Powis assisted the mothers when the sons were arrested for fighting, or for petty thefts or for stealing cars for a joyride. He also assisted when schools gave parents a difficult time about enrolling their children or when they were compelled to visit the welfare office, where it was difficult for them to argue their cases because the workers did not speak Spanish.

"There were just too many families coming at the same time," he later said.

MEANWHILE, EVEN THE lives of the established families were not as they once were. For Jose Sanchez this meant going with his father night after night to court, after word came that one of his three younger brothers was under arrest for yet another robbery or burglary that came from trying to find what money they could to support their heroin addictions.

It was only after he came home from Korea that he learned of his three brothers' drug habits; no one had written to tell him. He quickly learned the hard lesson his father, mother, and siblings had learned: that there was nothing he could do to stop his brothers from buying and using; their addictions were too far along. His brothers still lived at home and that was where the calls would come, at night, summoning his father to the precinct house. Sanchez, understanding his father's humiliation, talked with him about his brothers. His father, who continued preaching even while his sons were rifling through their sleeping siblings pockets, told him that saving one soul fulfilled a great mission, but "you can't save them all."

Sanchez did not know who was selling heroin to his brothers. The arrival in South Brooklyn of heroin and cocaine, he believed, may have coincided with the arrival of the newcomers, but he did not blame them for the coming of narcotics. Rather, he understood that while wealthy people had the money to buy their drugs, poor people needed to steal for theirs. The police had noticed the same thing: arrests were inching up for crimes involving narcotics; the police were not yet drawing a distinction between arrests for possession and sale, and arrests for crimes committed to buy narcotics. The numbers, however, were still modest—703 narcotics-related felony arrests in the first six months of 1956, compared to 604 for the same period in 1955. But in Brooklyn, District Attorney Edward Silver saw the beginnings of a scourge, and wanted to move quickly and forcibly to place drug-addicted criminals in "a quarantine type of confinement" where they might be cured of their habits—"It will isolate a dangerous contagion."

By the late summer of 1956, Jose Sanchez's brothers were spending time in jail. His sisters were coming home from school and telling of friends who had *their own rooms* and wondering when they might have them, too. Sanchez had never minded sharing with his brothers; it made everything feel closer, even if there were so many of them that they had to eat dinner in shifts.

"It wasn't like a family anymore," he would later say. "It was a happy feeling, until things started changing."

6 | LAST TRAIN TO PITTSBURGH

The 1956 Brooklyn Dodgers boarded a train for the last time on the night of September 20. They were bound for Pittsburgh. They were, as had been customary for most of the last ten years, a first place team. Though their lead was only a game, the Dodgers had reason to believe that another pennant was at hand: they were playing the Pirates, the sixth place team. And though the Pirates had played them well, the Dodgers had won five of their last six games. Milwaukee, meanwhile, had stumbled in Philadelphia, as well as against the Giants and Pirates, losing four of their last seven, blowing the slender lead they had carried from Ebbets Field. The Reds, who had seemed on the verge of making a run of their own, had been just as uneven. They'd had their chance at Ebbets Field. Twice they went into the ninth inning tied with the Dodgers. And twice the Dodgers beat them in their final at-bat. They left Brooklyn a sinking club, four and a half games out. Though the Dodgers finally lost one in the ninth against the Cardinals, they came back the following afternoon to flatten St. Louis 17 to 2.

A scattering of young men gathered at Track 14 at Pennsylvania Station to wish them well. It was late by the time the train pulled out and the Dodgers retreated to their sleeping compartments. Pee Wee Reese changed into a pair of striped pajamas, and was smoking a cigarette when Don Newcombe stopped in.

"You chow up?" Reese asked him.

"I had a bite," Newcombe replied.

"If I have any chow I can't sleep on a train," Reese said. "I just had a couple of beers."

The train's air-conditioning broke down, blowing cold air with such arctic ferocity that the Dodgers were left to plug the vents in their compartments with towels.

Jimmy Cannon, who had the columnist's luxury of choosing his own stories, decided to make the trip, perhaps to catch the aging fellows' pennant clincher in Pittsburgh. He walked among the Pullman cars sensing a team at ease with itself. The Dodgers had nine games to play, seven against the Pirates, and two against the Phillies. All they had to do was to keep winning.

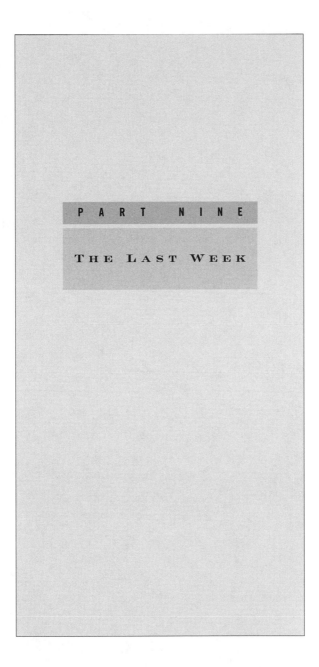

PART NINE

THE LAST WEEK

Sam Qualiarini had not been to a ball game all season. Years later he would think of the season and his teenage detachment from Ebbets Field and admit that it was probably nothing more than chance that drew him to the park on the night of September 25. He was back at school, having allowed his summer to run its course without once feeling compelled to make the short walk to Ebbets Field. The Dodgers remained for Sam and his friends a subject of conversation and a matter of concern. But there had been so many other things to do, like hanging out and seeing if the girls were hanging out, too.

For whatever reason Sam came to the park that night, it was surely not to see a pennant clincher. The one game lead the Dodgers had carried with them to Pittsburgh was gone. In its place was a half-game deficit. Milwaukee was back in first and Milwaukee was playing the Cubs.

The Dodgers had come to a rainy Pittsburgh with favorable tidings from the team's staff oracle, statistician Allen Roth. A few hours before game time, Roth assembled the traveling hacks at the Webster Hall Hotel and, having converted the lobby into Delphi, explained why the Dodgers *could not lose* that night's game. Sal Maglie was pitching and Maglie, he had calculated, had beaten Pittsburgh six times in a row, and twenty-five of the twenty-nine times he'd faced them. In fact, the Pirates had not beaten Maglie since 1953. There was more. Pittsburgh's starter, Ronnie Kline, had never beaten the Dodgers. He had never even completed a game against them. In fact, he had not completed a game in his last eight starts. The beat fellows and columnists took down Roth's words and headed to Forbes Field where in the course of the evening Sal Maglie would be gone in the seventh, Ronnie Kline would require no relief, and the Pirates would beat the Dodgers 2 to 1.

Things were worse still the next night, when the Pirates keelhauled Carl Erskine, 5 to 1. The loss dropped the Dodgers into a tie with Milwaukee, who let the advantage slip through their fingers when they lost in the tenth to the Cubs. Cincinnati, four and a half games out just five days before, beat St. Louis. The Reds were now only two games back with seven to play.

It was still raining on Sunday. It rained so hard the umpires halted play for two hours. The interminable delays only worsened the Dodgers' weekend: they were leading 8 to 3 at 6:59 P.M. when, in compliance with Pennsylvania's Sunday curfew law, the on-again-off-again game was suspended until the following day. Though Brooklyn did hold on to win the unfinished game on Monday, the victory provided no momentum: Pittsburgh took the nightcap, 6 to 5, leaving Jimmy Cannon to wonder whether the time had come to compose Brooklyn's epitaph. "Last night," he wrote, "might have been the one when the Dodgers lost the pennant."

The ease and calm with which the Dodgers had carried themselves to Pittsburgh was now replaced by grim and sour moods. The team flew back to New York on, of all things, an airliner dubbed the "Milwaukee Captain." They arrived early in the morning. Their wives were waiting for them at La-Guardia Airport, and so was the press. It was as if they'd come to cover a deathwatch, a fact not lost on Walter Alston, who said, "We don't have as many of you guys waiting when we win a series." Carl Furillo led his teammates past the photographers—"We might as well face it"—who captured nothing but long faces. Even the typically effervescent Roy Campanella could offer nothing more uplifting than, "We'll win tonight." As they waited for their bags, a photographer approached Duke Snider, who was standing with Carl Furillo.

"Watch what happens," the cameraman said to Furillo. And with that he snapped his flash in Snider's face.

Later, the man would say that Snider slugged him. But this the Duke vehemently denied: "After he took the shot I said to him, 'Now that you got it, you know what you can do with it.'" A fitting, if unpleasant coda to their last trip together.

THAT NIGHT, TUESDAY night, the twenty-fifth, Sal Maglie sat in the Dodger clubhouse and performed the ritual of anointing his pitching hand. First he applied a base of liquid rosin. Then he sprinkled the fingers with powdered rosin. And when he was done he was ready to pitch.

In Cincinnati the Braves had edged the Reds 6 to 5, and while it was the Phillies who had come to Ebbets Field it was difficult to find reason for confidence in playing a fifth place team: the Pirates were worse than the Phillies, and the Pirates had been the rudest of hosts. A loss would put the Dodgers a full game back, and with five games to play, and in the unenviable position of not only needing to win every game, but hoping that Milwaukee lost, too.

It was a chilly night, which made the appearance of Sam Qualiarini and fifteen thousand other souls all the more unusual: the team had not drawn this well on pleasant days. Still, the aging park was less than half full. Sal Maglie did not much mind the cold. He had once pitched a game in which snow fell for a full nine innings. That was in 1944, during his years of wandering in baseball's Canadian outback, wondering whether he would ever pitch in the big leagues again. Now, with the season in peril, the Dodgers furnished him with an electric blanket in which he could huddle in the dugout when Brooklyn came to bat.

The ball felt slippery in Maglie's hand and he worried about his control. In the first Marv Blaylock lined hard to left, but Sandy Amoros drew a quick bead and made the play look easy. In the second Willie Jones grounded to short and for a moment Pee Wee Reese struggled to get the ball out of his mitt before throwing him out. The Phillies surrendered quietly in the third and fourth. The Dodgers, meanwhile, scored five runs on only three hits, which the Phillies generously augmented with poor play in the field. Maglie pitched as he always did, using the fastball for show and his assortment of curves to keep batters guessing. The best view of his work belonged to Roy Campanella, and what he saw from behind the plate pleased him immensely: no tough outs. The Phillies hit only what Maglie allowed them to hit, and each time that was a pitch with which they could do little. Maglie had no need to worry about a cold hand gripping a slick ball; Reese, Hodges, and Robinson took turns rubbing up the ball for him. The fifth and sixth ended without incident and by the time Sam Qualiarini rose to stretch in the middle of the seventh, Sal Maglie, twenty years a professional pitcher, was allowing himself to contemplate the possibility of his first no-hitter.

WHEN HE CAME out for the ninth inning his right palm and fingers were stained black with rosin. Mayo Smith, the Philadelphia manager, was not about to concede a no-hitter; he sent Frankie Baumholtz, a left-handed batter, to pinch hit. Maglie stood on the mound, rosin bag in hand, with Jackie Robinson. "Should I watch the first pitch? He's a first ball hitter. Should I come in? Will he be taking?" Robinson listened and said nothing. Maglie started Baumholtz with a curveball strike over the outside corner. Baumholtz fouled his second pitch over the Dodger dugout and the wind appeared to be carrying it into the stands. Campanella chased the ball to the lip of the dugout and did not know who grabbed him under the arms and held him up long enough to make the catch.

Smith, wed to playing the percentages, next sent up Harvey Haddix, a pitcher but another lefty bat. Maglie later admitted to Milton Gross that the sight of Haddix perplexed him. "I didn't know what he hit. I only pitched to him once before." Forced to improvise, Maglie assumed that a pitcher would have trouble with his curve. Haddix, though, was game and fouled off the first pitch. Maglie took the new ball and flipped it to Reese to massage. Haddix fouled off this one, too. Robinson called for the new ball, and took his turn rubbing it down. Maglie wanted his next pitch to curve over the outside corner, and that is just what it did as Haddix waved and missed. Richie Ashburn was up next, and Ashburn, yet another lefty, was the best hitter on the team.

Maglie turned to Robinson and smiled, weakly. "This," he said, "is the guy I got to get."

Four times he threw outside and Ashburn held his ground, fouling off his curves. On the fifth pitch Maglie came inside, too much so. He clipped Ashburn on the leg, sending him to first and bringing Marv Blaylock to bat.

On the 110th pitch of his evening, Roy Campanella signaled for a fastball away, and Maglie, who'd shaken off his signs only twice all night, complied. He hit Campanella's target and Blaylock did what he was supposed to do, which was to reach to pull the ball only to ground it to second. Maglie watched the ball bounce to Jim Gilliam. "I watched that ball bounce all the way," he told Milton Gross. "I watched every damn hop until Gilliam got it and Hodges grabbed it and the ump's arm went up for the last out." And when it did Sal Maglie said to himself, "I got it. I got. My God, I got it."

2 | WEDNESDAY, SEPTEMBER 26

John Griffin, the clubhouse manager, was resting uncomfortably at Long Island College Hospital where he had been admitted the night before. Overwhelmed in his excitement over Maglie's no-hitter, Griffin fainted in the clubhouse, delaying but not postponing the celebration of The Barber's feat; Walter O'Malley even shoved a wad of hundred-dollar bills into Maglie's hand. Griffin, who had the soul and wardrobe of a clown, was wearing a long, blond wig when he passed out.

He was left to watch the Dodger-Phillie day game on television from his hospital bed. His wife, a nurse, told him that if he could not stay calm she would take the set away. She remained at his side, monitoring his blood pressure. His diastolic reading was acceptable in the first inning. But not so in the second.

Alston had sent Don Newcombe to pitch and though Newcombe had been Alston's stalwart all season he was throwing on a meager two days' rest. It was a sunny but chilly afternoon and later Newcombe would insist that he never quite got loose. Still, he retired the Phillies uneventfully in the first and seemed poised for good things in the second when, with a man on first, he induced an easy fly ball to left by Elmer Valo. Sandy Amoros settled beneath it, the glare reflecting off his sunglasses. At this point John Griffin's blood pressure caused his wife no concern. But as the ball hit Amoros's glove and then inexplicably fell to the ground she felt compelled to strap the monitor on her husband's arm and check. For all his foolishness, Griffin knew enough of the men who populated his clubhouse to begin fretting. For while Newcombe was enjoying the best season of his career, while he was leading the big leagues in wins, he was inclined to lose his sense of himself when things did not go well. Now Newcombe turned to face Solly Hemus. He hit him. Next came Roy Smalley, who doubled. The Phillies scored three and John Griffin's blood pressure shot up to 160 over 90.

A pitcher in Newcombe's position had two choices as he came to the dugout: he could accept the inevitability that even a terrific fielder like Amoros—he had saved the seventh game of the 1955 World Series with his running catch of a Yogi Berra liner—could muff the odd play; or he could rail against Amoros's blunder and thereby do further emotional harm to himself. Newcombe chose the latter path, and then went a step further. First he glared angrily at Amoros, who did not need an interpreter—he spoke almost no English—to measure the cost of his error. Then Newcombe went to Alston and demanded that he pull Amoros from the game. "Get him out of there," Newcombe roared. "Put in someone who can catch a ball." Alston declined, but the damage to Amoros, and to Newcombe, was done.

"You could see it coming," Jackie Robinson later said. "You could just sense it. After Sandy dropped the fly ball, Newk was boiling and Sandy went into his shell."

Amoros would commit two more errors that afternoon, both on throws, and fail to charge a ground ball single. Newcombe surrendered a fourth run in the third and was gone in the fifth. The Dodgers, meanwhile, could do little against Robin Roberts, the old Phillie ace who had beaten them on Opening Day. He struck out ten and allowed five hits and while Duke Snider did homer twice, his production could not compensate for his teammates' poor play. Philadelphia scored three more in the eighth after a bad hop grounder skipped past Jackie Robinson with two men out. John Griffin got permission to smoke one of his two daily cigars, but the moment brought him no pleasure. Milwaukee was heading to St. Louis with a one game lead, and the assurance that a sweep of the Cardinals would give them the pennant.

The writers took pity on Sandy Amoros, who they found sitting naked in front of his locker, pretending to read an English-language tax manual.

"The sun," he finally said. "No wind. Ball in sun."

Carl Furillo meanwhile was angry with Newcombe for having been so angry with Amoros.

"That guy saying they should take the kid out because Elmer Valo's ball got in the sun," he said. "Does he yell when he's lobbing them up and we're chasing them?"

"Didn't his arm stiffen up?" asked Jimmy Cannon.

"Was it his arm?" asked Furillo insistently. "His arm."

Jackie Robinson sat naked on an equipment box, disappointed with everyone, including himself. "We played like we didn't want to win the game," he said. "It started out wrong. It seems like we just knew it. Imagine

Smalley getting that hit. You know if Smalley gets a hit like that you're in trouble. Sandy played like he was sick."

He drank his beer, and when someone asked if the team was tight he snapped, "Of course we're not tight. It was just a lousy exhibition."

Walter Alston defended Sandy Amoros. Roy Campanella examined his ever more battered hands. "I got hit again today," he said. "And I got hit yesterday."

"What about Newcombe?" Cannon asked him.

"That dropped fly ball killed him," he replied.

Why it did was not a question for such a moment and in such a clubhouse. Only the following day, when Cannon raised the matter with Jackie Robinson, was he able to glean an insight into Newcombe's state of mind.

"I think part of it . . ." Robinson began. Then he started again. "I have a hunch that the press and sportscasters might have something to do with it this year. He's a very proud guy. I see where all the credit goes to Sal. Look, I know that without Sal we wouldn't be where we are. I'm not taking anything away from Sal. But along the way, they should have given some credit to Newk. He probably feels this way even though I haven't spoken to him about it. If I was in his spot, doing what he's been doing for the ball club and I wasn't given the credit, I'd be burned up, too."

Robinson may have been right about Newcombe's bruised pride; he was not even selected to the National League All-Star team. But he was wrong about the press: the writers had been reverential toward Newcombe. They portrayed him as a man of Bunyanesque proportions—"big Newk," "the gargantuan right-hander." They wrote about him as a pitcher so fearsome and dominating that it was surprising whenever he lost. That he had done so only six times all season, while winning twenty-six, only enhanced his reputation as a man who should not be beaten. Newcombe was six foot four inches tall, weighed 240 pounds, and approached his work in a manner that reflected his size: he threw very hard and did not mind working the inside part of the plate. Though his build gave him a great advantage on the mound, it put him in that unfortunate position of being the object of unreasonably high expectations: like all big men, he was *supposed* to beat lesser men. And when he did not his failure could not be dismissed as a physical limitation, say, like Carl Erskine's chronically sore shoulder. Worse still,

Newcombe's failures—like all pitchers, he did fail to win games his team needed—seemed to come in the big games. That is not to say that he had not won important games, many of them, and that he had been anything other than up to the task. But when the beat fellows broke out their record books and old scorecards it did not take long to notice that Newcombe had never won a game in a World Series.

It was difficult to know who began putting out the word that Newcombe lacked the nerve, the guts for the big games, that he was in the parlance of the trade, a "choke artist." Many believed the source to be Leo Durocher, who had managed him in Brooklyn and against him with the Giants and who possessed a cruel streak that he applied to good effect. It did not much matter whether, in fact, Newcombe choked, only that Newcombe be made to *feel* like he did when he pitched against New York. If Durocher was the source, he did his work well because by 1956 the book on Newcombe was that while he possessed terrific stuff he lacked the courage to use it when it most mattered. Durocher knew enough about Newcombe to know that while he blustered, ranted, and postured he was a sensitive man who looked at the strengths and triumphs of other men as indications of all that he lacked.

He had grown up in New Jersey a gifted athlete who wanted above all to be a truck driver. He played baseball well, but not seriously, assuming that if he did not make a living driving trucks he might become a drummer instead. His high school had no team, which did not much matter because by his senior year he dropped out after being told he would have to repeat a failed course. Instead he tried out for the Newark Eagles, a Negro League team, whose owner Effie Manley, signed him and sent him off to spring training. He was sixteen years old. He won sixteen and lost four and Branch Rickey, searching the Negro Leagues for talent, signed him and sent him to Nashua, New Hampshire, where he played for Buzzie Bavasi. In Nashua, Newcombe also met Roy Campanella, whom he admired as he did no one else.

Years later, when they were both playing in Brooklyn, Campanella was his roommate and best friend. In certain ways Campanella was his only friend. Newcombe was not close with Robinson. Robinson was hard on him, pushing him when he thought Newcombe's spirit was flagging. "I remember once I had an 11–1 lead in Pittsburgh," he told Ted Poston of the

Post, "and he came out and said, 'Get out there and pitch you lazy bastard. You gonna let these white guys win the game?' " Robinson, he conceded, was right and Newcombe did as he was told.

He turned to Campanella as a mentor and guide. Campanella, in turn, understood when Newcombe needed to be boosted and when he needed a swift kick—as he did when Newcombe refused Alston's order to pitch batting practice. He taught Newcombe many things, among them how to run a liquor store, which Newcombe did in New Jersey, just as Campanella did in Harlem. For his part Newcombe thought Campanella worried too much about business. "But me," he told Ted Poston, "I don't worry about nothing."

He did not see much of his teammates when the Dodgers were home. Instead, he drove home to New Jersey, to his wife, his young children, and his friends. On the road he and Campanella went to the movies together, to westerns and gangster movies, which Newcombe liked best. Roger Kahn once asked him in *Look* magazine whether he thought his other teammates liked him.

"If they took a popularity poll, I sure as hell wouldn't win," Newcombe replied. "Lots of guys don't like my attitude. Can't blame 'em. I don't like it myself."

"How so?" asked Kahn.

"I say things I shouldn't," Newcombe replied.

Campanella, an easy man, accepted Newcombe's moods and pouting, even if his teammates and the writers wearied of his sulking and the silences he imposed on people who upset him. But Campanella still saw the world from a catcher's perspective, which meant he was a student of flaws in hitters and in his pitchers. Newcombe's talent had once made Dizzy Dean, the great St. Louis pitcher of the 1930s, gush that Newcombe was the best pitcher in the game since he himself was on the mound. He was not alone in this assessment: by the summer of 1956 many considered Newcombe the finest pitcher in the game. Yet his approach to his work troubled Campanella.

"This game is easy some days," he once told Roscoe McGowan of the *Times*. "But then there are days when you got to push yourself. Trouble with Newk is he don't push hisself." The story was told again and again. And though the sight of Newcombe lumbering across the outfield between starts was a familiar one, Campanella's words stuck. They offered what seemed the only plausible explanation for why a man of such promise and accomplishment could fail to be wonderful at the very moments when everyone needed him to be nothing less.

The day after Newcombe humiliated Sandy Amoros for dropping Elmer Valo's fly ball, Robinson followed him into the back of the clubhouse.

"They're making a big fuss about that stuff you said yesterday," he said.

"What stuff?" asked Newcombe.

"About Sandy. You got to talk to Sandy right now. You apologize to him."

Newcombe dressed and went out to the field. He found Amoros at the batting cage.

"I said what they wrote," Newcombe told him. "But I shouldn't have said it."

3 | THURSDAY, SEPTEMBER 27

The Milwaukee Braves thundered into St. Louis's Chase Plaza Hotel careful to avoid tempting fate with predictions of a championship, but as young men are wont to do, counting their chickens just the same.

"How about that," said Gene Conley, the tall and grinning pitcher. "Even if we only got two out of three we've got at least a tie. And if we win three there's nothing they can do."

"I think they'll still lose another one," said Joe Adcock.

"I wouldn't mind if they lost all three and Cincinnati finished second," said Bob Trowbridge, greedy for more than a pennant alone.

"Just think of all that money," said Chuck Tanner. "We're just a couple of days away from it. I never saw that kind of money in my life." The Dodgers each made $9,768.21 for winning the 1955 World Series—the Yankee losers' shares were $5,598.58. "Our series shares," Tanner added, "might set a record." Ten thousand dollars—three years' salary at a decent wage.

The Chase felt like a convention center with the Shriners in town. Johnny Ray, "the civilized Elvis Presley," was playing the Chase's lounge and the reservation list was getting long. The out-of-town writers—"the Front Runners Association," the beat fellows called them—who'd been following the Braves all month threw a party for Fred Haney and the Milwaukee coaches. The Braves themselves strolled through the lobby, smiling and chatting, and when they went out to Busch Stadium to limber up, so many writers followed them that their numbers eclipsed those of the young men on the field. The Braves went through their workout with the nonchalance of men who believed they could afford to be a little goofy. Even the veteran pitcher Warren Spahn took a turn at sliding into third base, just to see if his roommate Lew Burdette, pretending to be an infielder, could tag him out. When they were done playing they lingered on the field so long that a handful had to be summoned to dress quickly because the bus back to the Chase was about to leave.

The numbers were propitious for the Braves. They'd beaten St. Louis twelve of the nineteen times they'd played, including the last six in a row. And though St. Louis's best hitters batted well at Busch Stadium, they had not done much at home with Milwaukee's pitching. Haney announced that Bob Buhl would start the first game, and Warren Spahn the second. He was not sure who would pitch on Sunday. But by then the question might well be moot: if the Braves took the first two and the Dodgers lost either of their first two games against the Pirates, the pennant would be Milwaukee's. No one needed to remind the Braves what the Pirates had done to Brooklyn the weekend before. The only way the Dodgers could win the pennant was by sweeping their three games with Pittsburgh and—this was too much to ask—hoping that St. Louis took two of three from Milwaukee. Brooklyn's best chance seemed a tie. But even that possibility rested on the remote chance of St. Louis taking one from Milwaukee, with the Dodgers still needing to win all three at Ebbets Field.

The math was so encouraging that in Milwaukee plans were well along for a victory celebration—all made, of course, with the clear understanding that the Braves had not won yet. Men dug the hole for the thirty-five-foot-tall Brave who would grace the city's skyline. Others hung flag holders on the light poles along Wisconsin Avenue; a Braves flag would fly in the middle, flanked by two American flags. The local chapter of the musicians' union volunteered to send a fifteen-piece band to the airport Sunday night to serenade the players and the throng expected to greet them when they came home in triumph. Plans were made to protect the players from the crush of the faithful: rather than have them walk through the terminal, the players would be introduced, one by one, as they disembarked. They would then be shuttled downtown by bus to the Schroeder Hotel for the official victory party. Six hundred members of the Braves Boosters fan club prepared to take a late-night train to St. Louis on Friday to catch the weekend's clincher. "Operation pennant," wrote Bob Wolf in the *Milwaukee Journal*, "is at hand."

IN BROOKLYN, WALTER Alston gave his players the option of coming to Ebbets Field for a workout or staying at home to rest. Buzzie Bavasi took a call from Frank Lane, his counterpart with the Cardinals. Lane, leaving open all his options, wanted fifty grandstand seats for the World Series—just in case the Dodgers somehow made it.

"We're out to beat Milwaukee three games," Lane told him.

"You do that," said Bavasi, "and you can have the entire grandstand."

4 | FRIDAY, SEPTEMBER 28

A light rain was falling in Brooklyn, not heavy enough for a certain washout and not misty enough to begin play. The Dodgers sat in their clubhouse playing bridge on an equipment trunk. They sat in their pants, their uniform shirts hanging in their lockers. They played loudly, fussing theatrically about the hands they held. John Griffin, released from the hospital, padded about in a long-curled wig.

Pee Wee Reese sat by his locker with nothing much to do but talk with Jimmy Cannon. The conversation veered toward the subject of Walter Alston for whom Reese admitted he felt admiration and pity.

"He's had a thankless job," he said.

"Why do you say that?" asked Cannon.

"He wins the pennant, he's supposed to," Reese replied. "This is supposed to be a great ball club. If he loses, he's no good, no matter what happens. The way people figure, he can't get any credit. No one wants to give him credit. On other teams a manager gets some credit. On this one the ballplayers get all the credit. This is not a ball club like Pittsburgh—high school kids."

His teammates, he went on, "know how to play the game. They have set ideas." The club might have been Reese's, had he wanted to manage in

1954. Instead the job went to Alston, and Reese recognized the great and inescapable burden that dogged Alston in his relationship with his players. "Holding this type of ball club together is no cinch," he said, "because this is a fellow who didn't play in the major leagues except for one time at bat with the Cards."

Across the changing room Sal Maglie had already slipped out of his uniform and was pulling on his sports jacket when someone called out, a little late, "The game's off."

Brooklyn and Pittsburgh would play two on Saturday, a change in plans that pleased the Dodgers immensely. Bob Friend would open the series for the Pirates and Friend, a strong pitcher, had beaten Brooklyn three of the four times he'd faced them. Alston had planned to start Roger Craig in the opener, but now, with an extra day's rest, he would use Maglie against Friend. The hitters, too, were relieved. Friend, explained Duke Snider, had a spin on his pitches unlike anyone else, a rotation on the ball that much harder to discern under the glare of klieg lights.

"That's right," said Reese. "I know I can see his pitches better in the daytime, anyway."

The bridge game ended. The Dodgers dressed. Walter Alston called for a team meeting. And a thousand miles away in St. Louis, the Cardinals scored three in the bottom of the first, knocking out Bob Buhl, who got only one man out.

Joe Adcock homered for one Milwaukee run in the second, and the Braves tied the game in the fifth. But in the sixth, four Cardinals in a row hit singles, scoring one run and then another on a wild throw. The Braves countered in the eighth. They scored one and seemed poised to score another when Eddie Mathews botched a bunt and Adcock and Andy Pafko left Henry Aaron stranded on first. Milwaukee went quietly in the ninth and, 5 to 4 losers, retreated to the visitors' clubhouse where no one thought it wise to joke. Their lead was down to a half game and worse still, they no longer commanded their own fate: now the Dodgers could force a one-game playoff, that is if the Dodgers could manage to sweep the Pirates.

Their defeat of Milwaukee brought little pleasure to the Cardinals who, one by one, admitted that they wanted to see the Braves win. "Everybody would," said Ken Boyer, the third baseman whose first inning double finished Bob Buhl. Indeed, the St. Louis papers were rallying behind

Milwaukee, even on their editorial pages: "The Brooklynese have been notoriously lax. Most people believe the Bums have won enough for the time being, at least."

But the view on the sports pages was less charitable. The box score showed two errors by the Braves. And though Fred Hutchinson, the Cardinal manager, did not believe the miscues were a result of fear or pressure, they were the sorts of mistakes, among them a pitcher failing to cover first, that did cost games. "We just beat them, or they beat themselves," Hutchinson said. "In any event, we'll be out there trying to do it again Saturday and Sunday."

5 | SATURDAY, SEPTEMBER 29

The Milwaukee Braves woke in their hotel rooms and rubbed the sleep from their eyes with the unsettling realization that their collective day would be one of waiting to see what fate had in store for them. Their game against the Cardinals was scheduled for the evening. An interminable day awaited them, a day spent, inevitably, hoping that the Pirates might rescue them from the mess they'd made of their pennant drive the night before. A Pittsburgh sweep would mean that those eager Milwaukee fans who had arrived in town for the weekend games might yet have a pennant clincher to celebrate. But if Brooklyn took two, the Braves would take the field that night a second place team, if only by a half game. The Reds, playing in Chicago, could only hope that everyone else lost.

The sun was shining in Brooklyn. Ebbets Field was packed. Sal Maglie made his way to the mound and just after 1:30 began where he had left off five days before. He retired the first two Pittsburgh batters, running his hitless streak to twenty-nine men. But the run ended with the next batter, Dale Long, who singled. A batter later, Maglie's scoreless stretch was over, too, when Frank Thomas homered. The Dodgers came to bat in the first down by two.

Jim Gilliam led off with a scratch single and it appeared as if he might end the inning at first base when Bob Friend struck out Reese and Snider. But Gilliam stole second and came home with Brooklyn's first run on Jackie Robinson's single to center. Now Sandy Amoros came to bat, his first appearance since wreaking such havoc on Wednesday afternoon. If Amoros still carried pain and doubt with him to the batter's box it was well hidden. His teammates, Don Newcombe included, had come to him before the game and reminded him what a good ballplayer they thought he was. Amoros confirmed all that they said: he homered to right, scoring Robinson ahead of him and giving Brooklyn the lead, 3 to 2. Amoros was smiling as he rounded the bases and his teammates mobbed him when he reached the dugout. Newcombe offered him a big, happy pat on the behind.

Emboldened, Maglie returned to work, if not quite in Tuesday's form, then close enough. The Pirates managed four more hits, but scored no more. Carl Furillo and Gil Hodges homered for the Dodgers. At the final out Maglie walked from the mound to a loud, standing ovation. The Dodgers retreated to their clubhouse 6 to 2 winners. The Milwaukee flag that had hung in center field to mark the league's leader came down. In its place flew Brooklyn's flag. This seemed presumptuous, at least to Red Smith who noted that while the Dodgers owned no more than half of first place, "management never studied fractions."

Alston had Roger Craig ready to pitch the second game. But instead he looked to his bull pen and called on Clem Labine. Labine seldom started, but when he did in big games he was splendid. The first two innings came and went with little fanfare. But in the Brooklyn third Roy Campanella managed to withstand the pain in his hands just long enough to homer and give the Dodgers a 1 to 0 lead. Labine went back to work and over the first six innings the Pirates managed only two hits. The Dodgers, meanwhile, were doing little against Pittsburgh's Ronnie Kline and were left to try to capitalize on what meager opportunities came their way.

In the fifth Campanella eked out a single, bringing Labine to bat for the requisite sacrifice bunt. Hank Foiles, the Pirate catcher, pounced on the ball and instead of going for the easy out at first, took the risk of throwing to second to keep Campanella from making his way to scoring position. Foiles' throw was so high that Dick Groat, the Pirate shortstop, had to leap to catch it as Campanella slid into second. Perhaps it was the dust and perhaps it was the view and perhaps it was a matter of interpretation of events, but umpire Vic Delmore called out the safe-by-a-light-year Campanella. Alston and Campanella hurried over to argue, but to no avail. The fans, however, were so incensed that they booed and waved white hankerchiefs. They carried their angry protest into the sixth inning with such passion that when they started hurling beer cans and paper on the field, Jocko Conlon, the umpiring crew chief, threatened to forfeit the game if they didn't pipe down. Quiet restored, Labine pitched out of a brief jam in the sixth, leaving the Pirates still scoreless. Brooklyn came to bat for what would turn out to be Pittsburgh's turn at feeling aggrieved.

Jackie Robinson was at first when Sandy Amoros, newly restored to heroic proportions, came at bat. Amoros was in midswing when Stan Landes, umpiring behind the plate, ruled that Foiles had tipped Amoros's bat, interfering with his swing. He awarded Amoros first base as Bobby Bragan, the Pirate manager, set off after Landes with such gusto that he was soon sent to an early shower. Foiles, equally upset, joined him. Gil Hodges came to bat and, his pallid hitting days seemingly behind him, tripled his mates home, giving Labine a 3 to 0 lead. This was useful because now Labine, used to facing only a few batters, was beginning to wear down. Pittsburgh pecked away at him in the seventh and eighth, getting men on base but not home. When they did finally score in the ninth their rally was too late and too modest. Labine, pitching a complete game for the first time in a year, struck out ten and made the fellow who'd hoisted the league-leader's flag look prescient. Brooklyn had first place to itself, at least for the rest of the afternoon. Now the Dodgers could wait, just as the Braves had, miserably, all afternoon.

WARREN SPAHN WAS thirty-six years old and there was no better left-handed pitcher in the game. He had been with the Boston Braves briefly in 1940 and, legend has it, was sent back down to the minors at Hartford after refusing to throw one at Pee Wee Reese's head during an exhibition game. Spahn's manager at the time, Casey Stengel, was not pleased with his insubordination. He was back pitching for Boston again in 1942 when his draft number came up. He saw action in Europe, earned a Purple Heart, and returned to the big leagues to stay in 1946. He won twenty games in all but four of the next eleven seasons, and late in the 1956 season he won his two hundredth. He threw with a big, sweeping motion that featured a magnificently high leg kick. Though he could never beat the Dodgers, he had much less trouble with most everyone else, and so it was fitting that on the night when their season of such lofty expectations was in jeopardy, Fred Haney handed him the ball.

He would have been perfect through the first five innings had he not walked Bobby Del Greco. Otherwise, the Cardinals could do nothing with him. The Braves scored once in the first on Bill Bruton's home run. But while they threatened time and again, Milwaukee could not score against St. Louis's Herman Wehmeier. Their leadoff man reached base in four of the next six innings, and while the percentages suggest a fifty-fifty chance of a leadoff baserunner coming home, the Braves botched two sacrifice bunts. The only Milwaukee runner to make it as far as second base was Johnny Logan, but his brief sojourn in scoring position ended with the embarrassment of getting picked off after taking too wide a turn.

Still, Spahn was all but flawless and had retired the first two batters in the sixth when Don Blasingame doubled home Alvin Dark, who had doubled right before him. The score was tied at one in the ninth when Eddie Mathews drove a Wehmeier pitch toward the wall in center field. Bobby Del Greco, the Cardinals fleet center fielder, managed to catch up with it at the warning track for a long out. Joe Adcock followed with a single. Jack Dittmer came to bat and quickly tested Del Greco again. He, too, drove one to the wall, but once again Del Greco was there to make the catch and send the game into extra innings.

The tenth ended quietly, as did the eleventh. Milwaukee went without causing a stir in the twelfth and when they took the field for the bottom of the inning Warren Spahn was still on the mound. He had given up only three hits. His teammates had managed nine against Herman Wehmeier, who was also still in the game and on this night at least was Spahn's equal. But they had only Bruton's home run, a lifetime ago in the first inning, to show for it. Spahn retired Alvin Dark and now faced his old friend, Stan Musial. Musial, as great a hitter as Spahn was a pitcher, had gone without a hit all night. But now he doubled off the wall in right and the Cardinals, much to their chagrin, found themselves in a position to win.

Spahn walked Ken Boyer, setting up a potential double play. The cartoon-hero-dubbed Rip Ripulski came to bat. Spahn started him with a pitch outside but Ripulski was not biting and let it go for ball one. Spahn next threw a change-up, high and inside. Ripulski chopped at the ball as if he were splitting a log. He sent the ball bouncing hard to third, where Eddie Mathews waited, on the edge of the grass. Mathews' glove was ready and the ball appeared headed for it, but when he looked down the ball had taken such a hideous bounce that it first glanced off his glove and then his leg before rolling into left field. Musial rounded third and came home with the run that would leave Warren Spahn in tears.

Afterward, in the St. Louis clubhouse, the Cardinals and their manager were lavish in their praise of Spahn—"He didn't give us the kind of chance we gave you," their manager, Fred Hutchinson, told the Milwaukee writers. And though no one suggested he was trying to be cruel, Hutchinson made it clear that this was a game the Braves could have won—"just like last night."

Like Friday night, the victory brought measured delight to the Cardinals, and a little guilt, too. "The whole country is going to be sore at us for spoiling it for the Braves," said Hank Sauer. "Everybody wanted them to win."

He may have been premature in putting this in the past tense. Milwaukee now trailed Brooklyn by a full game. They could still force a three-game playoff—but only if they won on Sunday afternoon, and Brooklyn lost.

In the Milwaukee clubhouse a photographer perched himself in front of Warren Spahn and tried to take his picture. Spahn threw his glove in his face. The photographer tried again and this time Spahn's teammates pulled him away.

Frank Lane, the Cardinals general manager, wanted to know whether it was true that Spahn had wept. Told that he had, Lane replied, "What the hell do they expect him to do after losing a game like that—whistle?"

6 | SUNDAY, SEPTEMBER 30

Carl Furillo was forbidden to listen to the Milwaukee–St. Louis game on the radio on Saturday night. His wife, Fern, had invited friends over and placed signs around the house reminding guests not to talk about baseball. Still, her husband had managed to catch the bottom of the twelfth inning.

Now, as he drove toward Ebbets Field, Furillo spotted Arthur Daley standing on a street corner in Flatbush. Daley, whose column appeared in the *Times*, was trying to capture the mood of Brooklyn on this, the season's last day. It was a chilly morning with temperatures hovering in the upper fifties. The sky was cloudy but no rain was in the forecast. Furillo pulled over and opened the door. "Get in," he told Daley. "Don't waste money on taxicabs."

At the ballpark the crowd was so thick that the police were turning away people who did not have tickets. The police had told ten thousand people to go home yesterday and would do the same today. Downtown Brooklyn was otherwise quiet. One newsvendor closed his stand, leaving a sign that read, "Sorry. In Bleacher Line Early."

Daley joined Furillo in the clubhouse where the Dodgers were talking about their sudden affection for Bobby Del Greco, the Cardinal center fielder.

"No doubt about it, Del Greco gets my vote as the most valuable player in either league," said Jim Gilliam.

"Either Del Greco made unbelievable catches or Vin Scully was laying it on too heavy in his radio descriptions," said a grinning Pee Wee Reese.

Buzzie Bavasi stopped by and Carl Erskine told him, "Listen, Buzz, the greatest deal Frank Lane ever made was the one that brought Del Greco to the Cards."

"It seemed that way last night," said Bavasi, who looked at his watch and turned to leave. "I got to go to church."

"Pray hard, Buzz," Clem Labine shouted after him.

Don Newcombe, still nursing the cold that kept him home on Friday night, got a shot of penicillin. He had had three days of rest and that, along with his medication and whatever prayers Buzzie Bavasi might offer, would have to get him through the afternoon.

On Eastern Parkway, a few blocks from Ebbets Field, Murray Schumach of the *Times* happened upon Jerry Levin, who was taking a walk with his wife and children. It did not take a street reporter of Schumach's skill to spot the story when he saw it: Jerry Levin had Eastern Parkway virtually to himself. The parkway, usually filled on a Sunday afternoon with strollers and bench sitters and children on bikes, was all but empty. The few people out were mostly older, or too young to understand what was taking place nearby. Jerry Levin helped steer his daughter's tricycle with one hand. In the other he held a big portable radio so he could follow the game. Schumach would spend the afternoon walking through Brooklyn. The streets would be deserted. As he walked Schumach would be able to follow the game just by listening: from window after window came the sound of baseball on television.

At two o'clock Newcombe completed his warm-up throws and turned to face Bill Virdon, who led off for the Pirates. Newcombe's cold had not affected his velocity, and he set Pirates aside easily in the first. His pitching counterpart, Vernon Law, was not so fortunate. He greeted the Dodgers with a walk to Jim Gilliam. Reese singled. Snider homered and Brooklyn had begun its afternoon with a 3 to 0 lead.

If the crowd that filled Ebbets Field settled back in their hard seats with the hope of finding entertainment in the dismemberment of the Pittsburgh Pirates they were to be disappointed; only those who took pleasure in anxiety would find happiness this afternoon because Don Newcombe, rested and pumped with antibiotics, did not have it.

Campanella was pleased with his speed but not with his control. Newcombe allowed the Pirate leadoff batter to reach base in five of the first six innings, among them a triple by Lee Walls. Walls might have scored, too, had Furillo not made a difficult catch on a foul ball. But in the third Newcombe surrendered a single to Jack Shepard, a walk to Dick Cole, and wild pitch that moved both runners into scoring position for Roberto Clemente, who singled them home. Newcombe's three-run cushion had been flattened to a single run.

His teammates, who had hit so poorly the weekend before, came to his rescue. In the bottom of the third Jackie Robinson homered, padding the Dodger lead to two. And Newcombe, perhaps the best-hitting pitcher in the game, helped himself in the fifth when he doubled, advanced to third on a grounder, and scored on Reese's sacrifice fly—typical of Reese, an out, but a productive one. Snider followed with his forty-third home run of the season onto Bedford Avenue. The Dodgers extended their lead to 7 to 2 an inning later when Sandy Amoros, who had already redeemed himself on Saturday, homered, too.

And that should have been that. Blessed with such good fortune, Newcombe took the mound in the seventh and served up a double to Dick Groat. Bill Mazeroski eked out a single and Jack Shepard bunted himself to first, loading the bases. Newcombe, however, was not about to capitulate. He induced a pop-up by Dale Long and struck out Clemente. He needed only to dispense with Bill Virdon to escape the trap he had set for himself. But Virdon doubled, scoring three and Brooklyn's fat lead shrank again.

Walter Alston was not looking to his bull pen when Bob Skinner came to bat, and for a brief and awful moment he might have wished he had. Newcombe wound and threw and Skinner swung and caught the ball flush. Its flight off the bat took it straight to center field where Duke Snider was already racing to the wall. A man in a coat, tie, and hat was beginning to reach down to catch what looked like a home run. In the press box, Tommy Holmes watched the ball and the Duke and as Snider began his leap Holmes was sure that he had taken to the air too soon. Later, Holmes would write that perhaps it was an "optical illusion" but Snider appeared to hang in the air just long enough to snag Skinner's drive in the outermost reaches of the webbing of his glove.

But Newcombe's generosity was not complete. Lee Walls, who'd already tripled, came to bat with a man out. This time he was not about to be stranded: he homered to the top deck in left, cutting the Dodger lead to 7 to 6 and leaving Walter Alston compelled to seek relief.

Clem Labine had gone a full nine yesterday. But Don Bessent was available, and Bessent had been more than equal to the challenge when he'd filled in during Labine's convalescence.

With a man out and a run in, Bessent came in and immediately surrendered a single to Dick Groat. He appeared to be out of the inning when Gene Freese grounded to Robinson at third, a sure double play. But Robinson fumbled the ball, and now Bessent had two runners on.

Bessent was not a pitcher of Maglie's complexity. He threw hard, and that, in essence, was his game. He threw hard to Jack Shepard, who flied out, and he threw hard to Dale Long, whom he fanned. For this he was rewarded with an extra run's cushion when Sandy Amoros homered again in the bottom of the eighth.

The score stood at 8 to 6 Brooklyn when Bessent climbed the dugout steps and took the mound in the ninth. The scoreboard now showed that Milwaukee was finally leading in St. Louis. If the Dodgers wanted to be sure of a pennant, they would need to end their season now, and end it well.

Roberto Clemente, however, was not inclined to oblige. He led off with a single. Bill Virdon, who'd already driven in three runs, stepped in. In right field Carl Furillo offered a silent prayer for a double play. "Nobody," Tommy Holmes later wrote, "will ever know what would have happened had Bill Virdon's smash been hit anywhere except directly at Junior Gilliam." But that is just where Virdon hit it, starting a double play that answered Furillo's prayer and brought the Dodgers to within an out of the National League championship.

AT FIRST BASE Gil Hodges could not stop berating himself. He had come to bat in the eighth after Amoros's home run. He'd singled and made it to third when Bessent blooped a fly ball to shallow left. Hodges had watched the Pirate fielders converge on the ball, unsure if anyone could make the catch. He drifted off third, hedging toward home before erring on the side of caution and easing back to third, ready to tag up if someone caught the ball. No one did. Hodges raced for the plate. But he had started too late and with too far to go and was out at home. "We could have had a big inning," he later told Milton Gross. "I loused it up. How dumb can you be?"

Hank Foiles stepped to the plate. Campanella trudged halfway out to the mound, close enough for Bessent to hear him say, "Reach back now and get a little extra on it. Give me everything you got."

Campanella squatted behind Foiles and called for a fastball. Foiles took it for strike one. He called for another, and Bessent was quickly ahead, no balls and two strikes. At third base Jackie Robinson, momentarily losing track of the count, charged in, mistaking the second strike for a third. The third base umpire laughed and Robinson retreated. Like Hodges he had not forgiven himself for his sloppy play in the eighth, when he botched Gene Freese's double-play grounder. "Maybe," he later admitted saying to himself, "I've blown the game."

Campanella called for a waste pitch, to see if Foiles might be too eager to hold off. Bessent performed the ruse of shaking off the sign. "Let him get thinking," he said to himself. Foiles took a fastball inside for ball one.

In the dugout Walter Alston's jaw hurt as he worked his chewing gum too hard. He had already decided that if Bessent could not get Foiles he would bring Labine in to face Frank Thomas. He did not like the idea of Thomas, a power hitter, taking a swing at Bessent's fastball. Better, he reasoned, to force him to hit Labine's curve.

Campanella called for a fourth fastball.

At shortstop Pee Wee Reese reminded himself of his place in the game—"Nobody on, no need to hurry if it comes here."

At second base, Jim Gilliam said to himself, "Get it yourself, Don, get it yourself."

Don Bessent went into his windup. The last thing he thought before releasing the ball was, he later said, "Tight, keep it tight."

Hank Foiles swung. The next thing he heard was the thud of the ball in Roy Campanella's mitt.

CAMPANELLA WAS THE first to reach Don Bessent, who was already leaping in the air. Campanella caught him around the waist and lifted him. The Dodgers surged toward the mound and the crowd surged toward the field and only Sal Maglie's quick grasp on Bessent kept him from being engulfed in all the teeming joy. "Thank God," Campanella said in silent prayer, "I could hang in there and play."

Three policemen stood at the clubhouse door, stopping no one. The members of the Dodger Sym-Phony made their way downstairs to play. Walter Alston led his players into the clubhouse, his customary reserve abandoned. He hurried around the room, shaking every Dodger's hand. Duke Snider poured champagne over Don Newcombe's head. Newcombe wore a silly hat pulled down to his eyebrows. "We're the champs," he called out. He spotted Jo Jo Deliao, a dwarf who played in the Sym-Phony, and danced with him. "We're the champs," he called out again.

Roy Campanella sat on a trunk gingerly holding a can of beer. The nail on his right forefinger was broken and peeling. His left hand was swollen but he held the ball that Don Bessent had thrown past Hank Foiles. The ball should have been Bessent's but Campanella had decided to keep it. "When I'm 97," he said, "I'll tell my sons, this is the toughest ball your daddy ever caught."

Sandy Amoros had a big unlit cigar in his mouth. Alston praised Sal Maglie. Newcombe paraded around in pink shorts. John Griffin put on a wig and smoked a cigar. Clem Labine rubbed Pee Wee Reese's wet head and told him, "They call you the old pro. You're a pro, that's enough."

"You did a hell of a job," said Reese.

"If I did half the job you did, I'd be proud of myself," replied Labine.

Snider retreated to his locker where he drank champagne from a bottle, with a beer chaser. Randy Jackson, who had never seen anything like this when he played for the Cubs, admitted that he had almost gotten trampled when he ran from the dugout to the mound. "Hot dog," Newcombe called out. "We're the champs."

Jackie Robinson, trying to talk above all the happy noise, predicted the Dodgers would win again in 1957, and that he was going to be part of it. There were so many young men who had seen how the older men played and won. "Then the old guys didn't do so badly, either did they," he said. "You're damn right I'll be here."

Reese, too, announced he would be back: "I'll quit when they make me."

The room was jammed and impossibly loud. Carl Furillo admitted he had seldom prayed as hard as he had when Bill Virdon came to bat in the ninth.

Reese joked with Labine. "I'm his idol," the captain said. "I mean I was his idol when he was a kid."

The Sym-Phony played on, badly. Newcombe paused his celebration to consider what he might have accomplished, had he only pitched better. "I can't get a big game," he said angrily. "Can't hold a five-run lead. Had a chance to be carried off the field. That's a great thing but I couldn't do it."

Buzzie Bavasi escaped the racket in the coaches' office, where he sat with Walter Alston. "If anybody told you last October that we would lose Podres, Loes and Spooner and that Campy would just barely hit .200 what would you have given us for chances?" he asked. "Not very much, I'll bet."

Outside, the line for World Series tickets was already forming, even though they would not go on sale until six o'clock the next night. First in line was George Schneider, who worked in a lumberyard and who insisted he was "married to the Dodgers." "I got to root them through," he said. "They lose unless I'm here." Behind him was a man from Connecticut who was willing to wait all night and day because, he said, "There's no fun watching it on TV." Further along was a fellow from Mexico who had admired Sal Maglie when he pitched in the Mexican League.

A telegram arrived from Mayor Wagner praising the team from "all New Yorkers." Walter O'Malley issued a statement, lauding Alston and adding that "real progress" was being made on the new stadium for downtown Brooklyn.

IT WAS APPROACHING five o'clock and in St. Louis, the scoreboard at Busch Stadium had already tolled the end of Milwaukee's season. The Cardinal fans booed, Eddie Mathews hit two home runs, and the Braves finally beat St. Louis, 4 to 2. The Braves retired to their clubhouse where they dressed for the flight home. Lew Burdette sat in front of his locker, smoking a cigarette. Lou Perini, the owner, walked through the clubhouse, shaking hands and saying, "Don't worry about a thing, boys."

Fred Haney placed his cap in his locker and did the talking for his players. "It's a terrible disappointment," he said. His team had been in first place for 124 days and yet when it most mattered, he said, "We just couldn't do it. It was almost as if we weren't supposed to do it." He thought of games during the season—fifteen came quickly to mind—that the Braves should have won, precluding any sort of race at all. He pulled a telegram from his pocket. It came from a fighter-bomber squadron based in Clovis, New Mexico. It read: "If you can't do it, Braves, we'll come and help."

"Fans all over the country were pulling for us," Haney went on. "I don't feel as badly for me as I do for all those people who rooted for us."

At Mitchell Field in Milwaukee, thousands were gathering to welcome the Braves home, even in defeat. They hung a sign that read, "We still love our Braves." And when the team plane finally landed at 7:30 that night, fifteen thousand people were waiting for them. Eight men in headdresses performed an exuberant war dance. The fans had hoped to see the players and perhaps still accompany them downtown to the Schroeder Hotel, which was to have hosted the victory party. But the players' wives were waiting for them and so only a few boarded the buses downtown. The players assumed that their party was canceled and so only Warren Spahn, Gene Conley, Ernie Johnson, and Andy Pafko made it to the hotel for dinner with their wives.

IN BROOKLYN DRIVERS honked their horns in celebration. Fifteen hundred people performed a snake dance near Borough Hall. In Bay Ridge the owner of a Finnish bar offered drinks on the house. The Italian patrons of a Norwegian bar called out "set the table all around" while outside the tavern people danced in the streets. Firemen raced across the borough, responding to false alarms from merry people who had signaled the alarms.

In downtown Brooklyn a great bonfire burned into the night. Firemen came and put it out. But when they left someone lit it again. The firemen returned and this time they doused the fire so that it would not burn again.

PART TEN

FALL

It is tempting to end the story of the 1956 Brooklyn Dodgers here. They had won a pennant people did not expect them to win, and many people did not want them to win, and they had won it dramatically. "This is the toughest one we ever won," Pee Wee Reese told Jimmy Cannon in the happy clubhouse that afternoon. "We're older."

The Dodgers had won this pennant as World Champions. In Brooklyn, where generations of baseball fans had come of age, or come to America, dreaming only of the day the Dodgers would merely be competent, the pennant had become an expected pleasure, noteworthy only in its absence. Fifteen thousand people did not descend upon Ebbets Field to salute the Dodgers, as had all those fans in Milwaukee. In his walk through Brooklyn, Murray Schumach could not help but feel that while people were pleased they were not floating with pleasure: the Dodgers had become a team that was *supposed* to win.

The Brooklyn teenage girl who threw open her window and called out "We did it," like the Norwegians and Italians and Swedes who bought each other drinks, and the people who snake danced at Borough Hall, could not have known that that night would be the last night for Brooklyn to celebrate the Dodgers. Because what happened next, and what would continue happening in the days, weeks, and months to come, would offer little for Brooklyn to celebrate. The story of the Brooklyn Dodgers is an often-told story that, as anyone who has heard it knows, ends sadly. That is why it is important to pause for a moment and take some final pleasure in what the Dodgers accomplished on the last weekend of the 1956 National League season. Because on Wednesday afternoon the New York Yankees would come to Ebbets Field and, with President Dwight Eisenhower in a field box to throw out the first pitch, begin the last World Series the Brooklyn Dodgers ever played.

Had that series ended badly but quickly—a four-game sweep for the Yankees, or four lopsided wins out of five—the end of the season would not have felt so cruel and haunting. But this was a good World Series. It went to seven games. It ended at Ebbets Field, on a cloudy afternoon ten days after the Dodgers had their last reason to smile at each other and embrace.

IT HAD TAKEN the Dodgers five tries before they beat the Yankees in a World Series. Now they would try to show that 1955 was not an aberration. The Yankees, meanwhile, had won the American League pennant with relative ease, ending the season nine games ahead of the Cleveland Indians. Their best player, Mickey Mantle, was enjoying one of the greatest seasons a ballplayer ever had—winning batting's "Triple Crown" with 52 home runs, 130 runs batted in, and a .353 batting average. He was surrounded by stars—catcher Yogi Berra, pitcher Whitey Ford—and solid men in the field: first baseman Bill Skowron, shortstop Gil McDougald, second baseman Billy Martin, and in the outfield Hank Bauer and forty-year-old Enos Slaughter. Tom Sturdivant, Johnny Kucks, and Bob Turley had pitched well. Don Larsen was a decent starter best known for hugging a lamppost with his car late one night in spring training. The oddsmakers liked the Yankees at seven to five.

The Yankees were New York's team, or rather Manhattan's team, even though they played in the Bronx. Their reputation was one of excess pride; no team had won as many championships and could boast such an alumni roster—Babe Ruth, Lou Gehrig, Joe DiMaggio, the list, in Brooklyn at least, felt interminable. They played in an immense park that only served to enhance their reputation as deities—not for Yankee Stadium the cozy intimacy between player and fan of Ebbets Field. At Yankee Stadium you came to admire and perhaps to worship if you were lucky enough not to get stuck with a pillar in front of your seat. It was not hard to hate the Yankees. It was easy and it was fun.

THE PRESIDENT ARRIVED at Ebbets Field for the opening game in an open-topped car. It was a chilly day and he wore a topcoat and rumpled fedora. He threw the ceremonial first pitch from his box and then settled down to watch, Walter O'Malley at his side. O'Malley had the whole afternoon to chat up the president, and by the end of the day was leaning close and talking as if the great man was a long-unseen fraternity brother from Penn.

Things did not begin well for Brooklyn, which was unusual because Sal

Maglie was pitching. Mickey Mantle came to bat in the top of the first with Enos Slaughter on first and promptly deposited a pitch on the Bedford Avenue side of right field. The Yankees were up by two before the president could even get cozy. The Dodgers could do nothing with Whitey Ford in the first. But in the second Robinson led off with a home run. Hodges followed with a single and Furillo doubled him home, tying the score. The Yankees seemed poised to cut deeper into Maglie in the third when Hank Bauer and Slaughter singled. But Maglie struck out Mantle on a rare fastball. Berra popped up and Skowron grounded out. And though the Yankees would nip at Maglie all day and score another on Billy Martin's home run, they had squandered their best chance to chase the Barber.

The Dodgers came right at Ford in the home third. Reese singled, and so did Snider. Hodges homered to left and Brooklyn had all the runs it would need. Inning after inning Maglie flirted with danger, most precariously in the fifth when Berra came to bat with two on and one out. Alston decided to visit the mound. Maglie's arm was tight but he beseeched Alston to let him pitch to Berra, a terrific hitter who would swing at anything, and often as not, hit it. Alston agreed and Berra flied to left. So did Skowron. Brooklyn scored again when Amoros singled home Campanella, who had doubled. Maglie pitched a full nine and while he and his teammates retired to their clubhouse pleased with their afternoon, they were not inclined to celebrate. "Hell, we've been through all this before," Reese explained to the reporters who were making more noise than the players. "We broke the ice on this deal last year."

Still, it was the best of all possible beginnings. Maglie, as had become his habit, had pitched well. Better still his teammates, batting slumpers all season, were hitting together. They had welcomed the Yankees by pummeling their best pitcher. And no one needed to remind them that they had won their World Championship after *losing* their first two games.

IT RAINED ON Thursday. This irritated Don Newcombe, who worried that the extra day's rest might take the precision off his pitches. He spent part of the afternoon doing his customary jogging across the Ebbets Field outfield. His father, meanwhile, announced that he had a good feeling that his son's moment of "big game" redemption was at hand: "I think this may be it," said James Newcombe, a frequent visitor to the Dodger clubhouse and a fixture in the seats behind home plate when his son pitched. He went on to explain that Don and his wife Freddie had adopted two children before the season and that the children "would bring him good luck."

The skies cleared on Friday and this time Adlai Stevenson, campaigning to defeat Eisenhower in November, arrived wearing Yankee and Dodger caps, one on top of the other. Walter O'Malley, who knew something of measuring a man's usefulness, let others sit by Stevenson's side. But just to keep the candidate from feeling too lonely, Randy Jackson, all but forgotten since cutting his hand on a shower handle, stopped by to visit: his father and Stevenson had been classmates at Princeton.

Furillo had a sore back. So did O'Malley, who with the president in tow had stumbled on the stairs at the Hotel Bossert. Don Newcombe, without any apparent ailments, was throwing hard but not accurately. The Yankees nicked him for a run in the first, and began nibbling at him again in the second—singles by Martin, Don Larsen, and McDougald for another run. A walk to Mantle loaded the bases and Yogi Berra came to bat. Just as Warren Spahn's struggles against the Dodgers could not be fully explained, neither could one batter's mastery of a pitcher who generally performed well against most everyone else. This was the case with Yogi Berra and Don Newcombe, who faced each other infrequently but always with the inexplicable advantage to Berra. Newcombe complemented him handsomely; his pitches made Berra look like the best hitter on earth. Now Newcombe slipped one past him. But not a second. This time Berra's drive sailed out to the gas station on Bedford, where the young boys chased a souvenir of his grand slam. Alston came to retrieve Newcombe, who trudged from the mound, leaving his teammates down by six.

He retreated to the clubhouse and, in a violation of protocol, stripped off his uniform, pulled on his civvies, and headed to his car, not bothering to wait for the end of the game and his teammates. He had parked his station wagon in the lot on the corner of McKeever and Sullivan, where Mike Brown was helping out his father-in-law, an attendant.

"What's the matter, Newk, a little competition too much?" Brown called out. "Do you fold up?"

Newcombe approached and said some harsh words. And then, Brown later told police, Newcombe punched him in the stomach. He told Brown he was tired of his taunts, that he had been needling him all season long.

Brown insisted that he only teased him twice, that he was only the fill-in guy. Newcombe apologized. The police arrived.

It was now the fourth inning and both Newcombe and Brown were missing a comeback of thunderous proportions. Ed Roebuck had staunched the bleeding in the second and, his workday done, watched as his teammates began slicing into Don Larsen. They were not hitting prodigiously, not yet at least, a single, a walk, sandwiched between some sloppy play in the field by the Yankees. Brooklyn scored a run, and when they loaded the bases Casey Stengel, the Yankee manager, replaced Larsen with Johnny Kucks. Reese singled home two. Stengel brought in a lefty, Tommy Byrne, to face Snider, who did nothing to restore Stengel's belief in his judgment when he homered to tie the game at six.

The Yankees would score two more against Don Bessent but Brooklyn would devour four more Yankee pitchers, scoring seven more times, and winning in a breeze 13 to 8. In the clubhouse the Dodgers maintained their muted pleasure. Alston said kind things about Don Bessent and admitted that Newcombe perplexed him. "He had good stuff," he said. "He just couldn't get his change-up where he wanted it." Meanwhile, Mike Brown, who at the parking lot seemed willing to let his confrontation with Newcombe drop, resurfaced at a precinct house with a lawyer at his side. The police referred them to the Flatbush Magistrate's Court, where the lawyer announced he would seek a warrant for Newcombe's arrest.

EBBETS FIELD HAD been packed for the first two games, which meant that grown men were left to find perches where they could—on the girders and railings, and along the ramps. They bent and stretched, moving with the pitches to follow the ball. They crammed together in the standing-room-only stretch along the third base line. Thirty-four thousand four hundred and seventy-three people squeezed themselves into Ebbets Field and even if their number was doubled it would still not equal the attendance at Yankee Stadium where 73,977 came to see if the Yankees could even things.

They left happy. Ford, back in form, beat Roger Craig in the third game 5 to 3. The Dodgers appeared poised for a comeback in the ninth when Furillo led off with a shot to center that eluded Mantle. By the time he reached second Furillo had his head down and was steaming for third. But Bauer had backed up Mantle and began the throwing relay that ended with the ball in McDougald's glove before Furillo's arrival. Still, the visitors club-house was not a gloomy place. "Sure, we're alright," said Alston, who chose Carl Erskine to start the fourth game.

But Erskine lasted only into the fourth when the Yankees scored two to break a 2 to 2 tie. They scored four more and the Dodgers could do little against Tom Sturdivant. Still, Alston had Maglie ready for the fifth game, a seeming advantage. Stengel had Don Larsen, who'd failed in game two.

MURRAY KEMPTON WAS a compassionate man who was not drawn to the winner's side. He wrote a column for the *Post,* and though sports were not generally his domain, he made the trip to Yankee Stadium that gray and chilly after-noon. Later, Kempton would come, as if he had known it all along, to the losers' dressing room. There he found Sal Maglie, who was naked and eat-ing a piece of Italian sausage. Maglie had pitched superbly. He had allowed only two runs and five hits. Don Larsen, however, had surrendered none.

Kempton had spent his afternoon watching Sal Maglie work. Larsen and his steady march toward a perfect game was incidental. Kempton typi-cally wrote about race and politics, about unknown people living noble lives and powerful people with no decency at all. Of Maglie he wrote, as so many others had that summer, about an old man going about the grim business of his difficult work. The writers had fallen in love with Maglie that season. He was no longer the menacing, headhunting Barber. Now, in twilight, he was a worn-down master of thousands of pitched innings, calling on every trick and skill to help carry a team that once despised him. With Maglie, age was always the context, age and what he used to be before he grew old and admirable. "There was the customary talk about the shadows of the years and the ravages of the law of averages when Sal Maglie went out to meet the Yankees yesterday afternoon," Kempton wrote.

He could not take his eyes off him. He noted the way Maglie blew on his hands, how he wiped the afternoon's first perspiration from his brow, and how he did not need to turn and look when a ball was hit past him, hav-ing long before learned the sound of an out and of a home run when he heard one. He surrendered one to Mantle in the fourth, the first hit of the game. He described the way Maglie, down by a second run, pitched through the Yankee seventh, striking out Larsen, Hank Bauer, and Joe Collins in succession. The Yankee Stadium crowd, understanding what he had been and what he still was, applauded. "It was the last inning of the most extraordinary season an old itinerant, never a vagrant, ever had," Kempton wrote. " 'I figured,' he later said, 'that for me, either way, it was the last inning, and I didn't have to save anything.' "

Kempton found him in the clubhouse unhappy with his afternoon— "How am I to be satisfied? But you got to adjust yourself." But Maglie, like his teammates, was gracious toward Larsen, a fellow pitcher whose perfect game had surpassed the no-hitter he himself had thrown just two weeks before. "I knew just how he felt in the ninth inning and, in a vague way, I didn't want to see his no-hitter ruined," Maglie said. "It would have been impossible, of course, but I wanted to see us win it without spoiling his performance."

He was dressed and heading to the crowded and happy Yankee clubhouse to congratulate Larsen when Roy Campanella called out after him. "I told you," he said, "that there would be days like this."

DON LARSEN'S PERFECT game brought Clem Labine the gift of pressure, a prize he coveted. The Dodgers had lost three in a row and now trailed by a game. A loss in Game Six at Ebbets Field and their season was done. Soon after Dale Mitchell struck out to end the perfect game, Alston announced Labine as his next starter. He had appeared in sixty-two games, but had started only three, most recently on the pennant-clinching weekend. The prospect of starting such a game, however, did not frighten Clem Labine. That night he slept, even if he was a bit nervous.

In the morning he drove to the ballpark with his teammates. He dressed and walked to the Dodger bull pen along the left field line. The stands pushed close to the field and Labine enjoyed having the children crowd close to railing to see how he was throwing.

He did not need much time to get warm, a gift as a reliever, who often needed to be ready in a hurry. Seven tosses were generally enough. Labine took the mound. It was a sunny day and there were no empty seats at Ebbets Field. Hank Bauer led off and Labine quickly sensed trouble. His pitches were not sinking. "If my ball isn't sinking well I get the ball up," he recalled years later, using the present tense. "If I get the ball up I worry." For Labine to succeed, he needed to keep the ball low. He had pitched well against the Yankees, especially to Mantle, against whom he seemed to be able to throw the ball just where he wanted. Berra worried him. Even if Labine was hitting his spots Berra was capable of hitting anything, even a waste pitch that any batter would otherwise be prudent to ignore.

He survived the first using his fastball and curve. His sinker was being hit, even though the Yankees were causing no damage. Between innings he asked Campanella whether they should just abandon the sinker. Campanella, knowing how essential the sinker was in forcing the Yankees to hit the ball on the ground, and not out of the park, advised patience. Labine and his Yankee counterpart, Bob Turley, pitched through painless first and second innings. Turley, who relied on the fastball, was beginning to record strikeouts. Meanwhile, Labine's arm was loosening with the work. His pitches were starting to drop. The timing was a blessing: he was now in the third and the Yankees would be coming to bat having already seen what he had.

Both men pitched through scoreless middle innings. The occasional Yankee, and the even rarer Dodger managed a hit. Only when Labine faced Berra did he throw a pitch he regretted. His strategy with Berra was one of home run avoidance: Berra tended not to hit the ball to left and so, Labine calculated, if he could keep the ball away from him he would not be able to pull it with power. But pitches, like children, do not always do as they are told and when Labine threw a curve the ball refused to break. Instead, it hung, a fat pitch with little behind hit. Berra caught it flush. Or rather, just as Labine had failed to apply just enough spin on the ball, Berra hit it hard, but not at precisely the right spot on the bat. The ball sailed to center and Labine sensed disaster until he turned to watch Duke Snider chase it down for an out.

The game was a scoreless tie in the ninth. Both starters were still pitching. The Yankees had seven hits against Labine. They had threatened but not scored; Labine had gotten Mantle out with two on in the third, stranded Berra on second in the sixth, and survived Joe Collins' one-out double in the eighth.

In section six, row three, seat thirteen, a Dodger fan named Henry Fleischman beat a steady tattoo on the drainpipe that blocked his view of home. He used a rolled up newspaper, as was traditional for the people who believed that by beating this drainpipe for the entire game they could summon the spirits who would make the Dodgers win. Henry Fleischman was thirty-nine years old. He was married, the father of three. He worked in Manhattan, an advertising man. He smoked without pause. And he believed in the powers of the drainpipe. "A lot of old-timers in this section know about it," he told Bard Lindeman of the *World-Telegram*. "I was here the first two days and that's why we won."

Bob Turley came to the mound for the bottom of the tenth, having struck out ten Dodgers and allowed only three hits, one of them a double by Labine himself that brought Stengel to the mound of a chat so long that Labine took the opportunity to sit down on second base for a breather. He advanced no further. When Gilliam struck out and Reese ended the inning by flying out a bugler in the stands played "Taps."

Now Turley made quick work of Labine and then undercut his advantage when he walked Jim Gilliam on four pitches. In section six Henry Fleischman had pounded his newspaper to tatters. He was beating the drainpipe with such fury that it was getting hot and beginning to vibrate. Reese came to bat. The infield was playing back, assuming that with a man out he would not be bunting to sacrifice Gilliam to second. But Reese, sensing opportunity, bunted just the same and though Turley threw him out at first, he had moved Gilliam into position to score on a single.

Snider was next and Stengel ordered him walked intentionally, bringing up Robinson, who jumped too hastily on Turley's first pitch, fouling it into the seats along the third base line. Turley came back with a fastball. Robinson's liner started low as it sailed to left and was rapidly gaining altitude when Enos Slaughter drew a bead. But Slaughter had judged its flight incorrectly and could only leap helplessly as the ball sailed over his mitt. Gilliam scored the game winner. Snider stepped on second and then turned back to first to join his teammates in pummeling Robinson on the shoulders.

In the clubhouse the newsmen descended first on Jackie Robinson who deflected their attention away from himself. "All I know," he said, "is that I am very happy for Clem Labine."

There would be a Game Seven. It would be the next day at Ebbets Field. Casey Stengel announced Johnny Kucks as his starter. Walter Alston had Don Newcombe.

2 | THE LONGEST NIGHT

Carl Erskine may have lost the fourth game but was in no mood to be pitied. He believed that his defeat was not in vain, that it was merely a stage in a greater plan. "There was a reason for it," he told a friend in the Dodger clubhouse that afternoon. He turned toward the locker where Newcombe sat. "There has to be another chance for him."

Don Newcombe did not sleep well the night before the deciding game. He woke four times, took a pill but still could not rest. His wife, Freddie, suggested that he move to another room, but he could not sleep there either. It was not the game that kept him awake, he told Milton Gross. "It was the other business I wanted to beat, but dammit I can't get away from it."

It was a brisk day but Newcombe was pleased with his warm-ups. Later, he would say that generally his troubles were early-inning troubles, that if he got through the first and second and found his rhythm he would be fine. Just before Hank Bauer stepped in, Reese approached the mound. He had already spoken to Newcombe in the clubhouse but wanted to repeat what he said—"I told him how he'd gotten us this far and told him that this was the payoff but whatever happens don't worry. Just go out there and pitch."

Bauer led off with a single. But Newcombe threw three strikes in a row past Billy Martin and did the same to Mantle. Bauer was still on first when Berra came to bat. Reese again came to the mound, this time to remind Newcombe to keep the ball away from Berra. Newcombe got two quick strikes. Campanella signaled for a waste pitch, high and inside. "I was getting the ball where I wanted," he later said. "Except the first one Yogi hit. I tried to brush him back but I didn't get it inside enough."

Later, Campanella would say that Berra "hit it off his ear." The ball found the seats and Brooklyn came to bat in the first, down by two. Snider singled, but that was all.

In the top of the second, Newcombe fell behind two balls and no strikes to Kucks, the pitcher. Robinson approached from third and asked whether Newcombe was aiming his pitches. Newcombe replied he did not believe he was. An aimed pitch is a tentative pitch, a pitch directed at a spot but delivered without authority. Newcombe was a fastball pitcher who had the control that eluded so many men who threw hard. He did not need to aim the ball unless he did not trust himself just enough to throw. Still, the Yankees did not score. Neither did Brooklyn. The Yankees were batting in the third when once again, Newcombe looked in to face Berra, this time with Martin on first. Again Newcombe got two quick strikes. He seemed poised for a strikeout when Berra nicked his third pitch for a foul tip. Campanella wanted the next pitch wasted inside.

Newcombe threw and kept his back to the scoreboard when Berra's pitch sailed onto Bedford Avenue. He stared at the ground. In the pressbox men trained their binoculars on him. His lips appeared to be moving and someone was sure that when he brought his hand to his face it was to wipe away a tear.

The Yankees led 4 to 0 when Newcombe came to bat to modest applause in the bottom of the third. Berra, a notorious chatterbox behind the plate, offered Newcombe some backhanded consolation. "I hit a perfect pitch," he said. "It was perfect—low outside fastball and I hit the hell out of it." The Dodgers went hitless in the third.

ELSTON HOWARD'S HOME run in the fourth finished him. Alston came to fetch him and as Red Smith wrote later that afternoon, a boo was the last sound Newcombe heard as he stepped from the field into the dugout.

Irving Rudd found him in the shower. "Go away," Newcombe told him. "You'll get all wet."

"Look Don," said Rudd, "I know what you're going to do and you'll regret it afterward. Finish your shower and get dressed and then sit down and cool off. It won't be more than half an hour and the game will be over."

But Newcombe did not want to stay. He dressed and walked out to his car with Rudd chasing behind. James Newcombe was waiting by the car and Rudd asked, "Pop, can't you talk to him?"

A man standing in the parking lot called out, "It's tough Newk. You can't win them all." Don Newcombe settled into the driver's seat of his station wagon. His father joined him. So did Milton Gross.

"I'm sorry, pop," Newcombe murmured.

"What?" asked his father, who could barely hear him.

"I'm sorry."

"What do you have to be sorry for?" said his father.

They drove along Washington Avenue, then over to Flatbush. They left

Brooklyn over the Manhattan Bridge and were driving through lower Manhattan when Newcombe switched on the radio. They heard Bob Wolf say, "After six innings it's Yanks 5, Dodgers 0. Roger Craig now takes over the mound." Gross was not sure whether Newcombe was listening. Twice he had to hit the brakes hard to avoid rear-ending other cars.

"You won 27," Gross told him. "You know there were some big ones."

"Remember that," said James Newcombe.

"I don't want to talk," Don Newcombe said. "I don't want to say anything."

He drove west toward the Holland Tunnel and New Jersey. He had his right hand on the wheel. In the left he clutched a handkerchief. He wiped his mouth and sometimes his eyes.

They lost the radio signal as they entered the tunnel. "Why didn't you change your shirt and go back to the dugout?" Gross asked.

"I don't know," Newcombe replied. "I don't know a lot of things."

Then, as they emerged into the light on the Jersey side of the tunnel, he said, "I felt good. I was throwing hard, real hard."

They were on the Pulaski Skyway when Bill Skowron came to bat with the bases loaded. The Dodgers had just walked Berra intentionally. Skowron's grand slam made it 9 to 0. Ebbets Field began emptying out.

"It can happen to somebody else, too," said James Newcombe. His son nodded.

"What about our hitters," said the father. "No hits the other day. Two hits yesterday and what have they got today." They had three.

Newcombe stopped at his father's house in Linden. He invited Gross in for a beer. In the kitchen his mother had the game on the television. "Get it over with," she said. "It's over and done."

"I'm sorry, ma," Newcombe said.

"What's to be sorry?" said his mother.

Newcombe poured beer for himself, his father, and Milton Gross. "Drink up," he said. "I want to call my wife."

Newcombe and Gross soon left. They drove on and Gross asked what he had been thinking of as they drove from Ebbets Field.

"I was thinking about what I do wrong," Newcombe replied. "But I can't put my finger on why I do it." He paused, and then went on. "I was running in the outfield at the stadium the other day and a guy called me a yellow-bellied slob. How do you take things like that?"

He told Gross what Reese had said to him in the clubhouse, about how vital he was to the team. "And other people say I choke up. I think it's rubbed off in the clubhouse."

He dropped Gross at the commuter rail station. Five boys were standing on the corner, four black, one white.

"That Newk?" one boy asked. He wanted to know why Newcombe was there; the game had just ended.

"He left early," Gross said. The white boy, he noted, giggled.

"Don't laugh," said one of the others. "Just don't laugh."

NEWCOMBE STOPPED AT home and then went out and by dawn his wife could not find him. "He was in a state of mind I've never seen before in our eleven years of marriage," she told a reporter who called. "He isn't here and I don't know where he is. He was only here about ten minutes, then he left." She had called the liquor store, but he was not there. She called his relatives, who had not seen him. "He said he wouldn't be home last night. He left the car in case I need it."

In Brooklyn that night a funeral director in Ridgewood loaned a coffin to a bartender so that Warren DeMontreaux of Cooper Street could pay off his Series bet by climbing in for a mock funeral. In Bedford-Stuyvesant, Dutch Pirozzi, who owned the Sportsmen's Café, placed a casket by the front door. Matty Bosco made a mock casket that he placed in front of his flower shop on Atlantic Avenue. Inside he placed a doll dressed in a baseball uniform and announced that the memorial would stand for three days. And in a gas station out on Pennsylvania Avenue, Harold Whetstone was reading the sad news in the bulldog edition when three teenagers stirred him from his gloomy reverie to tell him they had come to rob him. They took $135 and vanished into the night.

The Dodgers had a small party. The team had planned nothing elaborate, certainly nothing like the gala of the year before, and nothing like the Yankee victory party in Manhattan at the Waldorf-Astoria. The Dodgers had a 12:30 flight the next day that would begin their voyage to Japan. Newcombe did not appear at the team party and by morning Buzzie Bavasi was warning that he had best make the flight: "If he doesn't show up it'll be a matter for the Commissioner."

CARL FURILLO, WHO had fought in the Pacific, had refused to make the trip. So did Sal Maglie. Campanella announced that he would have surgery on his hand but would make the journey just the same. The Dodger wives were excited about visiting Japan, even if their husbands did not much want to go.

The players were milling around the gate at Idlewild Airport, drawing little attention, when Don Newcombe appeared. He wore a topcoat, a gray tweed suit, a red shirt, and a hat. He was chewing gum. He wore dark glasses over red-rimmed eyes. The reporters were on him quickly and he told them he had been home all night. "I told my wife not to tell anyone where I was," he said. "I felt terrible and didn't want to talk to anyone."

This was not true. Privately, he told Milton Gross that he had spent the night alone, walking. Gross had called the house. So had Jackie Robinson, Buzzie Bavasi, and the commissioner, Ford Frick. Newcombe admitted he had spent the night convinced he would break his contract and skip the Japan trip. He called his wife three times to let her know he was okay, but said nothing else. He wandered until dawn and then, at seven o'clock, called his lawyer. He was due in court to answer Michael Brown's charge that he had punched him in the stomach. A judge adjourned the case until November, after the team's return from Asia.

Newcombe left for the airport, bagless. When he arrived at Idlewild a crowd formed around the reporters who had gathered around Newcombe. Alston tried to buck him up. Campanella insisted his roommate did not choke. But Newcombe was on edge. "Where's my money for this trip," he said. "I'm not going until I get my check." A fellow from the front office took him by the arm and led him to the plane. His wife would take a later flight, and meet the team in Los Angeles.

He was loud on the plane. He sat near the front with Roy Campanella. Someone had brought a bottle on board and they were getting drunk. Walter O'Malley was on the plane with his wife. So were many of the other wives. Newcombe rose and on unsteady feet began noisily making his way to the bathroom. Walter Alston, who had seen and heard too much, got up. He was Newcombe's height and just as broad and now he stood in his path.

"Newk, I want you to go back to your seat and I want you to be quiet," Alston said. "You understand that?"

Clem Labine watched and listened as Newcombe replied. "Walter," he said, "get out of my way or I'm going to piss on you."

Alston stepped out of his way. But that, Labine later said, "was the beginning of the end for Newk. Newcombe was an alcoholic and none of us knew it."

3 | DEAL

Rosalind Wyman believed that a city could not be a place of consequence if it lacked a center for culture. She also believed that a city needed a team. Without "major league sports and major league arts" a city was destined to remain a "bush league" town, a fate she feared might visit her city, Los Angeles. Others in Southern California were at work on the cultural angle. Los Angeles had a football team, the Rams. But Rosalind Wyman had taken it upon herself to look for a baseball team.

Wyman was born in Los Angeles, unlike so many people who had come there from someplace else. Her parents had; they had moved west from Chicago. They owned a drugstore. Her mother loved the Cubs. Wyman became a baseball fan, too. She listened to the World Series on the radio. Los Angeles did have a couple of minor league teams—the Hollywood Stars and Los Angeles Angels. It had a baseball stadium, too, a small and rickety minor league park in South Central called Wrigley Field; her mother's beloved Cubs owned the minor league rights to Los Angeles. But major league baseball was almost two thousand miles away in Kansas City, and St. Louis.

In 1953, when she was just twenty-two, Wyman was elected the youngest member of the Los Angeles City Council. She ran, in part, on a campaign to bring baseball to the city, a theme she had printed on the three-by-five cards she handed out as she campaigned door-to-door. Wyman, a woman of self-described "wild ideas," did two things when she arrived at city hall. She started a World Series pool, a dollar-a-player sweepstakes just like her mother ran at the family drugstore. And she befriended a young Los Angeles County supervisor named Kenneth Hahn, with whom she began to talk about luring a ball club to Los Angeles. Hahn was already a believer. After his election the year before, he was approached by Vincent X. Flaherty, a sports columnist for the *Los Angeles Examiner*. Journalism in Los Angeles then was boosterish in nature, and Flaherty had for years been campaigning to bring a big-league team to the city. Not only had he encouraged other writers to join his crusade, but had told the young and eager Hahn, "If you want to stay in office for a long time, get a major league team to come to Los Angeles." Hahn stayed in office for forty years.

Rosalind Wyman was also busy writing—letters to owners who might be interested in talking of a move. She and Hahn had been emboldened in their campaign by Lou Perini's move to Milwaukee in 1953. That same year that Bill Veeck sold the woebegone St. Louis Browns to new owners in Baltimore, where the team was reborn as the Orioles. And Connie Mack's Philadelphia Athletics moved to Kansas City in 1955. Among the letters Wyman wrote was the one she had sent to Walter O'Malley in September 1955. The Dodgers, she later said, "were the crown jewel of baseball," and the possibility of luring them to Los Angeles seemed, at best, remote. O'Malley had just made his public play for a new Brooklyn stadium. He declined her offer to meet.

It might have made more sense had the plan to bring the Dodgers to Los Angeles begun at the highest levels of government and power—the Robert Moses equivalents in Los Angeles. But it was not until the Wyman and Hahn plan was well along that the powerful interests in Los Angeles took notice. It was one thing to have Dorothy Chandler, wife of *Los Angeles Times* publisher Norman Chandler, trolling for contributions from her monied friends for the great downtown arts and music center that would bear her name. The *Times* was the paper of power and influence. It fell to the second-tier paper, Hearst's *Examiner*, to beat the drum for major league baseball. Any club, it seemed, would do, even the Washington Senators, the worst team in the game.

Los Angeles was an old city, founded in 1781, before the United States Constitution was ratified. It was a large city, and in certain quarters an exceedingly wealthy one. It was also a city filling up more and more with people from elsewhere, who had left behind cold winters and aging city centers and row houses for the promise of a new and presumably better life in California. To be a school-age child in Los Angeles in the 1950s was to watch as new children came to class each fall, children whose parents had arrived from Cleveland, Chicago, Minneapolis, Detroit, and so many smaller cities in between. Moving vans, which Sam Qualiarini had begun noticing coming to Crown Heights to transport his neighbors to Long Island and beyond, were also arriving in places like Lakewood, Van Nuys, and Torrance, where life appeared so filled with promise. They left behind friends, neighbors, relatives, and baseball teams that they could only follow from afar.

But now, less than a year after he had rebuffed Wyman's overture, Walter O'Malley was pleased and excited by the interest Los Angeles was displaying in his team. Whatever details he might have learned in June of the city's "offer" he kept to himself: he shared none of this with Buzzie Bavasi, who heard no more mention of Los Angeles after the phone call that had shaken O'Malley out of his despair. The call had not come from either Wyman or Kenneth Hahn. Oddly, neither of them knew who had placed it. Bavasi believed it might have come from John Gibson, president of the city council. If it did, Gibson did not share this with Wyman or Hahn. Still, the call had given O'Malley reason to believe that he now might have what he so sorely lacked in his battle against Robert Moses: a suitor. Perhaps if the political and business people whom Moses courted and occasionally needed sensed that they would have to answer at the polls for losing the Dodgers to another city, they might convince Moses to soften his opposition.

As it happened Los Angeles did figure in the team's immediate plans, indirectly. The trip to Japan was a long one and would necessitate a stopover in Los Angeles.

KENNETH HAHN HAD been in New York for the World Series. He hoped to leave with a baseball team. The Washington Senators seemed interested in Los Angeles. Their owner, Calvin Griffith, had been talking of a new stadium for years. For this he needed not the approval of one man, as Walter O'Malley did from Robert Moses, but the assent of Congress. Congress had been deliberating about a new stadium for ten years. Griffith was growing tired of waiting. He had been approached by Los Angeles and by San Francisco and while no one thought a move was imminent, it seemed ever more likely that by 1958 California would have a major league baseball team.

Vincent X. Flaherty had helped arrange a meeting with Griffith and Hahn at Toots Shor's saloon. Hahn and John Leach, a Los Angeles County administrator, presented Griffith with a briefcase filled with statistics to bolster Los Angeles's claim as a wonderful place to move his team. Los Angeles would build him a stadium, and the stadium would have lots of parking. Hahn left Toots Shor's confident he had his team.

He was sitting with Griffith at Ebbets Field when an usher brought him a note. It was written on a napkin and struck Hahn as scribbled hastily. It came from Walter O'Malley. It asked Hahn to sign nothing until O'Malley could speak with him. "O'Malley," Hahn later wrote, "was interested in bringing the Dodgers to Los Angeles."

WALTER O'MALLEY ARRIVED in Los Angeles as a man with three options: he could drop to his knees and, in his morning prayers, beseech the Almighty to bring together the forces of money and politics and Robert Moses so that his new stadium might yet rise on the corner of Flatbush and Atlantic Avenues. Or, he could wait until the plan, whose prospects appeared ever more doubtful, sank and then take whatever alternative Moses deigned to extend to him. Or he could move.

On October 12 he met privately with Kenneth Hahn at the Statler Hotel in downtown Los Angeles. The team was spending the day in the city, en route to Honolulu and then, to Tokyo.

Years later Hahn would write and publish privately a brochure-sized story of how he, with the assistance of others, accomplished the seemingly impossible feat of bringing the Dodgers to Los Angeles. There was no mention in Hahn's account of the June phone call to O'Malley. In Hahn's telling of the story, Los Angeles's happy dance with the Dodgers began during the World Series and reached a quick, if nonbinding, consummation: "At that meeting," he wrote, "O'Malley told Hahn that he would move his team to Los Angeles in 1958." Hahn, who wrote of himself in the third person, went on, "O'Malley also told Hahn that if the move was announced publicly, he would deny it. As Hahn would later recall, O'Malley said the devoted Brooklyn fans 'would murder me' if they knew of the impending move."

Hahn did as he was told. The Dodgers boarded their DC-7 and flew west. Hahn told the Associated Press that while he had had breakfast with Walter O'Malley, the prospects of the Dodgers coming to Los Angeles were dim. "The Brooklyn authorities have promised the Dodgers a new stadium," he said. Then, carefully, he continued, "If this should fall through O'Malley says this would be the first place for him to move. But he thinks there is no likelihood of it not going through." Hahn portrayed himself as a man in despair; he was not even sure he could lure the Washington Senators to Los Angeles. Still, he added that O'Malley had offered wise counsel: to get a major league team, first build a major league park.

JAPAN WAS LIKE a family vacation with children too old to travel with their parents: not always pleasant. The players did not play well and, with rare exceptions, did not have fun. They dropped their first few games, which brought Walter O'Malley to the clubhouse to remind them that while they were goodwill ambassadors they should still—and this he said with a smile—"remember Pearl Harbor." The Dodgers won fourteen games in Japan, tied one and lost four, the first time a touring American team had ever lost more than a single game in Japan. Still, Gil Hodges took it upon himself to entertain fans in Osaka by imitating all the players on the field. Roger Craig and Ed Roebuck took a lot of pictures with the cameras each player got as a gift. Roy Campanella, the inveterate shopper, would come back to his hotel room and cover his bed with all the knickknacks he bought. Jan Roebuck got to know Rachel Robinson and enjoyed her company so much that she always regretted that the friendship did not continue once they came home.

Duke Snider bickered with his wife. Kazuhiro Yamauchi, a star of the Tokyo Orions, criticized the Dodgers for failing to play with the gusto of the New York Yankees. Don Newcombe pitched so poorly that the Japanese hitters, modest talents at best, treated him like a man tossing batting practice. "He'd come in the clubhouse and you could smell the liquor on his breath every morning," Labine later said. "O'Malley told him, if you want to go home you can go home. But he didn't. He stayed. I'll give him credit for that."

In Japan, Newcombe began telling about an injury he had suffered during the pennant clincher against the Pirates. He felt a twinge in his arm, he said, and afterward could not throw a curveball. "This choke-up and gutless talk is nonsense," he said. "I tried to win a game for them with a bad arm." He insisted that he had kept the injury a secret from everyone but Campanella. "He kept shaking off curves and throwing only his fastball," Campanella said. "I asked him once during the series why he wouldn't throw any curves and he said his arm hurt when he pitched a curve. After that, I wouldn't say another word. It was up to him if he wanted to see a doctor." He did not see a doctor. Nor did he turn to Doc Wendler, the team trainer.

Roscoe McGowan of the *Times* was dubious: why had Newcombe not told Alston, who could have started a healthy Don Bessent in the seventh game? McGowan's suspicions of Newcombe now bordered on contempt. He even wrote a poem about him in *The Sporting News*, a parody of a W. S. Gilbert verse—"When gigantic Donald Newcombe is a-pitching, And a-setting down the batters one-two-three, He never feels the slightest twinge or twitching, In elbow, sacroiliac or knee. . . ."

Still, Newcombe would return home to find consolation: a judge dismissed Michael Brown's charges against him. And he won not only the National League's Most Valuable Player but also the Cy Young Award as the best pitcher in the game. Buzzie Bavasi would always say that Don Newcombe in 1956 was the best pitcher for one season he ever saw. Bavasi chose the words carefully, knowing that Newcombe would have four more years in the big leagues and never approach what he was in 1956.

WALTER O'MALLEY WENT home the long way. His players and their wives flew home over the Pacific. O'Malley took his wife and children to Asia and Europe. They stopped in Karachi, where O'Malley had his picture taken riding a camel. They stopped in Italy and then in France and sailed for home from Cherbourg. They were gone for two months. But in his absence he had the club sell Ebbets Field to Marvin Kratter, a realtor, who announced plans to put a residential and commercial development on the site. The Dodgers could still rent the park for another three years while they waited to see where they might play next.

O'Malley came back to New York to continue his dance with the city, and with Robert Moses, over the new ballpark. But by the late fall this had dissolved into a sorry two-step that felt like a dance marathon in its twenty-second hour. In November the engineers submitted to John Cashmore, the borough president, their preliminary report on the site. They had drawn up plans just as O'Malley had hoped they would—a big, round stadium abutting Flatbush Avenue, right in the center of Brooklyn. Cashmore sent the report to the Brooklyn Sports Authority and the authority members announced they would go to the Board of Estimate to ask for more money to continue their work. But there was a problem: the plan recommended building the stadium not across from the Long Island Railroad station, but *above* it. In other circumstances this might have been a problem easily resolved. But Robert Moses did not think so. On December 7, he wrote to the mayor about the "obstacles" to building the stadium. First, he noted, the Board of Estimate was not going to allocate much money to the Sports Authority because the board believed that the financial burden for the stadium should be on the authority. And then there was the matter of the location. Moses, however, had a solution: separate the stadium from the rest of the development plan. He thought $100,000 should cover the cost of deciding how to make something of the neighborhood. He saw no need to boost the authority's allowance—"the only full time help needed would be a secretary."

Two weeks later the board met and did just what Moses recommended. The stadium was no longer a part of the redevelopment of downtown Brooklyn. It was a separate matter. The Sports Authority had asked for $278,000 to continue its work and study the feasibility of issuing bonds. The board gave it $25,000. And, just to make clear just where the currents were running, the mayor conceded that if the Sports Authority concluded it would not be able to issue bonds for the stadium, it would be "out of business." He insisted that he did not want people thinking the stadium plan was finished. But it was. And though it hardly seemed necessary, Robert Moses emerged to announce that while the authority be given "a run for its money"—the chance to prove it could actually raise the necessary funds—he was prepared to build a housing project on the site, with the federal government's Title I money that Walter O'Malley had coveted.

Finally, on December 28, O'Malley spoke: "There is still a short time before we could be forced to take an irrevocable step to commit the Dodgers elsewhere." And with that he announced that he was leaving town, first for Vero Beach, before heading on to Los Angeles. "We have done our part," he said. "We want to remain in Brooklyn and we should be allowed to continue there."

BUZZIE BAVASI, MEANWHILE, had a team to worry about, and there seemed little doubt that the Dodger club that had won the pennant would be a different one in 1957. Bavasi was not sure what to expect from Roy Campanella after yet another operation on his hands, nor did he know what he could expect from the aging Pee Wee Reese who, it turned out, was not thirty-eight but, in fact, forty. Johnny Podres would be back from the navy, and that would help the pitching. John Roseboro, who caught for the Dodger affiliate in Montreal, had promise, as did Don Demeter, an outfielder. Jim Gilliam was still young, as were Sandy Koufax and Don Drysdale. Sal Maglie was not. Carl Furillo might have another season left in him. Jackie Robinson had said he wanted to come back. But that was not going to happen.

In early December the team announced that O'Malley had met Horace Stoneham in Chicago and had sold him Jackie Robinson for cash and a little-known pitcher named Dick Littlefield. At first Robinson announced that while he was disappointed to be leaving the Dodgers, he was ready to play and play well for the Giants. He had no intention of signing. Later he wrote that he had already begun talking with the president of Chock full o' Nuts about an executive position. He was preparing to announce his retirement in *Look* magazine, which had agreed to pay him fifty thousand dollars for the exclusive. The story leaked three days before the magazine hit the newsstands, irking Bavasi no end. "Some of the writers damned me for having held out on the story," Robinson later wrote. "Others felt it was my right. Personally, I felt that Bavasi and some of the writers resented the fact that I outsmarted baseball before baseball had outsmarted me."

Free of a player whom he had wanted gone all season, Walter O'Malley gathered the men who worked in his front office for a meeting at the Hotel Bossert. He wanted to know what they thought about the possibility of moving to Los Angeles.

He went around the table, allowing each man to offer his reason for wanting to stay in Brooklyn. O'Malley listened as they told him of children in school, and mortgages, and the desire of New Yorkers to stay in New York.

Years later Buzzie Bavasi would recall how O'Malley first counted the votes, and then the words he spoke: "Everyone wants to stay except for me," said Walter O'Malley. "So we're going."

BUT THIS IS not where this tale ends. It ends later, much later. It ends in Brooklyn. And it ends well.

Just before four o'clock on the afternoon of October 8, 1957, Arthur "Red" Patterson, publicist for the Brooklyn Dodgers, stood before a group of reporters at the Waldorf-Astoria Hotel in Manhattan and, cigar in hand, distributed a fifty-two-word statement from his absent employer, Walter O'Malley. The typewritten statement was crafted with a lawyer's sense of prose. It began: "In view of the action of the Los Angeles City Council yesterday and in accordance with the resolution of the National League made Oct. 1, the stockholders and directors of the Brooklyn baseball club have met today . . ."

They were leaving.

The statement surprised no one. It brought expressions of regret from Mayor Wagner and John Cashmore. But in Brooklyn people did not take to the streets, nor did they gather in public places for the mock wakes that had followed the Dodgers' World Series loss almost exactly a year before. There had been one rally to keep the Dodgers in Brooklyn. But that was in April. Now, the sense among those who had covered the story and the borough was that people were so weary of the maneuvering to keep the Dodgers in Brooklyn that many were beyond caring. Merchants near Ebbets Field said they hoped the housing project planned for the site might bring them new customers. "I never figured them to go," said Lou Soriano, bandleader for the Dodger Sym-Phony. "The boys feel bad they're gone." Then, with a nod to the team offices on Montague Street, he added, "Let them all drop dead over there."

Walter O'Malley had set in motion a drama whose outcome he could not have predicted in November 1955, when he went to Princeton to see the first model of the stadium Billy Kleinsasser would build for him. He had told Mayor Wagner and Robert Moses in August 1955 that he could not stay in Ebbets Field much longer, and had used Jersey City to get their attention. He had rejected the first overture from Los Angeles in September 1955, believing he might find a way to acquire the land and build his stadium on the corner of Flatbush and Atlantic Avenues. And even after he secretly told Kenneth Hahn a year later that he was coming to Los Angeles, he never stopped trying to make things work in Brooklyn. At least that is how it appeared.

Walter O'Malley was a public man who kept his secrets well, which made it at times impossible to know what he was thinking. This made him a formidable man with whom to do business. But it did not help make his reputation as a man worthy of trust.

There are two ways to look at the story of Walter O'Malley's decision to abandon Brooklyn for Los Angeles: that he was, as the received wisdom has it, a man who cared only for money and not for the people who had, in fact, made his team profitable, year after year. Or that O'Malley was, in fact, a man not nearly as powerful as he would have liked to be, a man without the muscle and influence to get what he wanted. So he had to scheme, playing people and cities off each other because otherwise he would have ended up the loser, the owner of a team that fewer and fewer people were willing to go out of their way to see.

In the winter of 1957, Walter O'Malley was playing a game that, only in hindsight, he seemed destined to win. He had an invitation from Los Angeles. But Los Angeles had no major league ballpark for him, and no assurance that it would give him the land and the help to build one. In New York he had three men and a secretary comprising the Brooklyn Sports Authority that was somehow supposed to assist in pulling off the miracle of selling the bonds to finance a stadium on land he did not even own. He did not even have a ballpark anymore; Ebbets Field now belonged to Marvin Kratter, real estate magnate. In short, O'Malley had nothing but a team and himself. He had money in the bank, but the money was not enough.

So he went to work. In January 1957 he bought a forty-four seat plane for the Dodgers, an aircraft suitable for a traveling team. In February he announced that the Dodgers might play ten exhibition games in California. He also took out a new travel insurance plan for his team. And, most important, he convinced Philip Wrigley, the owner not only of the Cubs but also of the territorial rights to baseball in Los Angeles, to sell him the minor-league Los Angeles Angels and their stadium, Wrigley Field. Wrigley, it was said, was angry at Los Angeles over matters concerning his property on Catalina Island. Walter O'Malley did not need another farm team. But he did need the rights to a city in which he might want to move.

Mayor Wagner was paying attention to Walter O'Malley; he announced that he was concerned not only about the possibility of the Dodgers leaving the city, but the Giants, too. Others, whose opinion mattered less than the mayor's, also felt compelled to speak. In April, Abe Stark, the city council president, suggested the Parade Grounds, an expanse of playgrounds and ball fields in central Brooklyn, as the site of a new Dodger stadium. For once O'Malley and Robert Moses agreed: it was a terrible idea to rip out fields for children so that the professionals might have a new place to play. A group of investors from Queens offered to buy the Dodgers. O'Malley turned them down. In May, Stark suggested enlarging Ebbets Field. Stark, said O'Malley, "is a swell little fellow but he doesn't know what this is all about." Walter O'Malley was trying to work both coasts at once, and he did need the man who put the "hit-sign-win-suit" billboard in Ebbets Field gumming things up with alternatives.

Things were proceeding for O'Malley. In May the National League offered him and Horace Stoneham another important nudge to New York: permission for both teams to relocate. Now the talk was getting ever more serious. There were reports that Matty Fox's pay-per-view outfit, Skiatron, with which O'Malley was so enamored, was sweetening the prospects of moving to the West Coast: a reported $2 million fee to each team in return for pay-TV rights to their California games. O'Malley insisted that the possibility of moving had nothing to do with television. Matty Fox, however, did admit that he had set up escrow accounts for both the Dodgers and the Giants.

Finally, in June, the mayor invited O'Malley and Stoneham for a chat. The talk accomplished little, which was not surprising: Robert Moses had already spoken. In April, Moses announced *his* plan for professional baseball in New York: a new stadium in Queens, a fifty-thousand-seat arena set in the geographic center of the city on parkland known as Flushing Meadows. His Parks Department would build and own the stadium. A tenant could lease. Now, it turned out, this was what he had intended all along, long before Walter O'Malley had even become president of the Brooklyn Dodgers.

In the late 1930s, as Moses was working to build his vision of a new and greater New York, he saw in Flushing Meadows not only the 1939–40 World's Fair, but beyond that, a stadium. "We laid out on paper 20 years ago an all-purpose municipal stadium and sports center, roughly bounded by Flushing Bay and the Roosevelt Avenue elevated rapid transit line," he wrote. "No money is required for the land. The stadium can be built for $8 million without a roof and $10 million with." He explained his plan in a July article in *Sports Illustrated*. He also used the space to excoriate Walter O'Malley, whose scheme to use public money, or condemnation powers, to build his ballpark and make himself rich appalled him: "Walter honestly believes that he in himself constitutes a public purpose." And, "For years, Walter and his chums have kept us dizzy and confused." Moses made clear that there were, in his view, no alternatives to this plan, certainly not the one O'Malley favored. "Let me in my own words give you briefly what I believe will be the conclusion as to the Atlantic terminal site," he wrote. "It won't happen."

Nonetheless, two months later the Brooklyn Sports Authority unveiled plans for the site. The stadium and the land would cost not $12 million, as had originally been projected, but $20.7 million. The authority also reported that it would have a hard time issuing bonds to pay for it all, just as Moses had warned. Just to make clear to O'Malley and Horace Stoneham what would happen if they rejected his offer, Moses' associate at the Triborough Bridge and Tunnel Authority, George V. McLaughlin, the man who had first brought O'Malley to the Dodgers, announced a contingency plan should both teams move: a new National League team for New York, to be owned by a nonprofit corporation that would share its revenue with the players. The new team, of course, would play in Flushing Meadows.

BUT THIS WAS not 1956, when Buzzie Bavasi watched O'Malley gloomily lock himself away in his office. Now O'Malley had Los Angeles, and Los Angeles was being as generous and welcoming as New York was proving reluctant and, in Moses' case, intransigent. In May, O'Malley flew west for a visit. He met again with Kenneth Hahn, who this time invited him for a trip. They boarded a helicopter for a tour of the city. They flew over O'Malley's new property in South Central, Wrigley Field. And they flew over downtown Los Angeles, where from the air O'Malley, the former engineer, took in the largely vacant tract of hilly land along the Pasadena Freeway called Chavez Ravine.

Rosalind Wyman could not make the trip. But she spoke to Kenneth Hahn afterward. "Roz," he told her, "he saw the contours of the land and said, 'You could build a ballpark there.' "

And he could have it. He could have the three hundred acres and if there was, as some believed, oil in Chavez Ravine, they could talk about that, too. And if the poor Mexican people still living on the land did not want to move, they could be moved. And even if the land had once been designated as the site for public housing, they could make the very statutory changes that Robert Moses would not even consider in New York. It is easy, in retrospect, to believe that in its dealings with Walter O'Malley, Los Angeles assumed a prone position. But that is only because O'Malley ended up with such a beautiful stadium in such a convenient location, and because this made him so wealthy. The courting of O'Malley was not universally popular in Los Angeles; many believed that the city was being far too generous, and in the case of those people still living in Chavez Ravine, far too callous. It was by no means certain, then, that O'Malley would get what he wanted in Los Angeles. He had Kenneth Hahn behind him, and Rosalind Wyman, and John Gibson, the city council president. He also had the mayor, Norris Paulson, who was eager and passionate but who would never stand accused of possessing the keenest political mind. In Los Angeles, O'Malley had backers and possibilities. In New York he had neither. And yet he wanted to stay just the same. Or so it appeared.

In August 1957, Horace Stoneham announced that he was moving his Giants to San Francisco. The city was going to give him a new stadium where, in a bow to the team's storied past, a clump of sod from the Polo Grounds would be replanted. Stoneham admitted that while he felt badly about disappointing all the boys and girls who followed the Giants, he suggested their anger might be better directed at their parents, who were not taking them to his games anymore. Robert Moses greeted the news by announcing plans to expand a housing project onto the vacated site.

Walter O'Malley, however, was not done yet. That same month he announced that he would still be willing to buy the land on the corner of

Flatbush and Atlantic Avenues, if the city would condemn it. The city's corporation counsel, Peter Brown, issued an opinion suggesting that it might be legally possible for the city to do this. And though O'Malley was still short of cash, he now had a savior, a man with pockets so deep O'Malley could only look on in envy: Nelson Rockefeller wanted to help keep the Dodgers in Brooklyn.

Rockefeller was then a man of spectacular wealth as well as of political ambition; he would be elected New York's governor in 1958. In September he announced that for the past month he had been working in private, trying to craft an arrangement in which he might buy a part of the team, or might assist in raising money to help with the cost of buying land. Rockefeller met with the mayor and O'Malley. The Board of Estimate was said to be "kicking around" his proposal. "So far nothing has developed in these conversations to lend us positive encouragement," Rockefeller said. But others, in New York and in Los Angeles, saw in his arrival and with his money the key to keeping the Dodgers in Brooklyn.

Norris Paulson was crestfallen. "I'm very much afraid we don't have much of a chance to get the Dodgers," he said. "We want to make 'angels out of the bums' but we can't be Santa Claus like some of these big names." But they were trying. A week later the Los Angeles City Council voted to give O'Malley three hundred acres at Chavez Ravine if the club would be willing to pay for a recreation area. O'Malley had already decided not to press for the ravine's oil rights.

The Board of Estimate met to consider whether $2 million was a fair price to ask for land condemned on the proposed stadium site. Abe Stark reappeared to suggest that perhaps Ebbets Field could be modernized. In Los Angeles, Rosalind Wyman told a reporter she feared her city may have "lost" the Dodgers "because of the way negotiations were conducted."

No one was sure what, precisely, Nelson Rockefeller was offering, and what O'Malley was asking, and what the city was demanding. The reports on their talks were speculative: perhaps the Long Island Railroad might join in the deal; O'Malley was said to be willing to pay $10 million toward the stadium and the land. The Los Angeles City Council, meanwhile, voted to affirm its offer to O'Malley. It was September 18 and the Dodgers had until October 1 to inform the National League of its plans. O'Malley asked for more time, so that New York could still make an offer. The plan would require approval of the Board of Estimate, nine votes out of sixteen. "We haven't seen them yet," O'Malley said.

Robert Moses said nothing. He had made his offer. O'Malley's public response was vague: neither acceptance nor rejection. But the *World-Telegram* reported that the Flushing Meadows deal had fallen through. O'Malley was reported to be interested if Moses would drop the rent from $1 million to $500,000 and, to sweeten the deal, throw in the lucrative parking concession. Moses refused him. O'Malley, who always told Buzzie Bavasi that if he were going to move to Queens he might as well move three thousand miles away, passed.

The National League extended its October 1 deadline. But sensing the Dodgers were on the verge of slipping away, the Los Angeles City Council gathered to extend a full and final offer. On October 7 the council met for six hours. The outcome of its deliberations was in doubt. Before the council was a proposal to give the 300 acres of Chavez Ravine to O'Malley as well as have the city pay $2 million to prepare the hilly terrain for a stadium and $2.75 million for access roads. The city owned 185 of those acres but was prepared to buy the rest. In return, O'Malley would build his own $10 million stadium.

The debate was dragging on, angrily at times, when Norris Paulson summoned Rosalind Wyman. He needed to know that O'Malley would take the offer if their side could get the votes. Wyman resisted. Paulson told her that people were saying that O'Malley was using the city to get what he wanted in New York. Years later, Wyman would say, "No one knew if he really wanted it."

So she placed the call, and when she reached O'Malley she did what so many others had tried at and failed: she insisted on a clear answer: would he come to Los Angeles?

"Mrs. Wyman, I want to thank you for everything you've done, and I know it's been difficult," O'Malley replied. "I am a New Yorker. If I can get the best deal in New York I will stay in New York."

Rosalind Wyman hung up the phone and decided to keep the conversation to herself. "We had wobbly people," she later said. And if they knew what O'Malley had said, "we would have lost."

The council, unaware of O'Malley's reluctance, voted 10 to 4 to invite the Dodgers to Los Angeles.

The Board of Estimate never voted formally on Nelson Rockefeller's plan to keep the Dodgers in Brooklyn. It took no action on Peter Brown's opinion on condemning the stadium site land. There were reports that the board was balking when it learned that the final cost for the stadium would be closer to $30 million, and that Rockefeller had balked, too. On October 7, 1957, Walter O'Malley had no further offer from New York. And whether he was playing Rosalind Wyman or telling her the truth, his day ended with a choice between an appealing offer from Los Angeles and nothing more from New York.

On October 24, O'Malley arrived in Los Angeles and announced that the Los Angeles incarnation of his baseball team would be known by the same name it had used for eighty-one years in Brooklyn. There were no trolleys in Los Angeles. But the team would be the Dodgers just the same.

PEE WEE REESE came to play in Los Angeles, as did Gil Hodges, Duke Snider, Carl Erskine, Jim Gilliam, Carl Furillo, Clem Labine, and Don Newcombe. Walter O'Malley, who concerned himself little with his roster, had told Buzzie Bavasi to keep the aging stars on the payroll: Los Angeles wanted the Brooklyn Dodgers, and that is what the city would get.

But it was not the same team. Robinson was gone. Campanella, paralyzed in a horrific car accident at the end of the 1957 season, would never walk again. And, in time, the older men gave way to new stars, to Koufax, Drysdale, Roseboro, and Wally Moon. They won a World Series in Los Angeles in 1959. And in 1962, after hard negotiations, a close referendum, and ugly forced removals to clear the remaining people living at Chavez Ravine, the Dodgers moved into their new stadium.

Two years later Robert Moses presided at the opening of the ballpark he had always intended for Flushing Meadows, Shea Stadium, named for William Shea, the well-connected lawyer so instrumental in bringing the National League back to New York. Moses was now nearing the end of his career. He was an old man of diminishing power; Nelson Rockefeller, the new governor, was not nearly as intimidated by him as so many other powerful men had been. "When the Emperor Titus opened the Colosseum in 80 A.D.," Moses began at his vainglorious best, "he could have felt no happier." The new tenants, the Mets, borrowed a bit of the Dodger royal blue and the Giant orange for their team colors. Duke Snider came back to New York to play for the Mets, as did Gil Hodges, Roger Craig, Charley Neal, and Clem Labine. Like the Dodgers, the Mets were awful before they became champions. In 1969 they won a universally unexpected World Series title, managed by Gil Hodges.

WALTER O'MALLEY IS not the villain of this story. He is merely the player who set the drama in motion. Keeping the Dodgers in Ebbets Field was an option, but not in O'Malley's view an attractive one. Attendance was still over one million in 1956, but it was dropping. Only a sentimental man—or an heir or an otherwise wealthy man who did not make his money by owning a baseball club—would have stayed on in the hope he might yet lure people back. By the time O'Malley was ready to build a new stadium at a good location, he could not do as Charles Ebbets had done—spending years secretly buying small parcels of land from poor people ready to cash in. O'Malley needed help and New York was not going to extend it. O'Malley had not spent all his time and energy and divested himself of all his holdings but his baseball team in order to take Robert Moses' on-the-cheap deal in Flushing Meadows. Los Angeles courted him and wooed him and promised him more than New York would consider. Los Angeles was the smart move.

Walter O'Malley was a clever man. He was smart and he knew a lot more than did his counterparts about how to turn a handsome profit from the game. But he is still reviled in Brooklyn, and it is tempting when telling the story of the Brooklyn Dodgers' last good season to slip into the familiar refrain about Walter O'Malley, the greedy bastard. But that is too convenient. Walter O'Malley was not a bad man. He was devoted to his wife, and his children loved him. To this day his son, Peter, who ran the Dodgers after him, safeguards his father's reputation and his letters, especially when confronted by yet another writer from back east whom he has every reason to suspect will walk away and remind everyone what a louse his father was.

Walter O'Malley was nothing of the kind. He was a businessman and he was in the business of making money by owning a team and he decided that he could make a lot more money owning one in Los Angeles than in Brooklyn. O'Malley had a problem of a different sort. It dated to his years in military school, and Penn, where he presided over "O'Malley's Tammany":

He was a political man and political people believe they can seduce anyone. Often, they can. But people don't much like the feeling of being played. Why would anyone believe anything Walter O'Malley said when his stock-in-trade was the wink, the nod, and the empty smile?

But mendacity is a character flaw, not a crime. Walter O'Malley, however, was also a limited man. And it is in that limitation, not in his avarice or deceit that his sin resides. O'Malley should have never owned a baseball team because he could not see what he had. He could not see that a baseball team is more than a business, that it is a topic of conversation. People pay to go to games, and if they do not go in sufficient numbers the person who owns that team will not make money. But people also talk about the games and about the team. They think about the team and wonder about the team and share these thoughts with each other. Walter O'Malley, who sat apart from the "little people" in his private box, did not understand this. This did not make him unique among team owners. He was just the first to be so obvious about it.

This ignorance of the relationship between the team and its followers is the one thing that he and Robert Moses had in common: Neither man truly appreciated cities. They understood the things they could build in cities—housing, highways, and ballparks. But they did not understand people who lived in the cities. How could they, when at the end of their workdays they got in their cars and went home to the suburbs? They did not understand nor appreciate nor appear to give much thought to city life and city people and what is essential in making a city feel like a place where people know and get along with each other. Cities are not merely grand projects and the roads that connect them. They are places filled with neighborhoods where strangers have reason to talk to one another. Not intimately, but casually. They have things to share—the prices at the butcher and the lateness of the trash collector and the noise from the kids across the street.

Suburbs offer the gift of a home of one's own. But in the suburbs life often faces away from the street, and from the people on it. In city neighborhoods people are forced, whether or not they like it, to see each other and hear each other. Often this means that they have to acknowledge each other. There can be a certain pleasure in this, especially, as Jane Jacobs wrote, when people understand that just because a neighbor is being friendly that is not an invitation to ask too many questions. City life—street life, not high-rise life, which can be an anonymous existence—allows people to feel they are not alone, that they live among others who note their existence. A neighborhood offers company, strangers who find ways to live so close to each other. The ballpark is a temporary neighborhood, a gathering in of strangers who, for a few hours, do the same thing together—watch a game and maybe talk about it.

Robert Moses is the bad guy in this story. He was arrogant, imperious, and cruel. He also wrote unkind things about Brooklyn in *Sports Illustrated* in July 1957: "It is claimed that Brooklyn would not be Brooklyn without the beloved Bums. The same thing was said about the *Brooklyn Eagle*, which nevertheless folded. That was a damn shame, and so in some respects, would be the departure of the Dodgers, although a new location elsewhere on Long Island could hardly be classed as a tragedy. I shall leave it to people closer to politics and public opinion to prove what proportion of the 3 million and more Brooklyn residents really care a great deal in view of the slim attendance at Ebbets Field, the convenience of television, etc."

Moses was also a visionary who performed the remarkable feat first of envisioning a new New York and then actually building it. On the day the Dodgers announced their move to Los Angeles, Moses' slum clearance committee agreed on the final price for condemned land on the Upper West Side of Manhattan where his great arts complex, Lincoln Center, would rise. People lived in that neighborhood, and Robert Moses moved them away. If they were white people, especially middle- and working-class white people, they were lucky because they might find new and modern homes in the housing projects he was building. If they were poor, especially if they were black and Latino, they were often left to fend for themselves. Moses had about as much use for black people as Walter O'Malley did for Jackie Robinson. And here, again, was an instance where the limitations of such self-styled broad-thinking men blinded them to what was taking place in their city.

In the familiar telling of the last days of the Brooklyn Dodgers, the borough is cast as a wasteland. The white people are fleeing. Blacks and Puerto Ricans are moving in. The white people are the borough's soul, hundreds of thousands of William Bendix characters streaming out to Long Island, taking the heart of Brooklyn with them. The people who moved into the apartments they vacated were not Brooklyn people. They were new, and they were plentiful, and they were frightening.

That view, of course, is as simplistic as tracing Brooklyn's perceived demise to Walter O'Malley's greed. New people were moving in and many of them were poor and were blacks and Puerto Ricans who came looking for jobs that no longer existed. Many came from the countryside and brought rural ways with them. Crime did increase and, at times, its nature changed for the worse. But they were not the only people moving in. Joe Long moved to Brooklyn in 1954. He was seventeen years old. He came from New Bern, North Carolina. He was a "tar heel," a regional designation applied by the black people who had come before him, and as denigrating as the word "kike," which was what German Jews called their newly arrived brethren from Eastern Europe. Joe Long moved to Bedford-Stuyvesant. He moved in with his sister, who worked for a dry cleaning chain. He went to work there, too. In Bedford-Stuyvesant he was surrounded by "Alabams" and "Geegees,"—equally derogatory terms for people from Alabama and Georgia. They were fellow newcomers looking for wages better than they could find at home. Long worked and went to ball games at Ebbets Field and on Sundays he went to church. He did not join the gangs then proliferating in Bedford-Stuyvesant. His cousin was in a gang and protected him.

In time Long began augmenting his income by working part-time in a music store, Berdel's on Fulton Street, the commercial heart of Bedford-Stuyvesant. The owner was a Jewish man who liked Long and who, in 1968, sold him the store. The federal government assisted with a loan. Joe Long's story, of course, stands as evidence of a different and too-seldom-heard tale of the black migration to Brooklyn in the mid-1950s—the eager young man who works hard, sends money home to help send his sister to college, and who, by dint of desire and sweat becomes a merchant who, a generation later, would still be a prominent and respected man in the neighborhood. There is another way of seeing Joe Long, however, and that is a potential customer whom Robert Moses ignored. Long came to Ebbets Field, and not merely because black men played for the Dodgers. The Dodgers were the local team and they were good and he had heard of them, having caught the occasional game on the radio back home. At Ebbets Field he sat with white people and black people and, in his view, everyone got along fine.

They were not friends. They did not drink together at the Flatbush Avenue bars after the games. They sat together for nine innings and chatted and when the games were done they went their separate ways.

Long's story is not intended as a call for understanding and harmony. It is a statement of fact. Joe Long went to Dodger games. He was a paying customer. He would have kept going if the Dodgers had stayed in Brooklyn. He had simply taken the seat of someone who had moved away, just as the fellow before him had occupied the seat vacated by someone else. There were white people who did not want to sit near black people at the ballpark, let alone have them as neighbors. But there were others, whose views on race were not particularly enlightened, who like Sam Qualiarini had come to accept the presence of black people on their block. They played ball together. But they were not about to start dating each other's sisters. It was only when the balance in the neighborhood began shifting dramatically both in race and in class—read: many more poor black people—and when realtors warned white people of the fate that awaited the last whites left, that the panic and flight ensued. And with it ended the brief period where in places like Brooklyn, whites and blacks were slowly, if grudgingly at times, getting used to each other. Robert Moses either did not see or did not much care about that delicate balance. He was building parks for white people and highways to towns where white people lived. He did not want a ballpark in downtown Brooklyn. He wanted it on the highway to Long Island so that the people for whom he was building the city could come to take in a game.

In the end, Robert Moses did not so much transform Brooklyn as he made the transformation possible. He built the roads. The federal government supplied the loans for the distant homes on Long Island, but not for Brooklyn. But Moses did not have to sell people on the dream of a home of one's own. It was everywhere and it looked wonderful and the alternative in places like Brooklyn was not nearly so appealing.

It would take a generation before the children of the people who left began coming back to the cities, if not to live, then to come to the ballpark and capture some of the world their parents left behind.

A HOUSING PROJECT stands where Ebbets Field once stood. It is possible to walk through the project's grounds and find the spots where the players once stood—Carl Furillo's right field is a parking lot that continues as far as Duke Snider's center. So too is it possible to walk past a black wrought iron fence onto the spot where the marble rotunda rose up and walk straight ahead until the place where people first encountered the first great burst of stadium light and grass. A mile or so away, on the site where Walter O'Malley dreamed of building his stadium, stands a defunct appliance store. The site that Robert Moses had long before intended for the Dodgers or the Giants or any team he could find to fill the place is, of course, Shea Stadium in Queens. Shea itself is a much-despised park, a bland bowl whose only urban trappings are the auto parts stores that line the far side of the parking lot. There is talk of tearing the place down and building a replacement in the parking lot. The new park would be called Jackie Robinson Stadium. It would, if it is ever built, have a retractable roof but otherwise look like a replica of Ebbets Field.

The stadium, however, would sit at the confluence of highways, not city streets, which runs contrary to the idea of what Ebbets Field represented. It is an idea that other planners have incorporated in the new parks in Baltimore, Cleveland, Detroit, Seattle, Cincinnati, Milwaukee, San Francisco, and other cities that had built and then torn down parks like Shea. It is the reason Chicagoans fill Wrigley Field even when the Cubs are dreadful. Ebbets Field was a city ballpark, a ballpark to which people could walk. They could pass it on their way to work, and hear the noise from inside when they were heading someplace else. It sat in the middle of a place where many people lived.

Walter O'Malley built his dream ballpark three thousand miles away near the least archetypal of downtowns, Los Angeles. Dodger Stadium is a beautiful park, and unlike its contemporaries it has aged well. It is a wonderful place to see a game, in good measure because unlike the men who insisted, as Moses had with Shea Stadium, on multipurpose parks, O'Malley built his stadium only for baseball; the sight lines are for baseball, and baseball alone. The park and setting are so attractive that it is possible even for a visitor from the East Coast to sit above home plate at dusk on a summer's night, watch the sun set over the brown hills on the far side of the right field pavilion, and think what a clever man O'Malley was to have made the move.

But elsewhere across the country Robert Moses' urban vision is being repudiated, for a few hours at least, by baseball games at the new city ball-parks. The parks are small and were designed to feel reminiscent of the ballparks of a bygone America. They draw not only the city people, because passion about a team and about the baseball is not limited to people who live in town. The parks encapsulate the qualities about neighborhoods that urban romantics love to celebrate, qualities people often miss when they are lacking—the company and the conversation.

THE BROOKLYN DODGERS endure as a ghost. Many of the men who played for the 1956 team are dead. Hodges, Robinson, Gilliam, Drysdale died while still young men, in their forties and fifties. Don Bessent, who threw the last, glo-rious pitch of the pennant-clincher at Ebbets Field, drank himself to death. Walter Alston is dead, as are Irving Rudd, Sal Maglie, Carl Furillo, Rube Walker, Sandy Amoros, and Pee Wee Reese. Walter O'Malley died in 1979, and did not live to see his son Peter sell the team to the media baron Rupert Murdoch for $378 million. Billy Kleinsasser got back his model of the domed stadium he had designed for Walter O'Malley. He left it in the base-ment of his parents' home in Tennessee. It sat there for years. One day, about twenty-five years ago, they called to say they were cleaning the base-ment and found the model. They asked him what he wanted to do with it. He told them to throw it away.

The agony of Don Newcombe continued for years. His record dropped to 11 and 12 in 1957, when the team finished third, and 7 and 7 in 1958, their first season in Los Angeles. He pitched in the big leagues until 1960 and, ironically, last played in Japan where in 1962 he played the outfield for the Chunichi Dragons. Newk always could hit. It was only years later that he elevated his story to the realm of tragedy when he admitted to the alco-holism Labine had seen on sorry display on the flight from New York. He told of starting to drink beer when he was eight years old: his father, his greatest fan and booster, thought it would help him grow up big and strong. He never pitched drunk, but he did pitch hung over. Schaefer Beer, the team's sponsor, kept the clubhouse stocked. He would drink a six-pack and then stop and buy another for the drive home. By 1956 he was mixing liquor with grapefruit or grape juice. He stopped drinking in 1965, when his family found him passed out on the floor. They were preparing to leave him. He became an alcoholism counselor and was credited with assisting the young Los Angeles Dodger pitcher Bob Welch with his recovery. But even with sobriety Newcombe remained the same difficult man his teammates knew, generous one moment, bristling the next.

HIS TEAMMATES ASK after each other. They are scattered now. Roger Craig has a home in the desert east of San Diego. Randy Jackson lives in Georgia and Ed Roebuck outside of Los Angeles. Others live in the very places they left when they became baseball players—Snider in California, Erskine in Anderson, Indiana. Clem Labine lives in Rhode Island. They see each other at autograph shows and at funerals and at ceremonies honoring the surviving members of their storied team. Twice a year they meet in Vero Beach, at Dodgertown.

The team holds what are known as "fantasy camps," where men come to play baseball in Dodger uniforms in the company of men who used to be Dodgers. The older men are scattered among Los Angeles Dodgers, but they are easy to spot. Duke Snider's knee hurts too much to allow him to play. Labine's back gets sore after a day of coaching first base. Carl Erskine, trim and fit like the others, had lost none of his bounce, or the knot in his shoulder that hurt so much when he pitched.

It is one thing seeing them at home, or in a restaurant or in a hotel room. It is another to see them in uniform, together. They are back in Dodgertown. Their wives are with them but, like ballplayers, they spend their time in the company of other men. When they see each other they fall back on the familiar ways. Snider greets Erskine with "Hey, roomie." Labine, passing Snider, says, "Duker, Duker, Duker." And in that moment it is possible to see how they got along so well for so long. They were not all friends. They were teammates. They acknowledged each other. And that was enough.

Sam Qualiarini left Brooklyn for Staten Island. But when his first marriage ended he returned to Crown Heights, to Lincoln Place. He married a woman named Stella Moratta, who in the summer of 1956 used to watch him walk past her house on his way to St. John's Park. Abe and Ruth Steinberg still live in the same house in Oceanside that they bought in 1956. The Reverend Gardner C. Taylor retired but remained in Brooklyn, in a grand house that his congregation at Concord Baptist Church gave him to live in for the rest of his life. The younger George Clark became the fourth in his line to run the family real estate business in Gravesend and started training his son, George, to take over the firm. Lawrence Williams killed a man in a gang fight in 1961. He was convicted of manslaughter and spent three and a half years in prison. He returned to a very different Bedford-Stuyvesant than the one he'd left. The gangs as social entities were gone, replaced by the freelance terror of the drug dealers: "I came home to a monster here." He stayed in Bedford-Stuyvesant, never again ran afoul of the law, and eventually became a counselor for troubled teenagers.

John Powis became a priest. Later, as monsignor in the central Brooklyn neighborhood of Bushwick, he became one of the city's most vocal and effective champions of the poor. He also learned to speak fluent Spanish, believing it essential if he was to be able to speak with and for his many parishioners. Jose Sanchez also stayed in South Brooklyn. Years later, after he became a husband, and then a father and finally a grandfather, he would recall the summer of 1956 as a time when it was possible to believe that his neighborhood would remain as it always had been—safe and predictable, and nothing like the harsh and dangerous place it one day became. That he could think this way, that he could envision South Brooklyn's future with optimism and innocence, made even a wise and perceptive man like Jose Sanchez seem, in hindsight, naïve.

IN BROOKLYN THERE was no more baseball after the Dodgers left. But the team lived on, in stories, movies, books, and memorabilia—caps, shirts, and jackets purchased by a generation born after Ebbets Field was torn down. Taken together, they became emblems of a place and of a time when Brooklyn mattered. Because to grow up in Brooklyn after the Dodgers left was to live in a place that did not feel as if it mattered at all.

Brooklyn sank in the 1960s and 1970s but it is not a torpid place anymore. It is, in many ways, as it was in the best years—a mix of people from different places who have created a world apart from Manhattan: Russians in Brighton Beach, Haitians and others from the islands along Flatbush Avenue, middle-class blacks in Fort Greene, Orthodox Jews in Flatbush, but always with other people mixed in. Artists moved to Williamsburg. Bankers still live in Brooklyn Heights. And in 2001 a baseball team came to Brooklyn.

The team plays in Coney Island, in a new seventy-five-hundred-seat park that the city built for the New York Mets' entry-level minor league franchise. The team is called the Cyclones, after the old wooden roller coaster that still rumbles nearby. In its inaugural season the Cyclones sold out most every game and in Manhattan people who were used to getting good seats to sold-out events discovered they could do no better than bleacher seats for the Cyclones.

The return of professional baseball to Brooklyn was greeted with such enthusiasm that the Cyclones set up a website so that people could write their thoughts about its meaning. For all the entries that came from people who remembered the Ebbets Field of their youth, others came from younger people who wrote to tell that they had grown up hearing about the Brooklyn Dodgers but could now have a team just like them.

I took my wife and children to see the Brooklyn Cyclones. My children are both older now than I was in the summer of 1956. I was three, living in Midwood, and by the time I was aware of the world, and of baseball, the Dodgers were gone. My only association with Ebbets Field was the day the older boys from down the block came home from its demolition. They brought back bricks and sand.

We went on Russian Night: Oksana Baiul, the Ukrainian—close enough—Olympic skating champion threw out the first pitch and the concessionaires hawked Russian beer. I hurried into the park. It is a small stadium that brings most everyone close to the field. I did not know the players. I did not much care how well they played. A man behind us chanted, "Let's go Cyclones" and others took up the call. But then came an older man's voice, yelling, "Let's go Brooklyn."

I looked around me and could at last feel what I had missed.

The reporting for this book came largely, but not exclusively, from personal interviews. Roger Craig, Carl Erskine, Clem Labine, Randy Jackson, Ed Roebuck, and Duke Snider were especially generous with their time, and with their insights about the team and about themselves, as was their former teammate Ben Wade and batboy Stan Strull. Buzzie Bavasi possesses an encyclopedic baseball memory that he is only too happy to share. Tom Villante and Frank Graham, Jr., were equally helpful in giving a picture of life in Walter O'Malley's orbit. Terry Seidler, O'Malley's daughter, helped bring her father to life, as did Roy Campanella II on the subject of his father. Betty Erskine, Joan Hodges, Jan Roebuck, and Bev Snider were as generous in describing life as Dodger wives. Jim Brosnan, Andy Pafko, Daryl Spencer, and the late Bill Rigney explained a good deal about playing against the Dodgers.

In addition to those who lived in Brooklyn in 1956 and whose stories appear in the book—George Clark, Joe Long, Sam Qualiarini, John Powis, Jose Sanchez, Ruth and Abe Steinberg, the Reverend Gardner C. Taylor, and Lawrence Williams—others provided important details and insights about life in the borough at the time: Robert Bernstein, Nunzio D'Addona, Sebastiano Delgado, Jerry DiResta, Ozzie Fletcher, John Galea, Sal LaRocca, Ellen Langston, Stella Qualiarini, Jim Sempepos, Ron Schweiger, Ed Vargas, and Al and Evelyn Wasserman.

Maury Allen, Dave Anderson, Robert Creamer, Stan Isaacs, Sam Lacy, and Jack Lang shared their many stories and memories about covering the Dodgers. Filip Bondy and George Vecsey helped broaden, and to their credit, soften my picture of Dick Young. My education on the Braves and of Milwaukee came from Chuck Johnson, Jack Thompson, and most especially Bob Wolf. John Hall, Duane Esper, Ross Newhan, and Bob Oates helped round out my understanding of the Dodgers, and of Walter O'Malley in Los Angeles.

Jane Jacobs remains one of the great voices on the wonders of cities, although I suspect that she would find those words entirely too fulsome. Too bad. Her insights are as fresh and important today as they were a generation or two ago.

David Burney of the New York City Housing Authority provided a crash course on the history and architecture of public housing in New York. Louis Winnick was equally helpful on the general subject of housing. The architect Stan Meradith explained a great deal about the design of Ebbets Field. Sid Frigand, Frank Lynn, and Judge Milton Mollen, and historians Kenneth Jackson, Joel Schwartz, and Fred Seigel, taught me much about Brooklyn politics. Virginia Sanchez-Coro of Brooklyn College was very helpful on the subject of Puerto Rican migration to New York, and Robert McCrie of John Jay College of Criminal Justice helped mightily in understanding the nature of juvenile crime. Joseph Cerrell, Joan Milke Flores, Robert Gottlieb of Occidental College, Harold Meyerson, and Rosalind Wyman provided a portrait of Los Angeles. Mayor James Hahn generously offered a copy of his late father's written account of the Dodgers' move to Los Angeles. William Kleinsasser, now a retired architect, recalled in considerable detail his encounters with Walter O'Malley at Princeton.

THE ACCOUNT OF the battle between Robert Moses and Walter O'Malley was drawn primarily from their correspondence. The Robert Moses Papers, which are stored at the New York Public Library, and the papers of Mayor Robert Wagner at the New York City Archives, gave me the essential paper trail in understanding how and why the Dodgers ended up leaving Brooklyn. I am grateful to Ken Cobb of the city archives for his help in sifting through the Wagner papers, and to the staff at the Rare Books and Documents Room at the public library for their assistance. The Moses letters are a history in the form of correspondence. I cited the dates from the letters I quote, but wanted to offer a broader explanation about the letters.

The first mention of an O'Malley plan to replace Ebbets Field—at least one that Moses knew of—came in 1953. Moses wrote to and received letters from a host of people, many of whom are cited in the book. Taken together, those letters show Moses' increasing frustration with O'Malley and his desire to have the Dodgers matter resolved quickly and to his liking. The letters continue through 1954 and 1955, and by 1956 it was clear that O'Malley would not get what he wanted from Moses. There is no letter, nor any suggestion in any correspondence, that the plan to build a new stadium was merely a ruse by O'Malley to get a better deal in Los Angeles. If there was a secret offer from Los Angeles before 1956, no one close to O'Malley, including Buzzie Bavasi and Tom Villante, was aware of it. I should add that I tried without success to gain access to the O'Malley letters. His son Peter declined my requests for an interview and the family archivist would not grant me leave to see any of the documents, nor would he comment upon them.

In addition to those letters, I drew heavily on the newspapers and magazines of the time. The staff at the microforms division at Columbia University's Butler Library was generous with its assistance, and I am indebted to Joy Birdsong, Linda Wachtel, and Angel Morales at the *Sports Illustrated* library for helping me plow through the magazine's remarkable holdings, as well as to Susan Aprill of the Brooklyn collection at the Brooklyn Public Library, Bill Berdick of the National Baseball Hall of Fame library, and Sister Winifred Doyle, archivist for the Sisters of the Good Shepherd.

I have tried throughout the book to credit the writers whose work I have drawn from, and will expand on that in the breakdown that follows. But I wanted to cite the work of two writers in particular. I now believe, after having read every one of his accounts of the Dodgers' 1956 season, that no one ever wrote a better game story than Tommy Holmes of the *New York Herald-Tribune*. Nor have I ever read a columnist whose work displayed the mix of reporting and compassion like that of Milton Gross of the *New York Post*. In a town and at a time when the competition included such giants as Red Smith and Jimmy Cannon, Gross was every bit their equal and often outdid them. His account of driving home with Don Newcombe after the seventh game of the World Series stands as one of the great sports columns.

It's essential in reconstructing the story of a team and its season to avoid relying too heavily on a single view. Tommy Holmes, for instance, may have written marvelous accounts of the games themselves, but his pieces avoided any hint of controversy. The spice, the clubhouse intrigue came, of course, from Dick Young, but also from Sid Friedlander of the *New York*

Post, Roscoe McGowan—not in the *Times* but in *The Sporting News*—as well as Dan Daniel, Bill Roeder, and Joe Williams of the *New York World-Telegram*. Arthur Daley of the *New York Times* was that rare columnist who used dialogue as a way for his subjects to reveal themselves.

A more detailed explanation of sources follows. In those instances where I have not specified material, the sources are either interviews cited in the book or newspaper and magazine accounts. I drew heavily on the Brooklyn edition of the *New York World-Telegram* in creating a portrait of the borough at that time. The *New York Times* offered the most comprehensive reporting on the downtown Brooklyn stadium plan, as well as on Robert Moses' Lincoln Square project. In addition to these newspapers, I also drew upon articles in the *New York Post*, the *Daily News*, the *Journal-American*, the *Milwaukee Journal*, *Time*, *Newsweek*, *Life*, *Look*, the *Los Angeles Times*, the *Buffalo News*, *Newsday*, *The American Weekly*, *The New Yorker*, *Sport*, and *Sports Illustrated*.

THE EARLY HISTORY of the Brooklyn Dodgers in the Prologue and in Part One comes largely from Tommy Holmes' two books on the team: *Dodgers Daze and Knights*, and *The Dodgers*, as well as from Peter Golenbock's wonderful oral history, *Bums*. Brooklyn, of course, has been the subject of countless books, several of which I have drawn upon: *Brooklyn, An Illustrated History*, by Ellen M. Snyder-Grenier of the Brooklyn Historical Society; *Brooklyn USA: The Fourth Largest City in America*, edited by Rita Seiden Miller; *An Italian Grows in Brooklyn* by Jerry Della Femina; *Flatbush Odyssey: A Journey through the Heart of Brooklyn* by Allen Abel; *This Is Brooklyn*, by Andrew W. Dolkart; *The Brooklyn Reader*, edited by Andrea Wyatt Sexton and Alice Leccese Powers; *When Brooklyn Was the World, 1920–1957* by Elliot Willensky, and the indispensable *The Neighborhoods of Brooklyn*, by Kenneth Jackson and John Manbeck, both of whom were very helpful in broadening my understanding of the borough.

The Dodgers, too, have been the subject of many books, first among them Roger Kahn's *Boys of Summer*. His *Memories of Summer* is an important addition to Dodger, and baseball, literature. Carl E. Prince's *Brooklyn's Dodgers* explores the team's relationship with the borough. Christopher Jennison's *Wait 'Til Next Year* provides a history of baseball in New York from 1947 to 1957.

The portrait of Walter O'Malley is drawn from interviews with Buzzie Bavasi, Tom Villante, Terry Seidler, and Frank Graham, Jr. I learned a good deal of O'Malley's early life from interviews conducted in preparation for a 1958 *Time* magazine profile. Notes from those interviews are still kept in the O'Malley files at the *Sports Illustrated* library. John Helyer's *Lords of the Realm* not only provides additional history on O'Malley but on his relationship with baseball's other owners.

Neil J. Sullivan's *The Dodgers Move West* provided a good deal of background on the Flatbush Avenue project and on the events that followed O'Malley's fateful meeting with Moses and Wagner in August 1955. Sullivan also provides a wonderful account of O'Malley's dealings with Los Angeles.

All roads in reporting on Robert Moses lead to Robert Caro's seminal biography of Moses, *The Power Broker*. Caro's Moses is great, dark, vainglorious, brilliant, and often brutal—characteristics that come alive in Moses' own writings. Joel Schwartz's *The New York Approach* shows just how complicit New York's liberal political leadership was in abetting Moses' rebuilding of New York.

The portrait of Pee Wee Reese in Part Two is drawn from the recollections of his teammates, of the men who wrote about him, and from newspaper and magazine accounts that I have cited in the book. Despite his greatness as a leader and as a player, there is only one biography of Reese, Gene Schoor's *The Pee Wee Reese Story*, which was written for young readers. But because he was so accessible, and because the writers so admired him, he revealed a good deal in various comments made over the years, quotes that, taken together, tell much about the man.

I drew upon Kenneth Jackson's *Crabgrass Frontier* in the section on the push to the suburbs, and Taylor Branch's *Parting the Waters* in the section on the beginnings of the civil rights movement.

Several of the men who worked for Walter O'Malley wrote books, among them Irving Rudd's *The Sporting Life*, Frank Graham Jr.'s *A Farewell to Heroes*, and Harold Parrott's *The Lords of Baseball*. They had little if anything kind to say about him. Rudd was particularly tough on O'Malley. Taken together, however, the consistency of their portraits of him confirms the impression in Part Three that there were many better places to be than on the outer reaches of O'Malley's universe.

The background on the demographics of Crown Heights in Part Three comes from "The Crown Heights Neighborhood Profile" by Toby Sanchez, published in 1987 by Brooklyn In Touch Information Center, Inc., and from "Population Characteristics and Neighborhood Social Resources" published in 1959 by the Community Council of Greater New York. The demographic material on Bay Ridge in Part Four comes from the council's report of the same year. I also drew upon Joshua B. Freeman's *Working-Class New York*.

My view of Lewis Mumford's ideas on cities was drawn from two of his books, *The Culture of Cities* and *The City in History*. Jane Jacobs' arguments on what is best and worst about urban America is found in her *The Death and Life of Great American Cities*.

The portraits of Duke Snider and Carl Erskine in Part Four were broadened by the books each man wrote: *The Duke of Flatbush*, and Erskine's *Tales from the Dodger Dugout*.

I found a good deal of background on Skiatron and Matty Fox in the *New York Times* and the *Wall Street Journal*. In addition, Tom Villante explained the financial relationship between the team and television. Edgar Scherick spoke with me about the early days of sports television, a period covered extensively in *Sports for Sale* by Norman Marcus and my colleague, David Klatell.

I drew upon Tom Meany's *The Incredible Giants* for background on Sal Maglie's early years. Steve Acee, a baseball historian in Niagara Falls, was helpful in my reporting on Maglie.

The story of the relationship between Roy Campanella and Jackie Robinson in Part Five was drawn from interviews with their teammates, and, as noted in the book, from their own writing. The letters cited in the book appeared in Arnold Rampersad's biography *Jackie Robinson*. Rachel Robinson declined my requests to be interviewed. The story of the Dodgers losing Roberto Clemente came in the course of my interviews with Buzzie Bavasi.

Bob Wolf of the *Milwaukee Journal* provided the most complete view of the Braves. Wolf also authored the as-told-to *Batboy of the Braves* by Paul Wick, which offers not only a history of the team but portraits of its stars, especially Warren Spahn and Lew Burdette, and the managers, Charley Grimm and Fred Haney.

The history of Brooklyn's black neighborhoods in Part Six comes from *Blacks in Brooklyn from 1900 to 1960* by Harold X. Connolly, *Emerging Neighborhoods: The Development of Brooklyn's Fringe Areas, 1850–1930* by Eleanora W. Schoenebaum, and Gerald Sorin's *The Nurturing Neighborhood*.

The material on the Brooklyn, Milwaukee, and Cincinnati clubhouses in Part Eight was drawn from dispatches in *Sports Illustrated*. The material on Don Newcombe that appears in Parts Nine and Ten comes from interviews with his teammates that I cited in the book, as well as from articles written about him. Newcombe declined to be interviewed.

A C K N O W L E D G M E N T S

I am indebted to a good many people who helped make this book possible.

Every author should have the chance to work with Gerry Howard, who brings to the task of editing the rigor, passion, and ambition for his books that makes a writer want very much to please him. By the same token, no writer will ever find a greater, wiser, or more dedicated advocate than my agent, Barney Karpfinger, to whom this book is dedicated.

Kurt Dargis and Mark Shapiro at Classic Sports were generous in providing me with tapes of Dodger ballgames in 1956. My search for former ballplayers was assisted by Mark Langill and Brent Shire of the Los Angeles Dodgers press office, their counterparts at the press offices of the San Diego Padres and San Francisco Giants, as well as by Glenn Gough who runs the Brooklyn Dodger website, Marty Adler of the Brooklyn Dodgers Hall of Fame, baseball historian Lee Lowenfish, Andy McHugh of the Society for American Baseball Research, and Wade Denhartog of the Major League Baseball Alumni Association. Rick Curtis of the John Jay College of Criminal Justice helped in getting in touch with former gang members.

Miles Corwin, Sam Freedman, Mike Hoyt, Dan Sneider, and my brother James Shapiro offered invaluable advice on the manuscript. Rob Snyder was an essential sounding board on the history of New York.

Barbara Labine never lived in Brooklyn but was nonetheless a rapt and eager audience when her husband, Clem, spoke about his years there as a ballplayer. David Remnick maintained a steady stream of books and suggestions on all things Brooklyn and baseball. Pete Hamill offered valuable advice about Brooklyn and music.

I bent the ears of my parents Lorraine and Herbert Shapiro, both in the telling and in the asking about Brooklyn when they were young, and when I was young, too. So too did I inflict upon my children Eliza and Jake too many stories about people named O'Malley, Reese, and Robinson. They were remarkably patient in their indulgence of my enthusiasm and for that, and for more than I can express, I am grateful to them.

My wife, Susan Chira, read every word, vetted every idea, endured every complaint in the course of the work on this book. Saintly virtues. But more than these it is the everyday delight of her company that makes all things not only possible, but wonderful.

Michael Shapiro grew up in Brooklyn, where he attended Midwood High School and Brooklyn College. He is the author of four other books. His work has appeared in such publications as *The New Yorker*, the *New York Times, Sports Illustrated*, and *Esquire*. He is a professor at the Columbia University Graduate School of Journalism and lives in New York with his wife, Susan Chira, and their two children.